BUSINESS STATISTICS

'Sonia Taylor's book is a well presented, easy to read text underpinned with worked examples of statistical analysis relevant to the world of business. The book acknowledges and explores the different tools with which students are required to analyse data – Excel, SPSS and Minitab. For lecturers it offers a systematic approach, supported with a wealth of worked examples and student questions.'

Charles Leatherbarrow, Senior Lecturer,
University of Wolverhampton Business School, UK

Business Statistics
for non-mathematicians

Sonia Taylor

First edition 2001
Reprinted 3 times
Second edition 2007
Published by PALGRAVE MACMILLAN
Houndmills, Basingstoke, Hampshire RG21 6XS and
175 Fifth Avenue, New York, N.Y. 10010
Companies and representatives throughout the world

PALGRAVE MACMILLAN is the global academic imprint of the Palgrave Macmillan division of St. Martin's Press, LLC and of Palgrave Macmillan Ltd. Macmillan® is a registered trademark in the United States, United Kingdom and other countries. Palgrave is a registered trademark in the European Union and other countries.

ISBN-13: 978-0-230-50646-6
ISBN-10: 0-230-50646-1

This book is printed on paper suitable for recycling and made from fully managed and sustained forest sources.

A catalogue record for this book is available from the British Library.

A catalog record for this book is available from the Library of Congress.

10 9 8 7 6 5 4 3 2 1
16 15 14 13 12 11 10 09 08 07

Printed and bound in China

Contents

3 Numerical summary of data   35

4 Probability   59

5 Normal distribution 82

6 Estimation 102

7 Hypothesis testing   123

8 Analysis of variance   154

9 Correlation and regression   186

Appendix   334

Preface

Students:

- Are you a student, either undergraduate or postgraduate, who is studying statistics for the first time?
- Are you planning to do a course including statistics in the near future?
- Are you a researcher who will need to collect and analyse data?
- Do you lack confidence in mathematics or are you 'rusty'?
- Are you nervous about statistics?
- Are you looking for a user-friendly textbook?
- Do you want a textbook which keeps statistical theory, long formulae and mathematical calculations to a minimum?
- Would you like a website giving extra help and practice?

If you answer 'yes' to most of these questions then this is definitely the textbook for you.

Lecturers:

- Are you feeling overworked?

Don't despair: here is a publication which will cut down your preparation and ease your teaching considerably. *Business Statistics for non-mathematicians* is accompanied by lecturers' materials on a companion website, www.palgrave.com/business/taylor, which use the core material from each chapter of the textbook and provide masters for all the paperwork, overhead slides and PowerPoint presentations needed by the lecturer on a weekly basis. Revision questions, multi-choice questions suitable for in-class tests and examination type questions are provided in addition to the questions supplied to the students for revision purposes. (See Appendix F for a full list.)

 Business Statistics for non-mathematicians has been written as a practical response to the needs of the present-day student on a business studies or related course, who needs to obtain a reasonable grasp of basic statistics in the limited time available. This book is also suitable for students or researchers at any level who are not confident in the use of statistics or who are meeting the subject for the first time. It addresses the limitations imposed by modular courses for large teaching groups of students with uncertain mathematical ability. It is organised so that students can gradually build up the knowledge of statistics required, starting from a base of simple arithmetic. Many students experience problems initially, so the emphasis throughout is on understanding through practice, interpretation of results and their application rather than on depth of knowledge. Statistical theory, unhelpful jargon, the use of formulae and long mathematical manipulations are deliberately kept to a minimum. This encourages students who lack confidence in their own mathematical ability.

The main themes of this book are:

- Descriptive statistics: graphical and numerical.
- Inferential statistics: confidence intervals and hypothesis tests.
- Pairwise relationships between variables: correlation, regression and chi-square tests.
- Forecasting: modelling and use of time series.

More specifically:

- Chapter 1 introduces the topic of **statistics** generally, defines certain concepts with which you may or may not already be familiar, and concludes with a self check of the basic arithmetic required for this course.
- **Graphical and numerical description** of different types of data sets are covered in Chapters 2 and 3 with the emphasis on data **summarisation** as a means of communicating the information they contain to others.
- **Uncertainty** is a concept often first met in statistics. It is introduced in Chapter 4 as **probability** and enlarged upon in Chapter 5. This chapter describes and uses the **normal distribution** which fits much business data.
- **Inferential statistics** are introduced in Chapter 6 with the use of **estimation** in the form of **confidence intervals**. This subject is further developed with the **hypothesis testing of various parameters**. Chapter 7 is mainly concerned with a variety of t-tests and Chapter 8 with **analysis of variance**.
- Bivariate relationships between variables are analysed in the form of **correlation** and **regression** in Chapter 9 and **chi-square tests** in Chapter 10.
- **Index numbers** are studied in Chapter 11 to monitor and compare any changes over time. Various **time series** are modelled in Chapter 12 and are then extended into the future to produce **forecasts** in Chapter 13.
- Chapter 14 deals with the production of the **computer analysis** of data, in **SPSS**, **Minitab** and **Excel**, using all the methods covered in the previous chapters. The versions used are the current ones at the time of writing: SPSS 12.0.1, Minitab 14 and Microsoft Office Excel 2003.
- A continuous **case study** using real data runs through most of the chapters.

Each chapter includes the necessary theory but stresses the reasons for, and methods of, carrying out the various techniques and analyses. Plenty of practice is provided with tutorial exercises. Computer analysis by all methods using SPSS, Minitab and some Excel is described separately in Chapter 14.

A companion website

www.palgrave.com/business/taylor provides additional materials for the student:

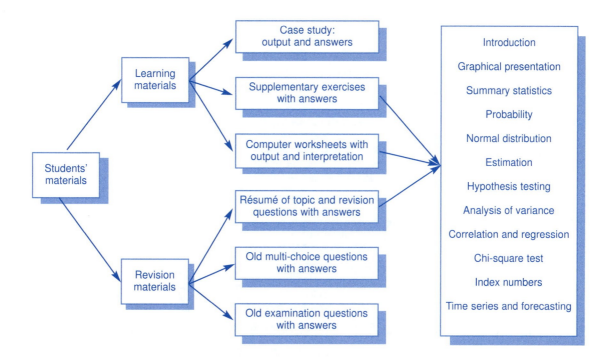

A complete set of lecturer's materials

For the lecturer there is provided on the companion website, www.palgrave.com/business/taylor, a very comprehensive set of all the materials necessary to run the course (see below).

Assuming that *Business Statistics for non-mathematicians* is the set textbook for your course, each student will already have all the subject material, tutorial sheets with answers for each topic and computer worksheets (both SPSS and Minitab for most topics, Excel for some). In addition, they have access to the students materials listed above on the Companion website.

The folders and files providing extra materials on the companion website www.palgrave.com/business/taylor (plus a user name and password) for the lecturer are shown overleaf. These materials are listed in full in Appendix F of this book. It is intended that lecture preparation time should be reduced to a minimum so that as much time as possible can be spent on communicating the subject matter to the students rather than on the increasing burden of administration.

This course material was originally written, in varying forms, for business, accountancy and computing students at the start of modularisation. It has been refined in order to allow for the increasing size of student groups and a lower standard of numeracy. The course has been run with the inclusion of Minitab or SPSS or neither and has always been well received by the students over many years. The use of Excel and the comprehensive website materials have also been included in this book.

It can be seen, therefore, that this book is intended as a practical approach to the problem of the restricted time available for both the student and the lecturer which limits both the range and the depth of topics taught. This book is an honest attempt to solve the very real problem created by increasing student numbers, increasing demands on lecturers' time and students' decreasing mathematical capability. From this point of view I freely admit that the basic approach is quite different to that of most text books!

I am indebted to many colleagues, particularly Linda Pryce, with whom I developed the

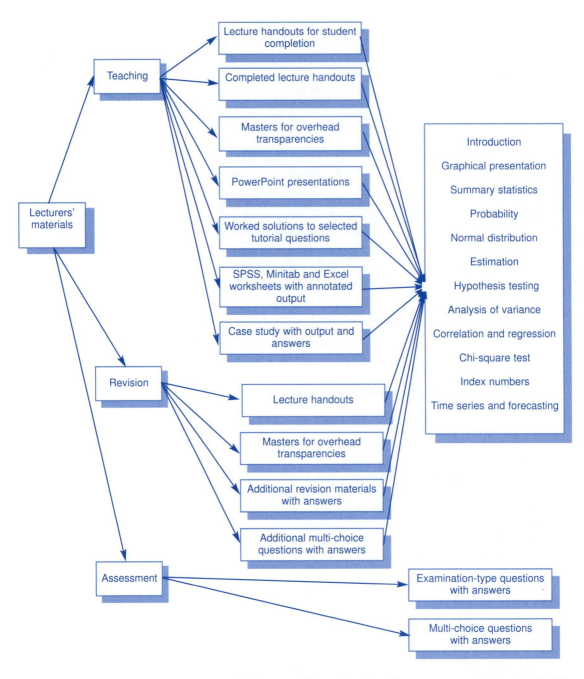

initial course, Jenny Kromer, Jon Blacktop and Jane Parkin who gave generously of valuable time for proofreading the first edition. Others have contributed to this book both willingly and, possibly, inadvertently as the origin of a few of the examples is lost in history!

I also thank Martin Drewe from Palgrave Macmillan for his prompt friendly assistance when required during the production of this second edition.

Mainly my thanks go to my husband, Geoff, for his tolerance during the writing of this book!

Sonia Ann Taylor (Formerly of the University of Huddersfield)

Introduction to statistics

1

Objectives of this chapter

In this introductory chapter no assumptions are made about any prior statistical knowledge. The main aim is to introduce you gently to the subject of statistics and its use of various types of data.

Having studied this chapter you should be aware, in general, of:

- different types of data
- methods of data collection
- reasons for displaying, summarising and analysing data.

Throughout the book, terms printed in **bold** are either occurring for the first time or are particularly important. They are described in the glossary in Appendix B.

1.1 What do we mean by statistics?

Statistics are numerical facts or figures. Therefore statistics, as a science, essentially deals with numbers. It is generally taken to include the systematic:

- collecting
- classifying
- analysing
- presenting

of data in order to get a better understanding of some given situation.

This may mean summarising the data in tabulated, graphical or numerical form.

A statistical study might range from simple exploration enabling us to gain an insight into a virtually unknown situation to a sophisticated analysis designed to produce numerical confirmation, or rejection, of some widely held belief.

1.2 Why do we need statistics?

In business, we may be interested in a set of data in its own right. In this case we could describe it both numerically and graphically in the most appropriate manner – **descriptive statistics**.

Alternatively, the set of data we have may be a sample drawn from a larger population. This population would be our target of interest. In this case we need to use the information held by the sample to tell us something about its parent population – **inferential statistics**. An example is a Gallup poll on a sample of the electorate before a general election.

In another instance we may be interested in the future and so use the data we have up to the present time to estimate the value of a quantity in the future – **forecasting**.

Statistics play a wide role in most aspects of the competitive business world, where they provide an essential tool in decision making. Any decision-making process should be supported by some quantitative measures produced by the analysis of collected data.

Useful data may be on:

- a firm's products, costs, sales or services
- its competitors' products, costs, sales or services
- measurement of industrial processes
- a firm's workforce.

Once collected, this data needs to be summarised and displayed in a manner which helps its communication to, and understanding by, its recipients. Only when fully understood can it profitably become part of the decision-making process.

During this course you will learn to:

- describe data, such as profits, in order to assist decision makers
- estimate a particular property of a large population of data from a comparatively small sample
- seek out relationships between pairs of variables such as advertising and sales
- use known data to forecast a quantity, such as future demand.

First we shall look at some basic considerations which we must always take into account when collecting or handling data. These considerations do not fit into any specific topic area but are applicable throughout.

1.3 Types of data and scales of measurement

The word **data** describes, in general, a collection of observations.

Any data you use can take a variety of **values** or belong to various **categories**, either numerical or non-numerical. The 'thing' being described by the data is therefore known as a **variable**. The values or descriptions you use to measure or categorise this 'thing' are the **measurements**. These are of different types, each with its own appropriate **scale of measurement** which has to be considered when deciding on appropriate methods of graphical display or numerical analysis.

A variable is therefore simply something whose 'value' can vary.

For example a car could be red, blue, green, etc. It would be identified by a registration number. It could be classed as small, medium or large. Its petrol consumption in mpg could be 30, 40, 50, etc. Its year of manufacture could be 1991, 1999, 2006, etc. It would have a particular length. These values all describe the same car but are measured on different 'scales'.

1.3.1 Categorical data

These are generally non-numerical data which are placed into **exclusive** categories and then counted rather than measured. People are often categorised by their occupation or sex. The car mentioned above can be categorised by its make or colour.

1.3.1.1 Nominal data

The scale of measurement for a variable is **nominal** if the data describing it are simple names or labels which cannot be ordered. This is the lowest level of measurement. Numbers may represent nominal data, such as 'codes' for computer analysis, but these can only be used as labels. Vest numbers identify athletes but make no value statements about them. A car registration number only serves to identify the vehicle.

Numbers representing nominal data cannot be used in any arithmetic. Your 'PIN number' allows you access to your bank account, as does your friend's to his, but the sum of them doesn't allow either, never mind both, of you access to either. All nominal data are placed in a limited number of exhaustive categories and any analysis is carried out on the **frequencies** within these categories.

1.3.1.2 Ordinal data

If the categories of data can be placed in a meaningful order without any measurements, then the data are classed as **ordinal**. This is one level up from nominal. We know that the members of one category are more, or less, than the members of another but we cannot say by how much. For example, the results of a race are decided by the finishing order of the athletes without any reference to their actual times. The vests they wear could be ordered as: 'small', 'medium' and 'large' without the aid of a tape measure.

Degree classifications are only ordinal because the difference between first and second-class degrees is not the same as the difference between a second and a third.

Questionnaires are often used to collect opinions using the categories: 'Strongly agree', 'Agree', 'No opinion', 'Disagree' or 'Strongly disagree'. The responses may be coded as 1, 2, 3, 4 and 5 for the computer, but the differences between these numbers are not claimed to be equal so the categories are only ordinal.

In order to analyse ordinal data, all individuals are placed in their relevant categories, the categories then ordered and calculations are performed on their frequencies.

1.3.2 Interval and ratio data

In interval and ratio scales of measurement all numbers are defined by standard units of measurement, such as metres or grams, so equal difference between numbers genuinely means equal distance between measurements. If there is **also** a meaningful zero, then the fact that one number is twice as big as another means that the measurements are also in that ratio. This data is known as **ratio data**. If, on the other hand, the zero has no mathematical meaning the data is **interval** only. Don't worry too much about this distinction as both sets of data are treated the same.

1.3.2.1 Interval data

There are very few examples of genuine interval scales. Temperature in degrees Celsius provides one example with the 'zero' on this scale being arbitrary. The difference between 30 °C and 50 °C is the same as the difference between 40 °C and 60 °C but we cannot claim that 60 °C is twice as hot as 30 °C. They are therefore **interval data** but not ratio data. Dates are measured on an interval scale as again the zero is arbitrary and not meaningful.

1.3.2.2 Ratio data

Ratio data must have a meaningful zero as their lowest possible value. For example, the time taken for athletes to complete a race would be measured on this scale. If we consider ages, a child at 12 years old is twice as old as his 6-year-old brother, and the age difference between them is the same as between his sisters who are 15 years old and 9 years old respectively. Their ages are ratio as well as interval but their dates of birth are only interval.

Suppose Bill earns £80,000, Ben earns £60,000 and Bob earns £40,000. The intervals of £20,000 between Bill and Ben and also between Ben and Bob genuinely represent equal amounts of money. Also the ratio of Bob's earnings to Bill's earnings is genuinely in the same ratio (1:2), as are the numbers which represent them. The value of £0 represents 'no money'. This data set is therefore **ratio** as well as interval.

The distinction between interval and ratio data is more theoretical than practical, as the same numerical and graphical methods are appropriate for both. They are usually referred to as **'at least interval'** data. Much of the data, such as money, that you will study will be measured on this scale.

We have therefore identified three measurement scales – 'nominal', 'ordinal' and 'at least interval'. The data measured on these scales are referred to in the same way, and this classification determines which methods of display and analysis are appropriate.

Any type of data may be analysed using methods appropriate to lower levels. For example: interval data may be analysed as ordinal but useful information is lost. If we know that Bill earns £80,000 and Ben earns £60,000 we are throwing information away by only recording that Bill earns 'more than' Ben.

Data cannot be analysed using methods which are only appropriate for higher-level data as the results will be either invalid or meaningless. For example it makes no sense to code the sex of students as 'male' = 1, 'female' = 2 and then report 'the mean value is 1.7'. It is however quite appropriate to report that '70 per cent of the students are female'.

1.3.3 Qualitative and quantitative data

Various definitions exist for the distinction between qualitative and quantitative data. Non-numerical (nominal) data are always described as being **qualitative** (non-metric) data as they describe some qualities without measuring them. **Quantitative** (metric) data which describe some measurement (or quantity) are always numerical. All definitions agree that interval or ratio data are quantitative. Some textbooks, however, use the term qualitative to refer to words only, while others also include nominal or ordinal numbers. Problems of definition could arise with numbers, such as house numbers, which identify or rank rather than measure. You don't need to worry about the 'grey areas'.

In the next two chapters we shall study the graphical and numerical methods appropriate to each type of data. The statistical techniques you will meet later are often divided into **parametric statistics,** which require data to be interval or ratio, and **non-parametric statistics,** which are appropriate for use at the lower levels.

1.3.4 Discrete and continuous data

Quantitative data may be **discrete** or **continuous**. If the values that can be taken by a variable change in steps, the data is **discrete**. These discrete values are often, but not always, whole numbers. If the variable can take any value within a range, so that you can imagine other values between those given, it is **continuous**. The number of people shopping in a supermarket is discrete but the amount they spend is continuous. The number of children in a family is discrete but a baby's birth weight is continuous. This is usually given to the nearest ounce but could be measured more precisely in half or quarter ounces. Some variables, such as money, are considered to be continuous even though they are measured in small discrete amounts.

1.4 Populations and samples

The **population** is the **entire group** of interest. This definition is not confined to people, as is usual in the non-statistical sense. A statistical population may include objects such as all the houses in a local authority area rather than the people living in them.

It is usually neither possible nor practical to examine every member of a **population**, so we use a **sample** – a smaller selection taken from that population – to **estimate** some value or characteristic of the whole population. Care must be taken when selecting the sample, as it must be representative of the whole population under consideration, otherwise it doesn't tell us anything relevant to that particular population.

Occasionally the whole population is investigated by a **census**, such as is carried out every ten years in the United Kingdom. The data are gathered from everyone in the population. A more usual method of collecting information is by a **survey** in which only a sample is selected from the population of interest and its data examined. Examples of this are the Mori polls produced from a sample of the electorate to forecast the result of a general election.

Analysing a sample instead of the whole population has many advantages such as the obvious saving of both time and money. It is often the only possible method, as the collecting of data may sometimes destroy the article of interest, for example the quality control of loaves of bread.

The ideal method of sampling is **random sampling,** in which every member of the population has an equal chance of being selected and each selection is independent of all the others. This ideal might not be achievable for a variety of reasons, and many other methods can be used (see Section 6.2).

1.5 Descriptive statistics

Descriptive statistics cover the analysis of the whole population of interest. The facts and figures usually referred to as 'statistics' in the media are very often a numerical and graphical summary of data from a specific group, for example unemployment figures. Much of the data generated by a business will be descriptive in nature, as will be the majority of sporting statistics.

1.6 Inferential statistics

If the information we have available is from a sample of the whole population of interest, we analyse it to produce the **sample statistics** from which we can infer (estimate) values for the parent population. This branch of statistics is usually referred to as **inferential statistics**. For example, we use the proportion of faulty items in a sample taken from a production line to estimate what proportion of all the items from the whole line are expected to be faulty. Pharmaceutical research is an example of the use of inferential statistics. Tests are necessarily limited to a small sample of patients, but inferences are applied to the whole relevant patient population.

A descriptive measure from the sample is usually referred to as a **sample statistic,** and the corresponding measure estimated for the population is referred to as a **population parameter**. The problem with using samples is that each sample produces a different sample statistic, giving us a different estimate for the population parameter. They cannot all be correct so a margin of error is generally quoted with any estimations.

1.7 Summary

In this short chapter you have been introduced to the different types of data we shall be using throughout the book. We shall be dealing mainly with interval data, such as money, which we shall learn to display, summarise and analyse. It is, however, important to be able to distinguish between the different types of data as this determines which methods of display and analysis are the most appropriate (see Table 1.1).

You have also been introduced briefly to the two main branches of statistics, descriptive and inferential statistics.

- Descriptive statistics result from gathering data about a whole group, or population, and reaching conclusions about that group only.
- Inferential statistics result from gathering data from a sample taken from a population and then reaching conclusions about the whole population from an analysis of the sample data.

Table 1.1 Scales of measurement

Scale of measurement	Non-numeric data	Numeric data
Nominal	Name or label only	Numbers only identify groups which cannot be ordered
Ordinal	Names or labels can be ranked	These numbers allow ranking but no arithmetic
Interval	Always numeric	Intervals between numbers are meaningful
Ratio	Always numeric	Intervals between numbers are meaningful and also their ratios as the lowest value is a meaningful zero.

1.8 Case study

A case study requiring you to investigate data in order to provide a quantitative basis for decision making runs throughout this book. Partial studies are to be found near the end of each chapter, requiring analysis from you as appropriate.

1.8.1 Scenario

You work for a company, Restful Restaurants, which is exploring the possibility of opening new premises in the expanding city of Lonbridge. The directors of your company need some quantitative evidence on which to base any decisions. If they open the company's standard type of restaurant, how big should it be? Might it be preferable to diversify and open a different type of food outlet, such as a large café or a takeaway? The directors have obtained survey data from the University of Lonbridge about existing food outlets in the city, and are asking you to analyse it in order to provide them with background information on the current situation regarding restaurants, cafés and takeaways.

More specifically, at the end of the case study, they would like to know for each type of establishment:

- its present frequency in Lonbridge
- how optimistic the owners feel about future sales
- how the estimated value of a business relates to (a) its gross sales, (b) its number of employees, and (c) the amount it spends on advertising
- how gross sales are related to the amount of new capital invested each year
- the proportion of sales revenue spent on (a) buying goods and (b) staff wages

- how effective advertising is in increasing sales
- how the number of employees is related to gross sales
- whether the size of an establishment relates to its type.

In order to build up a picture of the situation in Lonbridge you will be asked to carry out analysis in most chapters after you have studied specific topics, using your preferred computer package.

1.8.2 The data

This data originated as a survey of restaurants in Wisconsin, Canada, and was originally reproduced as a Minitab data set (Restrnt.MTW). The data set has been reduced in size and slightly adapted for this case study. This version will be found on the companion website in the folder 'Case study' in a file called 'Restaurants'.

It includes the following information on 255 eating establishments:

```
Variable  N       Label
OUTLOOK   255     Business Outlook
SALES     245     Gross sales (£'000)
NEWCAP    217     New capital invested (£'000)
VALUE     239     Estimated market value of business (£'000)
COSTGOOD  233     Cost of goods sold as % of sales
WAGES     233     Wages as % of sales
ADVERT    231     Advertising as % of sales
TYPE      254     Type of Outlet
OWNER     250     Type of ownership
FULL      248     Number of full-time employees
PART      248     Number of part-time employees
SIZE      246     Size of establishment in FTE equivalent
```

1.9 Check your course prerequisites

There is no exercise connected to the material in this introductory chapter. You should check, or revise, the basic mathematical knowledge that will be assumed when working through this book. This knowledge is fairly basic. In addition to a sound working knowledge of simple arithmetic you should be able to:

- work with fractions, decimals and percentages
- handle large and small numbers
- carry out simple algebraic manipulations
- solve fairly simple equations.

The following tutorial should enable you to check these prerequisites. If you find any question particularly difficult you should get some practice from any basic quantitative analysis or mathematics textbook.

Tutorial 1: Basic mathematics revision

1 Evaluate:

a) $\dfrac{3}{7} - \dfrac{4}{21} + \dfrac{5}{3}$ b) $1\dfrac{2}{3} + 2\dfrac{4}{5} - 3\dfrac{1}{2}$ c) $\dfrac{2}{7} \times \dfrac{14}{25} \times \dfrac{15}{24}$ d) $\dfrac{16}{21} \div \dfrac{4}{7}$

e) $\dfrac{4}{9} \times \dfrac{3}{16} \div \dfrac{7}{12}$ f) $4\dfrac{2}{5} \div \dfrac{11}{12} \times 1\dfrac{7}{8}$

2 a) Give 489 267 to 3 significant figures
   b) Give 489 267 to 2 significant figures
   c) Give 0.002 615 to 2 significant figures
   d) Give 0.002 615 to 1 significant figure
   e) Give 0.002 615 to 5 decimal places
   f) Give 0.002 615 to 3 decimal places

3 Retail outlets in a town were classified as small, medium and large and their numbers were in the ratio 6 : 11 : 1. If there were 126 retail outlets altogether, how many were there of each type?

4 Convert:
   a) 28% to a fraction in its lowest terms
   b) 28% to a decimal

   c) $\dfrac{3}{8}$ to a decimal

   d) $\dfrac{3}{8}$ to a percentage

   e) 0.625 to a fraction in its lowest terms
   f) 0.625 to a percentage

5 Express the following in standard form:
   a) 296 000 b) 0.000 296 c) 0.4590 d) 459.0 e) $\dfrac{1}{25\ 000}$ f) $\dfrac{1}{0.000\ 25}$

6 Reduce the following expressions to their simplest form, expanding brackets if appropriate.
   a) $3a + b + 2a - 4b$ b) $2a + 4ab + 3a^2 + ab$ c) $a^2(3a + 4b + 2a)$
   d) $(x + 2)(x + 4)$ e) $(x + 2)^2$ f) $(x + 1)(x - 1)$

7 Make x the subject of the formula and evaluate when $y = -3$.

   a) $y = 5x - 4$ b) $y = x^2 - 7$ c) $y = 2(3 + 6x)$ d) $y = \dfrac{3}{x}$

8 Find the value of x in the formulae in Question 7 when $y = -3$.

9 Evaluate the following when $x = -2$, $y = 5$ and $z = 4$.
   a) xy b) $(xy)^2$ c) $(xy + z)^2$
   d) $zy - x^2$ e) $(x + z)(2y - x)$ f) $x^2 + y^2 + z^2$

10 Solve for x:

a) $3x - 1 = 4 - 2x$ b) $2(x - 3) = 3(1 - 2x)$ c) $\dfrac{3}{x-1} = \dfrac{1}{2}$

Answers

1 a) $1\dfrac{19}{21}$ b) $\dfrac{29}{30}$ c) $\dfrac{1}{10}$ d) $1\dfrac{1}{3}$ e) $\dfrac{1}{7}$ f) 9

2 a) 489 000 b) 490 000 c) 0.0026 d) 0.003

   e) 0.002 62 f) 0.003

3 42 small, 77 medium, 7 large

4 a) $\dfrac{7}{25}$ b) 0.28 c) 0.375 d) 37.5%

   e) $\dfrac{5}{8}$ f) 62.5%

5 a) 2.96×10^5 b) 2.96×10^{-4} c) 4.59×10^{-1} d) 4.59×10^2

   e) 4.0×10^{-5} f) 4.0×10^3

6 a) $5a - 3b$ b) $3a^2 + 5ab + 2a$ c) $5a^3 + 4a^2b$ d) $x^2 + 6x + 8$

   e) $x^2 + 4x + 4$ f) $x^2 - 1$

7 a) $x = \dfrac{1}{5}(y+4)$ b) $x = \sqrt{y+7}$ c) $x = \dfrac{y-6}{12}$ d) $x = \dfrac{3}{y}$

8 a) 0.2 b) +2 or −2 c) −0.75 d) −1

9 a) −10 b) 100 c) 36 d) 16 e) 24 f) 45

10 a) $x = 1$ b) $1\dfrac{1}{8}$ c) 7

Graphical representation of data

2

Objectives of this chapter

So far you have considered four different types of data: nominal, ordinal, interval and ratio. In this chapter we shall investigate the different ways of presenting this data graphically in a meaningful manner. You are probably already familiar with **bar charts** and **pie charts** so they will be considered fairly briefly. The emphasis will be on **histograms** and **cumulative frequency diagrams**, plus an introduction to **stem-and-leaf plots** and **box plots**.

Graphs are potentially very good tools for communication, but they must be kept as simple as possible and never be presented so as to mislead the reader. If they can't be easily understood they are neither use nor ornament!

After studying this chapter you should be able to:

• draw appropriate graphs of given data
• interpret a variety of types of graph
• understand graphs presented in the media.

2.1 Introduction: why do we represent data by graphs?

What is your reaction if you are presented with a table full of figures? I'm sure that you are neither filled with delight nor an immediate understanding of the situation described by them! On the other hand, a fairly simple graph, if well presented, can quickly convey a general summary of a set of data to its reader. Further examination can then reveal more detail and produce a deeper understanding. If you always keep in mind that the purpose of drawing a graph is to convey information to its reader as easily and quickly as possible, you will not go far wrong. Simple graphs make for easy comparisons, so never put too much information in any one picture.

2.2 Tabulation

Immediately after collection, all new data (**raw data**) are in the form of individual figures. There may be pages of these, often far too many to convey any useful information as they stand, or they may be presented as a table. These individual data are ungrouped, so the first step in organising them is usually to produce **grouped data**: that is, collect like with like in order to reduce the total volume. This grouping can take a variety of forms – some students like to use tally charts – which all result in a **frequency distribution**. Various statistics can be calculated from the frequency distribution and suitable graphs produced.

First determine the range of the data: that is, the largest value minus the smallest value. Then decide on suitable **class intervals** to give a reasonable number of classes or groups. Somewhere between 5 and 15 is generally acceptable – too few classes will cause the loss of detail but too many classes may obscure the overall picture. In order to keep the work simple it is advisable to group in fives or tens, and in the first grouping you should use equal intervals. Data values must not fall into more than one class, so the class interval is usually described as, for example, '20 and under 30' so that 30 would go in the next class.

Now group the data by constructing a tally chart. In Example 2.1, record the first number, 55, next to the relevant interval, '55 and under 60', with a '|'. Then allocate the second, 64, to the '60 and under 65' interval, and so on until all the numbers have been recorded. After four strokes it is conventional to draw a diagonal through them for the fifth so that the number of 'fives' can easily be totalled. Total each 'tally' for the frequency in each interval.

Example 2.1

The following figures represent the examination marks (per cent) for 60 students on a business studies course. We shall first find the range, then decide the number of intervals to use, define the class intervals, and finally draw up a frequency table.

Table 2.1 gives Range: $84 - 37 = 47$. These figures would give us either 6 class intervals of 10 or 10 class intervals of 5. Either would be acceptable so we shall first group in classes of 5 and then combine into intervals of 10 and compare the results.

Table 2.1

55	64	74	53	66	40	52	39	70	59	53	57
62	60	40	45	54	72	47	42	38	60	43	37
61	65	41	54	69	47	80	66	52	78	43	72
44	84	61	67	74	57	60	61	60	56	66	49
54	59	59	60	57	70	61	54	67	54	65	56

Frequency distribution table

Class interval	Tally	Frequency
35 & under 40	|||	3
40 & under 45	⦀⦀ ||	7
45 & under 50	||||	4
50 & under 55	⦀⦀ ||||	9
55 & under 60	⦀⦀ ||||	9
60 & under 65	⦀⦀ ⦀⦀		11
65 & under 70	⦀⦀ |||	8
70 & under 75	⦀⦀		6
75 & under 80			1
80 & under 85	||	2

This gives us an overall idea of the 'shape' of the distribution. Does it look better if grouped in tens?

Frequency distribution table

Class interval	Tally	Frequency
30 & under 40	|||	3
40 & under 50	⦀⦀ ⦀⦀		11
50 & under 60	⦀⦀ ⦀⦀ ⦀⦀ |||	18
60 & under 70	⦀⦀ ⦀⦀ ⦀⦀ ||||	19
70 & under 80	⦀⦀ ||	7
80 & under 90	||	2

It is probably easier to interpret this second distribution: that is, it shows that 'most' of the students pass (40 per cent) but get less than 70 per cent. Have we lost any detail of interest? Probably not, in this case. There is no set rule about the number of classes, so just use a 'reasonable' number.

A frequency distribution already gives a good indication of the 'shape' of the data, but a well-drawn graph, such as a bar chart or histogram, communicates it better.

2.3 Graphs of non-metric (non-measurable) data

2.3.1 Bar charts

Bar charts are drawn as a pictorial summary of categorical data. Each bar, which is separated from its neighbours, represents one category, and the length of the bar represents the frequency in that category. Alternatively the length of the bar is proportional to the size of the items being considered, for example the Sales in Example 2.2. For nominal data the bars may be arranged in any order, but with ordinal data the categories are usually presented in ascending order. For comparative purposes the bars may be grouped, the frequencies stacked, or 'percentage charts' drawn, as in Example 2.2.

Example 2.2

A shop had sales from four departments for the last four quarters (£'000):

Table 2.2

Department	Spring	Summer	Autumn	Winter	Total
Food	160	180	180	200	720
Clothing	280	300	200	300	1080
Furniture	860	560	500	240	2160
Electrical	60	60	100	140	360
Total	1360	1100	980	880	4320

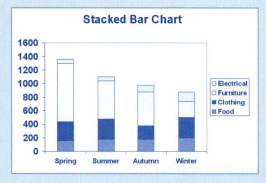

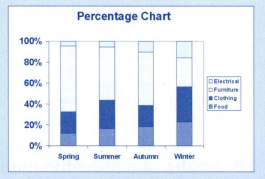

Figure 2.1 Bar charts for comparing the total and departmental quarterly sales (diagrams from Microsoft Excel 2003 – see Section 14.8, Excel Worksheets)

2.3.2 Pie charts

Pie charts are also drawn as a summary of categorical data. The total count of all the data represented is equivalent to 360° on the 'pie', and the frequency within each category is represented by the size of the angle of its sector: that is, its 'slice'. If pie charts are to be used for comparing **relative frequencies** between variables, then the area of the 'pie' describing each can be drawn so that it represents the total frequency of that variable.

Calculating the sector angles (refer to Table 2.2 for total sales):

$$\text{Food: } \frac{720}{4320} \times 360° = 60° \qquad \text{Clothing: } \frac{1080}{4320} \times 360° = 60° \text{ and so on}$$

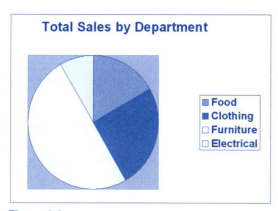
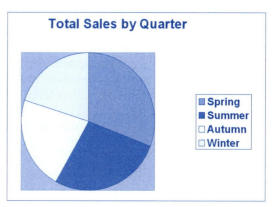

Figure 2.2

By hand, and some computer packages, all this information can be put onto one 'pie' by placing a second ring around, say, the simple departmental pie shown in the first diagram and then subdividing each departmental sector radially between the different quarters. These more complicated 'pies' can be difficult to interpret, and should be used with caution.

(For production of pie charts by computer see Sections 14.2.1, 14.5.1 and 14.8.1.)

2.3.3 Pictograms

You are not expected to draw pictograms but it useful to know how to interpret any shown in the media. You are probably familiar with the type of graph produced by the motor industry in which each little car drawn represents, for example, 1000 cars actually produced. Ten tiny cars might represent 10,000 real cars from one factory, and 20,000 real cars from another factory might be represented by 20 tiny cars. That method of pictorial comparison is fine as its meaning is clear. Other methods can be misleading.

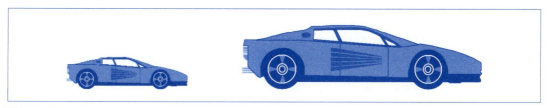

Figure 2.3

If the first car in Figure 2.3 represents 1000 real cars, how many does the second car represent? Its length is twice, its area four times and its volume eight times that of the first car. Does it represent 2000, 4000 or 8000 real cars? Diagrams of this type are open to misinterpretation and should be avoided. Published diagrams in the press need very careful scrutiny if they are not explained numerically.

2.4 Graphs of metric (measurable) data

2.4.1 Histograms

In Section 2.2 we grouped raw data to form a frequency distribution table. This gave a much clearer picture than did the individual data values. The most usual presentation of metric data is in the form of a **histogram**.

A histogram is a pictorial method of presenting frequency data. It appears similar to a bar chart but has two fundamental differences:

- The data must be measurable on a **continuous** scale, for example, lengths rather than colours.
- The **area** of a rectangle rather than its height is proportional to the frequency, so if one column is twice the width of another its height must be halved for the same frequency.

Histograms are produced by all statistical software packages but these often do not give you as much choice in presentation as is available when you draw them by hand.

Using the same data as in Example 2.1, we can look at the output from Minitab, one of the most commonly used educational packages, which is shown in Figure 2.4(a). Figure 2.4(b) has been grouped in 'tens' and the labelling has been moved to the class boundaries, which is always preferable. SPSS produces similar diagrams but does not allow the labelling to be moved. Excel does not produce genuine histograms but only contrived bar charts.

The histograms in Figure 2.4 both show equal class intervals, which is the default format in all packages. Neither Minitab nor SPSS will allow for the use of unequal intervals, so this will be described below in the method for hand-drawing histograms.

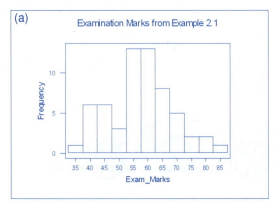

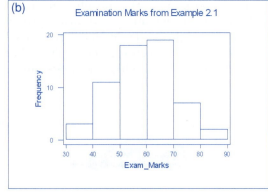

Figure 2.4

The construction of a frequency distribution table is shown again in Example 2.3. The data are first grouped in a frequency distribution table:

- Decide on sensible limits if the first or last class interval is left open, for example, 'less than 20', and also decide into how many classes you intend to group your data. Too few classes may hide information about the data; too many classes may hide its overall shape.
- Construct a frequency distribution table, grouping the data into a reasonable number of classes, (somewhere in the order of 10). Intervals are usually of the same width for the first summary.

Example 2.3

You are working for the transport manager of a large chain of supermarkets which leases cars for the use of its staff. She is interested in the weekly distances covered by these cars. Mileages recorded for a sample of hired vehicles during a given week yielded the following data for Fleet 1:

Table 2.3

138	164	150	132	144	125	149	157	161	150
146	158	140	109	136	148	152	144	145	145
168	126	138	186	163	109	154	165	135	156
146	183	105	108	135	153	140	135	142	128

Minimum = 105, Maximum = 186, Range = 186 – 105 = 81

Nine intervals of 10 miles width seams reasonable, but the first and last interval may be wider if data proves to be scarce at the extremes.

Frequency distribution table

Class interval		Frequency
100 & less than 110	||||	4
110 & less then 120		
120 & less than 130	|||	3
130 & less than 140	⊬⊤⊤ ||	7
140 & less than 150	⊬⊤⊤ ⊬⊤⊤ |	11
150 & less than 160	⊬⊤⊤ |||	8
160 & less than 170	⊬⊤⊤	5
170 & less than 180		
180 & less than 190	||	2
Total		40

It might be preferable to combine the two intervals at each end of the table and work with frequency density (per 10 mile interval).

Frequency distribution table

Class interval		Frequency	Freq/10 miles
100 & less than 120	||||	4	2.0
120 & less than 130	|||	3	3.0
130 & less than 140	ﾊﾞ||	7	7.0
140 & less than 150	ﾊﾞ ﾊﾞ |	11	11.0
150 & less than 160	ﾊﾞ |||	8	8.0
160 & less than 170	ﾊﾞ	5	5.0
170 & less than 190	||	2	1.0
	Total	40	

The histogram is then constructed:

- Frequencies are plotted in proportion to the area of each rectangle, so if the intervals (the rectangle bases) are not all the same width, their heights need to be calculated. These heights are known as the **frequency densities**, that is, frequency per constant interval. The most commonly occurring interval is often used.
- Construct the histogram, labelling each axis carefully. Hand-drawn histograms usually show the frequency vertically. (Computer output may be horizontal because it is more convenient for line printers.)

We shall return to histograms in the next chapter for the estimation of modal values.

Example 2.3 continued

If some intervals are wider than others care must be taken that the areas of the blocks are proportional to the **frequencies**, so heights are proportional to **frequency densities**. Figures 2.5 (a) and (b) illustrate the difference; (a) has the **frequency** plotted on the vertical axis and (b) has the **frequency density** with the two outside intervals combined at both of the extremes. It looks more aesthetically pleasing. (See Sections 14.2.1, 14.5.1, 14.8.1 for computer production of histograms).

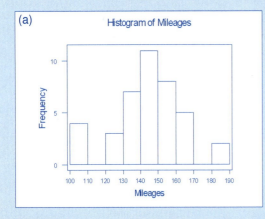

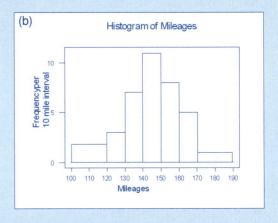

Figure 2.5

2.4.2 Frequency polygons

A **frequency polygon** is constructed by joining the midpoints at the top of each column of the histogram. The area under the polygon is the same as that under the histogram. Polygons can also be drawn without using a histogram. It is often easier to compare two frequency polygons than to interpret than a pair of histograms which tend to obscure each other. The polygons are drawn without the histograms, giving a clearer comparison.

For example if we wished to compare another fleet of 40 cars, Fleet 2, with the one in Example 2.3, Fleet 1, the diagram might look like Figure 2.6(b).

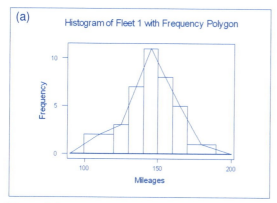
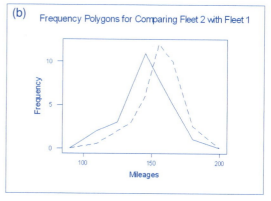

Figure 2.6

If we wish to compare two fleets of different sizes, comparing frequencies directly would not give a clear picture. Instead it would be advisable to compare **relative frequencies**. These measure the percentage of the total fleet which lies within each class interval.

For example for the interval 110 to 120 in Example 2.4, the relative frequency for Fleet 2 is $1/40 = 2.5\%$ and for Fleet 3 is $9/200 = 4.5\%$.

Example 2.4

Table 2.4

Class Interval	Fleet 2		Fleet 3	
	Frequency	Relative freq.%	Frequency	Relative freq.%
less than 100	0	0.0	0	0.0
100 & less than 110	0	0.0	9	4.5
110 & less than 120	1	2.5	9	4.5
120 & less than 130	2	5.0	35	17.5
130 & less than 140	4	10.0	70	35.0
140 & less than 150	6	15.0	40	20.0
150 & less than 160	12	30.0	23	11.5
160 & less than 170	10	25.0	12	6.0
170 & less than 180	4	10.0	2	1.0
180 & less than 190	1	2.5	0	0.0
Total	40	100.0	200	100.0

If we wished to compare our fleet, Fleet 2, with a much larger fleet, Fleet 3, we would calculate the relative frequencies for each fleet and plot those values instead of the frequencies (see Table 2.4). This makes the small and large fleets easier to compare as the areas under the graphs are equal.

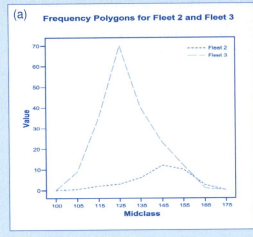

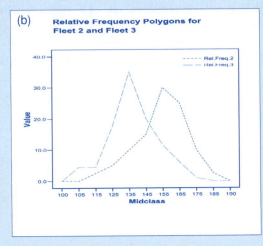

Figure 2.7

2.4.2.1 Shape of a distribution

We can also see whether the data distributions are symmetrical or not. If the 'peak' is towards the left and the longer tail towards the right, the data is referred to as 'positively [or right] skewed', and conversely if the 'peak' is towards the right and the tail towards the left, it is 'negatively [or left] skewed'. If neither is true, it is 'symmetrical'. The distribution of the Fleet 2 data set is seen to be slightly negatively skewed, and Fleet 3 positively, but both are nearly symmetrical. You will meet this concept again later in the course.

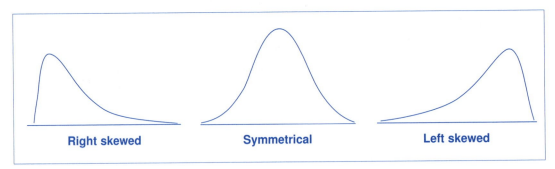

Figure 2.8

2.4.3 Stem-and-leaf plots

The **stem-and-leaf plot** displays the data in the same 'shape' as the histogram, although it tends to be shown horizontally. The main difference is that it retains all the original numerical information. The values themselves are included in the diagram so no information is 'lost'.

The stem-and-leaf plot in Figure 2.9 represents the Fleet 1 vehicles. The 'stem', on the left of the vertical line of dots, contains the first two digits (hundreds and tens), and the 'leaf' shows the units. The 'stem' contains the most significant digits. These might be all different, or grouped depending on the spread of the data (see 'Stem width' in Figure 2.9). The 'leaves', on the right of the vertical line, display the less significant digits. For small numbers these may be units (as in mileages), but for larger numbers they may represent tens, hundreds, etc. For

```
MILEAGES Stem-and-Leaf Plot

 Frequency     Stem &  Leaf
      4.00        10 .  5899
       .00        11 .
      3.00        12 .  568
      7.00        13 .  2555688
     11.00        14 .  00244556689
      8.00        15 .  00234678
      5.00        16 .  13458
       .00        17 .
      2.00        18 .  36

 Stem width:         10
 Each leaf:        1 case(s)
```

Figure 2.9 (from SPSS)

```
Salary Stem-and-Leaf Plot

 Frequency     Stem &  Leaf
      3.00         3 .  699
     12.00         4 .  000023333344
     17.00         4 .  5555666688888889
     17.00         5 .  01111122224444444
     13.00         5 .  5557777777788
     37.00         6 .  00000000000000000033333333333333333333
     15.00         6 .  666666666666999
      4.00         7 .  2222
      6.00         7 .  558889
      2.00         8 .  14
      5.00         8 .  57777
      1.00         9 .  3
      1.00         9 .  9
     23.00 Extremes    (>=102000)

 Stem width:    10000
 Each leaf:        1 case(s)
```

Figure 2.10 (from SPSS)

small data sets a leaf will represent a single number, but for larger sets it might represent many. (See 'Each leaf' in Figure 2.9.)

The first row in Figure 2.9 represents the values 105, 108, 109 and 109. We can see that the mileages travelled range from 105 to 186. Notice that the 'leaves' are arranged in numerical order so that it is easy to find the value of the middle mileage or the third largest, and so on. If you draw stem-and-leaf plots by hand, it is necessary to group the values in tens but also to arrange carefully the order of the leaves. Fortunately Minitab and SPSS do this for us. Excel does not produce these plots.

In the larger data set in Figure 2.10, describing the salaries earned by a firm's workers, each stem width of £10,000, as indicated by 'Stem width', has been split into two rows. The leaves will be one number less significant, in this case measured to the nearest thousand, so the first value is £36,000 to two significant figures. Extreme values may often be grouped together. In this case we have 23 salaries which are greater than or equal to £102,000. For larger data sets the leaves may represent more than one case, but we are informed in Figure 2.10 that each leaf in this stem-and-leaf plot represents just one case.

2.4.4 Dot plots

A useful quick picture of the data can be formed by keeping a running total of the situation by means of a **dot plot**. This would be suitable for the 'straw polls' which are invariably taken from voters entering polling stations on election days. All the candidates' names would be displayed on the horizontal axis and a 'dot' plotted against the appropriate name for each voter who favours them. After about the first hour of opening at one particular polling station the picture might look something like Figure 2.11.

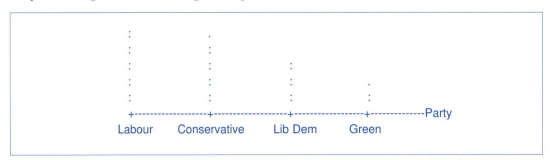

Figure 2.11

The advantage of this method, as opposed to using a bar chart or a pie chart is that the picture is built up gradually and does not need to wait for all the data to be collected before the diagram can be drawn.

2.4.5 Cumulative frequency polygons (ogives)

A **cumulative frequency polygon** is a graphical method of representing the accumulated frequencies up to and including a particular value. Think of it as a running total less than a stated value; for example, the proportion of a workforce earning up to £60,000 or cars doing up to 155 miles per week. These cumulative frequencies are often calculated as percentages of the total frequency. This method is used for estimating median and quartile values, and hence the interquartile or semi-interquartile range of the data (see Chapter 3). It can also be used to estimate the percentage of the data above or below a certain value. We shall construct the diagrams in this chapter and use them for estimating statistics in the next.

2.4.5.1 Method

- Construct a frequency table as in Section 2.4.1.
- Use it to construct a cumulative frequency table, noting that the **end** of the interval is the relevant value.
- Calculate a column of cumulative percentages if frequencies are to be compared.
- Plot the cumulative percentage against the end of the interval, and join the points with straight lines. Cumulative frequencies and percentages are plotted on the vertical axis.

In Example 2.5, using again the data from Example 2.3, we shall work through the method for drawing a cumulative frequency polygon. We shall then draw two on the same graph for comparison. In Chapter 3 we shall use these graphs to estimate the **median** mileage, the **interquartile range** and the **semi-interquartile range** of the data.

Example 2.5

Table 2.5

Interval less than	Fleet 1 frequency	Cumulative frequency
100	0	0
110	4	4
120	0	4
130	3	7
140	7	14
150	11	25
160	8	33
170	5	38
180	0	38
190	2	40

The cumulative frequency polygon is shown in Figure 2.12. As a picture in its own right, Figure 2.12 is not particularly informative.

For example we can read from it the number of vehicles which did less than, say, 155 miles in the week. This could be estimated from a hand drawn version on graph paper to be 29.

If, however, we use the same technique to compare Fleet 2 and Fleet 3, as we did with frequency polygons, it becomes more meaningful. As with the frequency polygons, you can see that comparing percentages is 'fairer' than comparing totals (see Table 2.6 and Figure 2.13).

All these cumulative frequency diagrams will be visited again in Chapter 3 when we will use them for various estimations. From the Figure 2.13(b) we can see, however, that Fleet 3 had many more low mileage vehicles than Fleet 2 as its steepest rise occurred sooner than that of Fleet 2.

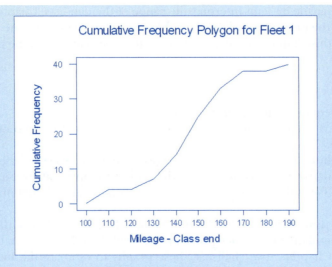

Figure 2.12

Table 2.6

Mileages less than	Frequency	Fleet 2 Cum. freq.	% C. f.	Frequency	Fleet 3 Cum. freq.	% C.f.
100	0	0	0.0	0	0	0.0
110	0	0	0.0	9	9	4.5
120	1	1	2.5	9	18	9.0
130	2	3	7.5	35	53	26.5
140	4	7	17.5	70	123	61.5
150	6	13	32.5	40	163	81.5
160	12	25	62.5	23	186	93.0
170	10	35	87.5	12	198	99.0
180	4	39	97.5	2	200	100.0
190	1	40	100.0	0	200	100.0

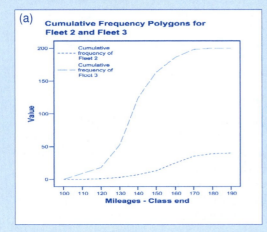

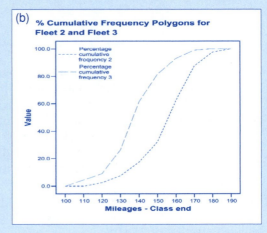

Figure 2.13

2.4.6 Box plots

Box plots can be constructed for ordinal, interval or ratio data. A box plot is a very useful diagram which summarises information about the location and spread of a set of data in one diagram. It is also referred to as a 'box and whisker plot'.

From Figure 2.14 we can see that the middle half of the data ranges from about 135 to about 155 miles, and that the highest value is an outlier at about 185, with the lowest also an outlier at about 105. The middle value is about 145.

This is a useful style of diagram for making comparisons. In Figure 2.15(a) we compare Fleet 1 with Fleet 2 and in Figure 2.15(b) we compare again the sales from the four different quarters from Example 2.2.

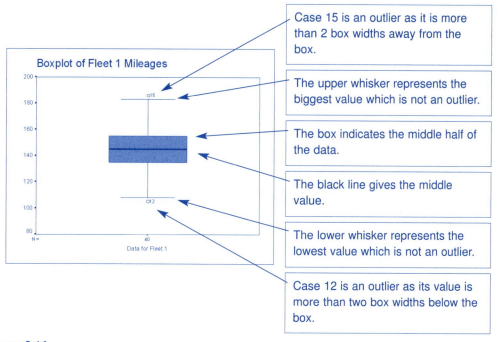

Case 15 is an outlier as it is more than 2 box widths away from the box.

The upper whisker represents the biggest value which is not an outlier.

The box indicates the middle half of the data.

The black line gives the middle value.

The lower whisker represents the lowest value which is not an outlier.

Case 12 is an outlier as its value is more than two box widths below the box.

Figure 2.14

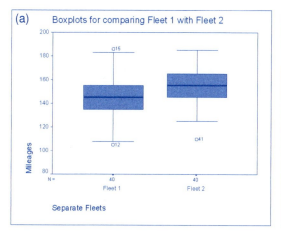

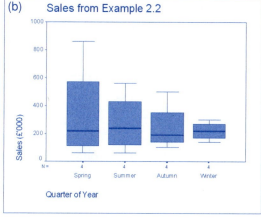

Figure 2.15

From Figure 2.15(a) we can see that the highest values for each of the two plots are similar but that the middle half, the box, is higher for Fleet 2 than for Fleet 1. The spreads, especially of the middle halves as shown by the boxes, are apparently the same.

For the sales of the combined departments for the separate quarters from Example 2.2 (Figure 2.15(b)), we can see that even though the lowest values are similar, especially for spring and summer, the highest ones are not. Looking at the boxes it is evident that the spreads are quite different. The sales cover a wide range of values in spring but are relatively constant in winter.

We shall interpret this type of diagram more fully in Chapter 3 when we again consider the black line and the box limits as measures of centrality and spread.

2.5 A continuous example using graphics

Example 2.6

You are interested in your firm's claim to promote equal opportunities for male and female workers. You therefore decide to select a random sample of the workforce, send them each a questionnaire and use the information produced to compare graphically male and female salaries. The information received on salaries has been tabulated in Table 2.7. The individual salaries, to the nearest thousand pounds, can be seen in Figure 2.18 showing the stem-and-leaf plots.

Table 2.7

Salary (£'000)	Frequency	
Class Interval	Male	Female
less than 20	4	21
20 and less than 30	12	48
30 and less than 40	36	58
40 and less than 50	64	42
50 and less than 60	77	21
60 and less than 80	35	8
80 and less than 120	18	2
over 120	4	0

We shall:

- close the open-ended intervals
- calculate frequency densities, i.e. frequency per £10,000 interval
- draw histograms
- calculate relative frequencies (per cent) to compare the samples of different sizes
- draw relative frequency polygons
- draw stem-and-leaf plots

- draw box plots
- calculate cumulative percentages
- draw cumulative percentage polygons.

Close open intervals

An employee is unlikely to work for less than £10,000 per annum. The top salary is more debatable, but £200,000 seems reasonable.

Calculate frequency densities

Table 2.8

Salary (£'000) Class Interval	Male employees		Female employees	
	Frequency	Frequency Density (per £10000)	Frequency	Frequency Density (per £10000)
10 and less than 20	4	4.0	21	21.0
20 and less than 30	12	12.0	48	48.0
30 and less than 40	36	36.0	58	58.0
40 and less than 50	64	64.0	42	42.0
50 and less than 60	77	77.0	21	21.0
60 and less than 80	35	17.5	8	4.0
80 and less than 120	18	4.5	2	0.5
120 and less than 200	4	0.5	0	0.0
Total	250		200	

Histograms

Both distributions (see Figures 2.16(a) and (b)) are positively skewed as might be expected for salaries. The peak for the men occurs between £50,000 and £60,000, that for the women between £30,000 and £40,000. The top female salary is under £120,000. which is estimated to be £80,000 less than that of the top male, even though the minimum values are the same.

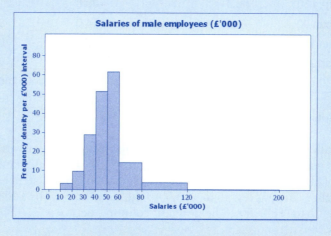

Figure 2.16(a)

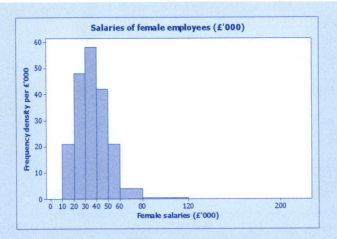

Figure 2.16(b)

Relative frequency polygons (see Section 2.4.2)

As would be expected, the frequency polygons lead to exactly the same interpretation as the histograms (see Table 2.9 and Figure 2.17). The polygons show both sets of data to be positively distributed, with the peak for males higher than that for females. The comparison is easier to make with polygons than with histograms, as the position of the peak is clearer.

Table 2.9

Salary (£'000)		Male employees		Female employees	
Class interval	Mid-interval	Frequency	Relative freq. (%)	Frequency	Relative freq. (%)
10 and less than 20	15.0	4	1.6	21	10.5
20 and less than 30	25.0	12	4.8	48	24.0
30 and less than 40	35.0	36	14.4	58	29.0
40 and less than 50	45.0	64	25.6	42	21.0
50 and less than 60	55.0	77	30.8	21	10.5
60 and less than 80	70.0	35	14.0	8	4.0
80 and less than 120	100.0	18	7.2	2	1.0
120 and less than 200	160.0	4	1.6	0	0.0
Total		250	100%	200	100%

Stem-and-leaf plots (see Section 2.4.3)

There is more data in this example than is usually illustrated by stem-and-leaf plots. The first plot is for the male salaries (sex = Male in Figure 2.18). For these data each leaf represents two cases. The units we are working with are £1000, so the stem width is £10,000. There are four cases earning less than £16,000; the next case earns £20,000. The last 22 cases earn more than £82,000. The longest column, between £50,000 and £60,000, contains 77 cases.

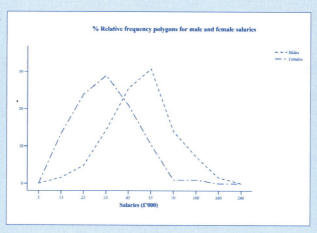

Figure 2.17 (from SPSS)

```
Salary Stem-and-leaf plot for sex= Male

Frequency   Stem &  Leaf
4.00 Extremes    (=<16)
12.00      2 .  02468
36.00      3 .  0002224446668888
64.00      4 .  00022222244444446666668888888888
77.00      5 .  00000000000000222222444444466666688888
14.00      6 .  00224&
21.00      7 .  224446688
22.00 Extremes   (>=82)


Stem width: 10
Each leaf: 2 case(s)


Salary stem-and-leaf plot for sex= Female

Frequency   Stem &  Leaf
21.00      1 .  000022446
48.00      2 .  0000222444444466668888
58.00      3 .  000022222224444444466666666888
42.00      4 .  0000222244446668888
21.00      5 .  2224446688
1.00      6 .  &
6.00      7 .  002
3.00 Extremes    (>=76)


Stem width: 10
Each leaf: 2 case(s)
& denotes fractional leaves.
```

Figure 2.18 Stem-and-leaf display: salary

The second plot, for the females (sex = Female in Figure 2.18), shows the salaries to range from £10,000 to more than £76,000, with the most common values between £30,000 and £40,000.

In this display format, the SPSS version, the left-hand column displays the cumulative frequency starting at each extreme.

Stem-and-leaf plots can be more informative if drawn 'back to back' with a common 'stem', but neither Minitab nor SPSS offers this format. Excel does not offer stem-and-leaf plots.

Box plots (see Section 2.4.6)

The box plots in Figure 2.19 illustrate both the centres of the data and the spreads.

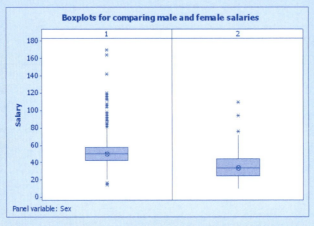

Figure 2.19 (from Minitab, 1 = males 2 = females)

The lowest values are similar for both sexes. The centre for the females is lower than that for the males. The total spread for the males is greater than that for females, but the width of the 'box' is wider for the females. We are mainly interested in the spread of the 'box', and this will be interpreted further in Chapter 3.

There are many more male outliers than female. The case numbers for these can optionally be included in the printout. Usually this numbering of cases is useful for identification purposes, but in this instance there are so many male outliers that their numbers overlapped and were indecipherable, and have not been included here.

Cumulative percentage diagrams (see Section 2.4.5)

Cumulative frequencies and cumulative percentages are first calculated. See Table 2.10. In order to compare male and female salaries the cumulative percentages are plotted on the same graph. See Figure 2.20.

We can see that for the female salaries (line 2), the steepest rise occurs first, showing that they peak at a lower salary than do the males (line 1). In Chapter 3 we shall produce much more information for comparing the salaries from these same graphs.

This graphical exploration of data has enabled us to see that males and females do not, in general, earn similar salaries. Do note that the data does not, however, tell us anything about their opportunities for advancement, so it should not be employed in this context.

Table 2.10

Salary (£'000) Interval	Male employees Freq.	Cum. freq.	Cum. %	Female employees Freq.	Cum. freq.	Cum. %
10 and less than 20	4	4	1.6	21	21	10.5
20 and less than 30	12	16	6.4	48	69	34.5
30 and less than 40	36	52	20.8	58	127	63.5
40 and less than 50	64	116	46.4	42	169	84.5
50 and less than 60	77	193	77.2	21	190	95.0
60 and less than 80	35	228	91.2	8	198	99.0
80 and less than 120	18	246	98.4	2	200	100.0
60 and less than 100	4	250	100.0	0	200	100.0
Total	250			200		

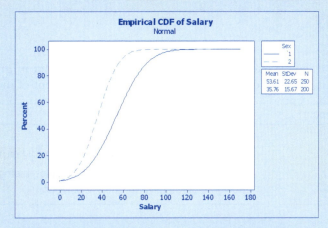

Figure 2.20 (from Minitab)

We have only used graphical comparisons in this chapter. In the next, numerical summaries will enable us to quantify any differences we have identified here.

2.6 Interpretation of published graphs

This section is included mainly as a warning. Take the greatest care when reading published graphs as the publisher may have a vested interest in their interpretation.

As stated previously for pictograms, you need to be clear how many dimensions are being used in any comparisons. If Box A is twice as long as Box B, does it indicate the ratio between them to be 2:1 for length, 4:1 for area or 8:1 for volume?

If comparing histograms, is zero frequency on the vertical axis or are just the column tops being shown? For example, 110 might appear to be double 105 if the base line is at 100. In line graphs the lack of an origin can lead to misinterpretation, making the gradient appear excessive.

The list is endless. Books on the misuse of statistics always devote quite a large section to graphs (see for example Reichman 1964 and Huff 1991).

2.7 Further methods of graphical description

This chapter has included most of the simple graphical presentations. These can be combined in various clever ways to include more information, but do be sure, before selecting one for use, that it also conveys this extra information to the recipient. Histograms and stem-and-leaf diagrams can be drawn 'back to back' very usefully for comparing, say, male and female earnings.

In this chapter we have considered only one variable at a time. In Chapter 9 you will meet scatter diagrams which look for associations between two variables. This can be extended using suitable software to three variables, though the graphics are not easy to interpret.

More sophisticated forms of statistical analysis, such as factor analysis, have their own graphical output, but these need not concern you.

2.8 Summary

In this chapter we have looked at various ways of presenting data in graphical form. The choice of presentation depends mainly on the scale of measurement of the data:

Scale of measurement	Suitable graphical presentation
Nominal	Bar chart, dot plot, pie chart
Ordinal	Bar chart, dot plot, pie chart, box and whisker plot
Interval or ratio	Box and whisker plot, stem-and-leaf plot, histogram, frequency polygon, cumulative frequency polygon

2.9 Case study (see Section 1.8 for background information)

You are asked to explore graphically, using your preferred computer package, some of the restaurant data provided by your employers, Restful Restaurants, to provide the directors with some insight into the survey data they have received from the University of Lonbridge:

Compare the three types of food outlet, restaurants, cafés and takeaways, in terms of:

- the numbers of each type of outlet
- their business outlook
- their size in terms of full-time employee equivalent
- their number of (a) full-time employees, (b) part-time employees
- the types of ownership
- the type of food outlet preferred by companies
- their gross sales
- the gross sales for the three sizes of outlets
- their market values.

The file you require is 'Restaurants', which you should download from the companion website (see book cover). It is in the students' materials in the case study folder from which you should select the version for your chosen software. The suggested corresponding output on the website is from SPSS, but this is only a suggestion of the appropriate diagrams, and yours may be (a) from a different statistics package or (b) a quite different selection. You are not expected, at this stage, to draw any conclusions, but just to get a feeling for your data.

Tutorial 2: Graphical presentation

Note: the diagrams drawn in this tutorial will be used in the next to estimate various summary statistics for the same sets of data.

The answers to all tutorial questions are to be found in Appendix A.

2.1 The following information refers to the number of defective components in 350 boxes.

No. of defective components:	0	1	2	3	4	5	6
No. of boxes:		25	85	99	70	51	14	6

a) Draw a histogram to represent this data.
b) Draw a cumulative frequency diagram to represent this data.

2.2 The following figures represent the ages of a sample of 60 male employees of a firm:

35	44	54	33	46	20	32	19	50	39	33	37
42	40	20	25	34	52	27	22	18	40	23	17
41	45	21	34	49	27	60	46	32	58	23	52
24	64	41	47	54	37	40	41	40	36	46	29
34	39	39	40	37	50	41	34	47	34	45	36

a) Form a grouped frequency distribution, using 10 year intervals.
b) Construct a histogram to illustrate the distribution of the data.
c) Add a frequency polygon to your histogram.
d) Construct a stem-and-leaf diagram with this data.
e) Draw a percentage cumulative frequency diagram of the data.

2.3 The following table refers to the height of 50 students in a class:

Height (inches)	Frequency
60" and less than 64"	2
64" and less than 66"	6
66" and less than 68"	11
68" and less than 69"	9
69" and less than 70"	10
70" and less than 72"	8
72" and less than 74"	2
74" and less than 80"	2

a) Form a frequency density distribution.
b) Draw a histogram to represent the data.
c) Draw a percentage cumulative frequency polygon of the data.

Notes

For SPSS/Minitab/Excel worksheets on graphical display see Chapter 14, Sections 14.2.1, 14.5.1 and 14.8.1 respectively. Worksheets with computer output and its interpretation are on the companion website.

The supplementary exercise for Chapter 2, with answers, is on the companion website.

Numerical summary of data

3

Objectives of this chapter

In Chapter 2 you learned how to represent a set of data by a single graph. In this chapter you will learn how to summarise the many values in a data set by just one or two values. This is known as **summary statistics**. This summary usually describes the centre of the data and how far the individual values are spread each side of that centre.

The measures of centrality we shall study are:

- mode
- median
- mean.

The measures of spread are:

- range
- interquartile range
- semi-interquartile range
- standard deviation.

We shall concentrate on the mean and standard deviation. You will learn to estimate these figures from graphs and calculate them from raw data, and how to use a statistical calculator.

After studying this chapter you should know:

- which measures of centrality and spread are appropriate for any given data set
- how to calculate them both by hand and on your calculator
- how to interpret the values produced.

3.1 Introduction: why do we need to summarise data numerically?

To repeat the question asked in Chapter 2, how do you react when faced with a large table full of figures? The graphs in the last chapter should have helped your understanding of given data sets. The problem is that a graph cannot be communicated very simply to another person either verbally or in writing. If, however, we make a statement such as that the average mark obtained in an examination was 65 and the marks ranged from 40 to 75, the recipient gains a reasonable understanding of the situation. In this example the figure of 65 gives an idea of the general **location** of the data, and the range of 40 to 75 a measure of its **spread** about its centre.

3.2 Measures of centrality (location)

In this section we are looking for a single figure to represent the whole data set. This is often referred to as the **average,** but in statistics different averages are calculated for different types of data, so we need to be more specific about which 'average' measure we intend to use.

3.2.1 The mode

The **mode** is the most commonly occurring value. (Think of the old-fashioned term 'mode' meaning fashion or that which is most commonly worn.) This measure of average is suitable for all different types of data from nominal to ratio (see Section 1.3).

We can count males and females and report the higher frequency; we can see from the charts which pop song is most popular, we know the most common degree classification awarded. Each of these results is a **modal** value, usually referred to simply as the **mode**.

To find the mode of a set of numbers, we just find which number has the highest frequency. For example, the set of numbers 1, 1, 1, 2, 2, 3, 4, 4, 6 would have a modal value of 1, as that number occurs more often than any other.

In a histogram the modal value occurs within the highest peak (see Section 3.4).

3.2.2 The median

Since the **median** is the 'middle member' of a data set, we must be able to place the data in some meaningful order to give this value. This measure is not, therefore suitable for nominal data. To specify the most popular, or modal, pop song is meaningful; but the middle, or **medial**, pop song is not. If a data set can be ordered, we can pick the middle member as being typical of it. We can find the degree classification of the middle member of a year group; we can identify the athlete who finished in the race in the middle of the field; we can find the middle child in a class placed in height order. To find the median of a set of numbers we just place them in order and find the middle one for an odd number of values, or the average of the middle two for an even number of values.

The number sequence 1, 1, 1, 2, 2, 3, 4, 4, 6 has a median of 2, as that is the middle value when they are placed in order.

In a histogram the median splits the area of the histogram into two equal halves. In a cumulative frequency polygon it is the 50th percentile (see Section 3.4).

3.2.3 The mean

The **mean** is the typical value usually referred to as the 'average'. It is found by adding all the values in a set and dividing their sum by the number of values. We do this using a formula:

$$\bar{x} = \frac{\sum x}{n} \qquad (3.1)$$

where $\bar{x}$ is the mean, x is a data value, $\sum$ (sigma) is the shorthand symbol for 'the sum of', and n is the number of values. The values must be measurable on an interval or ratio scale for the addition to be valid. For example it makes no sense to calculate the mean sex of the members of a class even if numerical codes are used to identify males and females separately. We can calculate a mode and median for degree classifications in a year group, but a mean value is not valid.

In business matters, the mean is the usual measure of financial average. It is the only average given by a statistical calculator, though the mode and median may be produced by a computer package. The mean is the measure of centrality that will be used throughout this course, although you should familiarise yourself with the median and the mode as well.

The set of numbers 1, 1, 1, 2, 2, 3, 4, 4, 6 would have a mean value of 24/9 = 2.67, as the sum of the nine values is 24.

In a histogram the mean can be considered as the 'centre of gravity' of the data.

Example 3.1

A small set of individual numbers

The following values represent the number of faulty garments returned each day to a store during a certain period.

13, 9, 10, 6, 7, 12, 4, 13, 14, 6, 9, 4, 8, 3, 10.

The store manager needs to find some useful measure of centrality, an average, in order to summarise them.

A useful step is to rewrite them in ascending order, giving:

3, 4, 4, 6, 6, 7, 8, 9, 9, 10, 10, 12, 13, 13, 14.

This data has five **modes** as the numbers 4, 6, 9, 10 and 13 all appear twice.

There are an odd number of values, (15), so the **median** is the middle number, that is the 8th, giving 9. The easiest way to find the middle position is to add one to the number of values and then divide the result by two, that is, (15 + 1)/2 = 8. Had there been only 14 values (an even number) the **median** would have been half way between the middle two, that is, the mean of the 7th and the 8th, giving 8.5.

The **mean** is found by adding all the returns together and dividing by the number of days during which they were returned.

$$\frac{3+4+4+6+6+7+8+9+9+10+10+12+13+13+14}{15} = \frac{128}{15} = 8.53$$

So 128 garments in total were returned during the period of 15 days.

Which of these measures is most useful to the store manager?

The mode is no use in this case because there are five modes in this data. The median is a reasonable measure because it is fairly central, but the mean is a better representation of all the daily returns because all the data have been used to calculate it.

Example 3.2

Discrete grouped data

If the number of returns were recorded for a whole year, the data would be summarised in a frequency table (see Section 2.2) rather than as individual values:

Table 3.1

Number of returns (x)	0	3	4	5	6	7	8	9	10	11	12	13	14
Number of days (f)	2	7	9	12	24	40	75	98	56	25	14	2	1
Running total of days	2	9	18	30	54	94	169	267	323	348	362	364	365

This is the first table of this type in the book so take time to understand it: on two days no garments at all were returned; on 7 days 3 garments were returned, and so on. The **mode** of this data is the most common number of returns made per day. We can see that 9 garments were returned on 98 occasions, so 9 is the modal number of returns.

The **median** is the number of returns on the middle day when the data is ordered. We have 365 days in total so the middle day will be $(365 + 1)/2 = 183$rd. A running total of days will show that 8 returns or less occur on 169 days, and 9 returns or less on 267 days, so 9 garments would be returned on the 183rd day.

In order to find the **mean** number of returns per day we need the total number of returns to be divided by the 365 days.

In symbolic form $$\bar{x} = \frac{\sum fx}{n}$$ (3.2)

where $\bar{x}$ is the mean and $\sum fx$ is the product of each data value and its frequency. This is an extension of Equation 3.1.

Table 3.2

Number of returns (x)	0	3	4	5	6	7	8	9	10	11	12	13	14
Number of days (f)	2	7	9	12	24	40	75	98	56	25	14	2	1
fx	0	21	36	60	144	280	600	882	560	275	168	26	14

$$\bar{x} \;=\; \frac{\sum fx}{n}$$

$$= \; \frac{21+36+60+144+280+600+882+560+275+168+26+14}{365}$$

$$= \; \frac{3066}{365} \;=\; 8.40$$

Fortunately we do not always need to find a mean by this type of calculation once the method is fully understood. It is preferable to use a statistical calculator in standard deviation (stat) mode. The processes of inputting the data values, x, and outputting the value for the mean, $\bar{x}$, will vary from one make of calculator to another, especially when dealing with frequency data, so make sure that you familiarise yourself with the method for your particular calculator from its instruction booklet.

Now try Examples 3.1 and 3.2 using your calculator. First work through Example 3.1 inputting the separate values, x, and outputting their mean value, $\bar{x}$, (its exact value is 8.53 recurring). Next work through Example 3.2, frequency data, making sure that you input the pairs of numbers in the order specified by your calculator instructions. Check that you get the same value, 8.40, for the mean.

Now work through Example 3.3 with a calculator. Once the mathematical method has been understood, it is preferable to use a statistical calculator in standard deviation (stat) mode. Calculators vary considerably in their methods of dealing with continuous frequency data, so be sure to consult your instruction booklet, and input the mid-point of each interval and its frequency as the pair of values in the correct order. Check that you get the correct answer, which is 57.2055, before rounding off to a more appropriate number of significant figures.

Further complete worked examples of each type follow in Section 3.3.

Example 3.3

Continuous grouped data

Suppose the previous store belonged to a company which had stores throughout the country, then the distribution describing the return of faulty garments for the year was:

Table 3.3

Number of returns	Number of days	Total no. of days
Less than 20	6	6
20 and less than 30	17	23
30 and less than 40	38	61
40 and less than 50	53	114
50 and less than 60	79	193
60 and less than 70	94	287
70 and less than 80	53	340
80 and less than 100	25	365
100 or more	0	365

The **modal class** is the class interval which occurs on the highest number of days, that is '60 and less than 70' returns which occurs on 94 days. We shall see in Section 3.4 how to estimate a more precise value within this interval.

The **medial class** is the one occurring on the middle number of days: $\dfrac{365+1}{2} = 183$

By calculating a running total of the number of days, we find that the 183rd day occurs in the interval '50 and less than 60' returns. This median will be estimated more precisely in Section 3.4.

The **mean** requires the total number of garments returned to be divided by the total number of days. As in Example 3.2 the frequency is the number of days on which a certain number of garments were returned. But what should we use for the value of x? We cannot input a range into the calculator so we use the mid-point of the interval to represent all the values within it. The total number of returns in any range can be calculated to be 'fx' as before. As previously $\sum fx/n$ gives the mean. A sensible lower limit for the lowest interval is zero and that for the highest interval is irrelevant in this case as its frequency is zero.

Table 3.4

Number of returns	Number of days	Midpoint (x)	fx
Less than 20	6	10	60
20 and less than 30	17	25	425
30 and less than 40	38	35	1 330
40 and less than 50	53	45	2 385
50 and less than 60	79	55	4 345
60 and less than 70	94	65	6 110
70 and less than 80	53	75	3 975
80 and less than 100	25	90	2 250
100 or more	0		0
Total	365		20 880

The mean value is therefore:

$$\frac{\sum fx}{n} = \frac{20\,880}{365} = 57.2 \text{ garments}$$

3.3 Measures of spread

A measure of centrality alone is not sufficient to describe a set of measurements. We also need to say how their values are dispersed about that centre. For example, the two sets of numbers 21, 22, 23, and 6, 22, 38 both have mean and median values of 22 but differ considerably in spread. In order for us to find any measure of spread, the data must be measurable on the ordinal scale at least. Nominal data cannot meaningfully be ordered so it is impossible to identify a spread. In this chapter we shall consider range, interquartile range and standard deviation as the main measures of dispersion (spread).

3.3.1 Range

The **range** of a set of data is simply the measure of the total width of its spread: that is, the largest value less the smallest value. The range is however a poor measure of spread as it only takes into account the two extreme data values. The two sets of data above (21, 22, 23 and 6, 22, 38) have ranges of 23 – 21 = 2 and 38 – 6 = 32 respectively. The second has a much larger spread than the first.

3.3.2 Interquartile range

The **interquartile range** avoids using only the extremes as it describes the spread of just the middle half of the ordered data. The ordered data is split into quarters with the same number of values in each. The quartiles are the values which divide the distribution into these four equal parts: the first quartile, Q_1, is the value below which 25 per cent of the observations lie; the second quartile, Q_2, is the median or middle value, and Q_3 has 75 per cent of the observations below and 25 per cent above it. The interquartile range is therefore the difference between the third and first quartile, $Q_3 - Q_1$. Some books also quote the **semi-interquartile range** which is, as its name suggests, $(Q_3 - Q_1)/2$.

As a simple illustration, consider the 11 ordered numbers 2, 2, 3, 5, 5, 5, 6, 6, 7, 7, 7. The first quartile, Q_1, [(11+1)/4] = the 3rd value = 3; the median, Q_2, is the [(11+1)/2] = the 6th value = 5; the third quartile, Q_3, is the [(11+1)3/4] = the 9th value = 7. The interquartile range is therefore 7 – 3 = 4. The semi-interquartile range would be 4/2 = 2. This idea has been demonstrated with a very small data set with a convenient number of observations; a larger data set is needed to make these measures more meaningful as they are less influenced by individual values.

Graphically, an interquartile range is estimated from a cumulative frequency diagram, as we shall see in Section 3.4.

3.3.3 Standard deviation

The **standard deviation**, as the name implies, is the standard measure of spread used in statistics. It is the measure of spread used throughout the following chapters of this book. We shall generally use a calculator in this course to calculate standard deviation, but first we shall work through a few examples by hand in order to aid understanding.

If we calculate the average deviation from the mean the answer would always be zero, because the positive and negative values would cancel out. We could just drop the negative signs and work with absolute values, but these are very difficult to manipulate arithmetically (see Section 3.5.2). We therefore remove the negative signs by finding the mean of the squared values and then finding its square root.

3.3.3.1 Population standard deviation

The **population standard deviation** is the figure calculated when we have all the data (the whole population of interest) in the analysis. It is most conveniently produced with the aid of a statistical calculator, by looking for the value of $x\sigma_n$:

The standard deviation is also known as 'root mean square deviation', and is calculated by squaring and then adding the deviations from the mean, finding the mean of the squared deviations, and then square-rooting the result.

$$\sigma = \sqrt{\frac{\sum(x-\bar{x})^2}{n}} \quad \text{or} \quad \sigma = \sqrt{\frac{\sum f(x-\bar{x})^2}{n}} \quad \text{for frequency data} \tag{3.3}$$

x represents the value of the data
f is the frequency of that particular value
$\bar{x}$ is the shorthand way of writing 'mean'
σ is the shorthand way of writing 'standard deviation'
$\sum$ is the shorthand way of writing 'the sum of'
$\sqrt{}$ means 'take the positive square root'. The negative root has no meaning for 'spread'.

The standard deviation is therefore a measure of how closely the data is grouped about the mean; the larger the value of the standard deviation, the wider the spread of the data. It is a measure of how well the mean represents the whole data set.

An equivalent formula which is often used is:

$$\sigma = \sqrt{\frac{\sum x^2}{n} - \left(\frac{\sum x}{n}\right)^2} \quad \text{or} \quad \sigma = \sqrt{\frac{\sum fx^2}{n} - \left(\frac{\sum fx}{n}\right)^2} \quad \text{for frequency data} \tag{3.4}$$

The first is the formula used by your calculator, but you don't need to worry about that.

We shall now find measures of spread for the data sets in Examples 3.1 to 3.3.

Example 3.1 continued

A small set of individual numbers

The small set of individual data for faulty garments returned is:

3, 4, 4, 6, 6, 7, 8, 9, 9, 10, 10, 12, 13, 13, 14 (as in Example 3.1).

The **range** is the largest value minus the smallest value = 14 – 3 = 11 garments.
For the inter-quartile range we must first establish which are the quartile values.
There are 15, an odd number of numbers, so: the quartiles, Q_1, Q_2, and Q_3 are the values of the $(15+1)/4$, the $2(15+1)/4$, and the $3(15+1)/4$ observations, that is the 4th, the 8th, and the 12th observations respectively. These have the values 6, 9 and 12 giving $Q_1 = 6$, $Q_2 = 9$ and $Q_3 = 12$ garments.
The inter-quartile range is therefore $Q_3 - Q_1 = 12 - 6 = 6$ garments
The **standard deviation** is a measure of the dispersion about the mean, $\bar{x}$, which we have already found to be 8.53 garments.

Table 3.5

x	$x - \bar{x}$ $(x - 8.53)$	$(x - \bar{x})^2$
3	−5.53	30.58
4	−4.53	20.52
4	−4.53	20.52
6	−2.53	6.40
6	−2.53	6.40
7	−1.53	2.34
8	−0.53	0.28
9	+0.47	0.22
9	+0.47	0.22
10	+1.47	2.16
11	+2.47	6.10
12	+3.47	12.04
13	+4.47	19.98
13	+4.47	19.98
14	+5.47	29.92
		Total 177.66

The standard deviation $\sqrt{\dfrac{(x-\bar{x})^2}{n}}$ is therefore:

$$\sqrt{\frac{177.66}{15}} = \sqrt{11.844} = 3.44 \text{ garments}$$

Using your calculator in standard deviation mode, following your instruction booklet carefully, input this individual data and output the **population standard deviation**, $x\sigma_n$. You should find that you get 3.40. This is the correct figure; the difference is due to rounding errors, particularly that of the mean.

Example 3.2 continued

Discrete grouped data

Table 3.1 has been repeated. The mean value is 8.40 returns.

Table 3.1

Number of returns (x)	0	3	4	5	6	7	8	9	10	11	12	13	14
Number of days (f)	2	7	9	12	24	40	75	98	56	25	14	2	1

The standard deviation is calculated using the formula for the frequency data.

Table 3.6

No. of returns (x)	No. of days (f)	$x - \bar{x}$ $(x - 8.40)$	$(x - \bar{x})^2$	$f(x - \bar{x})^2$
0	2	-8.40	70.56	141.12
3	7	-5.40	29.16	204.12
4	9	-4.40	19.36	174.24
5	12	-3.40	11.56	138.72
6	24	-2.40	5.76	138.24
7	40	-1.40	1.96	78.40
8	75	-0.40	0.16	12.00
9	98	+0.60	0.36	35.28
10	56	+1.60	2.56	143.36
11	25	+2.60	6.76	169.00
12	14	+3.60	12.96	181.44
13	2	+4.60	21.16	42.32
14	1	+5.60	31.36	31.36
Total	365		Total	1489.60

The standard deviation $\sqrt{\dfrac{(x-\bar{x})^2}{n}}$ is therefore:

$$\sqrt{\frac{1489.60}{365}} = \sqrt{4.0811} = 2.020 \quad \text{returns}$$

Check this figure using your calculator. The correct figure is 2.02017 giving 2.02 (to 3 significant figures).

Example 3.3 continued

Continuous grouped data

As for the calculation for the mean, the midpoint of each interval is first identified as its typical value, x. The mean number of returns was found earlier to be 57.2 garments.

Table 3.7

No. of returns	No. of days	Mid-point (x)	$\dfrac{x - \bar{x}}{x - 57.2}$	$(x - \bar{x})^2$	$f(x - \bar{x})^2$
Less than 20	6	10	-47.2	2227.84	13 367.04
20 & less than 30	17	25	-32.2	1036.84	17 626.28
30 & less than 40	38	35	-22.2	492.84	18 727.92
40 & less than 50	53	45	-12.2	148.84	7 888.52
50 & less than 60	79	55	-2.2	4.84	382.36
60 & less than 70	94	65	+7.8	60.84	5 718.96
70 & less than 80	53	75	+17.8	316.84	16 792.52
80 & less than 100	25	90	+32.8	1075.84	26 896.00
100 or more	0				0.00
Totals	365				107 399.60

The standard deviation $\sqrt{\dfrac{(x - \bar{x})^2}{n}}$ is therefore:

$$\sqrt{\frac{107\,399.6}{365}} = \sqrt{294.25} = 17.15 \quad \text{garments}$$

Check on your calculator. The exact figure should be 17.1536.

In practice the mean and standard deviation are found together using a calculator rather than separately, as we have done it. The next examples will be worked through calculating both parameters together.

Example 3.4

Grouped discrete data

The frequency distribution in Table 3.8 shows the time during which 95 costly machines in a computing laboratory were lying idle during a six-day week.
Find the mode, median, mean and standard deviation for the time they were lying idle from the following set of data: (Make sure you understand the data; we are finding answers in terms of idle time.)

Table 3.8

No. of idle days (x)	Number of machines(f)	fx	$x - \bar{x}$	$(x - \bar{x})^2$	$f(x - \bar{x})^2$
0	5	0	-2.29	5.244	26.22
1	24	24	-1.29	1.664	39.94
2	30	60	-0.29	0.084	2.52
3	19	57	+0.71	0.504	9.58
4	10	40	+1.71	2.924	29.24
5	5	25	+2.71	7.344	36.72
6	2	12	+3.71	13.764	27.53
Total	95	218			171.75

Mode	=	Most common number of idle days	=	2 days
Median	=	Middle, 48th, number of idle days	=	2 days
Mean	=	$\dfrac{\text{Total number of idle machine days}}{\text{Total number of machines}}$	=	$\dfrac{218}{95}$ = 2.29 days

or, by calculator, $\bar{x}$ = 2.294 74, rounded to 2.29 days (3 s.f.)

The standard deviation $\sqrt{\dfrac{(x - \bar{x})^2}{n}}$ is therefore: $\sqrt{\dfrac{171.75}{95}} = \sqrt{1.8079} = 1.34$ days (3 s.f.)

or, by calculator, standard deviation = 1.344 57, rounded to 1.34 days (3 s.f.)

Example 3.5

Grouped continuous data

A class of students were asked to keep a record of the time they spent at a computer during the course of a particular week.

Find the modal interval, the medial interval and the mean of these times.

Table 3.9

Time (minutes)	Number of students
Less than 20	2
20 and less than 40	5
40 and less than 60	4
60 and less than 90	6
90 and less than 120	5
120 and less than 180	7
180 and less than 240	3
240 and less than 360	2
360 or over	1

First it is necessary to close the top interval so that its mid-point can be found. A reasonable value might be set at any time over 480 min which would make its width at least the same as that of the previous interval. We shall go for that value giving a mid-value of 420 min.

Table 3.10

Time (minutes)	Mid-time (x)	No. of students(f)	fx	$x - \bar{x}$ $x - 116$	$(x - \bar{x})^2$	$f(x - \bar{x})^2$
Less than 20	10	2	20	-106	11 236	22 472
20 and less than 40	30	5	150	-86	7396	36 980
40 and less than 60	50	4	200	-66	4356	17 424
60 and less than 90	75	6	450	-41	1681	10 086
90 and less than 120	105	5	525	-11	121	605
120 and less than 180	150	7	1050	+34	1156	8092
180 and less than 240	210	3	630	+94	8836	26 508
240 and less than 360	300	2	600	+184	33 856	67 712
360 and less than 480	420	1	420	+304	92 416	92 416
Totals		35	4045			282 295

Modal interval = Most common interval = 120 to 180 minutes
Medial interval = Interval including middle, 18th, student = 90 to 120 minutes
Mean = $\dfrac{\text{Total time}}{\text{Total number of students}} = \dfrac{4045}{35}$ = 116 minutes (3 s.f.)

or, by calculator, $\bar{x} = 115.571$, rounded to 116 minutes (3 s.f.)

The standard deviation $\sqrt{\dfrac{(x-\bar{x})^2}{n}}$ is therefore $\sqrt{\dfrac{282295}{35}} = \sqrt{8065.6} = 89.8$ minutes

or, by calculator, $\sigma = 89.8075$, rounded to 89.8 minutes (3 s.f.)

3.3.3.2 Sample standard deviation

Much applied statistical work is based on the analysis of a sample, because the data from the whole population of interest is rarely available. It is therefore necessary to calculate the sample standard deviation as an estimate of the population standard deviation. It has been found that doing the calculation exactly as in the previous examples (Section 3.3.3.1) gives a biased result. An un-biased – more accurate – result is obtained using a slightly different formula which has 'n – 1' as the denominator instead of 'n' and 's', to distinguish the result as being produced from a sample rather than the population when we used σ. (Note that sample statistics are usually represented by roman letters (s) and population parameters by Greek letters (σ)).

The unbiased formulae are therefore:

$$s = \sqrt{\frac{\sum (x-\bar{x})^2}{n-1}} \quad \text{or} \quad s = \sqrt{\frac{\sum f(x-\bar{x})^2}{n-1}} \quad \text{for frequency data} \tag{3.5}$$

On the calculator we look for $x\sigma_{n-1}$. If the sample size is large there is very little difference between n and (n – 1), but for a small sample it can make a considerable difference.

Example 3.6

Calculating sample standard deviations for the Examples 3.1 to 3.5

Example 3.1 population standard deviation = 3.44 (3.40 from calculator)

Sample standard deviation

$$s = \sqrt{\frac{\sum(x-x)^2}{n-1}} = \sqrt{\frac{177.66}{14}} = \sqrt{12.69} = 3.56 \quad \text{(rounding errors)}$$

The calculator gives 3.5227 giving 3.52 (3 s.f.)

Example 3.2 population standard deviation = 2.02 (2.02 from calculator)

Sample standard deviation

$$s = \sqrt{\frac{\sum f(x-\bar{x})^2}{n-1}} = \sqrt{\frac{1489.6}{364}} = \sqrt{4.0923} = 2.02$$

The calculator gives 2.0229 giving 2.02 (3 s.f.)

Example 3.3 population standard deviation = 17.2

Sample standard deviation

$$s = \sqrt{\frac{\sum f(x-\bar{x})^2}{n-1}} = \sqrt{\frac{107399.6}{364}} = \sqrt{295.05} = 17.2$$

The calculator gives 17.177 giving 17.2 (3 s.f.)

Example 3.4 population standard deviation = 1.34

Sample standard deviation

$$s = \sqrt{\frac{\sum f(x-\bar{x})^2}{n-1}} = \sqrt{\frac{171.75}{94}} = \sqrt{1.827} = 1.35$$

The calculator gives 1.3517 giving 1.35 (3 s.f.)

Example 3.5 population standard deviation = 89.81

Sample standard deviation

$$s = \sqrt{\frac{\sum f(x-\bar{x})^2}{n-1}} = \sqrt{\frac{282295}{34}} = \sqrt{8302.8} = 91.1$$

The calculator gives 91.12 giving 91.1 (3 s.f.)

Notice that the sample standard deviations are each slightly larger than the corresponding population standard deviation. If you are not certain which of the two standard deviation buttons to use on your calculator, select the one that gives the larger value.

When the whole population is not available for analysis, as is usually the case, the sample standard deviation should be used. We shall use the **sample standard deviation** throughout the remainder of this course.

3.4 Estimation of summary statistics from graphs

In this section we shall use the histograms and cumulative frequency diagrams produced in Chapter 2. In practice it is obviously much quicker and more accurate to calculate the summary statistics directly from the raw data, if it is available. If, however, you only have the graphs it is important to be able to make estimates from them instead.

The mode can be estimated more precisely within the modal interval from a histogram of continuous data, and the median, other quartiles and interquartile range can be estimated from a cumulative frequency diagram.

3.4.1 Estimating the mode from a histogram

For discrete data the mode is simply the value that has the highest frequency. If the data is continuous or collected into a grouped frequency distribution, the mode must lie somewhere within the modal interval: that is, the interval with the highest frequency. The frequencies of the adjacent columns are used to estimate the mode within this interval, on the assumption that it is more likely to lie nearer to the column with the next highest frequency. Example 3.7 shows the modal class divided in the same ratio as the differences between the modal frequency and the frequency of the adjacent classes, by using crossed diagonals on the protruding part of the longest column.

Example 3.7

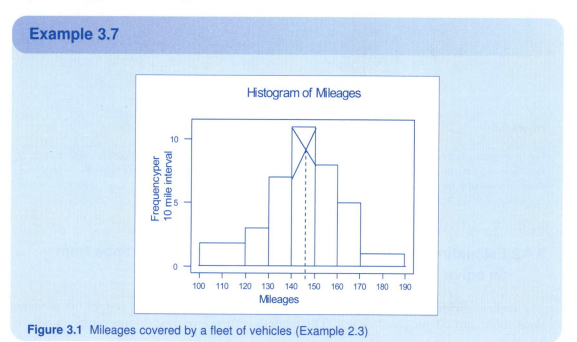

Figure 3.1 Mileages covered by a fleet of vehicles (Example 2.3)

Estimating the mode from a histogram

See Figure 3.1. Because the 150 to 160 interval has a higher frequency than the 130 to 140 interval we would expect the mode to lie towards the right of the modal interval, 140 to 150. By drawing the diagonals to the tops of the adjacent columns we can see that they intersect at about 146 miles giving a more precise estimate for the mode. A larger, hand-drawn histogram is preferable in order to produce a more accurate estimate.

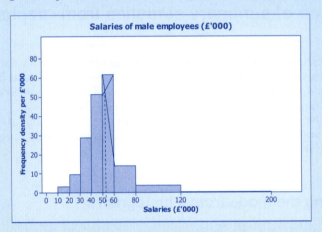

Figure 3.2

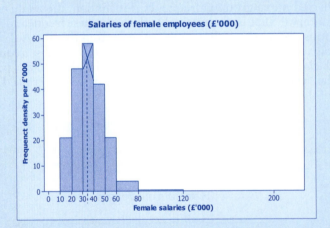

Figure 3.3

From Figures 3.2 and 3.3, using the crossed diagonals, the modes of the male and female salaries are estimated to be £5200 and £3400 respectively. As stated previously, a larger diagram would be preferable.

3.4.2 Estimating the median, quartiles and interquartile range from an ogive

The median divides the ordered data into two equal halves with 50 per cent of the observations above and 50 per cent below it. The median is therefore the 50th percentile. Similarly the lower quartile, Q_1, is the 25th percentile and the upper quartile, Q_3, is the 75th percentile. From a cumulative frequency diagram these values can be found by drawing horizontal lines from the 25 per cent, 50 per cent and 75 per cent positions, or their equivalent cumulative frequency values, on the vertical axis of the graph; then drawing vertical lines from the points of contact to the horizontal axis and reading off the values.

Example 3.8

Estimating the median, quartiles and interquartile range

1. Mileages covered by a fleet of vehicles

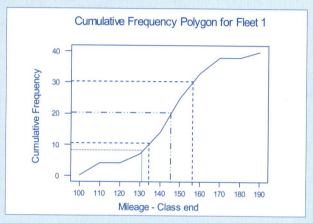

Figure 3.4 See Table 2.5 and Figure 2.12 in Example 2.5

Since there are 40 observations in this data we can take the 10th, 20th and 30th cumulative values to correspond to Q_1, Q_2, and Q_3 respectively. Estimating these values from the graph gives the figures 134, 145 and 156 miles respectively.

The median is therefore 145 miles, the upper quartile 156 miles, the lower quartile 134 miles and the interquartile range 156 – 134 = 22 miles. The semi-interquartile range is 22/2 = 11 miles.

We can also use this method for finding specific percentiles. For example, the number of vehicles travelling less than 131 hours = 8, or 20 per cent of the whole fleet.

2. Salaries of male and female employees

The values in Figure 3.5 are already plotted as percentiles. The estimated median salaries are £52,000 and £36,000 for the males (Sex = 1) and females (Sex = 2) respectively. For the males the upper and lower quartiles are £68,000 and £42,000, giving an interquartile range of £26,000 and a semi-interquartile range of £13,000. For the females the corresponding figures are £46,000 and £26,000, giving £20,000 as their interquartile range and £10,000 as their semi-interquartile range. This shows that even though the salaries of the females may have the lower location, they have the larger spread. (Again this graph is too small for any degree of accuracy.)

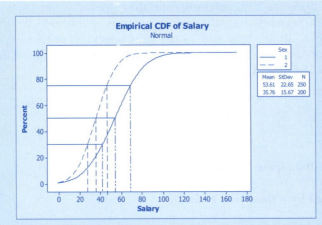

Figure 3.5 See Figure 2.20 in Example 2.6

3.5 Other summary statistics

3.5.1 Centrality

We have covered all the usual summary statistics in Sections 3.2 to 3.4. There are, however, a few more that are calculated in specialised circumstances.

In this chapter we have used the term 'mean' for the 'average', which is calculated by adding together all the values and dividing the result by the number of values, instead of the specific term **arithmetic mean**.

The **geometric mean**, which is often used when handling index numbers, is calculated by multiplying the n values together and then finding the nth root. The **harmonic mean**, which is defined as 'the reciprocal of the arithmetic mean of the reciprocals of the data', is sometimes used when analysing ratios. **Weighted means** are calculated when it is desirable for the contribution of some of the data to be greater than that of the rest, perhaps because of size or importance. This is similar to the method for dealing with frequency data when the value is multiplied by the frequency within each class, totalled, and divided by the total number of values.

3.5.2 Spread

As we have seen, the most common summaries of spread are **standard deviation** for interval or ratio data and **interquartile range** for ordinal data. Another measure often used is **variance**, which is the square of the standard deviation. This has the advantage of being easier to manipulate arithmetically than the standard deviation, but it is much more difficult to interpret in terms of units. For example, if the standard deviation of a group of salaries is in £'000 then the variance is in (£'000)².

The **mean absolute deviation** is the average size of deviation from the mean of each value. We cannot use the average deviation as a measure of spread, because the positive and negative deviations cancel out, but the size of deviation can be used if the signs are ignored. The mean absolute deviation is a sensible measure as it takes all the data into account, but absolute values are difficult to manipulate arithmetically, so it is not in general usage. One measure that is used, especially in financial circles, is the **coefficient of variation**. This measures relative dispersion, as it calculates the standard deviation as a percentage of the mean and so cuts out the effect of factors such as inflation.

3.5.3 Skewness

The ordering of the mode, median and mean determines the skewness of any data distribution. In Section 2.4.2 we looked at the skewness of a distribution as illustrated by a histogram or frequency polygon (see Figure 2.8).

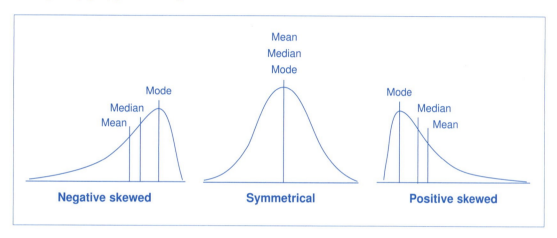

Figure 3.6

The **coefficient of skewness** is calculated from the formula: $\dfrac{3(\text{mean-median})}{\text{standard deviation}}$

You can see from the formula that the greater the deviation is between the mean and the median, the more skewed is the data.

These other summary statistics are described in more detail in many text books on statistics (see for example Weimer 1993, Chapter 3).

3.6 Computer numerical summary of Example 3.1

```
Descriptive Statistics: Returns

Variable Count   Mean  SE Mean  TrMean  StDev  Minimum
Returns    15   8.533   0.910   8.538   3.523    3.000


Variable   Q1    Median    Q3     Maximum
Returns  6.000   9.000  12.000    14.000
```

Figure 3.7 Minitab output

Descriptives			Statistic	Std. Error
Number of Garments returned	Mean		8.5333	.90956
	95% Confidence Interval for Mean	Lower Bound	6.5825	
		Upper Bound	10.4841	
	5% Trimmed Mean		8.5370	
	Median		9.0000	
	Variance		12.410	
	Std. Deviation		3.52272	
	Minimum		3.00	
	Maximum		14.00	
	Range		11.00	
	Interquartile Range		6.00	
	Skewness		-.004	.580
	Kurtosis		-1.120	1.121

Figure 3.8 SPSS output

Number of Garments returned	
Mean	8.533333
Standard Error	0.909561
Median	9
Mode	13
Standard Deviation	3.522715
Sample Variance	12.40952
Kurtosis	-1.11962
Skewness	-0.00424
Range	11
Minimum	3
Maximum	14
Sum	128
Count	15

Figure 3.9 Excel output

3.7 Summary

In this chapter we learned how to replace data sets by typical numbers – averages – representing them as an aid to better understanding.

We have seen that statistics such as the mean, mode and median can provide easy-to-calculate single measures of centrality, but that care must be exercised in selecting the most appropriate one to use for your particular type of data (see Table 3.11).

Measures of variability of a data set about its centre are also important but you may have found them more difficult to understand. The most appropriate statistic also depended on the type of data: for ordinal data it is usually the interquartile range about the median, and for interval or ratio data the standard deviation about the mean (see Table 3.11).

We also learned how to estimate summary statistics from graphically presented data, though these are not as accurate as those calculated directly from the original raw data.

Table 3.11

Scale of measurement	Suitable summary statistics
Nominal	Mode; no measure of spread.
Ordinal	Mode, median; Range, interquartile range, semi-interquartile range.
Interval or ratio	Mode, median, mean (any type); Range, interquartile range, semi-interquartile range, standard deviation, any of the other statistics in Section 3.5

3.8 Case study

You are asked to summarise numerically the same restaurant data as in Section 2.9, which has been provided by your employers, Restful Restaurants, to provide the directors with further insight into the survey data they have received from the University of Lonbridge.

Compare the three types of food outlet – restaurants, cafés and takeaways – in terms of:

- the numbers of each type of outlet
- their business outlook
- their size in terms of full-time employee equivalent
- their average number of (a) full-time employees, (b) part-time employees
- the types of ownership
- the type of food outlet preferred by companies
- their gross sales
- their market values.

Use whichever computer package you prefer. and the appropriate file 'Restaurants' from the students' materials on the companion website. You are still not expected to draw any conclusions, but your results will now be quantitative rather than qualitative, as in Section 2.9. Suggested suitable output is on the website in the case study output and answers folder. This is produced from SPSS, but either of the other packages would be equally suitable.

3.9 Calculator practice

Use your calculator in **standard deviation (stat) mode**, making reference to your instruction booklet until you are completely confident with the procedure. These questions are all asking for the calculation of the **mean** and the **sample standard deviation**.

1 The number of new orders received by a company over each of the last 25 working days were recorded as follows:

3 0 1 4 4 4 2 5 3 6 4 5 1 4 2 3 0 2 0 5 4 2 3 3 1

Use your calculator to estimate the mean and standard deviation for the number of orders received over all similar working days.

2 The mileages recorded for a sample of company vehicles during a given week yielded the following data:

138   164   150   132   144   125   149   157
146   158   140   147   136   148   152   144
168   126   138   176   163   119   154   165
146   173   142   147   135   153   140   135
161   145   135   142   150   156   145   128

Estimate the mean and standard deviation of the mileages of all the cars for the same week.

3 The number of breakdowns each day by your company's vehicles were recorded for a sample of 250 days as follows:

Number of breakdowns   0   1   2   3   4   5
Number of days   100   70   45   20   10   5

Estimate the mean and standard deviation for breakdowns on all days for the vehicles.

4 Determine the means and standard deviations of the whole of Marketing Departments A and B from which these two samples have been taken:

Annual sales (£)	No. from Dept. A	No. from Dept. B
150,000 but under 200,000	5	0
200,000 but under 250,000	17	19
250,000 but under 300,000	21	25
300,000 but under 350,000	3	4
350,000 but under 400,000	1	0
400,000 but under 500,000	1	0

Answers

1 Mean =   2.84 orders   Standard deviation =   1.70 orders
2 Mean =   146.8 miles   Standard deviation =   13.05 miles
3 Mean =   1.14 breakdowns   Standard deviation =   1.25 breakdowns
4 Mean =   (A) £250,600   Standard deviation =   (A) £50,110
              (B) £250,900   (B) £30,120

Tutorial 3: Data summary

The answers to all tutorial questions are to be found in Appendix A.

3.1 For the following set of sales:
State a) the range, b) the median.
Calculate c) the mean, d) the population standard deviation.

£210 £198 £204 £199 £192 £197 £201 £203 £196

3.2 A rope manufacturer has the choice of two heavy denier continuous filament polyester yarns which are identical apart from yarn strength. The manufacturer tests 12 bobbins from each type of yarn and obtains the following strengths (g/denier).

Yarn A 4.08 4.82 4.55 4.88 4.06 4.50 4.69 4.27 4.92 4.30 4.65 4.28
Yarn B 4.40 4.30 4.29 4.28 4.40 4.65 4.47 4.48 4.59 4.56 4.20 4.18

Calculate the mean, sample standard deviation and range for each yarn.

3.3 For the following information on the number of defective components in each of 1000 boxes, calculate the mean and standard deviation for the whole of the production.

No. of defective components	0	1	2	3	4	5	6
No. of boxes	25	306	402	200	51	10	6

3.4 From the frequency distribution of the monthly viewing times of a sample television audience, provided by a market research company and given below, calculate a) the mean and b) the standard deviation for the whole viewing audience.

TV sample audience monthly viewing times (hours)	Number of viewers (hundreds)
50 and less than 54	2
54 and less than 58	7
58 and less than 62	11
62 and less than 66	12
66 and less than 70	9
70 and less than 74	6
74 and less than 78	2
78 and less than 82	1

3.5 The following are the scores for a random sample of job applicants to your company. Calculate the mean and standard deviation for all job applicants.

Score (x)	80–84	85–89	90–94	95–99	100–104	105–109	110–114	115–119
Applicants (f)	8	13	22	24	11	10	7	5

3.6 For the data in Tutorial 2, Question 1, find the mode and median of the number of defective items produced.

3.7 For the graphs drawn for the data in Tutorial 2, Question 2, estimate the mode, median and interquartile range of the number of the ages of the employees. Find also the percentage of workers under 21 years old and the percentage of them who are over 50 years old.

3.8 For the graphs drawn for the data in Tutorial 2, Question 3, estimate the mode, median and interquartile range of the student heights. What percentage of the students are over 6 feet tall?

Notes

For SPSS/Minitab/Excel worksheets on summary statistics see Chapter 14, Sections 14.2.2, 14.5.2 and 14.8.2 respectively. Worksheets with computer output and its interpretation are on the companion website.

The supplementary exercise for Chapter 3, with answers, is on the companion website.

Probability

4

Objectives of this chapter

Many students find it difficult to make the transition from the certainty of mathematics to the uncertainty of statistics, so the main aim of this chapter is for you to gain some appreciation of the role played by probability in uncertain situations.

Having studied this chapter you should be able to make use of:

- symmetry
- past frequencies

to calculate

- probabilities
- expected values

and use these as decision-making tools in order to make choices concerning the uncertain future.

4.1 Introduction: the role of probability in statistics

We all cope with uncertainty in every day life by making risky decisions.

- Shall we carry an umbrella or risk getting wet as we think it is **unlikely** to rain?
- Do we allow 40 minutes for a journey as that will **probably** be long enough even if there is a hold-up en route, or can we **risk** 30 minutes by assuming there will be no hold-ups?
- Do we buy a particular share because we feel the **chances** are that its value will rise?

We make this subjective type of decision daily without the help of any quantitative evidence. In business it is preferable to make objective decisions on the basis of numerical evidence in order to minimise risk and uncertainty. If we can replace 'unlikely', 'probably', 'risk' and 'chance' with values, then comparisons can be made and a more logical decision-making process employed.

One of the main differences between mathematics and statistics is that mathematics deals with certainty whereas statistics is mainly concerned with uncertainty. In maths you carry out a calculation and state the answer as 'gospel' truth. In statistics, calculations are still performed but the answer usually includes some phrase such as "it is likely that ...", "there is a 95 per cent probability that ...", "we are 90 per cent certain that ...", and so on. In other words, black and white have been replaced by various shades of grey.

We may know the most probable life expectancy of the females in the United Kingdom but have no idea how long any one woman will live. Insurance tables are built up from what happens 'on average', but tell us nothing about individuals. The insurance company may possess a very good record of what has happened in the past, but cannot be certain of what will happen in the future, either 'on average' or in any individual case. A firm may know its monthly sales for many years past, but it cannot be certain as to what they will be for the next month; it can only make a reasonable **estimation**.

The role of statistics is to reduce this uncertainty to a minimum; to produce the **best estimations possible** and to accompany them with some **measure of their uncertainty**. If the sales of a non-seasonal commodity for the past 24 months are known, what is the most likely value next month, and how big a margin of error should be placed on that estimate? How do we choose between investments in two types of machinery which will probably produce different returns at different times during their different lives? What effect is this choice likely to have? Alternatively, would the expected returns be better if the money were simply invested?

In most circumstances we cannot analyse a whole population. For example, strength testing on textile fibres is done on only a very small proportion of the production, as the process results in their destruction. We know the average strength of the yarns that were tested, but what about all the others? Because we rarely have 'perfect knowledge' of an entire population, estimated measurements are unlikely to be completely accurate. Statisticians will not be completely sure of their results, so they will quote conclusions based on a sample and their confidence in those conclusions. This is usually quoted in terms of 'probability': for example, there is a high probability (0.95) that the mean strength will be 5.0 g per denier for the yarn. Alternative, a statistician might feel more comfortable stating that its mean strength lies somewhere between 4.8 g and 5.2 g per denier.

4.2 Probability as a measure of uncertainty

4.2.1 Measures of uncertainty

Probability **measures** the extent to which an event is likely to occur; it is the **numerical measure** of the **likelihood of its occurrence**.

- It can be measured by the ratio of favourable outcomes to non-favourable outcomes (**odds**).
- It is more generally measured by the ratio of favourable outcomes to all possible outcomes (**probability**).

Probability can be **calculated** from various sources:

- simple probability calculated from **symmetry**
- simple probability calculated from **frequencies**
- conditional probability calculated from **contingency tables**
- conditional probability calculated from **tree diagrams**.

4.2.2 Value of probability

Probability always has a value between 0 (impossibility) and 1 (certainty).

Probability of   0.0   corresponds to 'impossible'
                 0.1   corresponds to 'extremely unlikely'
                 0.5   corresponds to 'evens chance'
                 0.8   corresponds to 'very likely'
                 1.0   corresponds to 'certainty'

This can be summarised as $0 \leq P(E) \leq 1$ where $P(E)$ is the probability of an event occurring. An **event** may include more than one **outcome**, for example, for a die the event of 'an even number' includes the three outcomes '2', '4', and '6'.

4.2.3 Assessing probability

This can be done:

- from symmetry based on the geometry of the situation which gives an intuitive expectation – the **a priori approach**
- from past experience using relative frequencies – the **empirical approach**
- from 'gut feeling' – the **subjective approach**.

Let $P(E)$ be the probability of an event happening. With the a priori approach, '$P(E) = 1$' means that event E must always occur; there is no possible alternative outcome. With the empirical approach, this means that it has always occurred up to now but not that it is inevitable. With the subjective approach, it means that we feel certain the event will occur.

Let us take a numerical example. If a coin has landed 'heads up' ten times out of the last ten tosses, what is the probability of getting a head on the next toss of the same coin?

- The **a priori** method suggests 1/2, as half of the faces are heads.
- The **empirical** method: 10/10 = 1 as that has been the ratio of heads to all possible outcomes in the past.
- The **subjective** gut feeling is to doubt the fairness of the coin and so suggest that only a head is possible: that is, 1. Alternatively, the opposite gut feeling may be that a tail is definitely due, therefore 0!

4.3 Probability from symmetry

The 'theory of probability' was developed in the gaming situation, which depends upon the symmetry of dice, cards, roulette wheels and so on.

We can define the probability of an event E taking place as:

$$P(\text{event} E) = \frac{\text{Number of equally likely outcomes in which E occurs}}{\text{Total possible number of equally likely outcomes}} \quad (4.1)$$

Invoking symmetry, there is no need to actually do any experiments. This is the reason for the term 'a priori', which means deductive or without investigation.

If we had a single die with the number 6 on four faces and the number 2 on the other two, we would know from the geometry of the situation that the probability of getting an even number is **certainty**, that the probability of getting an odd number is an **impossibility**, and that the probability of getting 6 is four chances out of six. The definition in Equation 4.1 therefore seems quite satisfactory in this case.

The shorthand version of this is:

- P(even number) = 6/6 = 1
- P(odd number) = 0/6 = 0
- P(6) = 4/6
- P(2) = 2/6

Note that for a set of **exhaustive events** – that cover all possibilities between them – the probabilities always **sum to unity**: that is, they always add up to 1. In the example above, P(even number) + P(odd number) = 1, P(6) + P(2) = 1.

In general terms:

$$P(E) = \frac{r}{N} \quad (4.2)$$

where E is the event, r the number of favourable (in terms of the event E) outcomes, and N the number of possible outcomes. We shall look at some further examples from the gaming situation, even though their application is limited in the world of business, because this is the classic approach to probability.

Example 4.1

Coins

Tossing 1 coin:
Possibilities: Head, Tail.

P(a head) = 1/2 = 0.5   P(a tail) = 1/2 = 0.5

Tossing 2 coins:
Possibilities: Head Head, Head Tail, Tail Head, Tail Tail.

P(2 heads) = 1/4   P(2 tails) = 1/4   P(1 head and 1 tail) = 2/4

Tossing 3 coins:
Possibilities: head head head,   tail head head,   head tail head,   head head tail,
                   tail tail tail,   head tail tail,   tail head tail,   tail tail head.

P(3 heads) = 1/8   P(2 heads) = 3/8   P(1 head) = 3/8   P(0 heads) = 1/8
P(3 tails) = 1/8   P(2 tails) = 3/8   P(1 tail) = 3/8   P(0 tails) = 1/8

Note that the sum of all the possible probabilities is again one.
   This makes sense. These sets are exhaustive so one of these outcomes must occur and
P(certainty) = 1.

Example 4.2

Dice

Rolling a single die:
Possibilities: 1, 2, 3, 4, 5, 6.

P(6) = 1/6   P(anything but 6) = 5/6
P(an even number) = 3/6   P(an odd number) = 3/6

Again each pair of probabilities sums to 1.

Rolling a pair of dice:
All possibilities are shown in a possibility space diagram Figure 4.1.
This is useful as the regular pattern makes the answers easy to find in rows, diagonals
or columns. Make use of the fact that all possibilities sum up to 1, that is P(no 4s) =
1 − P(at least one 4)

1,1	1,2	1,3	1,4	1,5	1,6
2,1	2,2	2,3	2,4	2,5	2,6
3,1	3,2	3,3	3,4	3,5	3,6
4,1	4,2	4,3	4,4	4,5	4,6
5,1	5,2	5,3	5,4	5,5	5,6
6,1	6,2	6,3	6,4	6,5	6,6

Figure 4.1

P(any double) = 6/36   P(double 4) =1/36   P(exactly 4) = 3/36
P(less than 4) = 3/36   P(more than 4) = 30/36   P(at least one 4) = 11/36
P(no 4s) = 1 – 11/36 = 25/36   P(an even total) = 18/36   P(an odd total) = 18/36

Example 4.3

Suppose there are 100,000 tickets sold for a lottery with only one prize and you buy 50 of them, what is the probability that you will win the prize?

$$P(\text{winning}) = \frac{\text{Number of your tickets}}{\text{Total number of tickets}} = \frac{50}{100\,000} = 0.0005$$

In a more complicated situation, such as the rolling of three or four dice, it is more convenient to combine the probabilities from each die than to list all the possibilities.

4.3.1 Combining independent probabilities

If events are independent of each other, the probabilities are combined by multiplication. Events are independent if the outcome of one is not affected by the outcome of the others: for example, the result of rolling one die does not influence the result of rolling another die. The probability of throwing a 4 with one die is 1/6, so think of the probability of throwing a double 4 with two dice as being 'a sixth of a sixth': that is, $(1/6) \times (1/6) = (1/6)^2$.

Example 4.4

Calculate probabilities for multiple dice

One throw:
P(any one die scoring six in one throw) = 1/6
P(a score is not a six for one throw) = 5/6

Two throws:

P(two sixes in two throws) $= 1/6 \times 1/6 = (1/6)^2$

P(one six in two throws) $= 1/6 \times 5/6$, (if the first die is the six)
                                        $+ 5/6 \times 1/6$, (if the second die is the six)
                                        $= 2 \times (1/6)\,(5/6)$

P(no sixes in two throws) $= 5/6 \times 5/6 = (5/6)^2$

Three throws:

P(three sixes with three throws) $= 1/6 \times 1/6 \times 1/6 = (1/6)^3$

P(two sixes in three throws) $= 1/6 \times 1/6 \times 5/6 + 5/6 \times 1/6 \times 1/6 + 1/6 \times 5/6 \times 1/6$
                                      $= 3 \times (1/6)^2 \times (5/6)$

P(one six in three throws) $= 1/6 \times 5/6 \times 5/6 + 5/6 \times 1/6 \times 5/6 + 5/6 \times 5/6 \times 1/6$
                                      $= 3 \times (1/6) \times (5/6)^2$

P(no sixes in three throws) $= 5/6 \times 5/6 \times 5/6 = (5/6)^3$

Can you see the pattern emerging? The probability of one 6 in five throws is:

$$5 \qquad \times \qquad (1/6)^1 \qquad \times \qquad (5/6)^4$$

Number of dice   one dice showing 6   four dice not showing 6

In general if the probability of success in any one trial is p, the probability of getting r successes in n trials is:

$$P(r) = \frac{n!}{r!(n-r)!} \times p^r \left(1 - p\right)^{(n-r)} \tag{4.3}$$

where n! stands for factorial n, that is, n × (n–1) × (n–2) ... 2 × 1. (If you are not happy with this, use Pascal's triangle: see Figure 4.2.)

For example: P(three 6s in five throws) $= \dfrac{5!}{3!2!} \times \left(\dfrac{1}{6}\right)^3 \left(\dfrac{5}{6}\right)^2 \ = \ 10 \times \dfrac{5^2}{6^5} \ = \ 0.0322$

This makes use of the **binomial distribution** (see Section 5.7.1).

The coefficient n!/r!(n – r)! can be found directly from many calculators and also, without calculation, using **Pascal's triangle** (see Figure 4.2).

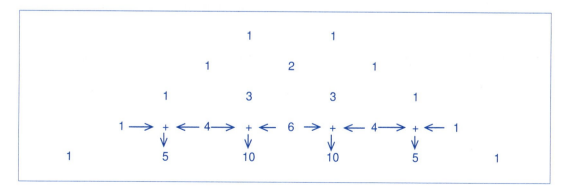

Figure 4.2 Pascal's triangle

Each line starts with the number 1, the next number is the sum of the numbers on either side of it in the previous line, and so on until it ends with another 1. So the sixth line would be:1, 6, 15, 20, 15, 6, 1. Therefore, if we threw six dice the sixth row of the coefficients would be used in calculating the probability of getting 0, 1, 2, 3, 4, 5 and 6 sixes respectively.

Find the following probabilities using the coefficients from the fourth row of Pascal's triangle:

P(four 6s with four dice) $= 1 \times (1/6)^4 \times (5/6)^0 = 1/1296 = 0.000\ 77$

P(three 6s with four dice) $= 4 \times (1/6)^3 \times (5/6)^1 = 20/1296 = 0.0154$

P(two 6s with four dice) $= 6 \times (1/6)^2 \times (5/6)^2 = 150/1296 = 0.1157$

P(less than two 6s with four dice) $= P(zero\ 6s\ ) + P(one\ 6)$

$= 1 \times (1/6)^0 \times (5/6)^4 + 4 \times (1/6)^1 \times (5/6)^3$

$= 0.4823 + 0.3858 = 0.8681$

Alternatively $= 1 - (0.0008 + 0.0154 + 0.1157) = 0.8681$

If you use Equation 4.3 you can calculate any combinations of independent probabilities:

P(getting three 6s with five dice) $= \dfrac{5!}{3!2!} \times (1/6)^3 \times (5/6)^2 = 0.0322$

P(getting three 6s with six dice) $= \dfrac{6!}{3!3!} \times (1/6)^3 \times (5/6)^3 = 0.0536$

4.4 Probability from relative frequency

An alternative way to look at probability is to carry out an experiment to determine the proportion of favourable outcomes **in the long run**.

$$P(E) \ = \ \frac{\text{Number of times E has occurred}}{\text{Number of times experiment was run}} \tag{4.4}$$

This is the **frequency definition of probability** and is referred to as the **empirical** (experimental) approach. There is no way of estimating the probability without doing an experiment or observing past data. (Section 4.4.1 merely illustrates the procedure.)

Relative frequency is the proportion of all the **possible times** it has **actually occurred**.

4.4.1 Estimating probability from long-term relative frequency

As the number of trials increases, the relative frequency demonstrates a long-term tendency to settle down to a constant value. This value is the probability of the event. But how long is this 'long term'? See Table 4.1.

We can see that the relative frequency values (the proportion of heads) are converging. If we carry on in this manner for as many flips of the coin as it takes for the relative frequency to settle down to two decimal places, and then plot the result on graph paper, we might get a picture similar to Figure 4.3.

By about the 14th toss the proportion has settled down to about 0.5, which gives the long-term probability for the next outcome being a head.

Table 4.1 Relative cumulative frequencies recorded from tossing a single coin

Total number of throws	Result	Number of heads	Proportion of heads
1	H	1	1.00
2	H	2	1.00
3	T	2	0.67
4	T	2	0.50
5	H	3	0.60
6	T	3	0.50
7	H	4	0.57

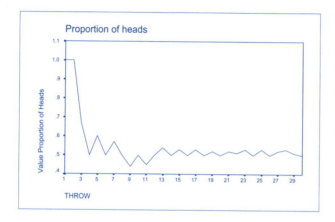

Figure 4.3

Note that:

- **the outcome of an individual trial is either 1 or 0 heads**
- **it is the long-term tendency that gives the estimated probability.**

More formally, If r trials out of n (a large number of trials) result in the event E, then the probability of the event E, assuming each outcome is equally likely, is:

$$P(E)=\frac{r}{n}$$

(4.5)

Note: n must be a large number because the accuracy of the estimate of probability improves as the sample size (number of trials) increases.

For example, suppose your company produces a new type of ballpoint pen and wishes to find the probability of any one pen being defective. The a priori approach is obviously no use, as the product is new and there is no prior knowledge of its deficiency rate. You therefore have to take the empirical approach of sampling the production, and using the proportion of defective pens in the sample to estimate the probability of any one pen being found faulty.

4.4.2 Estimating probability from frequency tables

Another alternative estimation of probability can be made from **frequency tables**. **Relative frequency** is calculated as before (see Section 2.3).

Example 4.5

Estimating probability from frequency

The data in Table 4.2 refer to the annual salaries of a group of workers. Since the figures are not simple enough for mental arithmetic, it is advisable to calculate relative frequency. Cumulative relative frequency might also be useful.

Table 4.2

Annual salary	No. of employees	Relative frequency	Cumulative rel. freq.
10 000 to < 11 000	3	0.03	0.03
11 000 to < 12 000	4	0.04	0.07
12 000 to < 14 000	7	0.07	0.14
14 000 to < 16 000	11	0.11	0.25
16 000 to < 20 000	18	0.18	0.43
20 000 to < 24 000	31	0.31	0.74
24 000 to < 30 000	22	0.22	0.96
30 000 to < 40 000	4	0.04	1.00
Total	100	1.00	

What is the probability that a worker chosen at random:
Earns £30,000 or over?   0.04 (from relative frequency.)
Earns less than £20,000?   0.43 (from (cumulative relative frequency.)
Earns between £20,000 and £30,000? 0.96 – 0.43 = 0.53
Earns between £12,000 and £24,000? 0.74 – 0.07 = 0.67

4.4.3 Estimating probability from histograms

A further alternative is that probability can be estimated from a **histogram** (see Section 2.5) based on frequency or frequency density. This method is particularly useful if the original data is not available.

Example 4.6

Figure 4.4 shows the time, to the nearest minute, it had taken an employee to get to work on 50 occasions. From this graph we can estimate the probability that the journey will take between any given lengths of time on the following day.

From Figure 4.4 the probability of the journey taking between 19.5 and 20.5 minutes can be estimated to be 25/50 = 0.5

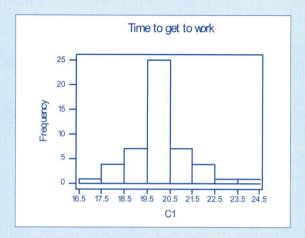

Figure 4.4

What is the probability of taking:

less than 19.5 min?	$(1 + 4 + 7)/50 = 0.24$
less than 20.5 min?	$(1 + 4 + 7 + 25)/50 = 0.74$
more than 20.5 min?	$1 - 0.74 = 0.26$
between 19.5 and 21.5 min?	$(25 + 7)/50 = 0.64$

4.5 Probabilities from contingency tables

If we have mutually exclusive data on two variables, the frequencies can be displayed in a **contingency table**. Mutually exclusive events can have only one outcome: for example, people are either experienced drivers, learners or non-drivers, but cannot be any two or three of these things at the same time.

Table 4.3

		Driver	
Gender	Driver	Learner	Non-driver
Male	70	0	10
Female	90	10	20

A contingency table displays all possible combined outcomes and the frequency of each observation. All contingencies – that is, all possibilities – are included in the table. No element can be placed in more than one cell, as the categories of each variable are mutually exclusive. Relative frequencies are calculated as estimations of equivalent probabilities.

As before, when looking for relative frequencies we are asking, how many fulfil the condition required out of how many possibilities? Since we are now combining probabilities we must be sure of the exact requirements for combination:

- 'And' requires both conditions to be satisfied.
- 'Or' requires either or both to be satisfied. Be careful not to include 'both' twice.

- 'If it is known that' or 'given that' limits the possibilities to just that specific subgroup.
- Remember that exhaustive probabilities add up to 1.

Example 4.7

A supermarket did a survey to investigate customers' spending on drink in relation to their mode of travel. The results are shown in Table 4.4.

Table 4.4 Expenditure on drink

Mode of travel	None	1p and < £30	At least £30
On foot	40	20	10
By bus	30	35	15
By car	25	33	42

The table is first completed by calculating all row and column totals.

Table 4.5 Expenditure on drink

Mode of travel	None	1p and < £30	At least £30	Total
On foot	40	20	10	70
By bus	30	35	15	80
By car	25	33	42	100
Total	95	88	67	250

What is the probability that a customer selected at random:
(a) will spend at least £30? $67/250 = 0.268$
(b) will travel by car? $100/250 = 0.400$
(c) will spend at least £30 and travel by car? $42/250 = 0.168$
(d) will spend at least £30 or travel by car? $(67 + 25 + 33)/250 = 0.500$
(e) will spend less than £30? $1 - 0.268 = 0.732$ from (a)
(f) will not travel by car? $(70 + 80)/250 = 0.600$ from (b)
(g) will not travel by car and will spend < £30? $(40 + 20 + 30 + 35)/250 = 0.500$
(h) will not travel by car or will spend < £30? $(250 - 42)/250 = 0.832$

It doesn't matter how you arrive at the subtotals. There are various methods using set notation and formulae, but the simplest way is just to total the cells that meet the required condition.

Example 4.8

A magazine subscription service conducted a survey to study the relationship between the number of subscriptions per household and family income. The survey, based on 1000 interviews, produced the results shown in Table 4.6.

Table 4.6

No. of subs. per household	Family income				Total
	Less than £30 000	£30 000 to £49 999	£50 000 to £69 999	At least £70 000	
0	28	54	78	23	183
1	29	151	301	73	554
2	15	31	69	57	172
>2	0	19	40	32	91
Total	72	255	488	185	1000

Find:

a) P(household had income < £50 000) $(255 + 72)/1000 = 0.327$

b) P(household had 1 subscription) $554/1000 = 0.554$

c) P(household having an income of £50 000 or more had no subscriptions) $(78 + 23)/(488 + 185) = 0.150$

d) P(household with < £30 000 had more than two subscriptions) $0/72 = 0.000$

e) P(household had at least one subscription) $1 - 183/1000 = 0.817$

f) P(household had either an income < £50 000 or more than one subscription) $(327 + 69 + 57 + 40 + 32)/1000 = 0.525$

Very often you will need to build up the contingency table from limited information which may appear to be incomplete but is often sufficient to build up a complete table. As each number is entered in the appropriate cell, it should be possible to infer others from the total or from a subtotal.

4.6 Conditional probability

If the probability of the outcome of a second event depends upon the outcome of a previous event, the second is **conditional** on the outcome of the first. This concept is easiest to understand when it is illustrated by a few examples.

Example 4.9

Cards

Two cards are selected from a full pack **without replacement**. Any probabilities concerning the second card depend on which card has previously been removed or, more to the point, which cards remain available for selection.

P(the first card being an ace) = 4/52
P(second card being an ace) = 3/51 if the first card was an ace but 4/51 if it was not
P(first card being a picture) = 12/52
P(second card being a picture given that the first was a picture) = 11/51
P(second card being a picture given that the first was not a picture) = 12/51

The word 'given' is usually represented by |. For example, P(second card a picture | first card was a picture).

Given information about the first card drawn from a pack of playing cards, find the probabilities of the second card being a heart? In each case there are 51 cards remaining but how many of them are hearts?

P(second a heart | first a heart)	12/51
P(second a heart | first not a heart)	13/51
P(second a heart | first a spade)	13/51
P(second a heart | first not a spade)	Here we do not know how many hearts remain after the first withdrawal so we cannot decide whether the answer is 12/51 or 13/51.

Example 4.10

200 workers, of whom 80 are male, were questioned about their driving capabilities. Three-quarters of the females were qualified drivers and two-thirds of the 30 non-drivers were female. 10 of the employees were learning to drive.

Table 4.7

Gender	Driver status Qualified	Learner	Non-driver	Total
Male				80
Female	3/4 of the females		2/3 of the non-drivers	
Total		10	30	200

First complete the contingency table and then use it to answer the questions below.

Table 4.8

Gender	Driver status Qualified	Learner	Non-driver	Total
Male	70	0	10	80
Female	90	10	20	120
Total	160	10	30	200

a) What is the probability of a any worker being a qualified driver?   160/200 = 0.800
b) What is the probability of a male worker being a qualified driver?   70/80   = 0.875
c) What is the probability of a qualified driver being male?   70/160 = 0.438
d) What is the probability of a female being a non-driver?   20/120 = 0.167
e) What is the probability of a non-driver being female?   20/30   = 0.667

Some examples that can be worked through using contingency tables may be even more easily solved by other methods. We shall solve Example 4.11 first using a contingency table, then with the aid of a **tree diagram**.

4.6.1 Tree diagrams

Tree diagrams provide a systematic approach to the listing of all the possible outcomes of combined events. They are also known as **probability trees**.

- Tree diagrams can be drawn for more than two events.
- All possible outcomes at each event are shown as branches.
- At each branching all the probabilities must sum to 1.
- Consecutive events follow along the branches.
- Combined probability along a series of branches is found by multiplication.
- Combined probabilities are added if more than one series of branches is favourable.
- For the complete tree all the combined probabilities must sum to 1.

Example 4.11

Your company is hosting a cricket match with one of its best suppliers tomorrow but is worried about the weather which has been poor in the recent past. Suppose the probability of rainfall tomorrow depends on today's weather. If it rains today, there is a probability of 0.7 that it will rain tomorrow, whilst if today is fine, there is a probability of 0.55 that it will rain tomorrow. Suppose further that the probability of rain today is 0.6. What are the probabilities that it will be fine tomorrow?

Let A be the event of rain today, $\bar{A}$ the event of no rain today, B the event of rain tomorrow, and $\bar{B}$ the event of no rain tomorrow

The word 'given' is represented by |. A horizontal line over an event means that it does not occur.

From the information above: $P(A) = 0.6$, $P(B|A) = 0.7$, $P(B|\bar{A}) = 0.55$

Solving using a contingency table

Insert these probabilities in a contingency table and calculate the other cell values.

Remember that, assuming the events are independent, the probability of two events happening is the product of their individual probabilities, and that, for any row or column the cell probabilities sum to the value under the total probability.

Table 4.9

Today's weather	Tomorrow's weather		
	Rain tomorrow (B)	Fine tomorrow ($\bar{B}$)	Total
Rain today (A)	0.7 x 0.6 = 0.42	0.6 – 0.42 = 0.18	0.6
Fine today ($\bar{A}$)	0.55 x 0.4 = 0.22	0.4 – 0.22 = 0.18	0.4(1 – 0.6)
Total	0.42 + 0.22 = 0.64	0.18 + 0.18 = 0.36	1.0

Find the corresponding conditional probabilities for it not raining tomorrow:

$$P(\bar{B}|A) = 0.18/0.6 = 0.3 \qquad P(\bar{B}|\bar{A}) = 0.18/0.4 = 0.45$$

This was not a very easy exercise with the information given, so we shall try another method.

Solution using a tree diagram

$$P(A) = 0.6 \qquad P(B|A) = 0.7 \qquad P(B|\bar{A}) = 0.55$$

First we insert the given probabilities into the tree diagram.

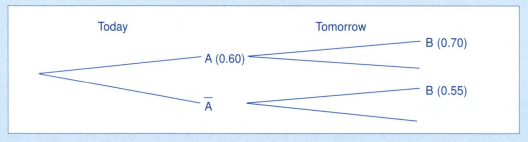

Figure 4.5

Next, using the fact that at any branching point the probabilities sum to 1, we insert the missing probabilities.

$$P(\bar{A}) = 1 - 0.6 = 0.4; \quad P(A \text{ and } \bar{B}) = 1 - 0.7 = 0.3; \quad P(\bar{A} \text{ and } \bar{B}) = 1 - 0.55 = 0.45$$

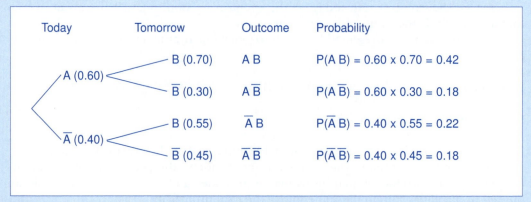

Figure 4.6

Always check that the probabilities sum up to 1.

P(A and B) = 0.42, P(A and $\bar{\text{B}}$) = 0.18, P($\bar{\text{A}}$ and B) = 0.22, P($\bar{\text{A}}$ and $\bar{\text{B}}$) = 0.18

From the diagram we can find other combinations:

P(A or B) = Probability of at least one rainy day = 0.42 + 0.18 + 0.22 = 0.82
P($\bar{\text{A}}$ or $\bar{\text{B}}$) = Probability of at least one day being fine = 1 − 0.42 = 0.58

For this example the tree diagram is more straightforward than the contingency table.

Example 4.12

A new office computer network has been installed and some of the employees are having diffi-
culty logging on to it. A technician is giving them some tuition and the problems encountered
during the practice session are recorded. These data result in the following probabilities:

* An employee has a 0.9 probability of logging on successfully (S) at her first attempt.
* If she is successful at any time, the same probability applies on her next two attempts.
* If she fails to log in at any time (F), she loses confidence and the probability of succeeding
  on any subsequent attempt is only 0.5.

Use a tree diagram to find the probabilities that:

(a) she is successful on all her first three attempts
(b) she fails at the first attempt but succeeds on the next two
(c) she is successful just once in three attempts
(d) she is still not successful after the third attempt.

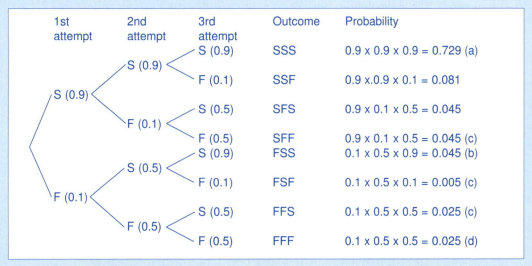

Figure 4.7

Using the tree diagram in Figure 4.7:

(a) P(she is successful on all her first three attempts) = 0.729
(b) P(she fails at the first attempt but succeeds
    on the next two)   = 0.045
(c) P(she is successful just once in three attempts)   = 0.045 + 0.005 + 0.025 = 0.075
(d) P(she is still not successful after the third attempt) = 0.025

4.7 Expected values

A commonly used method in decision-making problems is the consideration of **expected values**. The expected value for each decision is calculated and the option with the maximum or minimum value (dependent upon the situation) is selected.

The expected value of each decision is defined by:

$$E(x) = \sum px \tag{4.6}$$

where x is the value associated with each out outcome, $E(x)$ is the expected value of the event x, and p is the probability of it happening.

If you bought 5 out of 100 raffle tickets for a single prize of £25, the expected value of your winnings would be $(5/100) \times £25 = £1.25$. Clearly this is only a theoretical value as in reality you would win either £25 or £0.

Example 4.13

Two independent commercial operations of uncertain duration, A and B, are started simultaneously. The probabilities associated with each duration are given in Table 4.10:

Table 4.10

Operation A		Operation B	
Duration (days) (x)	Probability (p)	Duration (days) (x)	Probability (p)
1	0.0	1	0.1
2	0.5	2	0.2
3	0.3	3	0.5
4	0.2	4	0.2

Determine whether A or B has the shorter expected completion time.

Operation A

$$E(x) = \sum px = (1 \times 0.0) + (2 \times 0.5) + (3 \times 0.3) + (4 \times 0.2) = 2.7 \text{ days}$$

Operation B

$$E(x) = \sum px = (1 \times 0.1) + (2 \times 0.2) + (3 \times 0.5) + (4 \times 0.2) = 2.8 \text{ days}$$

Hence Operation A has the shorter expected completion time.

Example 4.14

A marketing manager is considering whether to distribute his company's product nation-wide or regionally. Use the data in Table 4.11 to decide on the more profitable method of distribution.

Table 4.11

	Distribution				
	National distribution			Regional distribution	
Level of Demand	Net profit £m (x)	Prob. that demand is met (p)	Level of Demand	Net profit £m (x)	Prob. that demand is met (p)
High	4.0	0.50	High	2.5	0.50
Medium	2.0	0.25	Medium	2.0	0.25
Low	0.5	0.25	Low	1.2	0.25

Expected profits

National distribution $E(x) = \sum px = 4.0 \times 0.5 + 2.0 \times 0.25 + 0.5 \times 0.25 = 2.625 \text{ (£m)}$

Regional distribution $E(x) = \sum px = 2.5 \times 0.5 + 2.0 \times 0.25 + 1.2 \times 0.25 = 2.050 \text{ (£m)}$

The marketing manager should opt for national distribution which is expected to produce the higher profit.

Example 4.15

A company which is considering leasing a computer has two models, A and B, in mind. The cost of computers A and B are £10,000 and £15,000 per annum, respectively. Estimates of the annual savings produced and their associated probabilities are shown in Table 4.12.

Decide which computer the company should lease in order to maximise savings.

Table 4.12

Savings from computer A	Savings from computer B
£5 000 with a probability of 0.3	£5 000 with a probability of 0.3
£10 000 with a probability of 0.3	£10 000 with a probability of 0.3
£15 000 with a probability of 0.4	£15 000 with a probability of 0.1
	£20 000 with a probability of 0.1
	£30 000 with a probability of 0.2

Expected savings (£'000)

Computer A: $0.3 \times 5 + 0.3 \times 10 + 0.4 \times 15 = 10.5$
Computer B: $0.3 \times 5 + 0.3 \times 10 + 0.1 \times 15 + 0.1 \times 20 + 0.2 \times 30 = 14.0$

Expected balance (£'000)

Computer A: $10.5 - 10 = 0.5$ An expected profit of £500
Computer B: $14.0 - 15 = -1.0$ An expected loss of £1000

The company should lease Computer A

4.8 Further work with probability

The use of tree diagrams can be extended into the field of decision making. Decisions are based on the probabilities of the outcomes at each branch combined with the costs involved.

Probability forms the basis of arguably the most important branch of statistics, inferential statistics. You will study three aspects of inference later in this book when we shall consider:

- **confidence intervals,** by which the most probable range for a population value is estimated from the analysis of a sample
- **hypothesis testing,** by which the probability that a hypothesised population value is correct or incorrect is based on the analysis of a sample
- **forecasting,** by which probable future values are inferred from the analysis of past values.

In addition to possibility space diagrams, contingency tables and probability trees, Venn diagrams are often used to illustrate combined probabilities. Because probability is considered so important a topic in statistics, much work has been done in this field. There are many standard probability distributions, and much can be inferred about the population of new data if it can be shown to follow one of these distributions. In Chapter 5 we shall study the normal distribution because it is widely applicable in the world of business. In later chapters we shall also use sets of probability tables constructed from other probability distributions. More advanced statistics textbooks can be consulted for information on standard distributions.

4.9 Summary

Our own actions are often subconsciously based on probability when we make choices or take risks. The role of statistics is to quantify the uncertainty so that we can make informed estimations and logical choices, particularly in the world of business.

In this chapter we have only introduced the basic concepts of probability. Probability can be studied in great depth in more advanced courses. Much of the work has been concerned with the methods of quantifying uncertainty in the form of numerical probabilities. These have been based on symmetry, or on relative frequencies from existing data. We have calculated combined probabilities with the help of contingency tables and tree diagrams, and we have calculated expected values as an aid to making choices and decisions.

Table 4.13

Number of events	Appropriate methods to use
1 event	Calculation
2 events	Calculation, contingency tables, probability trees, Venn diagrams.
> 2 events	Calculation, probability trees, Venn diagrams.

We shall continue to use probability throughout this course, and will make regular reference to tables which are based on specific probability distributions.

Tutorial 4: Probability

Answers in Appendix A.

4.1 If the probability of a successful outcome is 0.2, what is the probability of failure?

4.2 With a single die, what is the probability of scoring:
(a) 6, (b) an even number, (c) a number divisible by 3, (d) 0?

4.3 From a normal pack of 52 playing cards, on taking out one card at random, what is the probability of getting:
(a) an ace, (b) a club, (c) the ace of clubs, (d) an ace or a club, (e) a picture card (J, Q, K), (f) a red card, (g) a red king, (h) a red picture?

4.4 Three coins are tossed. List all the possibilities and use them to find:
(a) the number of possible outcomes, (b) P(3 heads), (c) P(2 heads), (d) P(1 head), (e) P(0 heads), (f) the sum of all the probabilities found.

4.5 Draw a space diagram to represent the sample space of the outcomes for throwing a pair of dice, one blue, one red. Use it to find:
(a) P(a score of 4), (b) P(a score of more than 7), (c) P(a double), (d) P(an even score), (e) P(both dice show even scores), (f) P(the score on the blue die is greater than that on the red).

4.6 A bag contains six red discs, four blue discs and two green discs. If a single disc is withdrawn at random, find:
(a) P(blue), (b) P(not red), (c) P(blue or red), (d) P(not blue or red).

4.7 Typing speeds of office workers have been found to vary considerably. In a recent dexterity survey the following typing rates were recorded:

Words per minute (wpm)	Number of workers
20 – 29	320
30 – 39	400
40 – 49	350
50 – 59	200
60 – 69	50
70 – 79	5

Calculate the relative frequencies of each group of workers, and find the probability that a worker selected at random:
(a) Is expert with a typing speed of ≥ 60 w.p.m.
(b) Needs practice, being slower than 40 w.p.m.
(c) Is in neither of these extreme groups?

4.8 Records were kept of 200 students enrolling for a degree course. The completed records showed the following frequencies:

Sex	Result Graduating	Not graduating
Male	90	20
Female	80	10

Find:
(a) Probability of any student graduating
(b) Probability of a male student graduating
(c) Probability of a female student graduating
(d) Probability of a graduate being female
(e) Probability of a graduate being male.

4.9 Some students, 50 male and 50 female, were asked whether they agreed with the proposition 'Statistics are often misleading'. 70 students, 30 of whom were male, agreed. Find using a contingency table:
(a) P(a student agreeing)
(b) P(a student being female)
(c) P(a student being male)
(d) P(a student agreeing given that he is male)
(e) P(a student agreeing given that she is female)
(f) P(a student who agrees is female)
(g) P(a student who agrees is male).

4.10 Consider the table below which shows the number (to the nearest hundred) of various kinds of dwellings found in the suburban area of Bradfield.

	Private dwellings	Council dwellings	Total
One bedroom	600	1000	1600
Two bedroom	3000	1700	4700
Three bedroom	4400	1800	6200
Total	8000	4500	12 500

Find:
(a) P(dwelling is private)
(b) P(dwelling has one bedroom)
(c) P(dwelling is private and has two bedrooms)
(d) P(dwelling is council and has three bedrooms)
(e) P(dwelling has least two bedrooms)
(f) P(dwelling is private or has two bedrooms)
(g) P(dwelling has three bedroom | it is private)
(h) P(dwelling has one bedroom | it is private)
(i) P(dwelling is private | it has three bedrooms)
(j) P(dwelling is a council property | it has three bedrooms)

Notes

The supplementary exercise for Chapter 4, with answers, is on the companion website.

Normal distribution

5

Objectives of this chapter

As we have seen in Chapters 2 and 3, data can be distributed symmetrically or can be skewed. The most commonly occurring distribution is a symmetrical one usually referred to as the **normal distribution**. If your data can be shown to follow this distribution, you can make use of standard statistical probability tables which describe the normal distribution in order to analyse the data. Other probability distributions will be described briefly, but the main aim of this chapter is to describe the use of the normal distribution in depth.

Having studied this chapter you should be:

- able to analyse completely any data shown to be 'normal'
- aware that similar methods can be applied to other, often skewed, distributions.

5.1 Introduction: importance of the normal distribution

Most naturally occurring phenomena have been found to follow a normal distribution. This describes many human characteristics and is also applicable in other situations, such as manufacturing, in which a target value is commonly hit but may be missed by small amounts. In this case the distribution of sample means is found to be normal, even if the underlying distribution is not (more of this in Chapter 6), and so the normal distribution plays a key role in the application of many statistical techniques.

The normal distribution describes continuous data, but it has been found to approximate to many discrete distributions also. It is, therefore, a useful tool for decision makers who meet both types of data in the field of business.

5.2 The characteristics of any normal distribution

The normal distribution is a symmetrical distribution centred on the mean of the data, with a spread depending on its standard deviation – the larger the standard deviation, the wider the spread. It is a suitable model for many naturally occurring variables which tend to be symmetrically distributed about a central modal value, the mean. A normal distribution approximately fits the actual observed frequency distributions of many naturally occurring phenomena, for example human characteristics such as height, weight and IQ; and also the output from many processes, for example weights and volumes.

As we saw in Section 5.1, this is a very important, widely occurring distribution which is extensively used when analysing business data. In Sections 5.2 to 5.5 we shall look first at all normal distributions, then at the standardised normal distribution, and finally see how this is used in the analysis of observed data. Strictly speaking any observed data should be checked for normality before this method of analysis is used. Standard tests are available in SPSS and Minitab but not in Excel.

The normal distribution is not a single normal curve, but a **family of curves**, each one defined by its mean, μ, and standard deviation, σ; μ and σ are called the parameters of the distribution.

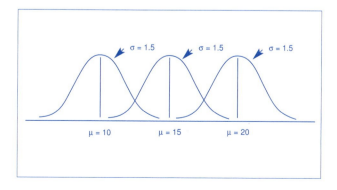

Figure 5.1

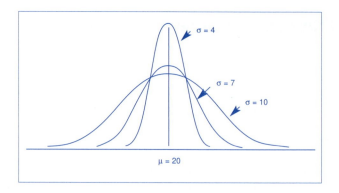

Figure 5.2

Figure 5.1 shows normal curves with the same standard deviation but different means, and Figure 5.2 shows three with the same mean but different standard deviations. The curves may have different centres and/or different spreads. The curves have several common characteristics:

- the curve is bell-shaped
- it is symmetrical about the mean (μ)
- the mean, mode and median coincide.

5.2.1 The area beneath the normal distribution curve

No matter what the values of μ and σ are for a normal probability distribution, the total area under the curve is equal to 1. We can therefore consider partial areas under the curve to represent probabilities. The percentage of the data between a stated number of standard deviation below and above the mean is the same for all normal distributions, as illustrated in Figure 5.3. For example 68.26 per cent of the data lies between points one standard deviation either side of the mean, which occur at the points of inflection of the curve.

Note that the curve neither finishes nor meets the horizontal axis at $\mu \pm 3\sigma$, it only approaches it and actually goes on indefinitely.

Although all normal distributions have much in common, they will all have different numbers on the horizontal axis depending on the values of the mean and standard deviation and the units of measurement involved. We cannot therefore make use of the standard tables at this stage.

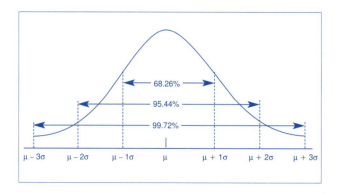

Figure 5.3

5.3 The standardised normal distribution

No matter what units are used to measure the original data, the first step in any calculation is to transform the data so that it becomes a **standardised normal variate** following the standard distribution which has a **mean of zero** and a **standard deviation of one**. The effect of this transformation is to state how many standard deviations a particular given value is away from the mean. This standardised normal variate is without units as these cancel out in the calculation.

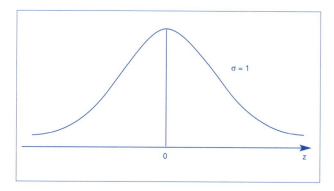

Figure 5.4

The **standardised normal distribution** is symmetrically distributed about zero; has a standard deviation of 1 and approaches the x-axis when the curve is three standard deviations away from the mean.

The formula for calculating the exact number of standard deviations (z) that the unstandardised value (x) is away from the mean (μ) is:

$$z = \frac{x - \mu}{\sigma} \tag{5.1}$$

The process of calculating z, the **standardised value**, is known as **standardising**.

In Figure 5.4, any point on the curve is described by the number of standard deviations it is away from the mean. The curve approaches the x-axis when the absolute value of z exceeds 3. The value of z enables us to find from the normal tables the area under the curve between the given value, x, and the mean. This is the probability of a value occurring between the given value, x, and the mean, μ, denoted by the letter Q, which stands for quantile. (This is easier to understand with numbers!)

For the standardised normal distributions the standard normal tables are used (see Appendix D, Table 1).

5.4 Finding probabilities under a normal curve

The steps in the procedure are:

- Draw a sketch of the situation.
- Standardise the value of interest.

- Use the standard tables to find its associated area under the curve.
- If necessary, combine the area found with another to give the required area.
- Convert this to:
  - a probability, using the area as found since total area = 1
  - a percentage, multiplying the area by 100 since total area = 100 per cent
  - a frequency, multiplying the area by the total frequency as required by the question.

Example 5.1

The manager of a new supermarket wished to estimate the likely expenditure of his customers. A sample of till slips from a similar supermarket describing the weekly amounts spent by 500 randomly selected customers was collected and analysed. This expenditure was found to be approximately normally distributed with a mean of £50 and a standard deviation of £15. Knowing this we can find the following information for shoppers at the new supermarket.

The **probability** that any shopper selected at random:
  a) spends more than £80 per week
  b) spends less than £50 per week.
The **percentage** of shoppers who are expected to:
  c) spend between £30 and £80 per week
  d) spend between £55 and £70 per week.
The **expected number** of shoppers who will:
  e) spend less than £70 per week
  f) spend between £37.50 and £57.50 per week.

a) The probability that a shopper selected at random spends more than £80 per week

We need **P(x > £80)**, the probability that a customer spends over £80.

Note: Sketches only guides – no need for accuracy.

$\mu = £50, \sigma = £15$

$x = £80$

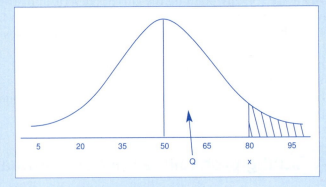

Figure 5.5

First standardise: $\quad z \; = \; \dfrac{x-\mu}{\sigma} \; = \; \dfrac{80-50}{15} \; = \; \dfrac{30}{15} \; = \; 2.00$

From Appendix D Table 1: $\quad z = 2.00 \Rightarrow Q = 0.4722$
$\qquad\qquad\qquad\qquad$ (z in the margin, Q in the body of the tables)

Note: The symbol $\Rightarrow$ stands for 'implies that', that is, if z = 2.00 then Q = 0.4772

Therefore: **P(x > £80)** = P(x > £50) – P(£50 < x < £80) = 0.5 – 0.4772 = 0.0228

(b) The probability that a shopper selected at random spends more than £50 per week

No need to do any calculations for this question! The mean is £50 and, because the distribution is normal, the median is also £50. Half the shoppers, 250, are therefore expected to spend more than £50 per week.

Using the frequency definition of probability: 250/500 = 0.5

(c) The percentage of shoppers who are expected to spend between £30 and £80 per week

We first need **P(£30 < x < £80)**, then we convert the result to a percentage.
   Our normal tables provide the area between a particular value and the mean so we need to split the area between £30 and £80 into partial areas, one on each side of the mean. The partial areas, £30 to £50 and £50 to £80 can be calculated separately and then the two parts recombined.

μ = £50, σ = £15

x_1 = £30, x_2 = £80

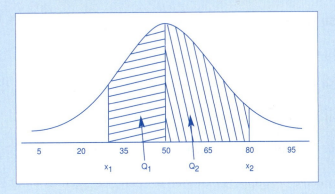

Figure 5.6

P(£50 < x < £80): From (a) x = 80 $\Rightarrow z_2$ = 2.00 $\Rightarrow Q_2$ = 0.4772

P(£30 < x < £50): $z_1 = \dfrac{x-\mu}{\sigma} = \dfrac{30-50}{15} = \dfrac{-20}{15} = -1.333$

(The table values are all positive, so when z is negative we invoke the symmetry of the situation and use its absolute value in the table.)

From tables: z_1 = –1.333 $\Rightarrow Q_1$ = 0.4088 (by interpolation)
   (Q_1 lies between 0.4082 (z = 1.33) and 0.4099 (Z = 1.34) and is one-third of the distance between them, 0.0017, being nearer to 0.4082, so 0.4082 + 0.0006 = 0.4088).

Therefore: **P(£30 < x < £80)** = $Q_1 + Q_2$ = 0.4088 + 0.4772 = 0.8860

The whole area is equivalent to 100% so 0.8860 of it = 88.6%

(d) Percentage of shoppers expected to spend between £55 and £70

We first need **P(£55 < x < £70)**, then we convert the result to a percentage.

$\mu = £50, \sigma = £15$

$x_1 = £55, x_2 = £70$

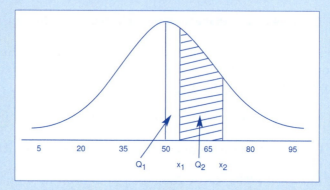

Figure 5.7

We now need to find the area between the mean and £70 (Q_2) and then subtract from it the area between the mean and £55, (Q_1).

P(£50 < x < £70): $\quad z_2 \; = \; \dfrac{x - \mu}{\sigma} \; = \; \dfrac{70 - 50}{15} \; = \; \dfrac{20}{15} \; = \; 1.333$

From tables: $Q_2 = 0.4088$ (by interpolation)

P(£50 < x < £55): $\quad z_1 \; = \; \dfrac{x - \mu}{\sigma} \; = \; \dfrac{55 - 50}{15} \; = \; \dfrac{5}{15} \; = \; 0.333$

From tables: $Q_1 = 0.1305$ (by interpolation)

Therefore: **P(£55 < x < £70)** $= Q_2 - Q_1 = 0.4088 - 0.1305 = 0.2783$

Percentage of shoppers expected to spend between £55 and £70 $= 0.2783 \times 100 = 27.8\%$

(e) The expected number of shoppers who will spend less than £70 per week

$\mu = £50, \sigma = £15$

$x = £70$

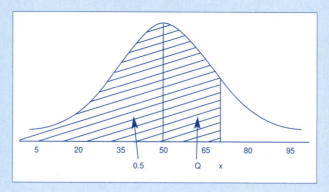

Figure 5.8

The area we need is that between the mean and £70 plus the 0.5 which falls below the mean.

P(£30 < x < £50):

First standardise: $z = \dfrac{x-\mu}{\sigma} = \dfrac{70-50}{15} = \dfrac{20}{15} = 1.333$

From tables: $z = 1.333 \Rightarrow Q = 0.4088$

Therefore: **P(x < £70)** = 0.5 + 0.4088 = 0.9088

The expected number of shoppers spending less than £70 is 0.9088 of the total = 0.9088 × 500 = 454.4, which is between 454 and 455 shoppers.

(f) The expected number of shoppers who will spend between £37.50 and £57.50 per week

We first need **P(£37.50 < x < £57.50)**. This is then multiplied by the total frequency.

μ = £50, σ = £15

x_1 = £37.50, x_2 = £57.50

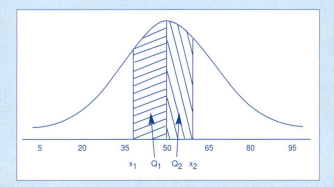

Figure 5.9

Our normal tables give the area between a value and the mean so we need to split the area between £37.50 and £57.50 into partial areas each side of the mean; calculate the partial areas separately and then recombine them.

P(£37.5 < x < £50): $z_1 = \dfrac{x-\mu}{\sigma} = \dfrac{37.5-50}{15} = \dfrac{-12.5}{15} = -0.833$

When z is negative use its absolute value in the table.

From tables: $z_1 = -0.833 \Rightarrow Q_1 = 0.2976$ (by interpolation)

P(£50 < x < £57.5): $z_2 = \dfrac{x-\mu}{\sigma} = \dfrac{57.5-50}{15} = \dfrac{7.5}{15} = 0.500$

From tables: $z_2 = 0.500 \Rightarrow Q_2 = 0.1915$

Therefore: **P(£37.50 < x < £57.50)** = $Q_1 + Q_2$ = 0.2976 + 0.1915 = 0.4891

Therefore the expected number of shoppers who spend between £37.50 and £57.50 is:

0.4891 × 500 = 244.55, which is 244 or 245 shoppers.

5.5 Finding values from given proportions

In Example 5.1, parts (a) to (f), we were given the value of x and had to find the area under the normal curve associated with it. Another type of problem gives the area, even if indirectly, and asks for the associated value of x.

Example 5.2

Using the data in Example 5.1, calculate the value of the shopping basket.

The value below which:
    g) 70 per cent of the customers are expected to spend
    h) 45 per cent of the customers are expected to spend.

The value expected to be exceeded by:
    i) 10 per cent of the till slips
    j) 80 per cent of the till slips.

The value below which:
    k) 350 of the shoppers are expected to spend
    l) 100 of the shoppers are expected to spend.

(a) The value below which 70% of the shoppers are expected to spend

$\mu = £50, \sigma = £15$

$x = £?$

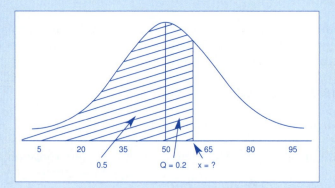

Figure 5.10

We first need to find the value of Q.
    Now 70% of the total area, 1.00, is below $x \Rightarrow$ 20% is between μ and $x \Rightarrow Q = 0.2000$

From tables, (used the other way round):
If $Q = 0.2000$ (in the body of the table) $\Rightarrow z = 0.524$ (in the margin of the table, by interpolation as z lies between 0.52 and 0.53 and is a little nearer to 0.52).

We now know the value of z and need to find x.

Using standardising formula:

$$z = \frac{x-\mu}{\sigma} \Rightarrow 0.524 = \frac{x-50}{15}$$

$$15 \times 0.524 = x - 50$$
$$7.86 = x - 50$$
$$7.86 + 50 = x$$
$$£57.86 = x$$

The value below which 70% of customers spend is £57.86

Alternatively, rearrange the formula first to give x = zσ + μ and then substitute the values into it directly.

If your algebra is a bit rusty try using the fact that this **positive** value of z, 0.524, tells us that x is 0.524 standard deviations **above** the mean.

Its value is therefore μ + 0.524σ = 50 + 0.524 × 15 = £57.86

(b) The value below which 45% of the shoppers are expected to spend

μ = £50, σ = £15

x = £?

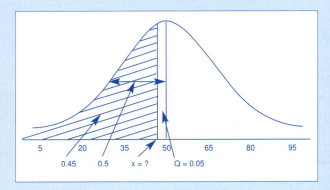

Figure 5.11

Now 45% below x is equivalent to 5% between x and μ, so Q = 0.05

From tables if Q = 0.05 $\Rightarrow$ z = 0.126 (by interpolation)
We know, however, that x is below the mean so z is **negative**, z = –0.126

Now x is 0.126 standard deviations **below** the mean:
x = μ – 0.126σ = 50 – 0.126 × 15 = £48.11 or using the standard formula:

$$z = \frac{x-\mu}{\sigma} \Rightarrow -0.126 = \frac{x-50}{15}$$

$$15 \times -0.126 = x - 50$$
$$-1.89 = x - 50$$
$$-1.89 + 50 = x$$
$$£48.11 = x$$

The value below which 45% of customers spend is £48.11

(c) The value expected to be exceeded by 10% of till slips

$\mu = £50, \sigma = £15$

$x = £?$

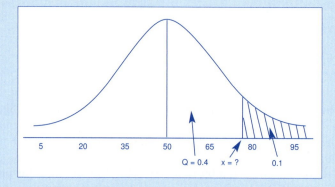

Figure 5.12

Now 10% above x $\Rightarrow$ 40% between x and μ so Q = 0.40

From tables if Q = 0.40 $\Rightarrow$ z = 1.282 (by interpolation)

Now x is 1.282 standard deviations above the mean:
$x = \mu + 1.282\sigma = 50 + 1.282 \times 15 = £69.23$

or using the standard formula:

$$z = \frac{x - \mu}{\sigma} \Rightarrow 1.282 = \frac{x - 50}{15}$$

15×1.282	=	$x - 50$
19.23	=	$x - 50$
$19.23 + 50$	=	x
£69.23	=	x

The value exceeded by 10% of the till slips is £69.23

(d) The value expected to be exceeded by 80% of the till slips

$\mu = £50, \sigma = £15$

$x = £?$

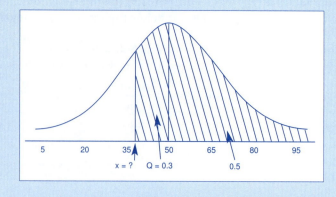

Figure 5.13

Now 80% above x $\Rightarrow$ 30% between x and μ so Q = 0.30

From tables if Q = 0.30 $\Rightarrow$ z = 0.842 (by interpolation)
    We know that x is below the mean so z is negative, –0.842

Now x is 0.842 standard deviations below the mean:
x = μ – 0.842σ = 50 – 0.842 × 15 = £37.37

or using the standard formula:

$$z = \frac{x-\mu}{\sigma} \Rightarrow -0.842 = \frac{x-50}{15}$$

$$15 \times -0.842 = x - 50$$
$$-12.63 = x - 50$$
$$-12.63 + 50 = x$$
$$£37.37 = x$$

The value exceeded by 80% of the till slips is £37.37

(e) The value below which 350 of the shoppers are expected to spend

Now 350 shoppers out of 500 is 70%, so once this conversion has been made the calculation is exactly the same as (a), giving an answer of £57.86.

(f) The value below which 100 of the shoppers are expected to spend

μ = £50, σ = £15

x = £?

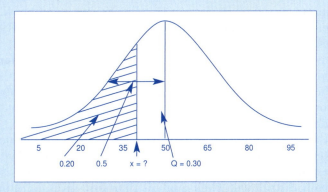

Figure 5.14

Now 100 customers below x $\Rightarrow$ 150 between x and μ so Q = 150/500 = 0.30

From tables if Q = 0.30 $\Rightarrow$ z = 0.842 (by interpolation)
    We know that x is below the mean so z is negative, –0.842

Now x is 0.842 standard deviations below the mean:
x = μ – 0.842σ = 50 – 0.842 × 15 = £37.37

or using the standard formula:

$$z = \frac{x - \mu}{\sigma} \Rightarrow -0.842 = \frac{x - 50}{15}$$

$$15 \times -0.842 = x - 50$$
$$-12.63 = x - 50$$
$$-12.63 + 50 = x$$
$$£37.37 = x$$

The value below which 100 shoppers are expected to spend is £37.37

In Examples 5.1 and 5.2 we have considered all the possible variations in the use of the normal distribution with a large set of data with given mean and standard deviation. Plenty of extra practice is provided in Tutorial 5 and on the companion website in the supplementary exercise for Chapter 5.

5.6 Further applications of the normal distribution

Any process or procedure that aims at a target but is not precise enough to hit it every time will produce errors which are likely to be normally distributed. Analysis of past errors is very important as it offers a reasonable estimate of the size of future errors and the probability of being able to hit the target within any given specification.

Many quality control models are based on the normal distribution, as production errors are often found to be normally distributed. What is the probability of being able to produce metal washers to meet the specification 15 ± 1 mm? This is another way of asking the question, ' What percentage of the production do you expect to meet this specification?'

Assuming the production is centred on the correct target, the precision of the production depends on the standard deviation of the errors – the **standard error** (standard error is considered in Chapter 6).

The normal distribution is similarly employed in stock control. Analysing previous demands on stock enables stores to be managed so that a balance is kept between overstocking goods and running out of supplies.

In modelling or forecasting, predictions (or 'fitted values') are produced but they are unlikely to fit the individual data completely accurately. The differences between the actual values and the model's fitted values are referred to as 'residuals', and these are usually normally distributed. Their analysis therefore gives an estimate of the accuracy of models or forecasts.

The normal distribution can be put to many other uses by statisticians. In this book we shall meet it again many times, with its uses ranging from estimation (Chapter 6) to forecasting (Chapter 13).

5.7 A brief look at other probability distributions

As we saw in Section 5.2, data that follow the normal distribution are continuous and reasonably symmetrical. Obviously the data you collect cannot be guaranteed to meet these criteria, so we shall briefly consider some other distributions which might describe real data, whether they are discrete or continuous, symmetrical or skewed.

You should be able to recognise whether the data is discrete or continuous (see Section 1.3), and a brief look at a histogram should give you some idea about its shape (see Section 2.4.1). Commonly occurring distributions for modelling data are given in Table 5.1.

Table 5.1

	Observed data			
Type	Discrete		Continuous	
Shape	Symmetric	Skewed	Symmetric	Skewed
Distribution	Binomial	Poisson	Normal	Exponential

A formula is known for each distribution, and standard tables have been produced giving information about the areas under any given section of each curve. Because these are all probability distributions, the area beneath their curves is always equal to 1. Once the appropriate distribution has been identified, the standard tables are used to calculate probabilities about the population from which the observed data has been drawn.

5.7.1 Binomial distribution

You have already met the binomial distribution in Section 4.3 Equation 4.3. We showed that for n trials, with the probability of success in any one trial being p, the probability of getting r successes is:

$$P(r) = \frac{n!}{r!(n-r)!} \times p^r (1-p)^{(n-r)} \tag{5.1}$$

where n! stands for factorial n, that is $n \times (n-1) \times (n-2) \dots 3 \times 2 \times 1$

Suppose we know from past experience that 15 per cent of a consignment of items are defective: $p = 0.15$. The probability of finding two defective items in a sample of seven is:

P(2 defectives in a sample of 7) =

$$\frac{7!}{2!5!} \times \left(\frac{15}{100}\right)^2 \left(\frac{85}{100}\right)^5 = 21 \times 0.15^2 \times 0.85^5 = 0.210$$

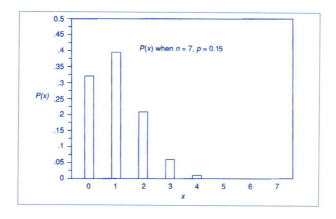

Figure 5.15

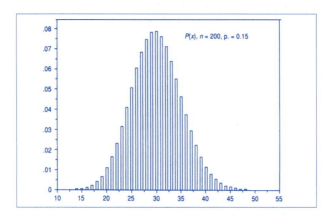

Figure 5.16

For a medium value of p, such as 0.15 above, the distribution will be skewed for small values of n, but will become symmetrical when n is large as for, say, 200 (see Figures 5.15 and 5.16).

If a binomial distribution has a large value for n and a very small value for p, so that the mean, np, is also small, then the binomial distribution approximates to a Poisson distribution (discussed below) with the same mean (see Section 5.7.2).

If a binomial distribution has a large value for n and p is not very small, so that the mean, np, is large, then the binomial distribution approximates to a normal distribution with the same mean and standard deviation (see Section 5.7.2).

5.7.2 Poisson distribution

The Poisson distribution describes random, discrete, rare events such as the occurrence of an accident on a particular stretch of motorway or the occurrence of a faulty item on a production line. The mean number, μ, is the expected number in a given time period.

The probability of a particular number, x, occurring is given by

$$P(x) = \mu^x \frac{e^{-\mu}}{x!} \tag{5.2}$$

where μ is the mean and $e \cong 2.718$ ($\cong$ means 'approximately equal to').

When the value of μ is very small, say $\mu = 0.001$, the distribution is very skewed, even for fairly large samples. For small values of μ the Poisson and the binomial distribution give very similar results (see Figure 5.17), but as μ gets larger the Poisson approximates to the normal distribution.

For any Poisson distribution with mean μ, its variance is also μ and its standard deviation is $\sqrt{\mu}$.

Figure 5.18 is a summary of all these approximations for discrete distributions.

Since the Poisson distribution is followed by random discrete variables, events that are found to follow the Poisson distribution, such as the arrivals of people joining a queue, can be shown to be random.

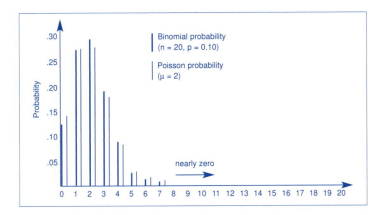

Figure 5.17

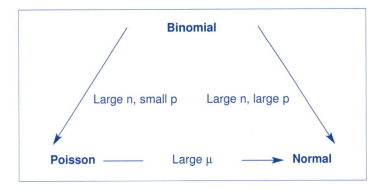

Figure 5.18

5.7.3 (Negative) exponential distribution

The probability distribution usually referred to as the exponential distribution is in fact the negative exponential distribution with the formula:

$$P(x) = \lambda e^{-\lambda x} \tag{5.3}$$

where λ (lambda) is the mean time between successive events.

The discrete Poisson distribution often describes the number of arrivals joining a queue in a given time. If this is the case, then the continuous negative exponential distribution describes the time between arrivals.

For this distribution the low probabilities predominate. Figure 5.19 shows the probability density function for $\lambda = 2$, 4 and 10. Note that the larger the value of λ the lower the main mass of the values, as is to be expected when the time between events is larger.

When the number of times an event occurs in a time interval has a Poisson distribution, with mean λ, the number of these time intervals between successive occurrences has an exponential distribution with

$$f(x) = \lambda e^{-\lambda x}$$

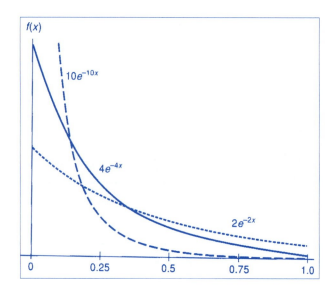

Figure 5.19

Section 5.7 has provided only a very short look at a few standard probability distributions other than the normal. More can be found in deeper statistics textbooks (such as Weimer 1993, Chapters 6 and 7).

5.8 Summary

You should now understand the importance of probability distributions in general, and that of the normal distribution in particular. We have concentrated on the use of the normal distribution but other probability distributions can be used if they fit your data better. Standard tables are available for all probability distributions. The most commonly used tables are published at the back of most statistics textbooks. They can be found here in Appendix D. A full range appears in specialised booklets such as *Elementary Statistics Tables* (Neave 1992).

If your data set approximately follows a normal distribution, with known mean and standard deviation, you should now be able to make use of the standardised normal distribution to analyse it. It is essential that you understand the normal distribution before you move on to other topics which make use of it.

5.9 Case study

In preparation for carrying out estimations and hypothesis tests at the end of future chapters, it is suggested that at this stage you produce histograms for:

- gross sales for all outlets together; gross sales for each type of outlet separately
- market value of all outlets together; market value of each type of outlet separately

- number of full-time employees for all outlets together; number of full-time employees for each type of outlet separately
- number of part-time employees for all outlets together; number of part-time employees for each type of outlet separately
- wages as percentage of sales for all outlets together; wages as percentage of sales for each type of outlet separately
- advertising as percentage of sales for all outlets together; advertising as percentage of sales for each type of outlet separately.

The data 'Restaurants' is in the case study in the students' materials on the companion website. (If you have forgotten how to separate the data into separate groups, or have not yet worked through Worksheets 14.2.1, 14.5.1 or 14.8.1, refer to Chapter 14, Sections 14.2.1.9, 14.5.1.10 or 14.8.1.9.)

Tutorial 5: Normal distribution

Answers are in Appendix A.

5.1 The lengths of steel beams made by a particular steel mill are normally distributed with a mean of 8.25 metres and a standard deviation of 0.07 metres.
   a) Find the probability that the length of a steel beam will be over 8.40 metres.
   b) Find the probability that the length of a steel beam will be between 8.20 and 8.40 metres.
   c) For a particular application, any beam less than 8.05 metres must be scrapped. What percentage of beams would expect to be scrapped?
   d) If the company expected to scrap 1 per cent of the production as being too long, what would be the maximum acceptable length?

5.2 The time taken by a student to walk to the university has been shown to be normally distributed with mean of 16 minutes and standard deviation of 2.1 minutes. He walks in once a day during term time, 180 days per year, and leaves home 20 minutes before his first lecture.
   a) Find the probability that he is late for his first lecture.
   b) Find the number of days per year he is likely to be late for his first lecture.
   c) If he arrives with 5 minutes to spare he has a cup of coffee. How many cups is he likely to manage during his three-year course?
   d) If he has 7½ minutes to spare he also has a bacon sandwich. How many of these is he likely to eat during his course?

5.3 For many years a company has been using a standardised test as a guide for hiring new secretaries. The test scores are normally distributed, with mean of 800 and standard deviation of 100. There has been an unusually high number of applicants in recent months, and it has been suggested that only the applicants who score in the upper 10 per cent should be considered further. What is the minimum test score an applicant would need for further consideration?

5.4 A commercial grower produces cabbages with masses that are normally distributed, with a mean of 1 kg and standard deviation of 0.15 kg. He sells these as 'small', 'medium' and 'large', and when they are weighed the ranges are found to be less than 0.75, between 0.75 and 1.20, and over 1.20 kg respectively.

From a plot producing 8000 of these cabbages, estimate how many are likely to be:
a) 'small',
b) 'medium'
c) 'large'?
d) If he wished to label 40 per cent of his production as 'large', to what weight should he reduce the lower limit of this group?

5.5 If a set of marks for a statistics examination is approximately normally distributed with a mean of 74 and a standard deviation of 7.9, find:
a) the lowest passing mark if 10 per cent of the students are failed
b) the highest mark getting B if the top 5 per cent get A.

5.6 A soft drink machine is regulated by its manufacturer so that it discharges an average of 200 ml per cup. If the amount delivered is normally distributed with standard deviation equal to 15 ml:
a) What percentage of the cups will contain over 225 ml?
b) What is the probability that a cup contains between 175 and 225 ml?
c) How many of the cups are likely to overflow if 250 ml cups are used for the next 10,000 drinks?
d) What percentage would fall below a permissible minimum of 150 ml?

5.7 A manufacturer finds that although it promises delivery of a certain item within 20 working days, the time it actually takes to deliver to customers is normally distributed with a mean of 16 and a standard deviation of 2.5 working days.
(a) What proportion of customers receive their deliveries late?
(b) What proportion of customers receive deliveries within 10 to 15 working days?
(c) To how many days should the delivery promise be amended if it is required that only 2 per cent of deliveries should be late?
(d) What proportion of customers will receive deliveries within 20 working days if the manufacturer manages to reduce the standard deviation of delivery time to 1.5 working days, keeping the mean time at 16 working days?

5.8 The mean life of one make of keyboard is typically 6 years with a standard deviation of 1.3 years. If the manufacturer wishes to replace no more than 3 per cent of keyboards under guarantee, how long should the guarantee be, to the nearest month?

5.9 Items coming off a production line are measured and have been found to have a mean diameter of 1500 mm and a standard deviation of 0.5 mm.
a) Quality control requirements are that the items should measure between 1498.5 mm and 1501.5 mm. What percentage of the items will meet these requirements?
b) Another part of the process produces items with holes which are normally distributed with a mean diameter of 1501 mm and a standard deviation of 1 mm. What percentage of the holes will have diameters between 1498.5 and 1501.5 mm?
c) What percentage of holes will need to be enlarged because they have diameters of less than 1498.5 mm?

5.10 A fertiliser is produced in '25 kg' plastic sacks. The filling process has been shown to have a mean weight of 26 kg with a standard deviation of 1.2 kg.
a) What is the probability of any sack being under the nominal weight?
b) What is the probability of a sack being more that 1 kg underweight?
c) To what mean weight should the process be set if only 1 per cent of the sacks are to be underweight, assuming the standard deviation remains unchanged?

Notes

The supplementary exercise for Chapter 5, with answers, is on the companion website.

Estimation

6

Objectives of this chapter

The subject of statistics is often more concerned with the grey area of what is **the most likely solution** than the ability to produce **an exact answer**. Frequently we do not have sufficient information to enable us to calculate an exact value of a parameter for a whole population of data; instead we have to make the best estimate we can of this value. This is generally done by taking a sample from the same population, calculating the required statistic from this, then using the result as an estimate of the true value for the whole population (see Section 1.4).

If many different samples are taken, it is inevitable that they will differ; for example they will have different means. All these results cannot be correct so one figure is usually quoted as being the most likely value. A margin of error surrounding this figure is also quoted. This margin of error is used to produce a **confidence interval**, centred on the sample value, which is considered to be the best we can manage with the limited data at our disposal.

After studying this chapter you should be able to:

- calculate point estimates
- calculate confidence intervals around the point estimates
- interpret confidence intervals correctly for such population parameters as:
  - means
  - proportions.

You should also appreciate the need for estimation and its use in preference to making rigid claims, which may be unjustified, about population parameters.

6.1 Why can't we find the exact answer?

In order to find a true answer about any population with absolute accuracy we need to have all possible relevant information about every member of that population. This is only rarely available, as for example in the ten-year **census** which enumerates the whole population of the United Kingdom and Northern Ireland. Most population data is estimated from the results of such **surveys** as the Mori polls in Britain and the Gallup polls in the USA.

More often, when we wish to know something about a **population**, we cannot possibly analyse all the cases belonging to it as either they are not available or the task of data collection is too costly in time and/or money. The larger the sample, the better the estimations will be, so a balance has to be struck between cost and accuracy. In industry the collection of data for analysis from a production line is often destructive, so large samples could reduce the profitability of the company. The science of quality control makes use of the techniques we shall study in this chapter.

By taking a representative **sample** from the population of interest and analysing it, we can find out all about the sample itself and also make **inferences** about the parent population from the results of this analysis.

This is the best we can do in the light of limited knowledge. We cannot infer an exact result, but instead a likely range of values together with a probability that this interval includes the 'true' population value. We generally wish, in the world of business, to be 95 per cent confident that the interval calculated will include the true value, but this admits a 5 per cent probability of being wrong! Sampling inevitably introduces error – **sampling error** – as each sample taken will produce a different estimate of the population value.

6.2 Taking a sample

Sometimes the whole population will be small enough to be included in a study. This is a census because data is gathered on every member of the population. Usually the population is too large for a researcher to question all its members, so a small carefully chosen sample is used to represent the population. Sampling allows statisticians to draw conclusions about the whole population by examining only a part of it.

Sampling theory is a whole subject in its own right. It is absolutely essential that the sample taken is as representative as possible of the population, because any result produced from the sample is used to estimate a corresponding value for the population. Common sense rightly suggests that larger samples will be more representative but more expensive to take and analyse.

There are two types of sampling methods:

- Probability sampling, in which every member has an equal chance of being selected and that chance can be quantified.
- Non-probability sampling, in which every member does not have an equal chance of being selected. It is useful when the whole population is not available.

Probability samples are ideal for statistical analysis, but for various reasons non-probability samples may be more convenient or cheaper to obtain.

Some sampling methods are described briefly below.

6.2.1 Simple random sampling

Simple random sampling assures that every member of the population has an equal chance of being independently selected, thereby minimising bias. Also, any combination of members of the population is equally likely to be selected. This is the 'best' method of sampling from the statistician's point of view as independence of sample members needs to be assumed by many statistical tests. All members of the population are labelled with a number, and random numbers (from random number tables or generated by a calculator) are used to select the sample.

A lottery draw is a good example of simple random sampling: a sample of six numbers is randomly generated from a population of 49; each number has an equal chance of being selected and each combination of six numbers has an equal chance of being generated.

Unfortunately simple random sampling is not always easy, or even possible, to achieve. All members of the population, the sampling frame, have to be identifiable and available for selection at the same time. This is rarely the case as the population may be widely dispersed geographically (people), not available at the same time (a production line) or difficult to identify if the population is constantly changing. Other sampling methods may be preferable for practical or economic reasons even they are not preferable to the statistician.

6.2.2 Systematic sampling

If the population is large and randomly distributed, systematic sampling will produce similar results to random sampling. This method is mainly useful when the whole sampling frame is not available. It is often used in industry when testing items from a production line to ensure that their quality is under control. The first item is selected randomly from the first n items off the production line (say from the first 20), and every nth (say 20th) member is included in the sample thereafter. This method has the obvious advantage that the whole of the production does not have to be complete before starting to select the sample. The main disadvantage is that the systematic sample might fail to include a regularly occurring fault in the production.

Interviewers conducting marketing survey often employ this method of selection, choosing the first house at random from the first n in a particular road and then interviewing the occupants of every nth house.

6.2.3 Stratified random sampling

If there is a systematic difference between groups in the population, for example male and female heights, stratified random sampling is preferable to simple random sampling. Stratified random sampling can produce less sampling error, especially where there is more difference between the subpopulations than within each of them. The population is split into these differing mutually exclusive subpopulations (strata), and a random sub-sample is then drawn from each, in proportion to the stratum size. Since each stratum has less variability than the overall population, the sampling error will be reduced.

The human population might be stratified by age and geographical area before each stratum is sampled separately, its size in proportion to the subpopulation of that stratum, analysed and the results from the separate strata recombined.

6.2.4 Cluster sampling

Cluster sampling is useful when the population consists of a very large number of similar clusters such as schools, factories or geographical areas. The clusters need to be similar so that there is more difference within the clusters than between them. Just a few selected clusters will therefore be representative of the whole population. The clusters to be included are randomly selected, and either every member of the selected clusters is included in the sample, or further random sampling takes place within each cluster, depending on the cluster size.

   The electorate might be sampled by this method, saving the expense of interviewing voters across the country when just a few typical subdivisions or wards could be visited instead.

6.2.5 Multi-stage sampling

Multi-stage sampling is another method which is useful when the population is very widely spread, making random sampling virtually impossible. This method is similar to cluster sampling but has at least two stages in the selection of clusters. The whole population is first split into a number of primary units and a sample of these units is randomly selected. Each of the selected primary units is composed of secondary units from which the final sample is randomly selected.

   A survey collecting educational information might adopt this method sampling geographical areas, then towns within those areas and finally schools within those selected towns.

6.2.6 Quota sampling

Quota sampling is a commonly employed method of non-probability sampling. The population is broken down according to certain controls: for example, age groups of men and women separately. Quotas are selected in sizes proportionate to these age groups in the population. Interviewers will then seek interviewees until their quotas have been filled. It is left to the interviewer to decide who is to be sampled, thereby making the sample non-random.

   Market research often makes use of this method in either telephone surveys or street interviewing. This is why you might be ignored by a researcher who is clearly looking for someone to interview: you do not fit his or her quota.

   For more detail on sampling see Groebner and Shannon (1993, Chapter 5).

6.3 Point and interval estimates

There are two types of estimate for a population parameter:

- a **point estimate** – one particular value
- an **interval estimate** – an interval centred on the point estimate.

6.3.1 Point estimate

Assuming the sample has been taken correctly, a point estimate for a population parameter is a single relevant statistic calculated from the sample, which serves as the best estimate for the population parameter of interest. Mori polls before a general election survey a sample of the electorate and use the results from the sample to estimate the proportion of the total electorate that is expected to vote for each political party. We shall concentrate on the point estimates, $\bar{x}$ for mean (μ), and p for proportion (π) (see Chapter 3). A shorthand way of indicating that a value is only an estimate is $\hat{\mu}$ (μ hat) or $\hat{\pi}$ (π hat).

6.3.2 Interval estimate (confidence interval)

Sometimes it is more useful to quote two limits between which the population parameter is expected to lie, together with the probability of it lying in that range. For example, 'There is a 95 per cent probability that the majority of the electorate will vote for Labour.'

The limits are called the **confidence limits**, and the interval between them the **confidence interval** (CI).

The **confidence interval** is therefore an interval centred on the point estimate, for example the mean, within which we expect a population parameter to lie. The size of the sample and its standard deviation are used to calculate the **standard error of the mean**, s/√n, which is also called the standard deviation of the mean. The number of standard errors included in the interval is found from statistical probability tables: **normal (z) tables** if we know the population standard deviation, **t-tables** if we do not know it and therefore need to estimate it from the sample. These tables show the number of standard errors to be included in half the confidence interval centred on the mean. For example for means, the interval would be: $\bar{x} \pm t$ or z standard errors (see Section 6.5.1).

The width of the confidence interval for a mean depends on three factors:

- the degree of confidence we wish to have in the result – the probability of it including the 'truth' – for example 95 per cent
- the size of the sample, n
- the amount of variation among the members of the sample: that is, its standard deviation, s.

The effect of sample size and confidence level are explored in Examples 6.2 and 6.3. Most of this chapter concentrates on the estimation of means but we shall first look briefly at the estimation of proportions or percentages.

6.4 Confidence intervals for a percentage or proportion

The only difference between calculating the interval for percentages or for proportions is that percentages add up to 100 and proportions add up to 1. The methods are identical even though the formulae differ. Percentage is more commonly used, so Examples 6.1 to 6.3 will estimate population percentages.

The confidence interval for a population percentage or a proportion, π, is given by:

$$\pi = p \pm z \sqrt{\frac{p(100-p)}{n}} \quad \text{for a percentage} \tag{6.1a}$$

or

$$\pi = p \pm z \sqrt{\frac{p(1-p)}{n}} \quad \text{for a proportion} \tag{6.1b}$$

where: π is the unknown population percentage or proportion
p is the sample percentage or proportion, that is, the point estimate for π
z is the appropriate value from the normal tables
n is the sample size.

The standard errors are $\sqrt{\dfrac{p(100-p)}{n}}$ for a percentage and $\sqrt{\dfrac{p(1-p)}{n}}$ for a proportion.

The samples must be large (>30) so that the normal tables may be used in the formula.

We therefore estimate the confidence limits as being at z standard errors either side of the sample percentage or proportion. The value of z from the normal tables depends upon the degree of confidence required. If the degree of confidence is 95 per cent we are prepared to be incorrect in our estimate 5 per cent of the time, and we look for α to be 5 per cent in the standard table. Confidence intervals are always symmetrical so we use the two-tail row for confidence intervals.

Example 6.1

In order to investigate shopping preferences at a supermarket, a random sample of 175 shoppers were asked whether they preferred the bread baked in-store to that from the large national bakeries. 112 of those questioned stated that they preferred the bread baked in-store. Find the 95% confidence interval for the percentage of all the store's customers who prefer bread baked in-store.

The point estimate for the population percentage, π, is $p = \dfrac{112}{175} \times 100 = 64\%$

Use the formula: $\pi = p \pm z \sqrt{\dfrac{p(100-p)}{n}}$ where p = 64 and n = 175

From Table 3 (Appendix D)
95% confidence $\Rightarrow \alpha = 5\%$, two tails gives z = 1.96

$p \pm z \sqrt{\dfrac{p(100-p)}{n}} \Rightarrow 64 \pm 1.96 \times \sqrt{\dfrac{64 \times 36}{175}} = 64 \pm 7.1$

The confidence limits for the population percentage, π, are 56.9% and 71.1% or

56.9% $< \pi <$ 71.1%

The percentage preferring the in-store baked bread is between 57% and 71%.

Confidence intervals do not have to be produced at the 95 per cent level of confidence. Let us see the effect of different levels of confidence in the above example.

Example 6.2

Use the data in Example 6.1 with p = 64% and n = 175 customers:

From the normal tables:
For 90% confidence z = 1.64; for 99% confidence z = 2.58

90% CI : $64 \pm 1.64 \times \sqrt{\dfrac{64 \times 36}{175}}$ $= 64 \pm 6.0$ $\Rightarrow 58.0\% < \pi < 70.0\%$

95% CI :   (from Example 6.1) $\Rightarrow 56.9\% < \pi < 71.1\%$

99% CI : $64 \pm 2.58 \times \sqrt{\dfrac{64 \times 36}{175}}$ $= 64 \pm 9.4$ $\Rightarrow 54.6\% < \pi < 73.4\%$

We can see that our confidence that an interval includes the true population percentage increases as the width of the interval increases. If 100 samples of size 175 were taken, we would expect 90 to include the true population percentage at the 90 per cent level, and so on.

What happens as we vary the sample size? Repeating Example 6.1 with various sample sizes:

Example 6.3

Substitute different sample sizes in Example 6.1 with p = 64% and keep the confidence level at 95%, so z will be 1.96 whatever the value of n.

n = 75: $64 \pm 1.96 \times \sqrt{\dfrac{64 \times 36}{75}}$ $= 64 \pm 10.9$ $\Rightarrow 53.1\% < \pi < 74.9\%$

n = 175:   (from Example 6.1) $\Rightarrow 56.9\% < \pi < 71.1\%$

n = 275: $64 \pm 1.96 \times \sqrt{\dfrac{64 \times 36}{275}}$ $= 64 \pm 5.7$ $\Rightarrow 58.3\% < \pi < 67.9\%$

Comparing the width of these three confidence intervals, we can see that our estimations become more precise as the sample size increases. If we know the precision required, the appropriate **sample size** can be calculated from the same formula.

Clearly the larger the sample size, the better from the statistical point of view, but the sampling exercise will be more expensive. Statistical sampling generally becomes a balancing act between precision and expense!

The effect of sample size and confidence level is the same whether we are investigating confidence levels for percentages or for means.

6.5 Confidence intervals for one mean

When calculating the confidence interval for a mean, the method is basically the same as the method for percentages. We first find the point estimate and then produce an interval around it with confidence limits equal to an appropriate number of standard errors. This number comes from either normal or t-tables depending on the answers to two questions:

- Do we know the population standard deviation?
- Is the sample a large one: that is, over 30?

If we know the population standard deviation, the normal tables are satisfactory. If we need to estimate the population standard deviation from the sample, there may be errors in its estimation, so a wider confidence interval is required. This is provided by the t-tables.

If we do not know the population standard deviation but the sample is large, generally taken to be over 30, the estimation error will be small, so again the normal table is appropriate. Both tables give similar results for large samples. Both the normal and the t-distributions are symmetrical, so if the data is very skewed the use of confidence intervals is not really appropriate. The problem is to decide from a small sample whether the population is symmetrical or not.

If we know the population standard deviation, σ, we make use of it in the calculation; if we do not know it then we use its point estimate, the sample standard deviation, s, instead.

The choice of statistical table is summarised in Table 6.1.

Table 6.1

Sample size	Population standard deviation	
	Known: standard error = $\sigma/\sqrt{n}$	**Unknown:** standard error = $s/\sqrt{n}$
Large	Normal tables	Normal tables
Small	Normal tables	t-tables

Do not be misled by Table 6.1 into thinking that the normal tables are used more often than the t-tables in estimation. We do not often know the population standard deviation, σ, and samples are not often as large as we would like, so the t-tables are more commonly used. We shall, however, first demonstrate the use of the normal tables before concentrating on the t-tables.

The convention is to assume, in the absence of the population data (and for statistical reasons not discussed on this course), that if the sample is not extremely skewed the population is likely to be normal (see Figure 6.1). In Figure 6.1(a) the population is definitely normal, but would you have judged it as such from the small sample of data in Figure 6.1(b) taken from it? Probably not! It is common practice to calculate confidence intervals even if the sample does not appear to be normal.

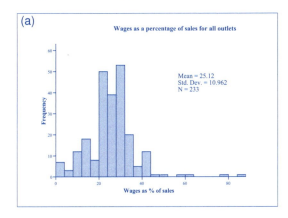
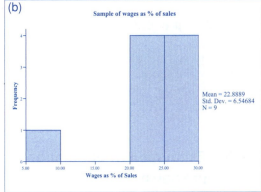

Figure 6.1

If the data is not normal it is customary to work with medians rather than means.

6.5.1 Estimation of population mean when σ is known

If the population standard deviation, σ, is known we use the normal tables in the estimation of the population mean, μ. The formula for μ is:

$$\mu = \bar{x} \pm z \frac{\sigma}{\sqrt{n}} \quad \text{that is the sample mean} \pm z \text{ standard errors} \qquad (6.2)$$

where: μ is the unknown population mean being estimated
            $\bar{x}$ is the sample mean, that is, the point estimate for μ
            z is the appropriate value from the normal tables
            σ is the known population standard deviation
            n is the sample size.

Example 6.4

For a **whole chain** of supermarkets it is **known** that the standard deviation of the hourly wages for part-time employees is £1.50.

A new supermarket is opened by the same chain in a new shopping precinct. The analysis of a random sample of the wages of 10 employees from this small supermarket gave a mean value of £6.15 per hour. Assuming the same standard deviation (£1.50), calculate the 95% confidence interval for the average hourly wage for employees of the small branch and use it to see whether the figure could be the same as for the whole chain, which is £6.50.

95% CI : $\bar{x}$ = £6.15, σ = £1.50, n = 10, α = 5%

$$\mu = \bar{x} \pm z \frac{\sigma}{\sqrt{n}} \quad \text{from the condensed normal tables } z = 1.96$$

$$6.15 \pm 1.96 \times \frac{1.50}{\sqrt{10}} = 6.15 \pm 0.930$$

So the mean wage of the small supermarket is likely to be between £5.22 and £7.08 per hour.

$$£5.22 < \mu < £7.08$$

This interval includes the mean for the whole chain, £6.50, so the average hourly wage could be the same.
   Note that the interval is rather wide because only a small sample was taken.

6.5.2 Estimation of population mean for large sample size and σ unknown

The calculation in this case is identical to that for Example 6.4. The usual practice is to use the normal tables. (If, however, you use the t-tables in error your result for a large sample will be the same.)

Example 6.5

A random sample of 100 sales invoices was taken from a very large population of sales invoices. The average value was found to be £47.50 with a standard deviation of £7.50. Find a 90% confidence interval for the true mean value of all the sales.

90% CI : $\bar{x}$ = £47.50, s = £7.50, n = 100, α = 10%

Now z, from the condensed normal tables = 1.64

$$\mu = \bar{x} \pm z \frac{s}{\sqrt{n}} = 47.50 \pm 1.64 \times \frac{7.50}{\sqrt{100}} = 45.7 \pm 1.23$$

So the mean of the sales invoices for the whole population is likely to be between £46.27 and £48.73.

£46.27 < μ < £48.73

6.5.3 Estimation of population mean for small sample size and σ unknown

The sample mean, $\bar{x}$, is used as the point estimate for μ as previously. The best estimate for the population standard deviation is s, the sample standard deviation, σ_{n-1}, from the calculator in statistical mode (see Section 3.3.3).

If the population standard deviation, σ, is not known we use the t-tables in the estimation of the population mean, μ. The formula for μ is:

$$\mu = \bar{x} \pm t \frac{\sigma}{\sqrt{n}} \quad \text{that is the sample mean} \pm \text{t standard errors} \tag{6.3}$$

In order to use t-tables, just as with normal tables, we assume the population to be normally distributed. When using the t-tables: ν (nu) refers to the **degrees of freedom** of the sample. It equals n – 1 for single samples, as here. If you look at Table 2 (Appendix D), you can see that the value of t varies with ν and therefore with the sample size. As the sample size increases, t approaches z, which is the value obtained from the normal tables.

Example 6.6

An accountant at a small branch of a large company wishes to obtain some information about all the invoices. In order to obtain an estimate of this information, a sample of 21 invoices is randomly selected from the whole population.

Use the results in Table 6.2 to produce point estimates for μ and σ and then find a 99% confidence interval for all the branch's invoices. If the average invoice value for the whole company is £38.50, is this small branch in line with the rest of the company?

Table 6.2 Sample of invoices (£)

32.53	25.27	31.47	25.11	38.05	42.04	41.47
22.27	26.78	38.00	43.48	24.11	38.07	32.92
33.38	30.97	43.16	32.93	29.05	38.06	22.20

99% CI :   From the calculator $\bar{x}$ = £32.92, s = £6.94, n = 21, α = 1%

From the t-table for $v = n - 1 = 20$ degrees of freedom, 2 tails, 1%, t = 2.85

$$\mu = \bar{x} \pm t\frac{s}{\sqrt{n}} \quad \Rightarrow \quad 32.92 \pm 2.85 \times \frac{6.94}{\sqrt{21}} \quad = \quad 32.92 \pm 4.32$$

£28.60 < μ < £37.24

This interval does not include £38.50, so the small branch is out of line with the rest of the company. Its invoices are smaller.

How do we interpret the 99% confidence interval? If 100 similar samples were taken and analysed then we are confident that 99 of the intervals calculated would include the true population mean.

A computer analysis of Example 6.6 using Minitab, SPSS and Excel is shown in Section 6.11.

Make sure you are happy with the use of the t-tables. The degrees of freedom, v, is one less than the sample size and this determines which row of the table you use to find the required value of t. The column is determined by α (100 minus the confidence level), $100 - 99 = 1\%$ in this case, and as stated earlier, for confidence intervals we will always use two tails.

6.6 Confidence intervals for two independent means

We are going to extend the previous method to see whether two populations could have the same mean, or alternatively whether two samples could have come from the same population as judged by their means, assuming that the standard deviations of both populations are the same.

There is a complicated formula for this but a simple approach can also be used. The confidence intervals for each sample mean can be found separately and compared to see if there is any overlap between them. If there is an overlap, the mean values could well be the same as they could both lie in the overlapping interval and so have a common value. If they do not overlap, then no common value exists and the samples are likely to have come from different populations. We assume, using this method, that both populations are normally distributed and independent of each other.

For example, if a supermarket chain wished to discover whether a local advertising campaign had been successful, it could sample customers' spending before and after the campaign and calculate confidence intervals for the mean spending of all customers at both times. If the intervals were found to overlap, the means could be the same, so the campaign might have had no effect. If on the other hand the intervals were separate, with the later sample giving the higher interval, then the campaign would appear to have effectively increased sales.

Example 6.7

The till slips of supermarket customers were sampled both before and after an advertising campaign and the results were analysed with the following results:

Before: $\bar{x}_B = £57.60, s_B = £6.70, n_B = 25$
After: $\bar{x}_A = £61.78, s_A = £5.30, n_A = 25$

Has the advertising campaign been successful in increasing the mean spending of all the supermarket customers? Calculate two 95% confidence intervals and compare the results.

For both, n = 25 so 24 degrees of freedom giving t = 2.06 for 5%, 2 tails, α = 5%.

Before (B): $\mu_B = \bar{x}_B \pm t \dfrac{s_B}{\sqrt{n_B}} \Rightarrow 57.60 \pm 2.06 \times \dfrac{6.70}{\sqrt{25}} = 57.60 \pm 2.76$

$£54.84 < \mu < £60.36$

After (A): $\mu_A = \bar{x}_A \pm t \dfrac{s_A}{\sqrt{n_A}} \Rightarrow 61.78 \pm 2.06 \times \dfrac{5.30}{\sqrt{25}} = 61.78 \pm 2.18$

$£59.60 < \mu < £63.96$

Interpretation: The sample mean had risen considerably but, because the confidence intervals overlap, the mean values for all the sales may lie in the common ground. There may be no difference between the two means so the advertising campaign has not been proved to be successful by this method.

We shall employ a preferable method in the next example.

6.7 Confidence intervals for paired data

If two measures are taken from each case, such as 'before' and 'after', in every instance then the data is '**paired**'. The 'change' or 'difference' for each case can be calculated and a confidence interval for the mean of the 'changes' calculated. This method should always be used for 'paired' data as it produces a smaller interval for the same sample size and confidence level, giving a more precise estimate.

CI : $\mu_d = \bar{x}_d \pm t \dfrac{s_d}{\sqrt{n_d}}$ (6.4)

where $\bar{x}_d$, s_d and n_d refer to the calculated differences for the mean, standard deviation and sample size respectively.

If the confidence interval includes zero, there is a possibility that no change has taken place. If both limits have the same sign, as in Example 6.8, then zero is excluded and some change must have taken place.

When interpreting any change look carefully at its direction, as this will depend on your order of subtraction. In Example 6.8 it is obvious that there has been an increase in the average spending.

Example 6.8

The supermarket statistician realised that there was a considerable range in customers' spending power, and that the increases in individual customer's spending would show a smaller spread. In other words the 'before' and 'after' populations are not independent, as high spenders before the campaign are likely to be high spenders after it.

Before the next advertising campaign at the supermarket, the statistician took a random sample of 10 customers, A to J, and collected their till slips. After the campaign, slips from the same 10 customers were collected and both sets of data recorded. Using the paired data, has there been any mean change at a 95% confidence level?

	A	B	C	D	E	F	G	H	I	J
Before	62.30	75.76	52.29	30.23	35.79	66.50	52.30	98.65	52.20	35.90
After	63.09	79.20	51.76	40.78	39.50	70.67	57.32	97.80	57.39	37.24

We first need to calculate the differences. The direction doesn't matter but it seems sensible to take the earlier amounts away from the later ones to find the changes:

	A	B	C	D	E	F	G	H	I	J
Diffs.	0.79	3.44	−0.53	10.55	3.71	4.17	5.02	−0.85	5.19	1.34

We can now forget the original data sets and just work with the differences.

From the differences $\bar{x}_d$ = £3.28, s_d = £3.37, n_d = 10, α = 5%

$$95\% \text{ CI}: \quad \mu_d = \bar{x}_d \pm t\frac{s_d}{\sqrt{n_d}} \quad \Rightarrow \quad 3.28 \pm 2.26 \times \frac{3.37}{\sqrt{10}} \quad \Rightarrow \quad 3.28 \pm 2.41$$

$$£0.87 < \mu_d < £5.69$$

This interval does not include zero so the possibility of 'no change' has been eliminated. Because the mean amount spent after the campaign is greater than that before it, there has been a significant increase in spending.

A computer analysis of Example 6.8 using Minitab, SPSS and Excel is shown in Section 6.11.

6.8 A continuous example using confidence intervals

Example 6.9

A large company was about to introduce a new training course to for office recruits. A previous course had produced a pass rate of 74% (p) on a standard test given to 1000 trainees and the company hoped that the new course would produce a better pass rate.

Find a 95% confidence interval for the percentage of trainees passing after the old training course.

95% CI : p = 74%, n = 1000, α = 5%

$$\pi = p \pm z \times \sqrt{\frac{p(100-p)}{n}} \;\Rightarrow\; 74 \pm 1.96 \times \sqrt{\frac{74 \times 26}{1000}} \;\Rightarrow\; 74 \pm 2.72$$

$$\Rightarrow\; 71.3\% > \pi > 76.7\%$$

During the first month with the new test a random selection of 18 candidates were each given the standard test before training and a similar one after training so that their progress could be monitored. These test results are given in Table 6.3.

Table 6.3

Trainee	A	B	C	D	E	F	G	H	I
Before (B)	42	56	64	57	45	43	62	51	39
After (A)	56	73	87	68	59	62	79	62	60

Trainee	J	K	L	M	N	O	P	Q	R
Before (B)	64	43	42	62	39	56	57	45	51
After (A)	87	62	56	79	60	73	68	59	62

Use two separate 95% confidence intervals to see if there has been a mean improvement.

Before the course (B): $\bar{x}_B = 51.0$, $s_B = 8.92$, $n_B = 18$, t = 2.11 (by interpolation)

$$\mu_B = \bar{x}_B \pm t \frac{s_B}{\sqrt{n_B}} \;\Rightarrow\; 51.0 \pm 2.11 \times \frac{8.92}{\sqrt{18}} \;\Rightarrow\; 51.0 \pm 4.44 \;\Rightarrow\; 46.6 < \mu < 55.4$$

After the course (A): $\bar{x}_A = 67.3$, $s_A = 10.1$, $n_A = 18$, t = 2.11 (by interpolation)

$$\mu_A = \bar{x}_A \pm t \frac{s_A}{\sqrt{n_A}} \;\Rightarrow\; 67.3 \pm 2.11 \times \frac{10.1}{\sqrt{18}} \;\Rightarrow\; 67.3 \pm 5.02 \;\Rightarrow\; 62.3 < \mu < 72.3$$

There is no overlap between these intervals, that is, no common ground, so the mean after the course must be different to the mean before the course and, looking at the two means, it is evident that an improvement has taken place.

Note: This approach assumes that the two samples are independent. Although the assumption is incorrect in this example, the example is a useful indicator of the method.

Assuming the data in Table 6.3 to be paired, use a 99% confidence interval for the mean improvement in the scores.

Differences: 14, 17, 23, 11, 14, 19, 17, 11, 21, 23, 19, 14, 17, 21, 17, 11, 14, 11.

From the sample: $\bar{x}_d = 16.3$, $s_d = 4.09$, $n_d = 18$, t = 2.91 (by interpolation)

$$\mu_d = \bar{x}_d \pm t \frac{s_d}{\sqrt{n_d}} \;\Rightarrow\; 16.3 \pm 2.91 \times \frac{4.09}{\sqrt{18}} \;\Rightarrow\; 16.3 \pm 2.81 \;\Rightarrow\; 13.5 < \mu < 19.1$$

Both limits are positive therefore there has definitely been an improvement in mean score.

Assuming the pass mark to be 60, find a point estimate for the percentage of the trainees who pass after the new course (Table 6.3). This is only a small sample, but is there any evidence that the pass rate has improved?

From the sample: $p = \dfrac{14}{18} \times 100 = 77.8\%$

This is above the 71.3% to 76.7% interval for the old course so it is likely that the pass rate of the trainees has been improved by changing to the new course.

6.9 Interpretation of confidence intervals

We have interpreted individual confidence intervals using specific examples, and now we shall take a more general look at the situation.

The mean of a population is a constant figure. Its value may be unknown but it does not change. The variability is produced by the fact that each sample taken from the constant population is different, as a result of sampling error, and so produces different sample statistics, $\bar{x}$, s and n. These sample values are used to calculate a confidence interval for each sample, and so these confidence intervals will vary from one sample to another. The confidence level states the percentage of confidence intervals, calculated from a very large number of samples, that we would expect to include the true population mean.

If we wish to be more sure of including the true value, but need to keep the sample size constant, then we have to use a higher confidence level (see Example 6.2), but this can make the interval so wide that it is meaningless.

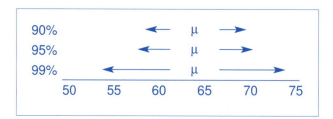

Figure 6.2

A preferable method is to keep the confidence level constant while increasing precision by taking larger samples (see Example 6.3), but this can be expensive in both time and materials.

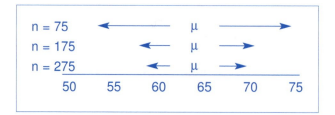

Figure 6.3

If we are comparing population parameters of independent populations by confidence intervals, our main interest centres on whether they overlap or not. If there is an overlap then there is common ground between them, and the samples could have come from the same population. Assuming the same standard deviation, this indicates, of course, that there is no difference between the population means.

If we are comparing population parameters of dependent, paired data, we will be interested in whether the resulting confidence interval includes zero or not. If zero is included then there might be no difference between the population means: for example, in a 'before' and 'after' situation no change has taken place. If zero is excluded, we know that some change has taken place, and looking back at the direction of the calculated differences and the sign of their mean, we can decide the direction of the change.

6.10 Further applications of estimations

Many decision-making applications involve estimating a population value from a sample taken from the same population. Estimations are widely used in quality control. Samples taken from a production line are analysed and the results used to estimate the quality of the whole of the production. These sample values, generally means, are plotted on a chart which is based on the expected distribution of the sample means when production is satisfactory. The 95 per cent and 99 per cent confidence limits are drawn on these charts to act as warning and action limits for the standard of the production. More information can be found in advanced textbooks on quality control or decision making.

Chapter 13 describes how confidence intervals are often applied to forecasting. The quality of a forecasting model depends upon its likely errors, as judged by how well the model fits past data. These errors are used in the construction of the confidence interval, so the forecast is stated with its expected precision.

Stock control is another useful application of confidence intervals to define the likely demand on stocks and indicate preferable stock-keeping levels.

6.11 Computer analysis of Examples 6.6 and 6.8

Example 6.6

See Figure 6.4 for Minitab and SPSS. Excel gives 3.900919 as half the confidence interval. Excel needs to be told the standard deviation, and sample size before producing this figure so you also need to find the mean to state the interval as $32.92 \pm 3.90 \Rightarrow £29.02 < \mu < £36.82$. This figure does not agree with the values produced, in common, by Minitab or SPSS because Excel incorrectly uses the normal tables instead of the t-tables.

Example 6.8

See Figure 6.5 for Minitab and SPSS. Excel gives 2.088709 as half the confidence interval. Excel needed to be given the standard deviation and the number of the differences. As in Example 6.6, the required interval is interpreted as being $3.28 \pm 2.09 \Rightarrow £1.19 < \mu < £5.37$. This does not agree with the values produced, in common, by Minitab or SPSS because Excel has used the normal tables instead of the t-tables. The difference is considerable because the sample size is so small.

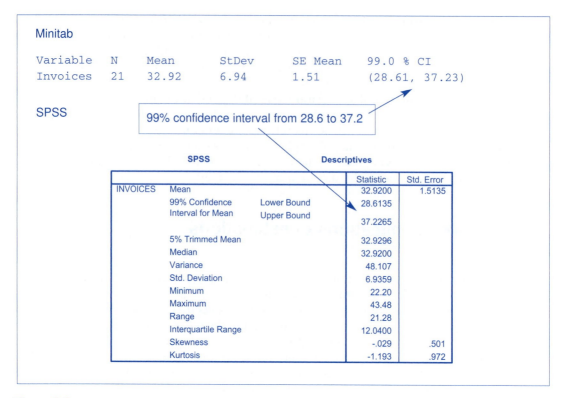

Figure 6.4

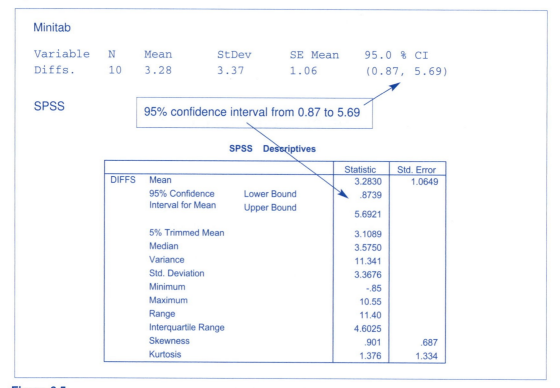

Figure 6.5

More computer output from confidence intervals is shown in Sections 14.2.3, 14.5.3 and 14.8.3.

6.12 Summary

In Chapter 6 we have introduced one of the most important concepts of statistics – estimating a population value from a sample taken from that population. We have looked at the inevitable sampling error introduced by this method, but concluded that this is the best we can do in the circumstances because the truth about the whole population is unavailable. We accept that estimations may not be accurate, so they are generally presented in the form of an interval which is expected to include the truth.

Confidence intervals can be calculated for all population parameters; in this chapter we have concentrated on means and percentages. We have used them as individual estimates, and in pairs for comparing population parameters or to see whether a particular value is acceptable as a likely population parameter.

Confidence intervals are centred on the point estimate of interest, with the confidence limits defined by a certain number of standard errors on either side. The width of an interval depends upon the sample size, the variability of the data within the population (or the

Table 6.4 Summary of formulae used in this chapter

Parameter	Number of samples	Population st. dev.	Data	Formula	Table
	one large →	known		$\bar{x} \pm z\dfrac{\sigma}{\sqrt{n}}$	normal table
		unknown		$\bar{x} \pm z\dfrac{\sigma}{\sqrt{n}}$	normal table
	one small →	known		$\bar{x} \pm z\dfrac{\sigma}{\sqrt{n}}$	normal table
		unknown		$\bar{x} \pm t\dfrac{s}{\sqrt{n}}$	t-table
Mean		unknown	paired	$\bar{x}_d \pm t\dfrac{s_d}{\sqrt{n_d}}$	t-table
	two small	unknown	unpaired	$\begin{cases} \bar{x}_1 \pm t\dfrac{s_1}{\sqrt{n_1}} \\ \bar{x}_2 \pm t\dfrac{s_2}{\sqrt{n_2}} \end{cases}$	t-table
Percentage →	one large ──────────────→			$p \pm z\sqrt{\dfrac{p(100-p)}{n}}$	normal table

sample as its best estimator), and the confidence level employed. The confidence level is a measure of the probability that an interval does include the truth.

Table 6.4 summarises the use of the different formulae introduced in this chapter.

Do note that there are really only three formulae from which to choose by answering two questions:

- Is the parameter being estimated a mean or a percentage?
- If it is a mean, do we know the population standard deviation?

There are many other situations in which confidence intervals can be calculated (see Weimer 1993, Chapter 9). We have confined ourselves in this chapter to those that are the simplest and most commonly used.

6.13 Case study

See 'Restaurants' in the folder case study in the students' materials on the companion website.

Even though there are obviously problems with normality (results of case study 5.10), your directors would like you to calculate confidence intervals for:

- gross sales for all outlets together; gross sales for each type of outlet separately
- market value of all outlets together; market value of each type of outlet separately
- number of full-time employees for all outlets together; number of full-time employees for each type of outlet separately
- number of part-time employees for all outlets together; number of part-time employees for each type of outlet separately
- wages as percentage of sales for all outlets together; wages as percentage of sales for each type of outlet separately
- advertising as percentage of sales for all outlets together; advertising as percentage of sales for each type of outlet separately.

Tutorial 6: Confidence intervals

Note: You may assume the populations to be normally distributed and of equal standard deviation where necessary. Answers to Tutorial questions are in Appendix A.

6.1 A sample of 100 observations is taken from a population with unknown mean, μ, and **known** standard deviation, $\sigma = 4.5$. If the mean of the sample is 28.3, construct a confidence interval for μ for each of the following confidence levels.
(a) 90% (b) 95% (c) 99%

6.2 The management of a large national chain of motels decided to estimate the mean cost per room of repairing damage caused by its customers during a bank holiday weekend. A random sample of 150 vacated rooms was inspected by the management, and indicated a mean repair cost of £48.10 and a sample standard deviation of £12.40. Construct a 95% confidence interval for the mean repair cost, μ, of all its rooms.

6.3 Repeated assessments on a chemical determination of human blood during a laboratory analysis are known to be normally distributed. Ten assessments on a given sample of blood yielded the values:

1.002 0.958 1.014 1.009 1.041 0.962 1.058 1.024 1.019 1.020

Find a 99% confidence interval for the true chemical determination in the blood for repeated assessments of the sample.

6.4 A survey of 672 audited tax returns showed that 448 resulted in additional payments. Construct a 95% confidence interval for the true percentage of all audited tax returns that result in additional payments.

6.5 Firm A claims that it pays its clerical staff on average more per week than its rival, Firm B. Firm B disputes the claim, so each firm examines a random sample of the salaries paid to its workers, with the following results:

Firm A: Mean £543.00, Standard deviation £13.20, n = 40
Firm B: Mean £538.50, Standard deviation £14.30, n = 50

Calculate two 95% confidence intervals and compare them to see which firm is correct.

6.6 The same 11 workers performed a task using two different methods. The completion times, in minutes, for each task are given below:

Worker	1	2	3	4	5	6	7	8	9	10	11
Method A	15.2	14.6	14.2	15.6	14.9	15.2	15.6	15.0	16.2	15.7	15.6
Method B	14.5	14.8	13.8	15.6	15.3	14.3	15.5	15.0	15.6	15.2	14.8

Construct a 99% confidence interval for the average of the time differences and interpret your result.

6.7 The following data resulted from two independent random samples taken from two normal populations:

Sample 1: $n_1 = 11$, $\bar{x}_1 = 14$, $s_1 = 2$
Sample 2: $n_2 = 9$, $\bar{x}_2 = 18$, $s_2 = 3$

Construct a 95% confidence interval for **each** sample.
What does this imply about the populations?

6.8 A training manager wishes to see if there is any alteration in the aptitude of his trainees after they have been on a course. He gives each a test before they start the course and an equivalent one after they have completed it. Their scores are recorded below:

Trainee	A	B	C	D	E	F	G	H	I
Score before training	74	69	45	67	67	42	54	67	76
Score after training	69	76	56	59	78	63	54	76	75

Find the 95% confidence interval for the average **change** in score. Interpret your answer for the training manager.

6.9   In a survey carried out in a large city, 170 households out of a random sample of 250 owned at least one pet. Find the 95% confidence interval for the percentage of house-holds in the city that own at least one pet.

   Does the result support a pet food manufacturer's claim that three-quarters of all households have at least one pet?

6.10 The personnel department of a company developed an aptitude test for screening potential employees. The person who devised the test asserted that the mean mark attained would be 100. The following results were obtained with a random sample of applicants:

$\bar{x} = 96, s = 5.2, n = 13.$

Calculate a 95% confidence interval for the mean mark for all candidates and use it to see whether the mean mark could be 100.

Notes

For SPSS/Minitab/Excel worksheets on estimation see Chapter 14, Sections 14.2.3, 14.5.3 and 14.8.3 respectively. Worksheets with computer output and its interpretation are on the companion website.

   The supplementary exercise for Chapter 6, with answers, is on the companion website.

Hypothesis testing

7

Objectives of this chapter

In Chapter 6 we used the analysis of samples taken from a population to estimate parameters, such as the unknown mean, of that population. In this chapter we use the same sample statistic to see whether a corresponding figure claimed – hypothesised – for the whole population is likely to be true or not. For example, instead of asking the question 'What is the range of values within which we expect the population mean to lie?' we ask, 'Is it probable that the population mean can take a particular hypothesised value?'

The uncertainty of using a sample value which caused us to quote interval rather than point estimates in Chapter 6 now requires us to state that we are only, say, 95 per cent sure that we have reached the right conclusion in rejecting any claim as being incorrect.

In this chapter we shall concentrate on the hypothesis tests concerned with means but shall start, as we did with estimation, by looking at the general concept and then testing for hypothesised percentages.

Having studied this chapter you should be able to:

- understand the general concept of hypothesis testing
- perform many of the simpler techniques for carrying out the procedure
- be aware of other techniques
- be able to interpret the results for non-statisticians in a business context.

7.1 General concept of hypothesis testing

When an estimate from a **sample** is used to test some belief, claim or **hypothesis** about the **population**, the process is known as **hypothesis testing**. A hypothesis is tested at a particular **significance level**, α, so the technique may also be called **significance testing**.

The **conclusions** we reach following the **analysis of the sample** are based on **probability** and so, as with confidence intervals, there is always a small **chance of their being incorrect**.

For example, in England a man who is charged with murder is assumed (hypothesised) to be innocent when he enters the courtroom. Clearly all the possible evidence will not be available (particularly if he is guilty!), so the jury have to reach a verdict (conclusion) from only a sample. After the sample of the evidence has been considered carefully, he may be found 'beyond reasonable doubt' to be 'guilty' when he is actually innocent, or 'not guilty' when he did, in fact, commit the crime. So two types of error could be made in reaching a conclusion, but the stress is always on avoiding a miscarriage of justice: that is, in not finding an innocent man guilty. Note that the possible verdicts, in England, are 'guilty' and 'not guilty'; a man is never proved to be 'innocent'. The hypothesis of 'innocence' is either rejected – 'guilty' – or not rejected – 'not guilty'.

Similarly in all hypothesis testing a claim, the **null hypothesis**, is stated and a conclusion is reached that is the most probably correct from the sample evidence. The conclusion is always recorded with the probability of its being incorrect for the whole population. (The p-value from computer output is defined in Section 7.2.) As in the courtroom example, the original hypothesised statement is the one that will be allowed to stand unless the evidence is strong enough to cause its rejection.

As considered in Section 6.2, the problem of sampling error can never be eliminated completely when a sample, instead of the whole population, is tested. The same precautions are taken to make sure that the sample is as representative as possible of the population to which the conclusion applies.

The process of hypothesis testing is so widely used that a **common methodology** has been adopted.

7.2 Common methodology

Remember that a claim, or hypothesis, is made about the whole **population**. A **sample** is taken from that population and analysed. The results of the analysis are used to decide whether the claim is reasonable or not.

The common method for all hypothesis tests comprises six steps. Suppose a claim has been made that the mean male salary in a particular firm is £25,000:

1 State the **null hypothesis (H_0)**
   This is a statement about the population which may, or may not, be true. It will be in the form of an equation making some claim about the population.

   The mean male salary is £25,000.
   H_0: μ = £25,000 where μ is the population mean.

2 State the **alternative hypothesis (H$_1$)**
This is the conclusion reached if the null hypothesis is rejected. It will include the terms: 'not equal to' ($\neq$) for two-tailed tests and 'greater than' ($>$), or 'less than' ($<$) for one-tailed tests.

The mean male salary is not, or is less than, or is greater than £25,000.
H$_1$: $\mu \neq$ £25,000, or H$_1$: $\mu <$ £25,000, or H$_1$: $\mu >$ £25,000

3 State the **significance level (α)** of the test
This is the proportion of the time you are willing to reject H$_0$ when it is in fact true. If not stated specifically, a 5 per cent (0.05) significance level is used. From computer output the p-value is the probability of H$_0$ being correct (see Section 7.11).

4 Find the **critical value**
This is the value from the appropriate table which the test statistic is required to reach before we can reject H$_0$. It depends on the significance level, such as 5 per cent or 1 per cent, and whether the test is one- or two-tailed. This value states the critical number of standard errors that the sample value needs to be away from the hypothesised value for the null hypothesis to be rejected. Any value greater than this lies within the critcal region.

5 Calculate the **test statistic**
This value is calculated from the sample statistics, such as the mean and standard deviation, which are substituted into the appropriate formula to find the value of the test statistic. (Each formula, which calculates a number of standard errors, is used in one specific type of hypothesis test only, and so needs careful selection.)

6 Reach a **conclusion**
Compare the values of the test statistic and the critical value. If the test statistic is greater than the critical value, then we have enough evidence from the sample data to cause us to **reject the null hypothesis** and conclude that the alternative hypothesis is true: for example, the mean salary is not £25,000. If the test statistic is not greater than the critical value, we do not have sufficient evidence on which to **reject the null hypothesis**. The mean salary for the whole firm could be £25,000.

Note: We can prove the null hypothesis to be false but we can never prove it to be true since we only have a sample of all the evidence.

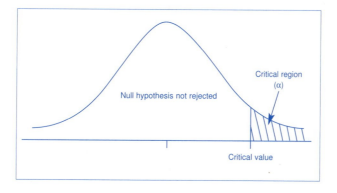

Figure 7.1(a) Graphical interpretation of conclusion – one-tailed test

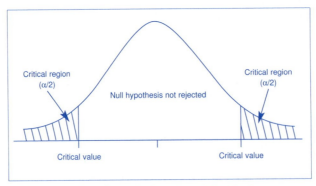

Figure 7.1(b) Graphical interpretation of conclusion – two-tailed test

If the test statistic falls into the critical region, there is sufficient evidence to cause the null hypothesis to be rejected. Many students find the use of this type of diagram to be helpful in deciding whether or not to reject the null hypothesis. The total shaded area is the significance level, α (alpha), given as either a percentage (5 per cent) or a decimal (0.05).

The methodology will seem simpler with specific examples so we shall first test some hypothesised proportions and then concentrate on means.

7.3 Testing for percentages or proportions

When we test for a population percentage or proportion, much that we learnt in Section 6.4 needs to be remembered: take large samples; the normal tables are appropriate for the critical value; the same method applies for both percentages and proportions.

Remember H_0 is shorthand for the null hypothesis. 'Null' means nothing so in this context it means 'no difference from' whatever value is being claimed. H_1 is shorthand for the alternative hypothesis, or the conclusion we shall reach if we have to reject the null hypothesis.

H_0: $\pi = c$ where π is shorthand for the population proportion and c is its hypothesised value.

H_1: $\pi \neq c$, $\pi < c$, or $\pi > c$ (that is, anything but equal to c.)

Significance level (α): as stated or 5 per cent by default.

Critical value: from normal tables (Appendix D, Table 3) using the appropriate number of tails and significance level.

Test statistic: calculated by $\dfrac{|p - \pi|}{\sqrt{\dfrac{\pi(100 - \pi)}{n}}}$ or $\dfrac{|p - \pi|}{\sqrt{\dfrac{\pi(1 - \pi)}{n}}}$ (7.1)

where p and π are the sample and population percentages or proportions respectively. This test statistic measures the number of standard errors (see Section 6.4).

Conclusion: H_0 is rejected if the test statistic is so large that the sample could not have come from a population with the hypothesised proportion: in other words there are too many standard errors.

Example 7.1

A company manufacturing a certain brand of breakfast cereal claims that 60% of all house-wives prefer that type to any other. A random sample of 300 housewives contains 165 who do prefer that type. At 5% significance, is the true percentage as the company claims or lower?

Given: π is claimed to be 60%, $p = \dfrac{165}{300} \times 100 = 55\%$, $n = 300$

(π is the hypothesises percentage and p the sample percentage.)

The claim is only wrong if the percentage is lower than π, so the test is one tailed.

H$_0$: $\pi = 60\%$ **H$_1$**: $\pi < 60\%$

Significance level (α): 5% (0.05)

Critical value: normal tables, one tail, 1.64

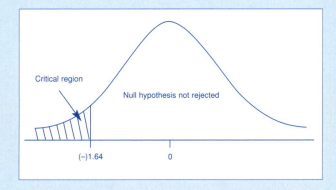

Figure 7.2

Because the test is one tailed and 'less than', we know that the critical region is in the lower tail. Most normal tables include only positive values. We need to compare the absolute value, shown by the use of two vertical lines, (| |), of the test statistic with the always positive critical value.

Test statistic: $\dfrac{|p - \pi|}{\sqrt{\dfrac{\pi(100-\pi)}{n}}} \Rightarrow \dfrac{|55-60|}{\sqrt{\dfrac{60(100-60)}{300}}} = \dfrac{5}{\sqrt{8}} = 1.77$

Conclusion: Test statistic exceeds critical value so reject H$_0$. The percentage using the brand is lower than 60%.

Example 7.2

An auditor claims that 10% of a company's invoices are incorrect. To test this claim a random sample of 200 invoices is checked and 24 are found to be incorrect. Test at the 1% significant level if the auditor's claim is supported by the sample evidence.

Given: π is claimed to be 10%, p $= \dfrac{24}{200} \times 100 = 12\%$, n $= 200$

The claim can be judged wrong in either direction so the test is two tailed.

H_0: $\pi = 10\%$ H_1: $\pi \neq 10\%$

Significance level (α): 1% (0.01)

Critical value: normal tables, two tails, $\alpha = 0.01$, 2.58

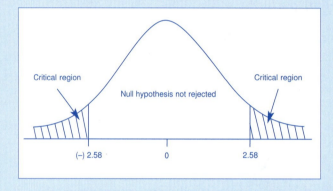

Critical region

Null hypothesis not rejected

Critical region

(−) 2.58   0   2.58

Figure 7.3

Test statistic: $\dfrac{|p-\pi|}{\sqrt{\dfrac{\pi(100-\pi)}{n}}} \Rightarrow \dfrac{|12-10|}{\sqrt{\dfrac{10(100-10)}{200}}} = \dfrac{2}{\sqrt{4.5}} = 0.943$

Conclusion: Test statistic is less than critical value so H_0 is not rejected. The percentage of incorrect invoices is consistent with the auditor's claim of 10%.

For each of these examples we have worked through the six steps described in Section 7.2. Had we decided to use proportions, rather than percentages, the method would have been the same except that $(100 - p)$ would have been replaced by $(1 - p)$ in Equation 7.1 and the values for p and π would have been decimals between 0 and 1 rather than percentages between 0 and 100.

7.4 Testing for one mean

The methods described in this section require the population to be measured on interval or ratio scales and to be normally distributed. You may assume this to be so for any data presented here. Testing for normality is covered later using a computer package, and the treatment of non-normal data is covered in Section 7.8.

As with Section 6.5 on confidence intervals, we have to ask whether the sample size is large or small, and whether the population standard deviation is known or has to be estimated from the sample, before deciding which test to use. The methods are basically the same but the answers to these questions, as in Section 6.5, determine the formula and table to be used (see Table 7.1).

Table 7.1

Sample size	Population standard deviation	
	Known: standard error = $\sigma/\sqrt{n}$	**Unknown:** standard error = $s/\sqrt{n}$
Large	Normal tables	Normal tables
Small	Normal tables	t-tables

7.4.1 Method of testing for one mean

A **mean value** is hypothesised for the population. A sample is taken from that population and its mean value calculated. This sample mean is then used to see whether the value hypothesised for the population is reasonable or not. If the population standard deviation is not known, the sample standard deviation is calculated and used to estimate it. The appropriate test to use depends on whether this estimated value has been used or not.

H$_0$: $\mu = c$

H$_1$: $\mu \neq c$, $\mu < c$, or $\mu > c$, where μ is the population mean and c is the hypothesised value.

Significance level: $\alpha = 5$ per cent, or as stated in the question.

Critical value: from normal (z) table or t-tables, significance level, number of tails, degrees of freedom.

The normal table is used if we know the population standard deviation and do not need to estimate it. If we need to estimate the population standard deviation then a slightly less stringent critical value is found from the t-table.

Test statistic: σ known

$$z = \frac{|\bar{x} - \mu|}{\sigma/\sqrt{n}} \qquad (7.2)$$

or σ unknown so s needed

$$t = \frac{|\bar{x} - \mu|}{s/\sqrt{n}} \qquad (7.3)$$

where $\bar{x}$ and μ are the means of the sample and population respectively and s and σ are their standard deviations.

Conclusion: Compare test statistic with critical value.
   Decide whether to reject H$_0$ or not.
   Conclude in terms of question.

7.4.2 Testing for one mean when σ is known

The population standard deviation, σ, is known so the z formula and the normal table are appropriate, as σ does not need to be estimated.

Example 7.3

A packaging device is set to fill detergent packets with a mean weight of 150g. The standard deviation is **known** to be 5.0g. It is important to check the machine periodically because if it is overfilling it increases the cost of the materials, whereas if it is underfilling the firm is liable to prosecution. A random sample of 25 filled boxes is taken and each weighed, giving a mean net weight of 152.5g. Can we conclude that the machine is no longer producing the mean net weight of 150g?

  Use a 5% (0.05) significance level.

Given: μ = 150g?, σ = 5g, n = 25, x̄ = 152.5g

The machine can 'no longer produce the mean net weight of 150g' by producing packets that are too heavy or too light therefore the appropriate test is two tailed.

Null hypothesis: The mean weight of all the packets is 150g. $\mathbf{H_0}$: μ = 150g
Alternative hypothesis: The mean weight of the packet contents is not 150g. $\mathbf{H_1}$: μ ≠ 150g

Significance level (α): 5% (0.05)

Critical value: σ known therefore use normal tables, 5%, two tailed, 1.96

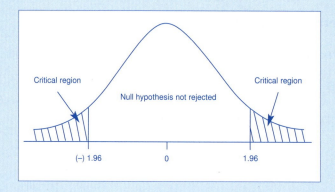

Figure 7.4

Test statistic: $z = \dfrac{|\bar{x} - \mu|}{\sigma / \sqrt{n}} \Rightarrow \dfrac{152.5 - 150}{5/\sqrt{25}} = \dfrac{2.5}{1} = 2.5$

Conclusion: The test statistic exceeds the critical value so reject H_0 and conclude that the mean weight produced is no longer 150g.

7.4.3 Testing for one mean when σ is not known and the sample is large

Because the sample is large the estimation of the population standard deviation will be accurate, so the z formula and the normal tables are appropriate.

Example 7.4

The mean and standard deviation of the weights produced by the packaging device set to fill detergent packets with a mean weight of 150g, are known to drift upwards over time due to the normal wearing of some bearings. Obviously it cannot be allowed to drift too far so a large random sample of 100 boxes is taken and the contents weighed. This sample has a mean weight of 151.0g and a standard deviation of 6.5g. Can we conclude that the mean weight produced by the machine has increased? Use a 5% (0.05) significance level.

Given: $\mu = 150g?$, $n = 100$, $\bar{x} = 151.0g$, $s = 6.5g$

We are only interested in whether the mean weight has increased or not so a one-tailed test is appropriate.

H_0: $\mu = 150g$ H_1: $\mu > 150g$

Significance level (α): 5% (0.05)

Critical value: σ unknown but sample large therefore normal tables, 5%, one tailed, 1.64

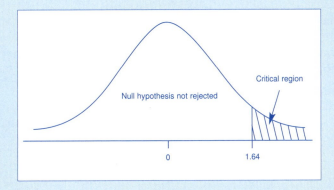

Figure 7.5

Test statistic: $z = \dfrac{|\bar{x} - \mu|}{\sigma/\sqrt{n}}$ $\Rightarrow$ $\dfrac{151.0 - 150}{6.5/\sqrt{100}}$ $=$ $\dfrac{1.0}{0.65}$ $=$ 1.54

Conclusion: The test statistic does not exceed the critical value so we do not reject H_0 but conclude that the machine may still be producing a mean weight of 150g.

7.4.4 Testing for one mean when σ is not known and the sample is small – one sample t-test

Since the population standard deviation is unknown it has to be estimated from that of the sample standard deviation. Because the sample is small, this estimate will not be very accurate and so the t-formula and tables are appropriate. This group of tests (see also Sections 7.5.2 and 7.6.1) are referred to as t-tests, and are the most widely used type of hypothesis tests.

Remember, from Chapter 6, that the t-tables (Appendix D, Table 2) require the use of degrees of freedom. For a single sample this is one less than the sample size, $n - 1$.

Example 7.5

One sample t-test

The personnel department of a company has developed an aptitude test for screening potential employees. The person who devised the test asserted that the mean mark attained would be 100. The following results were obtained with a random sample of applicants:
$\bar{x} = 96$, s = 5.2, n = 13

Test the hypothesis that the mean mark = 100 against the alternative that the mean mark is less than 100, at the 1% level.

Given: $\mu = 100?$, $\bar{x} = 96$, s = 5.2, n = 13,

H$_0$: $\mu = 100$ **H$_1$: $\mu < 100$**

Significance level (α): 1% (0.01)

Critical value: σ unknown so use t-tables at 1% significance, one tail, $n - 1 = 12$ degrees of freedom = 2.68

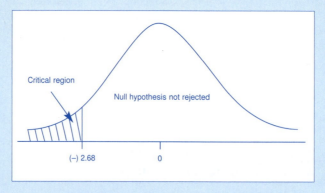

Critical region

Null hypothesis not rejected

(−) 2.68   0

Figure 7.6

Test statistic: $t = \dfrac{|\bar{x} - \mu|}{s/\sqrt{n}}$ $\Rightarrow$ $\dfrac{|96 - 100|}{5.2/\sqrt{13}}$ $=$ $\dfrac{4}{1.44}$ $=$ 2.77

Conclusion: The test statistic is larger than the critical value so reject H$_0$ and conclude that the mean mark is likely to be less than 100.

7.5 Testing for two independent means

If we have **two independent sets of data** we can test whether the difference between their means could be zero in a similar manner to the way we tested whether the mean from a single set of data could have a particular population value. In other words, could both samples have come from the same population?

The first four steps of the method of hypothesis testing are the same as those listed in Section 7.2: state the null hypothesis and the alternative hypothesis, state the significance level, and calculate the critical value. The test statistic needs to incorporate the parameters of both samples, and is calculated from a different formula (Equation 7.4). Again, the null hypothesis is rejected if the test statistic is greater than the critical value.

7.5.1 Testing the difference between two means – σ_1, σ_2 known

In this case we know the standard deviations of the populations which may, or may not, be the same. We do not need to estimate the standard deviations, so we use the normal table to find the critical value.

H$_0$: $\mu_1 - \mu_2 = 0$ (or c) or **H$_0$**: $\mu_1 = \mu_2$ **H$_1$**: $\mu_1 - \mu_2 \neq 0$ (or c) or $\mu_1 \neq \mu_2$

Significance level: as stated in question or $\alpha = 5$ per cent by default.

Critical value: from normal tables since population standard deviations are known.

Test statistic:

Calculated by
$$z = \frac{|\bar{x}_1 - \bar{x}_2|}{\sqrt{\dfrac{\sigma_1^2}{n_1} + \dfrac{\sigma_2^2}{n_2}}}$$
(7.4)

where $\bar{x}_1$, $\bar{x}_2$ are the sample means, σ_1, σ_2 are the known standard deviations, n_1, n_2 are the sample sizes.

Conclusion: H$_0$ is rejected if the test statistic is so large that the two samples could not have come from the same population.

Example 7.6

A retailing company wishes to see if there is any difference between the average sizes of the customer accounts in its Leeds and Bradford stores. Past experience has shown that the standard deviations for the two stores are £16 and £20 respectively.

Samples of 100 accounts taken from each branch gave mean values of £66.20 at Leeds and £70.40 at Bradford. Does this provide evidence, at 5% significance, that the mean account size at the two branches is different?

'Different' can be in either direction so a two-tailed test is appropriate.

Given: $\bar{x}_L = £66.20$, $\sigma_L = £16.00$, $\bar{x}_B = £70.40$, $\sigma_B = £20.00$, $n_L = n_B = 100$

H_0: $\mu_L = \mu_B$ H_1: $\mu_L \neq \mu_B$

Significance level: not stated so $\alpha = 5\%$ used by default.

Critical value: from normal tables since both σ values are known, two tails, 5%, critical value is 1.96

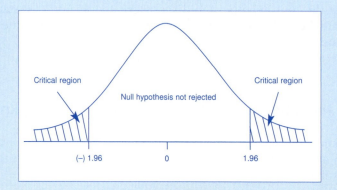

Figure 7.7

Test statistic:
$$z = \frac{|\bar{x}_1 - \bar{x}_2|}{\sqrt{\dfrac{\sigma_1^2}{n_1} + \dfrac{\sigma_2^2}{n_2}}} \Rightarrow \frac{70.40 - 66.20}{\sqrt{\dfrac{16^2}{100} + \dfrac{20^2}{100}}} = \frac{4.20}{2.561} = 1.64$$

Conclusion: H_0 not rejected as the test statistic is less than the critical value. The two samples could have come from the same population so the mean account size of the two stores could be the same.

7.5.2 Testing the difference between two means – σ_1, σ_2 unknown – two-sample t-test

Assumptions: The use of this test requires the samples to come from normal distributions and have equal standard deviation by testing their variance.

We must first test whether the standard deviations of the two sets of data are not too different from each other as indicated by the **F-test**.

An F-test is generally used to test for equality of sample variances, (standard deviation)^2.

This is a test for checking the ratio of the two variances against a table value to ensure that it is not too far from unity.

7.5.2.1 F-test

H_0: $\sigma_1 = \sigma_2$, H_1: $\sigma_1 \neq \sigma_2$

Significance level: as stated in question or $\alpha = 5$ per cent by default.

Critical value: from the F-tables (Appendix D Table 4) with $(n_1 - 1)$, $(n_2 - 1)$ degrees of freedom.

Test statistic:

$$F = \frac{s_1^2}{s_2^2}$$

(7.5)

where s_1 and n_1 refer to the sample with the larger standard deviation so that F is always greater than 1.

Conclusion: If the test statistic is less than the critical value, the variances, and therefore the standard deviations, can be assumed to be the same.

If the variances can be assumed to be the same, the standard deviations can be combined, or 'pooled', in order to get a better estimate of the population standard deviation.

If the data fails the F-test, a Mann–Whitney test (see Section 7.8.3) should be used rather than a two-sample t-test.

Most students prefer to calculate the pooled standard deviation separately so that a single figure can be substituted for the standard deviation, s_p, in the formula for the test statistic.

The formula used for pooling the standard deviations is:

$$s_p = \sqrt{\frac{(n_1 - 1)s_1^2 + (n_2 - 1)s_2^2}{n_1 + n_2 - 2}}$$

(7.6)

where s_1 and s_2 are the standard deviations of samples 1 and 2 respectively. This is really combining the sums of squares from which we originally calculated the separate standard deviations. Note that it is **not** the mean of s_1 and s_2.

7.5.2.2 Two sample t-test

H_0: $\mu_1 - \mu_2 = 0$ or $\mu_1 = \mu_2$ $(\mu_1 - \mu_2 = c)$

H_1: $\mu_1 - \mu_2 \neq 0$ or $\mu_1 \neq \mu_2$ $(\mu_1 - \mu_2 \neq c)$

Significance level: as stated or $\alpha = 5$ per cent by default.

Critical value: from t-tables, since population standard deviations are not known, with $(n_1 + n_2 - 2)$ degrees of freedom.

Test statistic:

Calculated by $\quad t = \dfrac{|\bar{x}_1 - \bar{x}_2|}{s_p \sqrt{\dfrac{1}{n_1} + \dfrac{1}{n_2}}} \quad$ or $\quad t = \dfrac{\left|\, |\bar{x}_1 - \bar{x}_2| - c \,\right|}{s_p \sqrt{\dfrac{1}{n_1} + \dfrac{1}{n_2}}}$

(7.7)

where s_p is the pooled standard deviation and c is the hypothesised difference.

Conclusion: H_0 is rejected if the test statistic is larger than the critical value; that is, so large that the two samples could not have come from populations with mean difference of zero (or c) as hypothesised.

Example 7.7

Firm A claims that it pays its clerical staff on average at least £10 per week more than its rival, Firm B. Firm B disputes the claim. Both examine a random sample of the salaries paid to their workers with the following results:

Firm A: μ = £443.00, σ = £13.20, n = 40   Firm B: μ = £438.50, σ = £14.30, n = 50

What conclusion can be drawn from this evidence at the 5% level of significance?

The F-test shows that the standard deviations are similar enough for pooling, s_p.

$$s_p = \sqrt{\frac{(n_1-1)s_1^2 + (n_2-1)s_2^2}{n_1+n_2-2}} \Rightarrow \sqrt{\frac{39 \times 13.2^2 + 49 \times 14.3^2}{88}} = £13.82$$

$H_0: \mu_A - \mu_B = £10$ $H_1: \mu_A - \mu_B < £10$

Significance level: α = 5%

Critical value: from t-tables, since population standard deviations are not known, with 88 degrees of freedom, one-tailed test = 1.66

Test statistic: calculated by $t = \dfrac{|(443-438.5)-10|}{13.82\sqrt{\dfrac{1}{40}+\dfrac{1}{50}}} = \dfrac{5.5}{2.93} = 1.87$

Conclusion: Test statistic > critical value so reject H_0, the difference is less than £10.

7.6 Testing for means of paired data

We may need to say whether there any difference between two sets of **paired data** or whether both sets could have come from the same population. As with confidence intervals (see Section 6.7), if the two sets of data represent two measurements in each case, a paired t-test is appropriate. In this test the 'difference' between each pair of data points is first calculated, then these differences are treated as a single set of data in order to consider whether there is any genuine difference, has been any significant change, or whether the observed differences could have occurred by chance.

7.6.1 Hypothesis test for mean of differences of paired data – paired t-test

If we have 'pairs' of measurements, the differences between each 'pair' can be calculated and the mean of the resulting values compared to zero, or some other hypothesised value, using the t-test for a single sample as used previously (Section 7.4.4).

This test is known as the **paired t-test**.

H_0: μ_d = 0 where μ_d is the mean of the differences.

H_1: $\mu_d \neq 0$, $\mu_d < 0$, or $\mu_d > 0$

Alternatively H_0: μ_d = c, where c is the value of the hypothesised change.

Significance level: α = 5 per cent, or as stated in question.

Critical value: t-table, degrees of freedom, significance level.

Test statistic: $t = \dfrac{\bar{x}_d - 0}{s_d / \sqrt{n_d}}$ (7.8)

Conclusion: Compare the test statistic with the critical value.
  Decide whether to reject H_0 or not.
  Conclude in terms of question.

Example 7.8

A training manager wishes to see if there has been any alteration in the ability of her trainees after they have been on a course. She gives each an aptitude test before they start the course and an equivalent one after they have completed it. The scores are recorded in Table 7.2. Has any change taken place at a 5% significance level?

Table 7.2

Trainee	A	B	C	D	E	F	G	H	I
Score before training	74	69	45	67	67	42	54	67	76
Score after training	69	76	56	59	78	63	54	76	75

First the 'changes' are computed and then a simple t-test is carried out on these differences.

Changes: −5, +7, +11, −8, +11, +21, 0, +9, −1

From sample changes: $\bar{x}_d$ = 5.0, s_d = 9.206, n_d = 9

H_0: μ_d = 0 H_1: $\mu_d \neq 0$

Significance level (α): 5% (0.05)

Critical value: t-table, 8 degrees of freedom, 5%, two tailed, critical value = 2.31

Test statistic: $t = \dfrac{\bar{x}_d}{s_d / \sqrt{n_d}} = \dfrac{5.0}{9.206/\sqrt{9}} = \dfrac{5.0}{3.07} = 1.63$

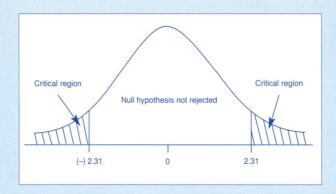

Figure 7.8

Conclusion: The test statistic of 1.63 is smaller than the critical value of 2.31 so do not reject H₀. There may be no change due to the training.

7.7 A continuous example using hypothesis testing

Example 7.9

A large company was about to be introduce a new training course for office recruits. Of the previous trainees, 74% had passed the aptitude test taken after the end of the previous course and the company hoped that the new course would produce a better pass rate. The pass mark for the test is 60%. (The same data was used in Example 6.8 for confidence intervals.)

During the first month with the new test a random selection of 18 candidates were each given a standard test before training and a similar one after training so that their progress could be monitored. These results are given in Table 7.3.

Table 7.3

Trainee	A	B	C	D	E	F	G	H	I
Before (B)	42	56	64	57	45	43	62	51	39
After (A)	56	73	87	68	59	62	79	62	60

Trainee	J	K	L	M	N	O	P	Q	R
Before (B)	64	43	42	62	39	56	57	45	51
After (A)	87	62	56	79	60	73	68	59	62

A random selection of 50 results later in the year gave a pass rate of 84%.

We shall use this data to test the following hypotheses:

- The pass rate has improved at the 1% significance level.
- The average mark after training is 75%, using $\alpha = 0.05$.
- The average increase in marks is more than 10%, using $\alpha = 0.01$.
- If the data were not paired, the increase in mean marks would be more than 10%, using $\alpha = 0.01$.

The pass rate has improved at the 1% significance level

$\pi = 74\%$, $p = 84\%$, $n = 50$

H_0: $\pi = 74\%$, H_1: $\pi > 74\%$ (only improvement is of interest)

Critical value: proportion, z-table, 1%, one tailed, 2.33

Test statistic:
$$z = \frac{|p - \pi|}{\sqrt{\dfrac{\pi(100 - \pi)}{n}}} \quad \Rightarrow \quad \frac{|84 - 74|}{\sqrt{\dfrac{74 \times 26}{50}}} = \frac{10}{6.20} = 1.61$$

Conclusion: The test static is less than the critical value so H_0 cannot be rejected. The pass rate might still be 74% and so it might not have increased for all the trainees.

The average mark after training is 75%, use $\alpha = 0.05$

$\mu = 75\%$? From sample: $\bar{x}_A = 67.3$, $s_A = 10.1$, $n_A = 18$,

H_0: $\mu = 75$, H_1: $\mu \neq 75$ (Claim can be proved incorrect at either end.)

Critical value: small sample, σ unknown, 5%, two tails, 17 degrees of freedom, critical value is 2.11

Test statistic:
$$t = \frac{|\bar{x} - \mu|}{s/\sqrt{n}} \quad \Rightarrow \quad \frac{|67.3 - 75|}{10.1/\sqrt{18}} = \frac{7.7}{2.38} = 3.23$$

Conclusion: The test statistic exceeds the critical value so H_0 is rejected the mean mark after training is not 75%. (Be careful not to conclude that it is less than because that was not the alternative hypothesis.)

The average increase in marks is more than 10%, use $\alpha = 0.01$

Paired t-test

Differences: 14, 17, 23, 11, 14, 19, 17, 11, 21, 23, 19, 14, 17, 21, 17, 11, 14, 11.

From the sample: $\bar{x}_d = 16.3$, $s_d = 4.09$, $n_d = 18$

H_0: $\mu_d = 10$ (No matter how the claim is phrased H_0 is always of equality.)
H_1: $\mu_d > 10$ (H_0 can be proved incorrect only at the upper end.)

Critical value: small sample, σ unknown, 1%, one tail, 17 d.f., 2.57

Test statistic: $t = \dfrac{|\bar{x}_d - \mu_d|}{s_d / \sqrt{n_d}}$ $\Rightarrow$ $\dfrac{|16.3 - 10|}{4.09/\sqrt{18}} = \dfrac{6.3}{0.964} = 6.54$

Conclusion: The test statistic exceeds the critical value so H_0 is rejected; the mean increase is over 10%.

If the data were not paired, the increase in mean marks would be more than 10%, use $\alpha = 0.01$.

Treating the scores before and after the course as independent samples, we first need their individual summary statistics.

Two-sample t-test

Before the course: $\bar{x}_B = 51.0$, $s_B = 8.92$, $n_B = 18$
After the course: $\bar{x}_A = 67.3$, $s_A = 10.1$, $n_A = 18$

Check that the standard deviations are similar enough to be pooled:

$$\frac{s_A^2}{s_B^2} = \frac{10.1^2}{8.92^2} = 1.282$$

From the F-tables at 5% significance with $(n_1 - 1)$, $(n_2 - 1)$ degrees of freedom:

$F_{0.05}(17, 17) = 2.28$ (See Table D4). The standard deviations pass the F-test.

Pool the standard deviations:

$$s_p = \sqrt{\frac{(n_B - 1)s_B^2 + (n_A - 1)s_A^2}{n_B + n_A - 2}} \quad \Rightarrow \quad \sqrt{\frac{17 \times 8.92^2 + 17 \times 10.1^2}{34}} = 9.53$$

This figure, s_p, is now used as the estimated common standard deviation.

Carry out the hypothesis test:

H_0: $\mu_A - \mu_B = 10\%$, H_1: $\mu_A - \mu_B > 10\%$

Significance level: $\alpha = 1\%$.

Critical value: from t-tables, since population standard deviations are not known, with 34 degrees of freedom, one tailed test = 2.44

Test statistic: $t = \dfrac{\left||\bar{x}_A + \bar{x}_B| - c\right|}{s_p \sqrt{\dfrac{1}{n_A} + \dfrac{1}{n_B}}}$ $\Rightarrow$ $\dfrac{||67.3 - 51.0| - 10|}{9.53\sqrt{\dfrac{1}{18} + \dfrac{1}{18}}} = \dfrac{6.3}{3.17} = 1.98$

Conclusion: Test statistic is less than the critical value so H_0 is not rejected. The increase could be 10%, that is, it has not been shown to be significantly more than 10%.

This extended example demonstrates that the paired test is better able to reject the null hypothesis and so should always be used when appropriate.

7.8 Non-parametric tests

These tests are not part of many course syllabuses but are very useful and are included here for completeness. If the **sample** is not normally distributed then we cannot assume that the **population** has a normal distribution. Alternatively if the information is only ordered, that is, ordinal, instead of being interval we cannot use the parametric tests, which **assume interval data and normality in the population**.

For this reason alternative tests have been produced which are less **powerful** but do not need the population to be normal. These non-parametric tests are also called 'distribution free' tests, as they need no assumptions to be made about the distribution of the parent population, and can be carried out validly on ordinal as well as quantitative data.

Each of the parametric tests that we use has a non-parametric equivalent. The most common ones are described briefly, with a single worked example of each, below.

- **The sign test** is used instead of the one-sample t-test.
- **The Wilcoxon matched pairs (signed rank) test** is used instead of the one sample and paired t-tests.
- **The Mann–Whitney U-test** is used instead of the two-sample t-test. This is also known as the **Wilcoxon rank sum test**.

If your data are ordinal, non-parametric tests are always appropriate as conclusions drawn from parametric tests will not be valid.

Non-parametric tests are used mainly for data that cannot be assumed to be normally distributed. Normality can be checked by examination of a histogram or a box plot of the sample data to see if they show symmetry. If using a computer package, a Kolmogorov-Smirnov, or equivalent, test for normality should be carried out.

Parametric tests are more powerful than their non-parametric equivalents and should always be used in preference if the data do not infringe any of the necessary assumed conditions.

Do note that for non-parametric – as opposed to parametric – tests we are looking for a result more extreme than could have taken place by chance, so the smaller of the two totals is the test statistic. The rejection region is therefore that which is **smaller than the table value**.

7.8.1 The sign test

This test, which is not powerful, compares the **sample median** with a **hypothesised median** by seeing how many sample members are above it (positive) and how many below it (negative). If the sample median is close to the hypothesised median, there will be the approximately the same number of **positive** and **negative** results.

Because orderings rather than actual measurements are involved, the sign test is acceptable if the distribution is not symmetrical; that is, when the mean would not be an appropriate measure of centrality.

The sign test is also used to detect significant change by comparing the number of positive changes with the number of negative changes. If for the whole population no change has taken place, the numbers of small random positive and negative changes can be expected to be nearly the same.

Example 7.10

Pre- and post-test scores after a particular training course are known to be non-normal in their distribution. A sample of the scores, with the calculated changes, is given in Table 7.4.

Table 7.4

Pre-test	67	71	83	69	68	36	52	72	56
Post-test	58	62	84	67	72	38	63	72	55
Changes	−9	−9	+1	−2	+4	+2	+11	0	−1
Pre-test	64	76	83	69	68	36	52	72	56
Post-test	59	76	84	69	72	38	63	74	66
Changes	−5	0	+1	0	+4	+2	+11	+2	+10

The sign test will be used to see if any significant change has taken place. **Equal values are ignored** for the purpose of this test.

H_0: There is no difference between the scores for the pre-test and the post-test.

H_1: There is a difference between them.

Significance level (α): 5% (0.05)

Critical region: Sign tables, Appendix D, Table 8, number of changes = 15, two tailed, critical region $S \leq 3$.

Test statistic: The number of positive changes is 10. The number of negative changes is 5. The test statistic, usually given the symbol S, is the smaller of these two totals, that is $S = 5$.

Conclusion: For 15 changes the totals needed to be more different, that is, 3 and 12, for a significant change to have taken place. In this case they were less extreme, 10 and 5, so we can conclude that no significant change has taken place.

7.8.2 Wilcoxon matched pairs (signed rank) test

The non-parametric equivalent of the paired t-test is the Wilcoxon matched pairs test. This test is carried out on the ranks of the differences between the pairs of data points. It is often used to identify a change in behaviour following an event such as an advertising campaign.

The basic premise is that the rankings of individual changes will be random if there has been no overall change. Where there has been an overall change, the rankings of those changes in a positive direction will be different from the changes in a negative direction.

Example 7.11

A small panel of 8 members have been asked about their perception of a product before and after they had an opportunity to try it. Their perceptions, measured on an ordinal scale, gave the results in Table 7.5.

Table 7.5

Member	A	B	C	D	E	F	G	H
Before	8	3	6	4	5	7	6	7
After	9	4	4	1	6	7	9	2

Have the perception scores changed, at 5%, after trying the product?

H_0: There is no difference in perception.
H_1: There is a difference in perception.

Significance level (α): 5% (0.05)

Critical region: Wilcoxon matched pairs, Appendix D Table 9, 5%, two tailed, n = 8, critical region ≤ 3.

Test statistic: Find the difference between the two scores and rank these differences in absolute size. There are seven differences so the smallest difference is ranked 1 and the largest 7. Ties are given the mean of their rankings.

Table 7.6

Member	Before	After	Difference	Rank
A	8	9	+1	2
B	3	4	+1	2
C	6	4	−2	4
D	4	1	−3	5.5
E	5	6	+1	2
F	7	7	0	ignore
G	6	9	+3	5.5
H	7	2	−5	7

Sums of ranks: T+ = 11.5, T− = 16.5. The smaller is the test statistic: T = 11.5

Conclusion: The test statistic is less extreme than the critical region, do not reject H_0, there has been no change after trying the product.

7.8.3 Mann–Whitney U test (Wilcoxon rank sum test)

The Mann–Whitney U test is used if two samples have unequal variance, as judged by the F-test (see Section 7.5.2). This test is also appropriate if the data are only ordinal.

The basic premise of the Mann–Whitney U test is that if both the samples come from populations with the same medians, and if all the values from the two samples are put into a single ordered list, then the members of Sample 1 and Sample 2 will be ranked at random. If the two samples come from different populations, the rankings of the values from the samples will not be random, and there will be a tendency for one of the samples to have lower ranks than the other.

The smallest sum of ranks possible is:

$$\frac{n(n+1)}{2}$$

where n is the number of items being ranked. (Try this for just the five numbers one to five – they add up to 15 which is $(5 \times 6) / 2$.)

Test statistic: $U \;=\; R - \dfrac{n_1(n_1+1)}{2}$ (7.9)

where R is the smaller sum of ranks and n_1 the size of the same sample.

The test statistic measures its deviation from the smallest possible sum: that is, the most extreme position.

Example 7.12

Samples have been taken from two branches of a chain of stores. The samples relate to the daily takings of both branches, which are situated in city centres. We wish to find out if there is any difference in turnover between the two branches. (With such small samples it cannot be assumed that the data are normally distributed.)

Branch 1   £4350 £4550 £5550 £3950 £4440 £4400 £4360 £4590 £4600.
Branch 2   £4400 £3980 £4200 £4150 £4450.

H_0: Both samples come from the same population and so have the same median.
H_1: The two samples come from different populations and have different medians.

Significance level (α): 5% (0.05)

Critical value: Mann–Whitney, Appendix D Table 10, 5%, sample sizes 5 and 9, two-tailed test (α_2), $U \leq 7$

Test statistic: All the sample values are ranked in one ordering in Table 7.7.

Sum of ranks of branches: $R_1 = 78.5$, $R_2 = 26.5$, so $R = 26.5$ (the smaller value).

$$U \;=\; R - \frac{n_1(n_1+1)}{2} \;=\; 26.5 - \frac{5(5+1)}{2} \;=\; 11.5$$

Conclusion: Test statistic, 11.5 > critical value, 7, so the situation is not so extreme that we need to reject H_0. We can conclude that the two samples could come from the same population, that is, there is no difference between the turnovers of the two branches.

Table 7.7

Branch 1	Order	Branch 2	Order
4350	5	4400	7.5
4550	11	3980	2
5550	14	4200	4
3950	1	4150	3
4440	9	4450	10
4400	7.5		
4360	6		
4590	12		
4600	13		

With non-parametric tests the data has to be very extreme before the null hypothesis will be rejected; we were not able to reject any of the null hypotheses above. This is because these tests are less powerful than the parametric ones, so should only be used when the assumptions needed for the parametric tests are not true (see Weimer 1993, Chapter 15).

7.9 Other hypothesis tests

We shall cover more hypothesis tests in the next three chapters. In Chapter 8 you will study **analysis of variance,** with which we shall investigate the differences between more than two means. Chapter 9 covers **chi-square tests** which look for associations between two categorical variables, and in Chapter 10 we shall look for significant **correlation** between two continuous variables before identifying the relationship between them in the form of a **regression equation**.

There are numerous other non-parametric tests which have been developed comparatively recently. Many have been produced independently by more than one statistician, and like the test described in Section 7.8.3, they bear more than one name. Some statisticians have been prolific in their production of tests, and so have numerous tests named after them (Siegel and Castellan, for example) This can lead to some confusion, so if you are looking for a particular test, be very careful!

In this course we have so far studied only single variables. Later we shall study bivariate data, but we shall not venture into the realms of multivariate analysis (see Weimer (1993), Everitt and Dunn (2001)). Many of the simpler tests used have multivariate equivalents which are only appropriate for analysis by computer packages such as Minitab, SPSS and SAS.

7.10 Further considerations

There are various other considerations common to all types of hypothesis tests. You should be aware of them but need not study them in detail on this course.

7.10.1 Types of error

When testing any hypothesis there are four possible outcomes, as illustrated in Table 7.8.

Table 7.8

Action	H$_0$ is true	H$_0$ is not true
Reject H$_0$	Incorrect decision – Type I error	Correct decision
Do not reject H$_0$	Correct decision	Incorrect decision – Type II error

A **Type I error** occurs if the null hypothesis is rejected when it is actually true. This is the most common situation, and has been illustrated in all the previous examples. In the courtroom example it is the case when the accused is found 'guilty' when in fact he or she is 'not guilty'. The probability of committing a Type I error is the familiar significance level, and is usually symbolised by the Greek letter α (alpha). If the probability of committing a Type I error is α, then the probability of not committing it is $(1 - \alpha)$, which is of course the familiar **confidence interval**. In this course we are only concerned with Type I errors.

A **Type II error** occurs if the null hypothesis is not rejected when it is in fact false. (This is the conclusion of 'not guilty' when in fact the man is 'guilty'.) This leaves the status quo unchanged, so it is considered preferable to making a Type I error.

7.10.2 The power of a test

The main purpose of hypothesis testing is to reject the null hypothesis when it is incorrect, so we need **powerful tests**. Remember that the parametric tests are more powerful than their non-parametric equivalents, so should always be used if the data are appropriate.

The power of a test is the ability of that test to reject the null hypothesis correctly: that is, to avoid Type I errors. Any test must of course be **valid** for the given circumstances.

7.10.3 The validity of a test

For a test to be **valid** it must assess what it is intended to assess.

Among other things, the validity of a test depends on the data to which it is being applied. Are they quantitative, qualitative, interval, ordinal, or merely nominal? Are they normally distributed or skewed?

Tests are available for use on any type of data, and will only be valid as long as the data are appropriate for that particular test, because validity depends on the data being appropriate to the standard probability distribution giving the critical value.

The importance of using non-parametric tests when the data are not interval or not normally distributed has already been stated but not fully explained. Each hypothesis test has its own set of assumptions based on the distribution from which the test statistic is assumed to come. Each test has a particular probability associated with its value if the null hypothesis is correct.

Similarly if the data are skewed or with large kurtosis ('peakedness') the probability associated with any particular test statistic is not the same as for the normal distribution.

Another obvious point is that the probability changes with the number of tails, so the number used in the conclusion must agree with that in the alternative hypothesis. For example, we

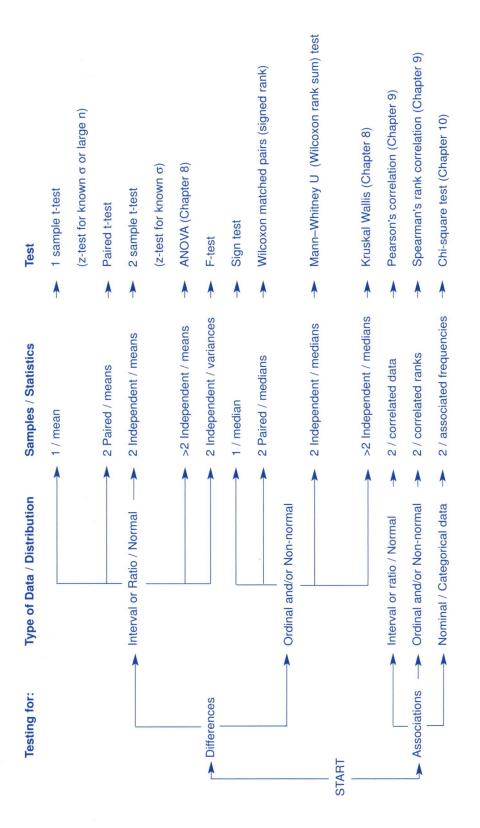

Figure 7.9 The selection of a hypothesis test, including those from later chapters

cannot infer a direction from the results of a two-tailed test. This is why both hypotheses should be established **before** any evidence is collected or any given data analysed.

You should now understand the importance of selecting appropriate tests so that you have confidence in any conclusions you reach.

7.11 Summary

In this chapter we first considered the concepts common to all hypothesis tests and then studied many different tests in more detail. The reason for the formal method of hypothesis testing with its six essential steps and its logical ordering should now be evident.

- The two hypotheses establish the framework for the whole test.
- The critical value assumes a certain distribution and lays down the region of rejection of the null hypotheses with a predetermined probability.
- The test statistic establishes whether rejection is appropriate or not.
- The conclusion states which of the two hypotheses is most likely to be true.

At this stage you are probably thinking that the main problem is the selection of the appropriate test to use in any given circumstances. Figure 7.9 summarises the situation for all the tests considered on this course. All the tests given there, apart from the chi-square test, need continuous data.

These tests all share the same overall methodology but differ mainly in the calculation of the test statistic and the tables from which the critical value is obtained. The required formulae and distribution tables needed for each are given in Appendices C and D.

Finally, if the analysis has been carried out by a computer package, such as Minitab, SPSS or Excel, the output will include a p-value which is the probability of H_0 being correct. If you are testing at 5 per cent (0.05) this needs to be < 0.05 if H_0 is to be rejected.

7.12 Computer output for Example 7.9

7.12.1 T-test of the mean

See Figure 7.10. Excel does not produce a one sample t-test.

7.12.2 Paired t-test and confidence interval

See Figures 7.11 and 7.12. In the Excel output in Figure 7.12 the test statistic is 't Stat'. The absolute value of 27.3 does not agree with Minitab or SPSS.

7.12.2 Two-sample t-test and confidence interval

See Figures 7.13 and 7.14. For Excel (Figure 7.14), even though the t Stat and the one tailed probability does not agree with Minitab or SPSS the same conclusion of rejecting the null hypothesis is reached.

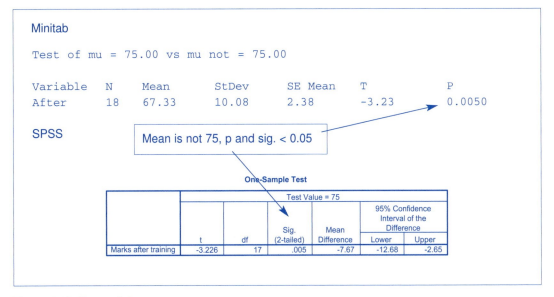

Figure 7.10 T-test of the mean

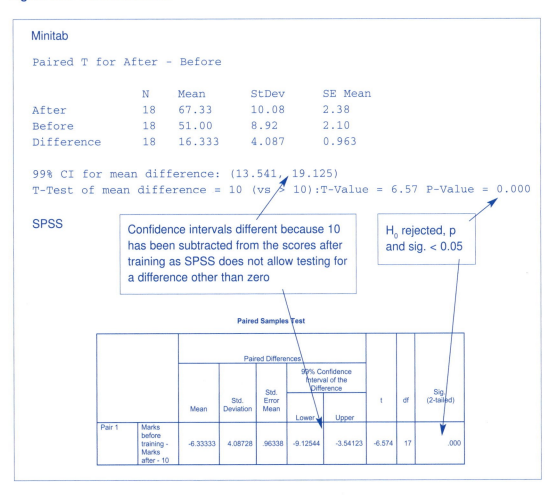

Figure 7.11 T-test and confidence interval – Minitab and SPSS output

Excel

t-Test: Paired Two Sample for Means

	Variable 1	Variable 2
Mean	51	67.33333333
Variance	79.52941	101.6470588
Observations	18	18
Pearson Correlation	0.914633	
Hypothesized Mean Difference	10	
df	17	
t Stat	-27.3343	
P(T<=t) one-tail	8.62E-16	
t Critical one-tail	1.739607	
P(T<=t) two-tail	1.72E-15	
t Critical two-tail	2.109816	

Figure 7.12 T-test and confidence interval – Excel output

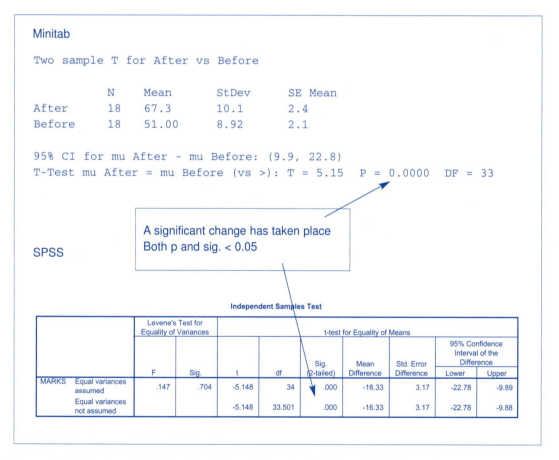

Minitab

Two sample T for After vs Before

	N	Mean	StDev	SE Mean
After	18	67.3	10.1	2.4
Before	18	51.00	8.92	2.1

95% CI for mu After - mu Before: (9.9, 22.8)
T-Test mu After = mu Before (vs >): T = 5.15   P = 0.0000   DF = 33

A significant change has taken place
Both p and sig. < 0.05

SPSS

Independent Samples Test

		Levene's Test for Equality of Variances		t-test for Equality of Means						
									95% Confidence Interval of the Difference	
		F	Sig.	t	df	Sig. (2-tailed)	Mean Difference	Std. Error Difference	Lower	Upper
MARKS	Equal variances assumed	.147	.704	-5.148	34	.000	-16.33	3.17	-22.78	-9.89
	Equal variances not assumed			-5.148	33.501	.000	-16.33	3.17	-22.78	-9.88

Figure 7.13 Two sample t-test and confidence interval – Minitab and SPSS output

Excel

t-Test: Two-Sample Assuming Equal Variances

	After	Before
Mean	67.33333	51
Variance	101.6471	79.52941176
Observations	18	18
Pooled Variance	90.58824	
Hypothesized Mean Difference	10	
df	34	
t Stat	1.996263	
P(T<=t) one-tail	0.026982	
t Critical one-tail	1.690924	
P(T<=t) two-tail	0.053964	
t Critical two-tail	2.032244	

Figure 7.14 Two sample t-test and confidence interval – Excel output

7.13 Case study

Your directors are interested in comparing three different types of food outlets, so the testing that we shall study in the next chapter is more appropriate than the tests studied in this chapter, which only consider one or two groups of data.

As there are obviously problems with normality (see the results of the case study in Section 5.9), the directors would like you, at this stage, to carry out a Kolmogorov-Smirnov test (in SPSS or Minitab) to see which, if any, of the variables listed below are normally distributed. These are the ones we shall explore further in the next case study:

- gross sales for all outlets together; gross sales for each type of outlet separately
- market value of all outlets together; market value of each type of outlet separately
- number of full-time employees for all outlets together; number of full-time employees for each type of outlet separately
- number of part-time employees for all outlets together; number of part-time employees for each type of outlet separately
- wages as percentage of sales for all outlets together; wages as percentage of sales for each type of outlet separately
- advertising as percentage of sales for all outlets together; advertising as percentage of sales for each type of outlet separately.

Tutorial 7: Hypothesis testing

Answers to tutorial questions are in Appendix A.

7.1 A newspaper article stated that students at a particular university spend an average of £95 on beer. A student investigator who believed this average was too high polled a random sample of 50 students and found that $\bar{x}$ = £92.25 and s = £10. Use these results to test at the 5% significance level the statement made by the newspaper.

7.2 Clerical officers are expected to spend 30% of their time on the telephone. Pamela, who was suspected of spending longer, was found to be on the phone during 90 out of 200 on random spot checks.

Test at the 5% level whether she did use the phone more often than expected.

7.3 Eleven cartons of sugar, each nominally containing 1 kg, were randomly selected from a large batch of cartons. The weights of sugar they contained were:

1.02 1.05 1.08 1.03 1.00 1.06 1.08 1.01 1.04 1.07 1.00 kg

Does this support the hypothesis, at 5%, that the mean weight for the whole batch is over 1.00 kg?

7.4 The expected lifetime of electric bulbs produced by a given process was 1500 hours. To test a new batch a sample of 10 was taken. This showed a mean lifetime of 1455 hours. The standard deviation of the production is known to still be 90 hours. Test the hypothesis, at 1% significance, that the mean lifetime of the electric light bulbs has not changed.

7.5 A sleeping drug and a neutral control were tested in turn on a random sample of 10 patients in a hospital. The data below represent the differences between the number of hours sleep under the drug and the neutral control for each patient:

2.0 0.2 –0.4 0.3 0.7 1.2 0.6 1.8 –0.2 1.0 hours

Test, at 5%, the hypothesis that the drug would give more hours sleep on average than the control for all the patients in the hospital.

7.6 A coin is suspected of being biased. It is tossed 200 times and 114 heads occur. Carry out a hypothesis test to see whether the coin is indeed biased at 1% significance.

7.7 The times taken to complete a task were recorded for a sample of eight employees both before and after a period of training (minutes):

Employee	1	2	3	4	5	6	7	8
Before training	15	14	18	14	15	17	13	12
After training	13	15	15	13	13	16	14	12

Test at 5% to see whether the training is effective or not.

7.8 A dairy advertises that a tub of ice cream produces on average 84 scoops. An ice-cream seller who buys wholesale from the dairy found that an average of 81.5 scoops were obtained from 72 tubs. The standard deviation was found to be 11.43 scoops, so she thinks that the claimed quantity is too high. Carry out a test at the 5% level of significance to see who is correct.

7.9 After treatment with a standard fertiliser, the average yield per hectare is 4.2 tonnes of wheat. A super fertiliser is developed and administered to 10 hectares. The yields from the hectares are:

4.3 6.0 4.9 6.1 6.2 5.4 4.1 4.2 3.8 and 3.9 tonnes.

Test the hypothesis that this fertiliser would give a higher yield, if a farmer changed over to it, at 1% significance.

7.10 A new method of study for management has been introduced. In order to test its effectiveness equivalent tests are given to the same students both before and after they have taken the course. Their test scores are shown below:

Student	A	B	C	D	E	F	G	H	I	J
Before	596	610	598	613	588	592	606	619	600	597
After	599	612	607	610	588	610	607	623	591	599

Assuming the score changes to be normally distributed, is this method of study effective at 5% significance?

Notes

For SPSS/ Minitab/ Excel worksheets on hypotheses testing see Chapter 14, Sections 14.2.3, 14.5.3 and 14.8.3 respectively. Worksheets with computer output and its interpretation are on the companion website.

The supplementary exercise for Chapter 7, with answers, is on the companion website.

Analysis of variance

8

Objectives of this chapter

In Chapter 7 we investigated variation among cases in terms of group means. Do males and females have different earnings in a particular company? Do students' aptitude marks improve after training? We calculated the summary statistics for each group from the samples, then used them to answer questions about the population.

In this chapter we continue with the same theme but extend it to investigate more than two groups of cases. If a factory works shifts, is there any difference between the production of the morning, afternoon and night shifts? Is the production level higher on any day of the week? Production can also be analysed using the shifts and days of the week in combination. Is Friday afternoon production worse than that on any other shift?

Analysis of variance, or ANOVA, can be quite a complex topic. We shall use it in its simplest form, **one-way ANOVA**, to investigate the variation between three or more groups. We then extend this to **two-way ANOVA** to split the variation between two sets of groups, and briefly discuss more complex analysis. (In practice ANOVA is generally carried out using software.)

Having completed this chapter you should be:

- able to do the simpler analysis
- aware of the potential of the method for carrying out more detailed work.

8.1 Introduction – why do we need analysis of variance?

We cannot carry out repeated t-tests on pairs of the variables. If many independent tests are carried out pairwise, **the probability of being correct for the combined results is greatly reduced**. For example, if we compare the average marks of two students at the end of a semester to see if their mean scores are significantly different we would have, at a 5 per cent level, a 0.95 probability of being correct. Three students need three pairwise tests, and so on. Table 8.1 shoes how the probability of being correct decreases even for a small number of students.

Table 8.1

Students	Pairwise tests	P(all correct)	P(at least one incorrect)
2	1	0.95	0.05
3	3	$0.95^3 = 0.857$	0.143
10	45	$0.95^{45} = 0.10$	0.90 etc.

For a large group of n students this process clearly produces a very high probability of being incorrect.

We need to use methods of analysis which will allow the variation between **all n means to be tested simultaneously**, giving an **overall** probability of 0.95 of being correct at the 5 per cent level. This type of analysis is referred to as analysis of variance or ANOVA. It measures the overall variation within a variable, finds the variation between the group means, combines these to calculate a single test statistic, then uses this to carry out a hypothesis test in the standard manner.

The traditional terminology of ANOVA reflects its origins in agriculture. It refers to 'levels of treatment', 'blocking factors', and so on. This book aims to avoid these terms as much as possible, calling treatments and blocks by names specific to a particular example.

8.2 One-way analysis of variance

8.2.1 Assumptions needed to be met for ANOVA

ANOVA can be thought of as an extension of the two-sample t-test to more than two groups. As with the two-sample t-test:

- the population should be normally distributed
- the groups should be independent of each other
- the groups should be of similar variance.

The distribution of the sample can be checked by drawing a histogram, or carrying out a Kolmogorov-Smirnov test for normality if a computer package is available. The need for independence is usually satisfied by the random selection of the samples. The equality of variance can be checked by the F-test as described in Section 7.5.2. In practice, the method is fairly robust to departures from the ideal situation.

8.2.2 The one-way ANOVA model

The total variation between all the cases is split between **variation caused by the difference between groups** and the **remainder** or **residual** error which is caused by chance. The variation is quantified as 'sums of squares', which is total variance.

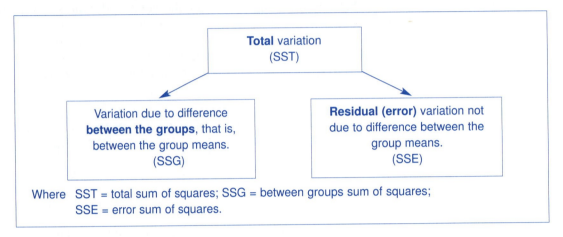

Figure 8.1

The method of measuring this variation is **variance** (see Section 3.5.2).

Total variance = between groups variance + variance caused by errors

It follows that:

Total sum of	=	Sum of squares between	+	Sum of squares due
squares (SST)		the groups (SSG)		to the errors (SSE)

If we find any two of the three sums of squares, the other can be found by difference. In practice we calculate SST and SSG, then find SSE by difference.

The method will be explained in stages by reference to a numerical example. Examples 8.1, 8.3 and 8.4 use the same data, building up its complexity.

8.2.3 Sums of squares as a measure of deviation from the mean

The sum of squares is the total of the squares of the deviations from the mean, that is, $\Sigma(x - \bar{x})^2$ (SST), where x is the value for each case and $\bar{x}$ is the mean. The classical method for calculating this sum is to tabulate the values, subtract the mean from each value, square the results, and finally sum the squares. It is much easier to use a statistical calculator!

In Section 3.3.3 we saw that the standard deviation is calculated by:

$$s_n = \sqrt{\frac{\Sigma(x-\bar{x})^2}{n}} \quad \text{so } \Sigma(x - \bar{x})^2 = ns_n^2 \text{ with s from the calculator using } [x\sigma_n]$$

or $$s_{n-1} = \sqrt{\frac{\Sigma(x-\bar{x})^2}{n-1}} \quad \text{so } \Sigma(x - \bar{x})^2 = (n-1)s_{n-1}^2 \text{ with s from the calculator using } [x\sigma_{n-1}]$$

Example 8.1

An important factor in selecting software for word processing and database management systems is the time required to train users. In order to evaluate three database management systems, a firm devised a test to see how many training hours were needed for five of its word processing operators to become proficient in each of the three systems.

Table 8.2

System A	16	19	14	13	18
System B	16	17	13	12	17
System C	24	22	19	18	22

Using a 5% level, is there any difference between the training time needed for the three systems?

In this case the groups are the three database management systems, A, B and C. Differences between the groups account for some of the variance but the remainder is due to the errors, that is, the variance unaccounted for by the groups.

Method

Calculate the total sum of squares (SST)

Input all the data individually and output the values for n, $\bar{x}$ and s_n from the calculator in statistics mode. Use these values to calculate s_n^2 and ns_n^2.

n	$\bar{x}$	s_n	s_n^2	ns_n^2
15	17.33	3.419	11.69	175.3 = SST

Calculate the sum of squares between the groups (systems) (SSSys)

Calculate n and $\bar{x}$ for each of the systems separately:

Table 8.3

	n	$\bar{x}$
System A	5	16
System B	5	15
System C	5	21

Input as frequency data, using a frequency of 5 in your calculator. Output n, $\bar{x}$ and s_n.

n	$\bar{x}$	s_n	s_n^2	ns_n^2
15	17.33	2.625	6.889	103.3 = SSSys

Find the sum of squares due to the errors (SSE)

SSE is found by difference SSE = SST − SSSys = 175.3 − 103.3 = 72.0

8.2.4 ANOVA table

Table 8.4 shows the general format of an analysis of variance table. You may find it helps you to follow the sequence of calculations. If not, please ignore it and work with the numbers for a specific example.

Table 8.4 (For k groups and total sample size N)

Source	Sum of squares (SS)	Degrees of freedom (df)	Mean sums of squares (MSS)	Test statistic (F)
Between groups	SSG	$k - 1$	$\dfrac{SSG}{k-1} = MSG$	$\dfrac{MSG}{MSE} = F$
Errors	SSE	$(N - 1) - (k - 1)$	$\dfrac{SSE}{N-k} = MSE$	
Total	SST	$N - 1$		

8.2.4.1 Method

- Calculate the total sum of squares, SST, and the between-groups sum of squares, SSG; find the sum of squares caused by errors, SSE, by difference.
- The degrees of freedom, df, for the total and the groups are one less than the total number of values and the number of groups respectively; find the errors df by difference.
- The mean sums of squares, MSS, is found in each case by dividing the sum of squares, SS, by the corresponding degrees of freedom, df.
- The test statistic, F, is the ratio of the mean sum of squares caused by the differences between the group means (MSG) and that caused by the errors (MSE).

Example 8.1 continued

In this example: (k = 3 systems, N = 15 values)

Table 8.5

Source	SS	df	MSS	F
Between systems	103.3	$3 - 1 = 2$	103.3/2 = 51.65	51.65/6.00 = 8.61
Errors	175.3 − 103.3 = 72.0	$14 - 2 = 12$	72.0/12 = 6.00	
Total	175.3	$15 - 1 = 14$		

8.2.5 The hypothesis test

The methodology for carrying out the hypothesis test is as described in Section 7.2.

Null hypothesis, H$_0$, is that all the group means are equal. H$_0$: $\mu_1 = \mu_2 = \mu_3 = \mu_4$ and so on.

Alternative hypothesis, H$_1$, is that at least two of the means are different.

Significance level is as stated or 5 per cent by default.

Critical value is from the F-tables, Appendix D Table 4, $F_\alpha(v_1,v_2)$, with the two degrees of freedom being those between the groups, v_1, and the errors, v_2.

Test statistic is the F-value calculated from the sample in the ANOVA table.

Conclusion is reached by comparing the test statistic with the critical value and rejecting the null hypothesis if the test statistic is the larger of the two.

Example 8.1 continued

H$_0$: $\mu_A = \mu_B = \mu_C$

H$_1$: At least two of the means are different.

Critical value: $F_{0.05}(2,12) = 3.89$ (df from between systems is 2 and errors is 12).

Test statistic: 8.61

Conclusion: test static > critical value so reject H$_0$. There is a significant difference between the mean times taken to learn at least two of the three systems.

8.2.6 Where does any significant difference lie?

We can calculate a **critical difference** (CD) which depends on the mean sum of squares caused by errors (MSE), the sample sizes and the significance level. Any difference between means that exceeds the CD is significant, and any difference that is less than it is not.
    This critical difference formula is

$$CD = t\sqrt{MSE\left(\frac{1}{n_1}+\frac{1}{n_2}\right)}$$

where t has the error degrees of freedom and one tail (see Appendix D Table 2).

Example 8.1 continued

$$CD = t\sqrt{MSE\left(\frac{1}{n_1}+\frac{1}{n_2}\right)} \implies 1.78\sqrt{6.00\left(\frac{1}{5}+\frac{1}{5}\right)} = 2.76$$

From the samples $\bar{x}_A = 16$, $\bar{x}_B = 15$, $\bar{x}_C = 21$. System C takes significantly longer to learn than Systems A and B which have similar training times.

Example 8.2

A company, intending to alter its logo, sent questionnaires to a sample of its employees asking their opinions about three possibilities. The employees were asked to award each of the three logos (A, B and C) a score out of five on six different aspects of design, colour, and so on. The total scores awarded by the eight employees are given in Table 8.6.

Table 8.6

Logos	1	2	3	4	5	6	7	8
				Employees				
A	22	19	14	18	21	18	23	20
B	24	22	18	20	21	21	18	19
C	20	16	16	19	18	15	19	18

Is there a significant difference between logo preferences?

Sums of squares

Total SS: Inputting all the individual values into the calculator gives the following summary statistics: $n = 24$, $\bar{x} = 19.125$, $s_n = 2.403 \implies ns_n^2 = 138.63$

Between logos SS: The mean scores are $\bar{x}_A = 19.375$, $\bar{x}_B = 20.375$ and $\bar{x}_C = 17.625$.
  Each of these means came from 8 values so inputting the means with a frequency of 8 gives: $n = 24$, $\bar{x} = 19.125$, $s_n = 1.1365 \implies ns_n^2 = 31.00$ (n and $\bar{x}$ for checking purposes).

Error SS: $138.63 - 31.00 = 107.63$

ANOVA table (In this example: k =3 logos, N =24 values)

Table 8.7

Source	SS	df	MSS	F
Between logos	31.00	3 − 1 = 2	31/2 = 15.50	15.50/5.13 = 3.02
Errors	107.63	23 − 2 = 21	107.63/21 = 5.13	
Total	138.73	24 − 1 = 23		

Hypothesis test

H_0: $\mu_A = \mu_B = \mu_C$ H_1: At least two of them are different.

Critical value: $F_{0.05}(2,21) = 3.47$ (degrees of freedom from 'between logos' and 'errors'.)

Test statistic: 3.02

Conclusion: test statistic < critical value so H_0 not rejected. There is no significant difference between employee preference for the logos.

8.3 Two-way analysis of variance

In Section 8.2, using one-way ANOVA we investigated whether there was a difference in the time taken to learn three different database management systems. We found that System C took longer to learn than either of Systems A or B, which took similar lengths of time. System C took, on average, at least 5 hours longer, and since the standard error of the difference between the means – the critical difference – was 2.76 we concluded that System C was significantly more difficult to learn.

We might suspect that some of the variation left in the errors from one-way analysis of variance was not, in fact, down to random chance but was caused by some other measurable factor. For instance in Example 8.1 we might feel instinctively that some of the variation in time needed to learn a database management system was because of the different learning ability of the operators. If so, this accountable variation was incorrectly included in the error sum of squares (SSE), and caused the mean error sum of squares (MSE) to be too large. The calculated F-value would then be too small and would make the rejection of the null hypothesis more unlikely.

Two-way analysis of variance can be used in various ways. We can:

- Explore just one factor of interest in a more realistic manner by removing the accountable variation and allowing a truer conclusion to be reached by this more powerful test. (When individual learning ability is taken onto account, are the database learning times any different?)
- Investigate two factors of interest at the same time by also testing the difference in means between levels of the second set of groups. (Is there any difference between the three systems and also between the five operators?)
- Consider any interaction between the two variables. Do the levels of one factor react differently to the levels of the other? (Are any operators faster at learning any particular system?)

We shall look at just these three uses in turn, but you should be aware that analysis of variance is a very powerful analytical tool which can be used effectively to do other types of analysis with very large sets of data. However this is only practical using computer packages.

8.3.1 Randomised block design

In this section we shall treat the two-way ANOVA method as an extension of one-way ANOVA but also include a blocking factor to remove the unwanted accountable variation which we shall assume to be of no interest. (The term 'blocking' comes from the agricultural origins, when each trial would have been applied to each 'block' of ground, for example those having different degrees of slope.)

This design ensures that each group is measured under the same conditions by removing the variation because of these conditions by the use of a blocking factor. In the case of the database management systems in Example 8.1, each system was learned by all the operators in the sample. This removed the variation because of differing operator learning ability and gave a better indication of the variation that was genuinely caused by random errors.

We shall again consider the theory in tandem with the calculations in order to make the method easier to follow.

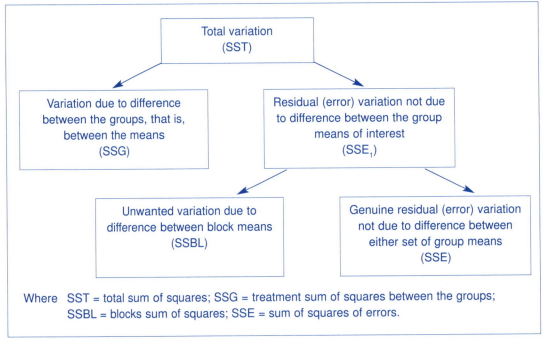

Figure 8.2 Two-way random blocked ANOVA model

Example 8.3

Example 8.3 uses the same data as Example 1 but the operators are identified. Since operator variability was believed also to be a significant factor, each of the five operators was trained on each of the three database management systems. The training hours needed for each are as shown in Table 8.8

Using the system means calculated in Example 8.1, also calculate mean time for each operator:

Table 8.8

	Operators					
	1	2	3	4	5	Means
System A	16	19	14	13	18	16.00
System B	16	17	13	12	17	15.00
System C	24	22	19	18	22	21.00
Means	18.67	19.33	15.33	14.33	19.00	17.33

In this two-way model, in the context of the management systems and operators example:

Total variance = between systems variance + between operator variance + error variance.

It follows that:

Total sum of squares (SST)	=	Sum of squares between systems (SSSys)	+	Sum of squares between Operators (SSOps)	+	Sum of squares of errors (SSE)

SST: (from the individual data, as Example 8.1) = 175.3

SSSys: (inputting treatment means as frequency data, as in Example 8.1) = 103.3

SSOps: Inputting the operator means from Table 8.8 as frequency data (frequency = 5) gives:

n	$\bar{x}$	s_n	s_n^2	ns_n^2
15	17.33	2.078	4.317	64.7 = SSOps

A generalised ANOVA table for k treatments, b blocks and total sample size N is shown in Table 8.9. The error df is generally calculated as: $(N - 1) - \{(k - 1) + (b - 1)\}$, that is, the remainder. (Again, ignore this if you don't find it helpful.)

Table 8.9

Source	SS	df	MSS	F
Between groups	SSG	$k - 1$	$SSG/(k - 1)$ = MSG	MSG/MSE
Between blocks	SSBL	$b - 1$		
Errors	SSE	$(k - 1)(b - 1)$	$SSE/(k - 1)(b - 1)$ = MSE	
Total	SST	$N - 1$		

Example 8.3 continued

A two-way ANOVA table, including both systems and operators, is shown in Table 8.10.

Table 8.10

Source	SS	df	MSS	F
Between systems	103.3	3 − 1 = 2	103.3/2 = 51.65	51.65/0.91 = 56.8
Between operators	64.7	5 − 1 = 4		
Errors	7.3	14 − 6 = 8	7.3/8 = 0.91	
Total	175.3	15 − 1 = 14		

Hypothesis test

Method as Example 8.1 (assuming no interest in operator difference).

H_0: $\mu_A = \mu_B = \mu_C$ H_1: At least two of them are different.

Critical value: $F_{0.05}(2,8) = 4.46$

Test statistic: 56.8 (Note how much larger this is than for the one-way analysis.)

Conclusion: test statistic > critical value. so reject H_0. There is a significant difference between at least two of the times needed for training on the different systems, after we have allowed for operator variability.

8.3.2 Main effects only

In this model we assume that there are two factors of interest but no interaction between them. The only difference from the previous model is that the 'blocks' are now of interest and so the second factor is also tested for significance. See Table 8.11. The error df is generally calculated as: $(N − 1) − \{(k − 1) + (b − 1)\}$, that is, the remainder.

Table 8.11

Source	S	df	MSS	F
Between groups	SSG	k − 1	SSG/(k − 1) = MSG	MSG/MSE
Between blocks	SSBL	b − 1	SSBL/(b − 1) = MSBL	MSBL/MSE
Errors	SSE	(k − 1)(b − 1)	SSE/(k − 1)(b − 1) = MSE	
Total	SST	N − 1		

Example 8.4

Example 8.4 continues Example 8.3 by testing for significance of operator difference.

Two-way ANOVA table (Including both Systems and Operators)

Table 8.12

Source	SS	df	MSS	F
Between systems	103.3	3 − 1 = 2	103.3/2 = 51.65	51.65/0.91 = 56.8
Between operators	64.7	5 − 1 = 4	64.7/4 = 16.18	16.18/0.91 = 17.8
Errors	7.3	14 − 6 = 8	7.3/8 = 0.91	
Total	175.3	15 − 1 = 14		

We test now for two separate hypotheses, one that the systems can be learnt in the same time and the second that the operators take the same mean time to learn them.

Hypothesis Test for Systems (As for Example 8.3)

H_0: $\mu_A = \mu_B = \mu_C$ H_1: At least two of them are different.

Critical value: $F_{0.05}(2,8) = 4.46$

Test statistic: 56.8

Conclusion: test statistic > critical value so reject H_0. There is a difference between at least two of the mean times needed for training on the different systems.

Hypothesis test for Operators

H_0: $\mu_1 = \mu_2 = \mu_3 = \mu_4 = \mu_5$ H_1: At least two of them are different.

Critical value: $F_{0.05}(4,8) = 3.84$

Test statistic: 17.8

Conclusion: test statistic > critical value so reject H_0. There is a significant difference between at least two of the operators in the mean time needed for learning the systems.

Where does this significant difference lie? The calculations are as in Example 8.1, but the degrees of freedom and mean square errors are different.

Now t has the error degrees of freedom = 8, one tail only, giving 1.86

$$CD = 1.86\sqrt{0.91\left(\frac{1}{3}+\frac{1}{3}\right)} = 1.45$$

Table 8.13

	n	$\bar{x}$
Operator 1	3	18.67
Operator 2	3	19.33
Operator 3	3	15.33
Operator 4	3	14.33
Operator 5	3	19.00

Absolute differences between operator mean training times

Table 8.14 shows that it is not necessary to list all possible pairs.

Table 8.14

Operators	1	2	3	4	5
1	0				
2	0.66	0			
3	**3.33**	**4.00**	0		
4	**4.33**	**5.00**	1.00	0	
5	0.33	0.33	**3.66**	**4.66**	0

This is not so easy to interpret. It looks as though operators 1, 2 and 5 are very similar. Operators 3 and 4 are not significantly different from each other but are from the others.

   We conclude that operators 3 and 4 are significantly quicker learners than operators 1, 2 and 5.

Example 8.5

Using the same data as Example 8.2 but we are now interested in employees as well as logos. One-way ANOVA found no significant difference between logo preferences. Can this more powerful method detect any? Is there any difference between the scoring of the different employees. Are some more generous than others?

Table 8.15

Logos	Employees							
	1	2	3	4	5	6	7	8
A	22	19	14	18	21	18	23	20
B	24	22	18	20	21	21	18	19
C	20	16	16	19	18	15	19	18

As calculated for Example 8.2:

Total SS: = 138.63

Between logos SS: = 31.00

Between employees SS:
$\bar{x}_1 = 22.0$, $\bar{x}_2 = 19.0$, $\bar{x}_3 = 16.0$, $\bar{x}_4 = 19.0$, $\bar{x}_5 = 20.0$, $\bar{x}_6 = 18.0$, $\bar{x}_7 = 20.0$, $\bar{x}_8 = 19.0$

Sums of squares

n	$\bar{x}$	s_n	s_n^2	ns_n^2
24	19.13	1.62	2.61	62.63 = SSEmps

ANOVA table

Table 8.16

Source	SS	df	MSS	F
Between logos	31.00	3 − 1 = 2	31/2 = 15.50	15.50/3.21 = 4.83
Between employees	62.63	8 − 1 = 7	62.63/7 = 8.95	8.95/3.21 = 2.79
Errors	45.00	23 − 9 = 14	45.0/14 = 3.21	
Total	138.63	24 − 1 = 23		

Hypothesis test for logos

H_0: $\mu_A = \mu_B = \mu_C$ H_1: At least two of them are different.

Critical value: $F_{0.05}(2,14) = 3.74$ (degrees of freedom from 'between logos' and 'errors').

Test statistic: 4.83
(Note that this test statistic is much larger than that produced by one-way ANOVA.)

Conclusion: test statistic > critical value so H_0 is now rejected. There is a significant difference between logo preferences. This test has been powerful enough to reject the null hypothesis which was not rejected by one-way ANOVA.

Hypothesis test for employees

H_0: $\mu_1 = \mu_2 = \mu_3 = \mu_4 = \mu_5 = \mu_6 = \mu_7 = \mu_8$ H_1: At least two of them are different.

Critical value: $F_{0.05}(7,14) = 2.76$ (df from 'employees' and 'errors'.)

Test statistic: 2.79

Conclusion: test statistic > critical value so H_0 is rejected. There is a difference between employee scores.

The critical difference can be calculated and the means inspected as previously to see which logo was significantly preferred and which employees scored more generously than the rest. For eight employees a matrix of means is definitely recommended!

8.3.3 Main effects and interactions

You are not expected to carry out this type of analysis by hand as it can be executed more conveniently by means of a computer package. However you need to know that replicate (two or more) data values are always needed for the analysis. For single values, the method assumes that any variation not caused by the main effects is the result of their interaction, so the value of the error sum of squares would be zero. This means that the ANOVA table cannot be completed and so no conclusion can be reached. It is always necessary therefore to collect duplicate or triplicate samples if the interaction between the main effects is to be of interest.

What do we mean by interactions? In Example 8.4 we concluded that System C took longer to learn than the other two, and in Example 8.5 that Operators 3 and 4 were significantly quicker learners than the Operators 1, 2 and 5. But it might be possible that a particular operator related better to one of the systems, even though the rest had trouble with it, and he or she might have had problems with a different one.

A graph of the situation may make it easier to understand.

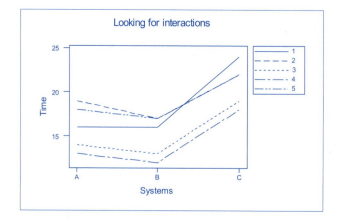

Figure 8.3

We can see that Systems A and B were mastered by the operators in the same order; operator 4 finished first followed by 3, 1, 5 and 2. System C followed the same pattern except that Operator 1 seemed to have particular problems with it. In other words, there was an interaction between this operator and System C which accounted for some of the variation between the main effects.

In a sketch of this type parallel lines indicate no interactions, but marked differences in gradient or lines crossing each other indicate that some interaction has upset the pattern. If the lines were drawn for the systems, rather than the operators, it would be seen that all three are parallel except in the section for System C, which would have a different gradient between Operators 1 and 2.

8.4 Further analysis using ANOVA techniques

If a large amount of data is available it is more sensible to use a computer package for these more advanced techniques. It is, however, difficult to know exactly what is happening between putting in the data and looking at the ANOVA table, so Examples 8.6 and 8.7 are produced here.

We have only considered two sets of main effects, but many more can be investigated in computer analysis providing that sufficient data are available. The main effects and interactions of interest can be selected so that the models do not become too cumbersome. Try to avoid the 'throw everything in and see what comes out' attitude because it can lead to some very difficult interpretation.

More than one variable can also be considered simultaneously in MANOVA – multivariate analysis of variance (but not on this course).

8.4.1 Factorial model

The factorial model has been discussed briefly in Section 8.3.3. We shall now work through a question by hand.

Example 8.6

The transport manager in a haulage company wished to improve the fuel consumption of her fleet. She knew that there were a variety of fuel additives on the market which might improve the performance of the vehicles. Four different additives were used on long journeys with three different types of vehicle.

There are simultaneously three different hypotheses under test:

$H_0(1)$: There is no difference between the mean fuel consumption produced by the four different additives.

$H_0(2)$: There is no difference between the mean fuel consumption of the three different types of vehicle.

$H_0(3)$: There is no interaction between the different vehicles and the different additives.

H_1: In each case is that at least two of the mean fuel consumptions are different.

The experiment

In this experiment the average consumption for 24 long journeys was measured. Three different types of vehicle were used. Duplicate journeys were recorded for each combination of additive and vehicle, giving the data shown in Table 8.17.

First calculate the mean values for each additive, each vehicle, each interaction and the overall mean. Add them to the table, giving Table 8.18.

Next the sums of squares are all calculated. The main effects of additive and vehicle are input and calculated as in previous examples.

For the interaction sum of squares (Vehs × Adds) the mean of each cell is input with a frequency of 2 since two values contributed to it. The figure produced from the standard deviation includes the main effects sums of squares which then have to be subtracted from it. See Table 8.19.

Table 8.17 Fuel consumption (m.p.g.)

Vehicle	Fuel additive			
type	1	2	3	4
A	34.0	30.1	29.8	29.0
	32.7	32.8	26.7	28.9
B	32.0	30.2	28.7	27.6
	33.2	29.8	28.1	27.8
C	28.4	27.3	29.7	28.8
	29.3	28.9	27.3	29.1

Table 8.18 Mean fuel consumption (m.p.g.)

Vehicle	Fuel additive				
type	1	2	3	4	Mean
A	34.0	30.1	29.8	29.0	
	(33.35)	(31.45)	(28.25)	(28.95)	30.500
	32.7	32.8	26.7	28.9	
B	32.0	30.2	28.7	27.6	
	(32.60)	(30.00)	(28.40)	(27.70)	29.675
	33.2	29.8	28.1	27.8	
C	28.4	27.3	29.7	28.8	
	(28.85)	(28.10)	(28.50)	(28.95)	28.600
	29.3	28.9	27.3	29.1	
Mean	31.600	29.850	28.383	28.533	29.592

Table 8.19 Sums of squares

	n	$\bar{x}$	s_n	s_n^2	ns_n^2
Total	24	29.592	1.9545	3.8200	91.68 = SST
Vehicles	24	29.592	0.7779	0.6051	14.52 = SSVehs
Additives	24	29.592	1.2925	1.6704	40.09 = SSAdds
Interactions	24	29.592	1.7885	3.1987	76.77
Vehs × Adds	76.77 − (14.52 + 40.09) = 22.16 = SS(Vehs × Adds)				

Table 8.20 ANOVA table, including both vehicles and additives

Source	SS	df	MSS	F
Between vehicles	14.52	2	14.52/2 = 7.26	7.26/1.24 = 5.85
Between additives	40.09	3	40.09/3 = 13.36	13.36/1.24 = 10.77
Between vehicles × adds	22.16	6	22.16/6 = 3.69	3.68/1.24 = 2.98
Errors	14.91	12	14.91/12 = 1.24	
Total	91.68	23		

F-table values for comparison: $F_{0.05}(2,12) = 3.89$ $F_{0.05}(3,12) = 3.49$ $F_{0.05}(6,12) = 3.00$

Since the interaction proves to be insignificant the small amount of variance accounted for by it should be included with the error variance and the F-values recalculated:

Table 8.21

Source	SS	df	MSS	F
Between vehicles	14.52	3 − 1 = 2	7.26	3.52
Between additives	40.09	4 − 1 = 3	13.36	6.49
Errors 14.91 + 22.16 =	37.07	23 − 5 = 18	2.06	
Total	91.68	24 − 1 = 23		

F-table values for comparison : $F_{0.05}(2,18) = 3.55$ $F_{0.05}(3,18) = 3.16$

Conclusion: So there is a significant difference between effects of the additives but not between the types of vehicle.

Additives: $CD = 1.73 \times \sqrt{2.06\left(\dfrac{1}{6} + \dfrac{1}{6}\right)} = 1.43$

Table 8.22

Absolute differences	1	2	3
2	1.75		
3	3.22	1.47	
4	3.07	1.32	0.15

Additive 1 is significantly different from (produces better mileage than) additives 2, 3 and 4 and 2 is better than 3.

8.4.2 Latin square model

The Latin square model is a very efficient method of resource allocation. The experimental area, or its theoretical equivalent, is divided into rows and columns, and each treatment must appear once in each row and once in each column. (Think about Sudoku, which is similar regarding rows and columns.) The most important property of this arrangement is that any comparison of treatments is unaffected by the average differences which exist between rows or between columns, since all treatments have been applied to each row and each column. This design is described as being 'fully balanced'.

The analysis follows the normal procedure of analysing the differences between rows, columns and treatments.

Example 8.7

The same transport manager as in Example 8.6 wants to test the relative efficiency, in miles per gallon with the four different additives A, B, C and D using four different types of vehicle (Mini, Volkswagen, Rover, Porsche) on four different types of road (country lane, city street, trunk road and motorway).

Test to see, at the 5% level, if there is any difference between the fuel consumption of the different brands, vehicle makes or road types.

A Latin square experiment was carried with each type of car using each type of additive on each type of road and the results in Table 8.23 were obtained (note that each additive appears in every row and every column):

Table 8.23

Type of car	Type of road			
	Country lane	City street	Trunk road	Motorway
Mini	(A) 30	(B) 33	(C) 36	(D) 40
Volkswagen	(B) 32	(C) 32	(D) 35	(A) 38
Rover	(C) 24	(D) 26	(A) 23	(B) 26
Porsche	(D) 23	(A) 21	(B) 23	(C) 24

Table 8.24 Means (miles per gallon)

Cars:	Mini	Volkswagen	Rover	Porsche
Means	34.75	34.25	24.75	22.75
Roads:	Country lane	City street	Trunk road	Motorway
Means	27.25	28.00	29.25	32.00
Brands:	A	B	C	D
Means	28.00	28.50	29.00	31.00

Table 8.25 Sums of squares

	n	$\bar{x}$	s_n	s_n^2	ns_n^2
Total	16	29.125	5.925	35.109	561.75 = SSTotal
Cars	16	29.125	5.424	29.422	470.75 = SSCars
Roads	16	29.125	1.807	3.266	52.25 = SSRoads
Brands	16	29.125	1.139	1.297	20.75 = SSBrands

Table 8.26 ANOVA table

Source	SS	df	MSS	F
Between cars	470.75	3	156.92	52.31
Between roads	52.25	3	17.42	5.81
Between brands	20.75	3	6.92	2.31
Errors	18.00	6	3.00	
Total	561.75	15		

F-table values for comparison: $F_{0.05}(3,6) = 4.76$

The main source of variation is between the types of car used and there is also some between the type of roads travelled but none between the additive brands.

Which cars are significantly different?

Cars: $CD = 1.94 \times \sqrt{3.00\left(\dfrac{1}{4}+\dfrac{1}{4}\right)} = 2.37$

Observed differences between means

Table 8.27

	Mini	VW	Rover
VW	0.5		
Rover	10.0	9.5	
Porsche	12.0	11.5	2.0

We clearly have two pairs of cars in terms of petrol consumption: the Mini and the Volkswagen are more economical then the Rover and the Porsche.

8.5 A continuous example using ANOVA

In this example we shall carry out:

- a one-way analysis of variance
- a two-way analysis of variance where only the main factor is of interest
- a two-way analysis of variance where both factors but no interaction are of interest
- a two-way analysis of variance where both main effects and the interaction are of interest – a factorial design.

Example 8.8

An engineering component is produced by a process which involves it being baked at a fairly high temperature for a short while. This baking may take place in any one of four ovens each of which tends to run at different temperatures.

The production manager in charge of this process suspects that the working lifetime of these components may depend upon the temperature at which they are baked and runs an experiment to investigate.

Duplicate sample components are baked at each of three controlled temperatures in each of the four types of oven and their working lifetimes found in a testing laboratory. We shall analyse the results by the different methods of analysis of variance met in this chapter in order to see if the production manager is correct.

Table 8.28 Working lifetime of component in hours

Temperature °C	Oven			
	1	2	3	4
250	220 224	207 252	218 229	253 222
275	187 208	181 179	232 198	246 273
300	174 202	198 194	178 213	206 219

Does the baking temperature have any effect on a component's working lifetime?

One-way analysis of variance

Table 8.29 Mean lifetimes for each temperature and overall mean

Temperature	250	275	300	All
Mean	228.1	213.0	198.0	213.0

Table 8.30 Sums of squares

	n	$\bar{x}$	s_n	s_n^2	ns_n^2
Total	24	213.0	25.32	641.0	15383 = SSTotal
Temps	24	213.0	12.29	151.0	3624 = SSTemps

Table 8.31 ANOVA table

Source	SS	df	MSS	F
Between temps.	3624	2	1812	3.24
Errors	11759	21	560	
Total	15383	23		

Hypothesis test for temperatures

H_0: $\mu_{250} = \mu_{275} = \mu_{300}$ H_1: At least two of them are different.

Critical value: $F_{0.05}(2,21) = 3.47$ (degrees of freedom from 'between temps' and 'errors').

Test statistic: $= 3.24$

Conclusion: test statistic < critical value so H_0 is not rejected. There is no significant difference between the lifetimes of the components baked at the different temperatures.

Does the baking temperature have any effect on a component's working lifetime if the effect of the different ovens is removed from the analysis?

Two-way ANOVA using a blocked design

Table 8.32 Mean lifetimes for each temperature, each oven and overall

Temperature	250	275	300	All
Mean	228.1	213.0	198.0	213.0

Oven	1	2	3	4
Mean	202.5	201.8	211.3	236.5

Table 8.33 Sums of squares

	n	$\bar{x}$	s_n	s_n^2	ns_n^2
Total	24	213.0	25.32	641.0	15383 = SSTotal
Temps	24	213.0	12.29	151.0	3624 = SSTemps
Ovens	24	213.0	14.06	197.7	4745 = SSOvens

Table 8.34 ANOVA table

Source	SS	df	MSS	F
Between Temps.	3624	2	1812	4.65
Between Ovens	4745	3		
Errors	7014	18	390	
Total	15383	23		

Hypothesis test for temperatures

H_0: $\mu_{250} = \mu_{275} = \mu_{300}$ H_1: At least two of them are different.

Critical value: $F_{0.05}(2,18) = 3.55$ (df from 'between temps' and 'errors'.)

Test statistic: 4.65

Conclusion: test statistic > critical value so now H_0 is rejected. There is a significant difference between the mean lifetimes of the components baked at the different temperatures if the effect of the different ovens is eliminated from the analysis.

The lower the temperature of baking the longer the life, within the range of temperatures tested.

Is there a significant difference between the mean working life of components baked in the different ovens?

Completing the ANOVA table for the ovens as well as for the temperatures:

Table 8.35 ANOVA table

Source	SS	df	MSS	F
Between temps.	3624	2	1812	4.65
Between ovens	4745	3	1582	4.06
Errors	7014	18	390	
Total	15383	23		

Hypothesis test for ovens

H_0: $\mu_1 = \mu_2 = \mu_3 = \mu_4$ H_1: At least two of them are different.

Critical value: $F_{0.05}(3,18) = 3.16$ (df from 'ovens' and 'errors').

Test statistic: 4.06

Conclusion: test statistic > critical value so H_0 is rejected. There is a significant difference between the lifetimes of the components baked in different ovens.
    Oven 4 seems preferable to the others in terms of life expectancy.

Is there a significant interaction between the ovens and the temperature of baking as regards life expectancy?

Table 8.36 Working lifetime of component in hours – cell means

Temperature °C	Oven 1	2	3	4
250	222.0	229.5	223.5	237.5
275	197.5	180.0	215.0	259.5
300	188.0	196.0	195.5	212.5

Table 8.37 Sums of squares

	n	$\bar{x}$	s_n	s_n^2	ns_n^2
Total	24	213.0	25.32	641.0	15383 = SSTotal
Temps	24	213.0	12.29	151.0	3624 = SSTemps
Ovens	24	213.0	14.06	197.7	4745 = SSOvens
T + Ov + T × Ov	24	213.0	21.95	481.6	11560
Interaction		$11560 - (3624 + 4745) = 3191$ = Temp × OvenSS			

Table 8.38 ANOVA table

Source	SS	df	MSS	F
Between temps.	3624	2	1812	5.69
Between ovens	4745	3	1582	4.97
Temp × oven	3191	6	532	1.67
Errors	3823	12	318.6	
Total	15383.0	23		

Checking the significance of the interactions: $F_{0.05}(6,12) = 3.00$

Conclusion: Since 1.67 is less than this there is no interaction between the ovens and the temperature at which they are run. The final analysis is therefore that shown in Table 8.35.

8.6 The Kruskal-Wallis test

The Kruskal-Wallis test is the non-parametric equivalent of the one-way ANOVA. It is appropriate for use if the data is either ordered or not normally distributed. It is not necessary to work through the method by hand as it is rather laborious; it is much more efficient to use SPSS or Minitab.

Repeating again the training times taken by the operators in Example 8.1:

Table 8.39

System A	16	19	14	13	18
System B	16	17	13	12	17
System C	24	22	19	18	22

If these times were shown to be non-normal, the use of ranks rather than means would be more appropriate in the analysis. The one-way analysis of ranks is used in the Kruskal-Wallis test.

Let's look at the SPSS analysis of this data:

Ranks

	File management system	N	Mean Rank
Training hours	A	5	6.60
	B	5	4.80
	C	5	12.60
	Total	15	

Test Statistics[a,b]

	Training hours
Chi-Square	8.430
df	2
Asymp. Sig.	.015

a. Kruskal Wallis Test

b. Grouping Variable: File management system

Figure 8.4

It can be seen that the mean rank of Operator C is higher than that of A or B. The significance of the test is 0.015, which would cause the null hypothesis of equality of medians to be rejected at the 5 per cent level, showing that there was a difference between at least two of the operators.

There is no non-parametric equivalent of two-way ANOVA.

8.7 Summary of analysis of variance (ANOVA)

The technique known as ANOVA can be employed at a range of levels. The simpler methods make up most of this chapter, with the more complex variations confined to Section 8.4.

We used one-way ANOVA to see whether there was a significant difference between three or more group means, in the three file management systems in Example 8.1. We then used two-way ANOVA to remove any accountable variation which might prove a nuisance during analysis in a blocked design. If the second grouping, such as the operators in Example 8.3, was itself of interest, it was analysed simultaneously with the main factor and both tested for significance.

Any interaction between the two factors could be tested for significance using a factorial design, but that method is beyond the scope of this course and has been confined to the further analysis. We just considered a graphical description of the situation.

Finally we used the non-parametric equivalent of one-way ANOVA, known as the Kruskal-Wallis test.

The textbooks by Groebner and Shannon (1993) and Weimer (1993) both have plenty of ANOVA examples, but both calculate sums of squares by the tedious tabulation method.

8.8 Computer analysis of Examples 8.1, 8.3 and 8.5

Example 8.1

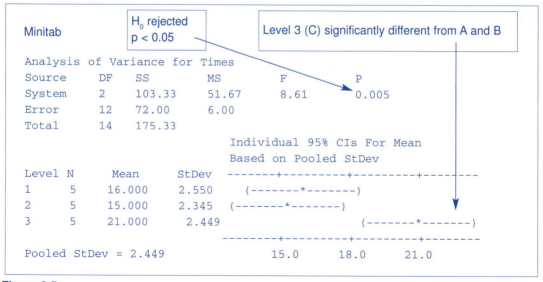

```
Minitab          H₀ rejected              Level 3 (C) significantly different from A and B
                 p < 0.05

Analysis of Variance for Times
Source      DF    SS          MS          F          P
System      2     103.33      51.67       8.61       0.005
Error       12    72.00       6.00
Total       14    175.33

                              Individual 95% CIs For Mean
                              Based on Pooled StDev
Level  N       Mean      StDev   -------+---------+---------+---------
1      5       16.000    2.550          (-------*-------)
2      5       15.000    2.345   (-------*-------)
3      5       21.000    2.449                         (-------*-------)
                                 -------+---------+---------+---------
Pooled StDev = 2.449                   15.0      18.0      21.0
```

Figure 8.5

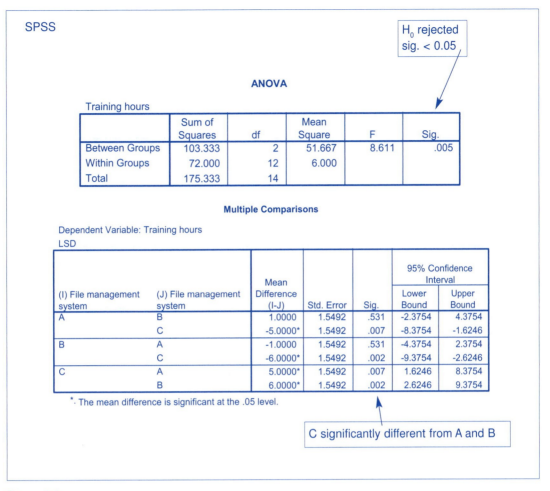

SPSS

H₀ rejected
sig. < 0.05

ANOVA

Training hours

	Sum of Squares	df	Mean Square	F	Sig.
Between Groups	103.333	2	51.667	8.611	.005
Within Groups	72.000	12	6.000		
Total	175.333	14			

Multiple Comparisons

Dependent Variable: Training hours

LSD

(I) File management system	(J) File management system	Mean Difference (I-J)	Std. Error	Sig.	95% Confidence Interval Lower Bound	Upper Bound
A	B	1.0000	1.5492	.531	-2.3754	4.3754
	C	-5.0000*	1.5492	.007	-8.3754	-1.6246
B	A	-1.0000	1.5492	.531	-4.3754	2.3754
	C	-6.0000*	1.5492	.002	-9.3754	-2.6246
C	A	5.0000*	1.5492	.007	1.6246	8.3754
	B	6.0000*	1.5492	.002	2.6246	9.3754

*. The mean difference is significant at the .05 level.

C significantly different from A and B

Figure 8.6

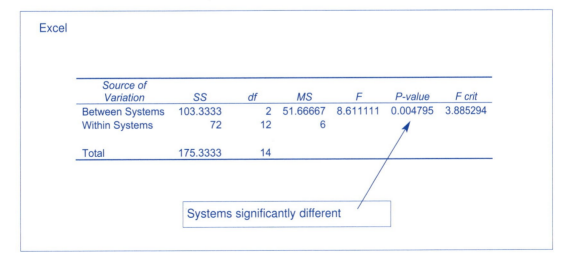

Excel

Source of Variation	SS	df	MS	F	P-value	F crit
Between Systems	103.3333	2	51.66667	8.611111	0.004795	3.885294
Within Systems	72	12	6			
Total	175.3333	14				

Systems significantly different

Figure 8.7

Example 8.3

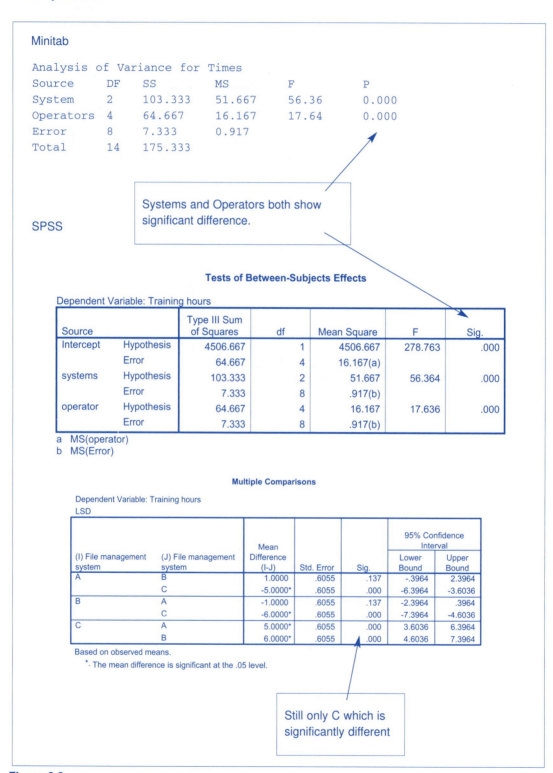

Minitab

```
Analysis of Variance for Times
Source      DF   SS        MS       F        P
System      2    103.333   51.667   56.36    0.000
Operators   4    64.667    16.167   17.64    0.000
Error       8    7.333     0.917
Total       14   175.333
```

Systems and Operators both show significant difference.

SPSS

Tests of Between-Subjects Effects

Dependent Variable: Training hours

Source		Type III Sum of Squares	df	Mean Square	F	Sig.
Intercept	Hypothesis	4506.667	1	4506.667	278.763	.000
	Error	64.667	4	16.167(a)		
systems	Hypothesis	103.333	2	51.667	56.364	.000
	Error	7.333	8	.917(b)		
operator	Hypothesis	64.667	4	16.167	17.636	.000
	Error	7.333	8	.917(b)		

a MS(operator)
b MS(Error)

Multiple Comparisons

Dependent Variable: Training hours
LSD

(I) File management system	(J) File management system	Mean Difference (I-J)	Std. Error	Sig.	95% Confidence Interval	
					Lower Bound	Upper Bound
A	B	1.0000	.6055	.137	-.3964	2.3964
	C	-5.0000*	.6055	.000	-6.3964	-3.6036
B	A	-1.0000	.6055	.137	-2.3964	.3964
	C	-6.0000*	.6055	.000	-7.3964	-4.6036
C	A	5.0000*	.6055	.000	3.6036	6.3964
	B	6.0000*	.6055	.000	4.6036	7.3964

Based on observed means.
*. The mean difference is significant at the .05 level.

Still only C which is significantly different

Figure 8.8

Excel

Source of Variation	SS	df	MS	F	P-value	F crit
Operators	64.66667	4	16.16667	17.63636	0.000494	3.837853
Systems	103.3333	2	51.66667	56.36364	1.93E-05	4.45897
Error	7.333333	8	0.916667			
Total	175.3333	14				

Systems and Operators both show significant difference.

Figure 8.9

Example 8.6

Minitab

Analysis of Variance for Consumpt, using Sequential SS for Tests

Source	DF	Seq SS	Adj SS	Seq MS	F	P
Vehicle	2	14.326	14.326	7.163	5.75	0.018
Additive	3	39.871	39.871	13.290	10.67	0.001
Vehicle *Additive	6	22.447	22.447	3.741	3.00	0.050

Vehicles and Additives both significantly different.
Interaction not significant at 5% level

SPSS

Tests of Between-Subjects Effects

Dependent Variable: Fuel consumption (m.p.g.)

Source	Type III Sum of Squares	df	Mean Square	F	Sig.
Corrected Model	76.768(a)	11	6.979	5.617	.003
Intercept	21016.002	1	21016.002	16914.287	.000
vehicle	14.523	2	7.262	5.844	.017
additive	40.082	3	13.361	10.753	.001
vehicle * additive	22.163	6	3.694	2.973	.051
Error	14.910	12	1.242		
Total	21107.680	24			
Corrected Total	91.678	23			

a R Squared = .837 (Adjusted R Squared = .688)

Figure 8.10

Excel

Source of Variation	SS	df	MS	F	P-value	F crit
Vehicles	14.52333	2	7.261667	5.8444	0.016898	3.885294
Additives	40.08167	3	13.36056	10.75296	0.00102	3.490295
Interaction	22.16333	6	3.693889	2.972949	0.051168	2.99612
Within	14.91	12	1.2425			
Total	91.67833	23				

Vehicles and Additives both significantly different.
Interaction not significant at 5%

Figure 8.11

Example 8.6 – Kruskal-Wallis test (not available in Excel)

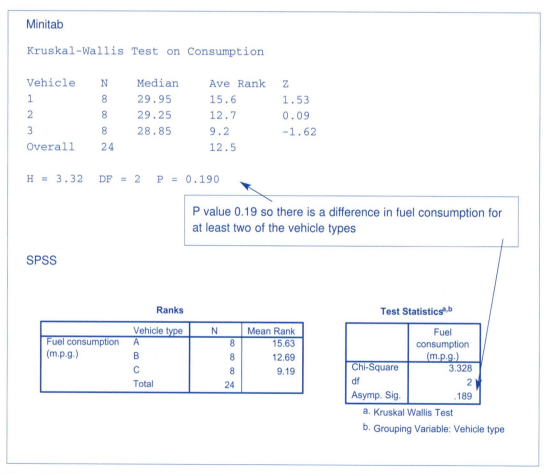

Minitab

Kruskal-Wallis Test on Consumption

Vehicle	N	Median	Ave Rank	Z
1	8	29.95	15.6	1.53
2	8	29.25	12.7	0.09
3	8	28.85	9.2	-1.62
Overall	24		12.5	

$H = 3.32$ $DF = 2$ $P = 0.190$

P value 0.19 so there is a difference in fuel consumption for at least two of the vehicle types

SPSS

Ranks

	Vehicle type	N	Mean Rank
Fuel consumption (m.p.g.)	A	8	15.63
	B	8	12.69
	C	8	9.19
	Total	24	

Test Statistics[a,b]

	Fuel consumption (m.p.g.)
Chi-Square	3.328
df	2
Asymp. Sig.	.189

a. Kruskal Wallis Test
b. Grouping Variable: Vehicle type

Figure 8.12

8.9 Case study

As you should by now have realised, we have reached the method of analysis most useful to your directors, who are interested in the differences between three types of food outlet – takeaways, cafés and restaurants.

Bearing in mind the results of the normality tests you carried out in Section 7.14, test at the 5 per cent level whether there is any difference between the three types of food outlet in terms of:

- gross sales
- market value
- number of full-time employees
- number of part-time employees
- wages as percentage of sales
- advertising as percentage of sales.

Tutorial 8: analysis of variance

(Answers in Appendix A)

8.1 The accompanying table contains the number of words typed per minute by four office trainees at five different times using the same word processor.

A	B	C	D
82	55	69	87
79	67	72	61
75	84	78	82
68	77	83	61
65	71	74	72

At the 5% significance level, determine whether the typing speeds of the four trainees differ. Summarise your findings in an ANOVA table.

8.2 Three equivalent training courses were taught by three different instructors. A common final examination was given. The test scores are given in Table 8.40.

Assume that the populations of test scores are normally distributed with equal variance. By using the 0.5 significance level, test to determine if there is a difference in the average marks gained by the students of the three instructors. Summarise your calculations in an ANOVA table.

8.3 Four laboratories, A, B, C and D, are used by food manufacturing companies for making nutrition analyses of their products. The data in Table 8.41 are the fat contents (in grams) of the same weight of three similar types of peanut butter.

Table 8.40

Instructor 1	Instructor 2	Instructor 3
75	90	17
91	80	33
83	89	55
45	93	70
82	53	61
75	87	43
68	76	50
62	58	73
47	82	73
95	98	93
38	78	58
79	64	81
	80	70
	81	
	79	

Table 8.41

Peanut Butter	Laboratory			
	A	B	C	D
Brand 1	16.6	17.7	16.0	16.3
Brand 2	16.0	15.5	15.6	15.9
Brand 3	16.4	16.3	15.9	16.2

Analyse the data at 5% significance by (a) carrying out a one-way ANOVA to see if there is a difference between the fat content of the three brands; and (b) performing a two-way ANOVA to see if there is any difference between the brands using the laboratories as blocks. (c) Do you think there is any evidence that the results were not reasonably consistent between the four laboratories?

8.4 An electronics manufacturing firm operates 24 hours a day, five days a week. Three eight-hour shifts are used, and the workers rotate shifts each week. A management team conducted a study to determine whether there is a difference in the mean number of 14" video monitors produced when employees work on the various shifts. A random sample of five workers was selected, and the number of 14" video monitors they produce for each shift is recorded in Table 8.42.

Is there a difference in the mean production by worker and/or the mean production by shift? Use a two-way analysis of variance for both variables which you may assume to exhibit no interaction. Test at the 5% level.

Table 8.42

Employee	Monitors produced		
	Morning	Afternoon	Night
A	10	4	14
B	12	5	12
C	7	3	9
D	9	8	7
E	7	5	6

8.5 The manager of a large department store conducted an experiment to determine whether there is a difference between the average weekly sales of three members of the staff in the same department. The following data indicate sales (in £100) for seven consecutive weeks for the three employees.

Week	Employee		
	A	B	C
1	27.6	28.7	26.4
2	31.2	29.3	30.3
3	28.8	28.4	28.0
4	30.6	29.8	28.7
5	30.0	31.0	32.3
6	28.4	29.9	29.6
7	30.9	29.5	31.1

a) Carry out a one-way ANOVA to see whether there is any difference between the sales of the three employees.
b) Carry out a two-way ANOVA to see whether there is any difference between the sales of the three employees when using the weeks as blocks.
c) If you find a significant result, test pairwise to see where the difference lies.

Notes

For SPSS/Minitab/Excel worksheets on analysis of variance see Chapter 14, Sections 14.2.4, 14.5.4 and 14.8.4 respectively. Worksheets with computer output and its interpretation are on the companion website.

The supplementary exercise for Chapter 8, with answers, is on the companion website.

Correlation and regression

9

Objectives of this chapter

So far we have only been interested in one variable at a time. In this chapter we consider two quantitative variables and look for any bivariate association between them. If a relationship is found to exist, the next step is to describe it both graphically and by an equation which can be used for predictive purposes.

Once you have completed this chapter you should be able to

- describe bivariate data graphically
- represent them by an equation describing the dependent variable as a function of the independent one
- use the equation for predictive purposes
- give an indication of the expected accuracy of the prediction.

9.1 Introduction

If we have information available on more than one variable, we might be interested in seeing if there is any connection – any association – between them. The method for doing this depends upon the type of data we have. Are they nominal, ordinal or interval?

Methods for analysing the association between two **nominal** variables will be described in Chapter 10, which covers the use of contingency tables and chi-square tests. In this chapter we first consider pairwise association between **interval** data using scatter diagrams, and Pearson's method of correlation. We then look at associations between **ordinal** variables using Spearman's method.

If a pairwise correlation is found to be significant, the relationship between the variables will be investigated by producing a regression model in the form of a linear equation. If we wish to use the regression equation for making predictions we also need to know how good our predictions are likely to be. On the assumption that the lack of fit for the predicted values will be similar to that for the data from which the regression model was constructed, we shall analyse the residuals (the lack of fit), and quote estimates of accuracy with the predictions.

Example 9.1

An ice-cream manufacturer wishes to estimate how much ice-cream he is likely to be able to sell in the coming month. Common sense suggests that his sales vary with the climatic conditions and, now that long-term weather forecasts are available, he realises he can obtain an estimate of the average temperature for one month ahead. Can he find an association between average monthly temperature and his sales in the past, then use this association to predict his likely sales for the coming month?

Table 9.1

Month	Average temp. (°C)	Sales (£'000)
January	4	73
February	4	57
March	7	81
April	8	94
May	12	110
June	15	124
July	16	134
August	17	139
September	14	124
October	11	103
November	7	81
December	5	80

In order to help him we need to find out:

• If there is any association between average monthly temperature and ice-cream sales.
• If there is an association, is it strong enough to be useful to him?
• If so, what form the relationship between the two variables takes.
• How we can make use of the relationship for predictive purposes, that is, forecasting.
• How good any predictions about his sales will be.

The sample of information collected by the manufacturer about his sales for the previous twelve months and the corresponding average monthly temperatures from the weather office for his locality are recorded in Table 9.1.

9.2 Scatter diagrams

Some initial insight into the relationship between two continuous variables can be obtained by plotting a **scatter diagram** (scatter plot) and looking at the resulting graph. Does there appear to be any relationship between the two variables? See Figure 9.1.

We are looking for a **linear** relationship with the bivariate points lying reasonably close to a straight **line of best fit**. Scatter diagrams are usually plotted on graph paper, and although at this stage no causality is implied, it makes sense to use the same diagram for the addition of the regression line later. The dependent variable, y, should be identified at this stage and plotted on the vertical axis, with the independent variable, x, on the horizontal axis.

9.2.1 Independent and dependent variables

The decision as to which variable is which sometimes causes problems. Often the choice is obvious, as in Example 9.1 because it make no sense to suggest that monthly temperature could be dependent on ice-cream sales! The temperature has to be the independent variable, x, and the ice-cream sales the dependent variable, y.

If you are unsure, here are some pointers that might be of use:

• If you have control over one of the variables then that is the independent, x. For example, a manufacturer can decide how much to spend on advertising and expect his sales to be dependent upon how much he spends.
• If there is any lapse of time between the two variables being measured, then the latter must depend upon the former; it cannot be the other way round.
• If you want to predict the values of one variable from your knowledge of the other variable, the variable to be predicted must be dependent on the known one.

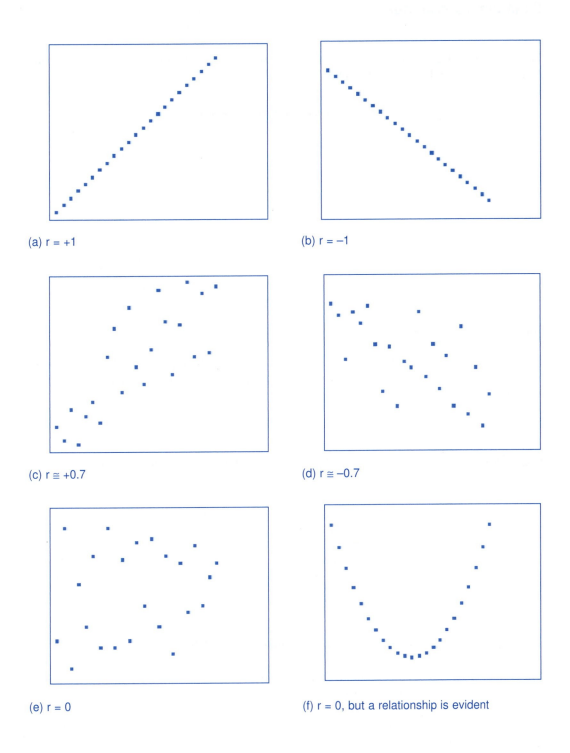

(a) r = +1

(b) r = −1

(c) r ≅ +0.7

(d) r ≅ −0.7

(e) r = 0

(f) r = 0, but a relationship is evident

Figure 9.1 Scatter diagrams for various relationships and their correlation coefficients (r)

Example 9.1 continued

Plot a scatter diagram with average temperature as the independent variable and ice-cream sales as the dependent variable.

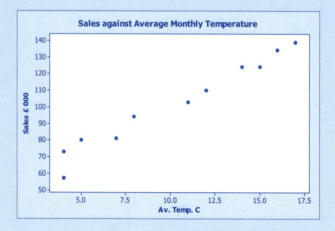

Figure 9.2 Scatter diagram (from Minitab)

Figure 9.2 seems to indicate a straight line relationship, with all points fairly close to a line of best fit. The strength of the relationship can be quantified by calculating the coefficient of correlation which will then be tested for significance.

9.3 Pearson's product moment correlation coefficient

Pearson's product moment correlation coefficient is generally just referred to as the correlation coefficient, r. It describes the strength of a **linear** relationship between two variables measured on an interval or ratio scale.

Pearson's correlation coefficient compares how the variables vary together with how they each vary individually, and is independent of the origin or units of the measurements. Note that it is not concerned with 'cause' and 'effect'. Perfect correlation would give a value of 1.

9.3.1 Calculation of Pearson's correlation coefficient

The value of the correlation coefficient, r, is most easily found using a calculator in linear regression mode. (See Section 9.14 or, preferably, consult your calculator booklet for the method.)

The Tutorial for this chapter will also provide practice in the use of your calculator. Make sure that you are happy and confident in its use. If not, ask for help from your lecturer or tutor. (If you do not have a calculator capable of carrying out correlation and regression calculations use the formulae shown in Section 9.15.)

Example 9.1 continued

For the ice-cream data the value of the correlation coefficient from the calculator is r = 0.9833

Is the size of this correlation coefficient large enough to claim that there is a **significant** relationship between average monthly temperature and sales of ice-cream? The test statistic seems very close to 1, but is it close enough to decide that the amount of association between the two variables justifies the use of temperature to estimate sales?

We need to compare the correlation coefficient with a table value to see if it is significantly high. The correlation table is reproduced as Table 6 in Appendix D. The table (critical) value is found by using n − 2 degrees of freedom, 5 per cent significance and two tails, where n is the number of data pairs in the sample.

If you have studied Chapter 7 on hypothesis testing you should carry out the formal test in Section 9.3.2. If not, just compare the sample correlation coefficient with the table value. If the value from the sample is higher than the table value, the correlation is significant. If it is lower, any association between the two variables is not significant and could have occurred by chance.

9.3.2 Hypothesis test for Pearson's correlation coefficient

Null hypothesis H_0: $\rho = 0$. There is no association (correlation) between ice-cream sales and temperature. ρ is the population correlation coefficient.

Alternative hypothesis H_1: $\rho \neq 0$. There is an association (correlation) between them.

Critical value: Pearson's correlation tables (Appendix D Table 6), usually 5 per cent (0.5), two tails, n − 2 degrees of freedom, where n is the number of data pairs in the sample.

Test statistic: the sample correlation coefficient.

Conclusion: compare the test statistic with the critical value.

If the test statistic is larger, reject the null hypothesis and conclude that the correlation is significant. If it is smaller, accept the null hypothesis that there is no significant correlation.

Example 9.1 continued

Null hypothesis H_0: $\rho = 0$. There is no association between ice-cream sales and temperature.

Alternative hypothesis H_1: $\rho \neq 0$. There is an association between them.

Critical value: 5%, (12 − 2) = 10 degrees of freedom gives 0.576

Test statistic: 0.983

Conclusion: The test statistic exceeds the critical value so we reject the null hypothesis and conclude that there is a significant association between ice-cream sales and temperature.

Because we have found significant association between average monthly temperature and ice-cream sales it is reasonable to try to identify this relationship by a regression model in the form of a linear equation. This can then be used to estimate sales.

9.4 Regression equation (least squares)

As we now know there is a significant relationship between the two variables, the next obvious step is to define it by a 'least squares regression' equation. We can then draw the line described by the equation on the scatter diagram and also use it to estimate a value for the dependent variable from a given value of the independent.

The term 'least squares regression' comes from the method of calculating the equation (see Section 9.15). It is the method used by the calculator even though we are not aware of it!

The regression line is described, in general, as the straight line with the equation:

$$y = a + bx$$

where x and y are the independent and dependent variables, respectively, a is the intercept on the y-axis, and b the slope of the line. (You may be more familiar with a straight line equation in the form $y = mx + c$, in which c the intercept on the y-axis, and m the slope of the line.)

As with the correlation coefficient, the coefficients a and b of the regression equation can be found directly from the calculator in linear regression mode or calculated (see Section 9.15).

To draw the regression line on the scatter diagram, plot any three points and join them up. The points should be widely spaced on your diagram and in the region of the observed data, so choose one low value of x and one high value of x, substitute them in your equation, and find the corresponding values of y. For any value of x the corresponding value of y can be calculated from the equation. Alternatively, while the data is still in your calculator, inputting any value of x and selecting $\hat{y}$ will produce the corresponding value of y. The centroid $(\overline{x}, \overline{y})$, which can be found directly from your calculator, is often plotted as the third point, but any third point will do.

Example 9.1 continued

Plot the regression line to find the expected values of ice-cream sales for a forecast average temperature.

The values of a and b produced from a calculator in linear regression mode are a = 45.52 and b = 5.448, giving the regression equation when rounded off to three significant figures:

$$y = 45.5 + 5.45x$$

That is the predicted ice cream sales (£'000) are:

45.5 + 5.45 × average monthly temperature (°C)

To draw this line on the scatter diagram, give x a low value and a high value and calculate the corresponding y values, for example:

If x = 5 then y = 45.5 + 5.45 × 5 = 72.8
If x = 15 then y = 45.5 + 5.45 × 15 = 127.3

Alternatively, while the data is still in your calculator, inputting the value of 5 for x and requesting $\hat{y}$ will produce the corresponding value of y, 72.8.

The centroid $(\bar{x}, \bar{y})$ is the point (10.0, 100.0). Plot these three points on your graph and join them with a straight line.

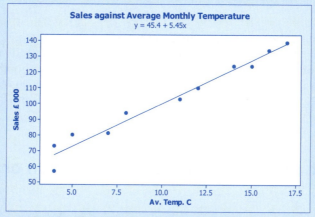

Figure 9.3 Scatter diagram with regression line added (Minitab)

9.4.1 Interpretation of regression equation

The constant, a, is interpreted as the value of the dependent variable, y, if the independent variable, x, is zero: that is, the intercept on the y axis. The gradient, b, can be interpreted as the marginal increase in the dependent variable: that is, the change in the dependent variable, y, per unit change in the independent variable, x. The model is only applicable within the range of the sample data.

Example 9.1 continued

Mathematically we interpret the coefficients of the equation y = 45.5 + 5.45x as:

* For a month during which the average temperature is 0°C we would expect sales of £45,500.
* For every extra 1°C in average monthly temperature we can expect an extra £5450 in sales.

These interpretations do not necessarily apply in real life. An average temperature of 0°C is a most unlikely situation in this country! Also zero is outside the range of the sample data.

9.5 Goodness of fit

How well does the regression line fit the data? Goodness of fit is measured by (r^2 x 100)%. This indicates the percentage of the variation in the dependent variable that is attributed to the variation in the independent variable.

Example 9.1 continued

For the ice-cream data the correlation coefficient, r, was 0.983 so we have a goodness of fit of $(0.983)^2 \times 100 = 96.6\%$ fit. This high value indicates that any predictions made about sales from a value of the average monthly temperature will be very good.

The variation in the average monthly temperature accounts for 96.6% of the variation in sales leaving only 3.4% to be accounted for by other unknown factors.

9.6 Using the regression model for prediction or estimation

All predictions lie on the regression line, so the **regression equation**, the model, is used to calculate their values. Substituting the known or estimated value of the independent variable, x, into the equation allows the calculation of the corresponding dependent value, y.

Sales can also be estimated directly from **your graph** using the regression line. For any given value of x, what is the value on the line of the corresponding value of y?

The corresponding value of y for any value of x can be produced directly from a calculator in linear regression mode by typing in the x value and using $\hat{y}$ to find the estimated value of y.

Example 9.1 continued

The ice-cream manufacturer knows that the estimated average temperature for the following month is 14°C, what would he expect his sales to be?

By substitution:

Estimated sales
      =   45.5 + 5.45 × average temperature
            45.5 + 5.45 × 14
      =   121.8

Expected sales would be £122,000 (only 3 significant figures appropriate for this data)

From the graph:
What is the value on the line of y when the x value is 14?
    You will find that is about 122. The number of significant figures to which you can read the value depends on the scale of your graph.

Using a calculator:
While the original data is still in your calculator, type in 14 and then output $\hat{y}$. This will produce the value of 121.8 giving estimated sales of £122,000.

9.6.1 Precision of predictions

Correlation coefficients can be used directly for comparing the degree of association of bivariate variables provided the sample sizes are the same. The higher the coefficient, the closer the regression points are to the regression line. As we expect the future to reflect the past, any predictions will be good if past data plots are close to the regression line. The goodness of fit is measured by ($r^2 \times 100\%$). This figure is included in the output from regression analysis, as is the standard error of the residuals. The confidence interval describes what is expected to happen on average, and the prediction interval indicates the range of values expected to be taken by individual predictions.

Example 9.1 continued

(This Minitab output has been edited for ease of interpretation)

```
The regression equation is

Sales £ 000 = 45.5 + 5.45 Av. Temp. C

R-Sq = 96.7%    R-Sq(adj) = 96.4%


Predicted Values for New Observations

Av.Temp.C Fit        SE Fit     95% CI                 95% PI
15.0        127.24     2.16       (122.43, 132.05)       (115.03, 139.45)
```

Figure 9.4

The predicted sales for an estimated average temperature of 15°C are £127,240.
On average sales are expected to be between £122,430 and £132,050.
Any individual prediction may be between £115,030 and £139,450.

9.7 Residual analysis

The residual is the difference between the measured value and the predicted value: that is, the value on regression line: **Residual = Sales – Predicted (Fitted) value.**

The sizes of the residuals are a measure of the 'misfit' of the model. In each case the residual is the quantity not accounted for by the regression model. Graphically it is the vertical distance between the plotted point (the actual value) and the regression line (the model value). These residuals therefore need to be small, as is the case when the points on the scatter diagram are all near to the line. They also need to be randomly scattered about zero, with a much smaller standard deviation than that of the dependent variable, normally distributed and random when plotted against the dependent variable.

A package such as Minitab or SPSS is usually employed for residual analysis. If you are not using a computer package, just use 'goodness of fit' ($r^2 \times 100\%$) as a comparative measure of the accuracy of your model. Obviously the higher the goodness of fit value, the better the model.

Example 9.1 continued

Analysis of the residuals from the ice-cream model in Minitab produced the following:

```
          N      MEAN      STDEV
Sales     12     100.00    26.41
RESI1     12     0.00      4.80
```

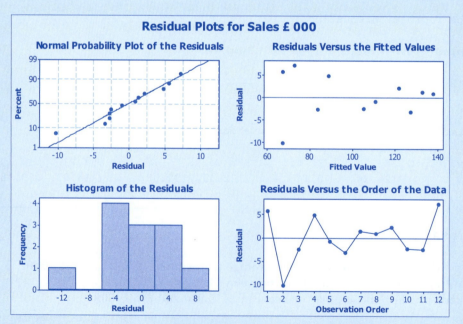

Figure 9.5

We can see that the mean of the residuals is zero and their standard deviation is much smaller than that of the original sales. Also from Figure 9.5 the residuals appear to be approximately normally distributed, random against sales (fitted values), and random in order.

9.8 A continuous example using correlation and regression

Example 9.2

The gross monthly sales volume for a corporation is not subject to substantial seasonal variation. We are interested to see if a relationship exists between sales volume and the amount spent on advertising in the previous months and, if so, how we can use this amount to predict sales.

The data in Table 9.2 represent a sample of advertising expenditures and sales volumes for ten randomly selected months.

Table 9.2

Month	Advertising X (£0'000s)	Sales Volume Y (£0'000s)
1	1.2	101
2	0.8	92
3	1.0	110
4	1.3	120
5	0.7	90
6	0.8	82
7	1.0	93
8	0.6	75
9	0.9	91
10	1.1	105

Scatter plot

Plot a scatter diagram by hand on graph paper. You will see that the result suggests a fairly loose linear relationship. In general the larger the amount spent on advertising the larger the sales volume. See Figure 9.6.

Correlation coefficient

The correlation coefficient, r, from the calculator is 0.8754.
   Testing it for significance:

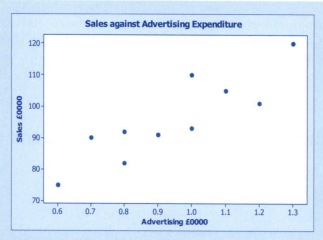

Figure 9.6 Minitab output

H₀: $\rho = 0$. There is no association between advertising expenditure and sales volume.
H₁: $\rho \neq 0$. There is an association between them.

Critical value: 5%, $(10 - 2) = 8$ degrees of freedom $= 0.632$

Test statistic: 0.875

Conclusion: The test statistic exceeds the critical value so we reject the null hypothesis and conclude that there is a significant association between advertising expenditure and sales volume.

Regression equation

From the calculator a = 46.5, b = 52.6, so the regression equation

$$y = 46.5 + 52.5x$$

is calculated from the sample to estimate:

Sales = 46.5 + 52.5 × advertising expenditure (£0'000) for the whole corporation.

Plot the line

To plot the line y = 46.5 + 52.6x on your graph by hand:

Plot the centroid $(\bar{x}, \bar{y})$	(0.94, 95.9)
Plot a point for a low value of x, say x = 0.60.	
y = 46.5 + 52.6 × 0.60 = 78.1	(0.60, 8.06)
Plot a point for a high value of x, say x = 1.30.	
y = 46.5 + 52.6 × 1.30 = 114.9	(1.30, 114.9)

By eye, the regression line shows a reasonable fit. (see Figure 9.7)

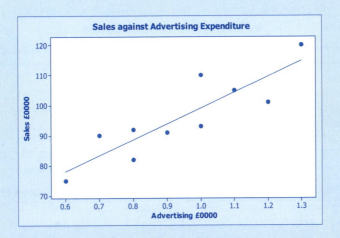

Figure 9.7

Interpretation of coefficients

We need to interpret the coefficients of the equation y = 45.5 + 52.6x.

    If no money were to be spent on advertising we would expect sales to be £455,000. For every extra £10,000 spent on advertising we expect an extra £526,000 in sales – not bad!

Goodness of fit

r = 0.875 gives a goodness of fit measurement of $0.875^2 \times 100 = 76.6\%$

Estimating values

What value would you estimate for the gross monthly sales if you decided to spend £12,000 on advertising in a particular month?

Substitute 1.2 for x in the equation and calculate the corresponding value of y:

y = 46.5 + 52.6x ⇒ y = 46.5 + 52.6 × 1.2 ⇒ y = 109.6

By spending £12,000 on advertising the firm would expect, on average, sales of £1,100,000

Residual analysis

	N	MEAN	STDEV
Sales	10	95.90	13.34
RESI1	10	0.00	6.45

Figure 9.8(a) (Minitab output)

The residuals have a mean of zero, low standard deviation, appear random and normal.

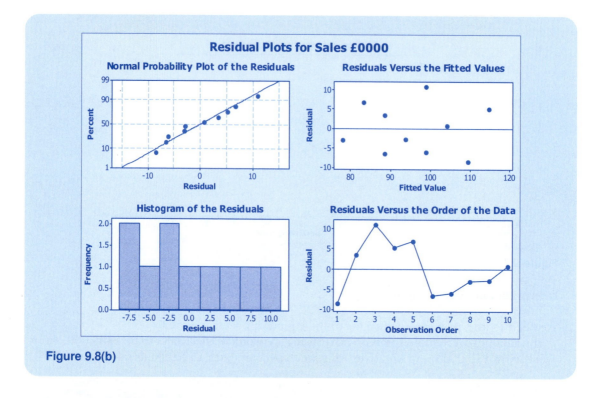

Figure 9.8(b)

9.9 Spearman's rank correlation coefficient

If data are neither interval nor ratio but can be ranked in some manner, such as in qualitative replies to questionnaires, then the use of Spearman's rank correlation coefficient, r_s, is preferable to Pearson's coefficient.

9.9.1 Calculation of Spearman's rank correlation coefficient

The formula for calculating Spearman's rank correlation coefficient is:

$$r_s = 1 - \frac{6\sum d^2}{n(n^2 - 1)} \tag{9.1}$$

where d is the difference in ranking of each pair and n the sample size.

The coefficient is then tested against a table value from the Spearman's rank correlation table (Appendix D Table 7). As for the Pearson's correlation, the amount of correlation is considered to be significant if its value exceeds the table value.

If hypothesis testing (Chapter 7) has been included in your course, then the following test should be carried out. If not just compare the two values. If the test statistic is the larger, the correlation is significant.

9.9.2 Hypothesis test for a Spearman's correlation coefficient

Null hypothesis, H$_0$: $\rho_s = 0$. There is no association (correlation) between the two variables.

Alternative hypothesis, H$_1$: $\rho_s \neq 0$. There is an association (correlation) between them.

Critical value: Spearman's correlation tables (Appendix D Table 7), usually 5 per cent, for n pairs of data points.

Test statistic: the sample correlation coefficient, r$_s$.

Conclusion: compare the test statistic with the critical value.
   If the test statistic is the larger, reject the null hypothesis and conclude that there is significant correlation.
   If it is smaller, accept the null hypothesis that there is no significant correlation present.

This test is not as powerful as the Pearson's test as the original data values are not taken into consideration. However, it is always better to carry out a valid test rather than a more powerful one that is invalid. (See Groebner 1993, Chapter 13 for more detail.)

Example 9.3

An office manager ranked his staff on their understanding of computer technology. He then tested their speed of word processing input, in words per minute, to see if there was any association between these two abilities. The ranked variable indicates that Pearson's correlation coefficient would not be valid so Spearman's will be calculated instead. The results he obtained are in Table 9.3.

Table 9.3

Employee	A	B	C	D	E	F	G	H	I	J
Computer understanding	9	4	6	5	2	1	7	8	3	10
Speed (wpm)	45	85	50	65	80	75	60	50	65	55

In order to carry out Spearman's test both variables have to be ranked. In Table 9.4 the speed is ranked, the differences in ranking calculated and the sum of the squared differences found as required by Equation 9.1. Ties take the average of the ranks involved, signs are ignored.

Table 9.4

Employee	A	B	C	D	E	F	G	H	I	J
Computer understanding	9	4	6	5	2	1	7	8	3	10
Speed (wpm)	45	85	50	65	80	75	60	50	65	55
Ranked speed	10	1	8.5	4.5	2	3	6	8.5	4.5	7
Difference in rankings (d)	1.0	3.0	2.5	0.5	0.0	2.0	1.0	0.5	1.5	3.0
d^2	1.00	9.00	6.25	0.25	4.00	4.00	1.00	0.25	2.25	9.00

Using Equation 9.1 to calculate the test statistic:

$$r_s = 1 - \frac{6 \sum d^2}{n(n^2-1)} \Rightarrow 1 - \frac{6 \times 37}{10 \times 99} = 1 - 0.224 = 0.776$$

Hypothesis test

Null hypothesis, H$_0$: $\rho_s = 0$. There is no association (correlation) between the understanding of computers and speed of word processing input.

Alternative hypothesis, H$_1$: $\rho_s \neq 0$. There is an association (correlation) between them.

Critical value: Spearman's correlation tables (Appendix D Table 7), at 5% significance with 10 pairs of data gives 0.632

Test statistic: the sample correlation coefficient, r_s, gives 0.776

Conclusion: The test statistic is the larger than the critical value so we reject the null hypothesis and conclude that there is significant correlation between understanding of computers and word processing input.

9.10 Further methods and applications of regression

Simple linear regression can be extended in three ways:

- as non-linear regression which deals with 'curved' data, that is, data which cannot be fitted by a straight line
- as multiple regression in which there is more than one independent variable
- as log-linear regression in which categorical variables can be investigated.

Linear regression can also be used in the analysis of a time series, and the resulting model used for forecasting (see Chapter 13).

9.10.1 Non-linear regression

If a scatter plot indicates that a curved line would fit the data better than a straight one, the problem is to decide what function best describes the line. Is it a quadratic or a cubic? Is a logarithmic function better either of these? Fortunately the answer can readily be found in SPSS or Minitab.

Using the non-linear curve fitting facility in SPSS or Minitab a variety of functions can be tried very quickly. The graphs of the functions are plotted from the data so that an assessment of their fit can be made. The goodness of fit can also be compared numerically. By this method it is easy to see which non-linear equation best fits your data.

9.10.2 Multiple regression

It may be preferable to use more than one predictor variable, if available, in predicting the value for the dependent variable. Explaining the behaviour of one dependent variable in terms of several independent variables often produces a much better-fitting model.

The use of a computer is essential for this technique or the mathematics becomes very cumbersome. With the use of Minitab or SPSS any number of predictor variables can be introduced into the equation, the contribution of each to the overall model compared, and the quality of the finally selected model assessed.

9.10.3 Log-linear regression

Log-linear regression is an extension of the two-dimensional contingency table for more than two categorical or ordinal variables, in which frequencies are examined for independence. By taking logs the ratios are converted into a linear combination of the variables so that a model similar to that used in regression can explore the relationships between the original variables. (See Groebner and Shannon 1993, Chapter 14 for more detail.)

9.11 Summary

- We have considered the association between two variables measured on a continuous scale.
- We drew a scatter diagram to check whether the data seems to follow a straight line. If it does not, the correlation methods of analysis used in this chapter are not appropriate.
- We calculated Pearson's correlation coefficient, r, if the variables were measured on an interval scale, or Spearman's correlation coefficient, r_s, if the data were only ordinal.
- We tested the correlation coefficients for significance using hypothesis tests (or just compared the sample correlation coefficient to a table value).
- For interval data with a significant Pearson's correlation coefficient:
  - We carried out regression analysis in order to produce the best-fitting model in the form of a regression equation.
  - We plotted the regression line on the original scatter diagram.
  - We used the regression model in order to estimate the value of the dependent variable, y, for a given value of the independent variable, x.
  - We checked, roughly, how good this estimation was likely to be.
  - We analysed the residuals from the model in order to check that they were random, with smaller standard deviation than the dependent variable, normally distributed, and random when plotted against the dependent variable.
  - We looked briefly of more sophisticated regression methods.

9.12 Computer output for regression – Example 9.1

See Figures 9.9 and 9.10.

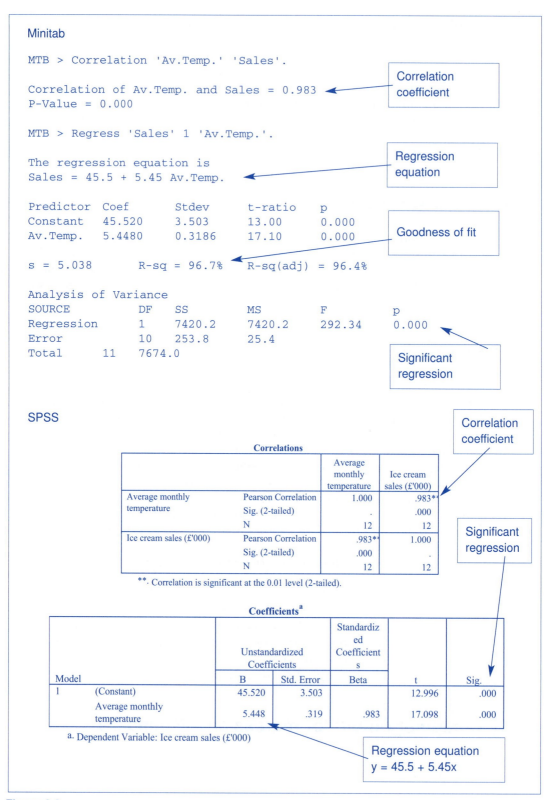

Figure 9.9

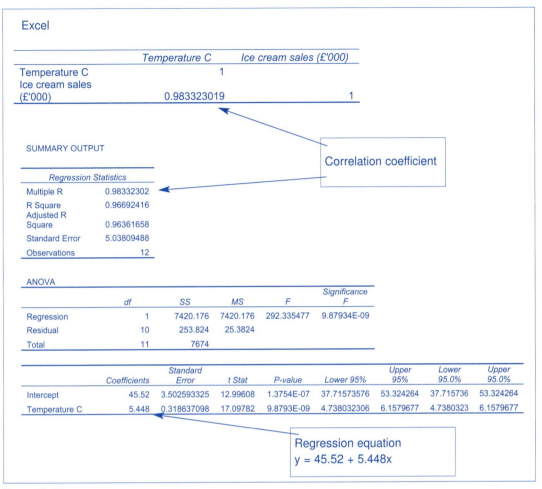

Figure 9.10

9.13 Case study

Your directors are mainly interested in which of the other variables have most effect on (a) the market value and (b) the gross sales of food outlet they might open. They would also like to know how the gross sales affect the market value of the establishment. (Use the file 'Restaurants' in the case study folder in the students' materials on the companion website.)

Ignoring the results of previous normality tests for each of the three types of outlet:

a) Find the Pearson's correlation coefficient between the market value and any other continuous variables you think may influence it. For the most significant association found, calculate the goodness of fit and state the regression equations.
b) Find the Pearson's correlation coefficient between the gross sales and any other continuous variables you think may influence gross sales. For the most significant association found, calculate the goodness of fit and state the regression equations.
c) Find the Pearson's correlation coefficient between the market value and gross sales. If significant, calculate the goodness of fit, the regression equation, and carry out residual analysis.

9.14 Calculator use and practice for regression

Enter the data from datasets 1–4 below as pairs of numbers. Within the many memories of the calculator these numbers and their squares are accumulated, and the correlation coefficient and the values of 'a' and 'b' in the regression equation are then calculated using the formulae as shown in the notation in Sections 9.15.1 and 9.15.2 from these stored sums.

You need a statistical calculator working in regression mode. The characteristics of your model determine the method of entering the pairwise data and outputting the results of the analysis carried out by the calculator. All the required instructions will be in the calculator handbook. The output you will need to produce should include: r, A, B, $\hat{x}$, $\hat{y}$, $\bar{x}$, $\bar{y}$.

1. Clear all memories.
2. Enter linear regression mode.
3. Input variables x and y for each case using one of the data sets below. Repeat to end of data.
4. Check number of pairs entered.
5. Output correlation coefficient (r).
6. Output intercept (A) and slope (B) of regression line.
7. Output $\hat{y}$ value for plotting line when x is given value within the data range.
8. Output the coordinates of the centroid: $\bar{x}$, $\bar{y}$.
9. Estimate the dependent value for the independent value = 8.

9.14.1 Practice

For each of the sets of numbers following, calculate:

- the value of the correlation coefficient
- the regression equation
- the value of y when x = 8

1	x	3	5	4	7	8	6	9	10	12
	y	5	6	9	8	11	13	14	16	19
2	x	15	13	9	10	7	6	4	5	3
	y	7	7	9	9	11	15	14	13	18
3	x	4	5	4	7	6	6	10	5	2
	y	5	6	7	8	4	8	9	6	7
4	x	7	4	4	10	11	8	7	9	14
	y	10	6	9	15	9	12	13	15	20

Answers	1	r = 0.898	y = 1.03 +1.43x	12.5
	2	r = −0.922	y = 18.3 − 0.858x	11.4
	3	r = 0.470	y = 4.86 + 0.331x	7.51
	4	r = 0.781	y = 3.77 + 1.01x	11.9

9.15 Use of formulae for calculating correlation and regression coefficients

9.15.1 Pearson's product moment correlation coefficient

The value of the correlation coefficient, r, is best produced directly from a calculator in linear regression mode. Otherwise the following calculations are necessary:

The formula used to find the Pearson's product moment correlation coefficient is: (least squares method)

$$r = \frac{S_{xy}}{\sqrt{S_{xx}S_{yy}}} \qquad \left(-1 \leq r \leq +1\right) \tag{9.2}$$

where

$$S_{xx} = \sum x^2 - \frac{\sum x \sum x}{n}$$

$$S_{yy} = \sum y^2 - \frac{\sum y \sum y}{n}$$

$$S_{xy} = \sum xy - \frac{\sum x \sum y}{n}$$

where Σx means the sum of all the x values, and so on.

9.15.2 Regression equation

As with the correlation coefficient, the regression equation can be produced directly from a calculator in linear regression mode. Otherwise further use is made of the values of Σx, Σy, Σx^2, Σy^2, Σxy, n (all produced previously).

The **regression line** is described, in general, as the straight line with the equation:

y = a + bx

where **x** and **y** are the independent and dependent variables respectively, **a** the intercept on the y-axis, and **b** the slope of the line.

The **gradient, b**, is calculated from :

$$b = \frac{S_{xy}}{S_{xx}} \quad \text{where} \quad S_{xy} = \sum xy - \frac{\sum x \sum y}{n} \quad \text{and} \quad S_{xx} = \sum x^2 - \frac{\sum x \sum x}{n} \tag{9.3}$$

Since the regression line passes through the centroid, both means, its equation can be used to find the **value of a**, the intercept on the y-axis:

$$a = \bar{y} - b\bar{x}$$

Example 9.3

The data in this example is the same as Example 9.1.

Ice-cream sales per month against mean monthly temperature (Celsius) are shown in Table 9.5. The sums of columns, are also calculated.

Table 9.5

Month	Average temp. (x)	Ice cream sales (y)	x^2	y^2	xy
Jan	4	73	16	5329	292
Feb	4	57	16	3249	228
Mar	7	81	49	6561	567
Apr	8	94	64	8836	752
May	12	110	144	12100	1320
Jun	15	124	225	15376	1860
Jul	16	134	256	17956	2144
Aug	17	139	289	19321	2363
Sep	14	124	196	15376	1736
Oct	11	103	121	10609	1133
Nov	7	81	49	6561	567
Dec	5	80	25	6400	400
Sums	120	1200	1450	127674	13362

Correlation coefficient

$$\sum x = 120, \quad \sum y = 1200, \quad \sum x^2 = 1450, \quad \sum y^2 = 127674, \quad \sum xy = 13362, \quad n = 12.$$

$$S_{xx} = 1450 - \frac{120 \times 120}{12} = 250$$

$$S_{yy} = 127674 - \frac{1200 \times 1200}{12} = 7674 \qquad r = \frac{1362}{\sqrt{250 \times 7674}} = 0.9833$$

$$S_{xy} = 13362 - \frac{120 \times 1200}{12} = 1362$$

r = 0.983

From previously: (Sales now assumed to be dependent on temperature)

$$S_{xy} = 1362 \quad S_{xx} = 250 \quad so \quad b = \frac{1362}{250} = 5.448 \qquad a = \frac{1200}{12} - 5.448 \times \frac{120}{12} = 45.52$$

The values of a and b are therefore 45.5 and 5.45 respectively, giving the regression line:

y = 45.5 + 5.45x

Tutorial 9: correlation and regression

Answers are in Appendix A.

9.1 A small retail business has determined that the correlation coefficient between monthly expenses and profits for the past year, as measured at the end of each month, is r = 0.56. Assuming that both expenses and profits are approximately normally distributed, test at the 5% (0.05) level of significance the null hypothesis that there is no correlation between them.

9.2 Plot a scatter diagram and calculate the correlation coefficient for the following data.

Firm	Annual % increase in advertising expenditure	Annual % increase in sales revenue
A	1	1
B	3	2
C	4	2
D	6	4
E	8	6
F	9	8
G	11	8
H	14	9

If appropriate find the least squares regression line, plot it on your graph and use it to estimate the increase in sales revenue expected from an increase in advertising of 7.5%.

9.3 The following data relates to the annual sales of petrol (in gallons) of eight garages and their expenditure on coupons that they give away to customers.

Expenditure on coupons (£'000)	Sales of petrol (0'000 galls)
15	35
5	40
25	30
30	45
20	40
40	50
50	25
55	55

a) Plot a scatter diagram. (First decide which variable is independent.)
b) Calculate the correlation coefficient and see whether it is significantly high.
c) If appropriate find the least squares regression line.

d) Calculate percentage goodness of fit.

e) If appropriate estimate the sales of petrol if £25,000 is spent on coupons.

9.4 A training manager wondered whether the length of time his trainees revised for an examination had any effect on the marks they scored in the examination.

Before the exam, he asked a random sample of them to estimate honestly how long, to the nearest hour, they had spent revising. After the examination he investigated the relationship between the two variables.

Trainee	A	B	C	D	E	F	G	H	I	J
Revision time	4	9	10	14	4	7	12	22	1	17
Exam mark	31	58	65	73	37	44	60	91	21	84

a) Plot the scatter diagram in order to inspect the data.

b) Calculate the correlation coefficient and test it for significance.

c) If significant calculate the regression model to fit the data and interpret its coefficients.

d) Plot the regression line on the scatter diagram.

e) Calculate the percentage goodness of fit.

f) Predict the examination mark for a trainee who revises for 15 hours.

g) Predict the examination mark for a trainee who revises for 35 hours.

h) Do you have any reservations about your answer to (g)?

9.5 In an effort to determine the relationship between annual wages, in £'000, for employees and the number of days absent from work because of sickness, a large corporation studied the personnel records for a random sample of 12 employees. The paired data are provided below:

Employee	Annual wages (£'000)	Days missed
1	25.7	4
2	27.2	3
3	23.8	6
4	34.2	5
5	25.0	3
6	22.7	12
7	23.8	5
8	28.7	1
9	20.8	12
10	21.8	11
11	35.4	2
12	27.2	4

Determine the correlation coefficient and test to see whether the number of days missed is related to annual wages, at the 5 per cent level of significance. If it is, find the regression equation for predicting the number of likely absence in days. Interpret its coefficients and use it to predict the likely absence of an employee earning £25,000.

9.6 The turnover and profit levels of ten companies in a particular industry are shown below (in £ million).

Company	A	B	C	D	E	F	G	H	I	J
Turnover	30.0	25.5	6.7	45.2	10.5	16.7	20.5	21.4	8.3	70.5
Profit	3.0	2.8	1.1	5.3	0.6	2.1	2.1	2.4	0.9	7.1

Test whether the variables are significantly correlated at the 1 per cent level.

If they are correlated, calculate the regression line for predicting expected profit from turnover and explain the coefficients of your equation.

Notes

For SPSS/ Minitab/ Excel worksheets on correlation and regression see Chapter 14, Sections 14.2.5, 14.5.5 and 14.8.5 respectively. Worksheets with computer output and its interpretation are on the companion website.

The supplementary exercise for Chapter 9, with answers, is on the companion website.

Contingency tables and chi-square tests

10

Objectives of this chapter

In Chapter 9 we looked for association between measurements on two continuous variables. We calculated the correlation coefficient between the two variables and then tested it to see if there was a significant association between them.

In this chapter we shall again look for association but now between categorical variables. The calculations are based on the frequencies in the cells of a cross-tabulation, as in Chapter 4 on probability. This is a very useful technique as it deals with the type of bivariate data often collected from questionnaires for which correlation is not appropriate as the data are often only categorical or, at best, ordinal.

Having completed this chapter you will be able to:

- construct cross-tabulations from given information
- test to see if a significant association exists between the two variables
- revise some of the previous work on probability.

10.1 Introduction

In this type of analysis we have two characteristics, such as gender and eye colour, which cannot be measured but which can be used to group people by variations within them. These characteristics may be associated in some way or they may be completely independent of each other. How can we decide?

We can take a random sample from the population, note which variation of each characteristic is appropriate for each case and then cross-tabulate the data. It is then analysed in order to see if the proportions of each characteristic in the sub-samples are the same as the overall proportions – easier to do than to describe! As an example if there is no relationship between gender and eye colour we would expect similar proportions of males and females to have blue eyes.

The variables are usually nominal, (described by name only) and the frequencies may be cross-tabulated by each category within the variable. Ordinal variables may be used if there are only a limited number of orders so that each order can be classified as a separate category. Continuous variables may be grouped and then tabulated similarly, although the results will then vary according to the grouping categories and useful information may be lost.

10.2 Contingency tables (cross-tabs)

You have met this type of table before as a contingency table when calculating probabilities. Cases are allotted to categories and their frequencies cross-tabulated. In the gender and eye colour example there might be blue-eyed males, blue-eyed females, brown-eyed males, brown-eyed females. These tables are known as contingency tables. All possible 'contingencies' are included in the 'cells' which are themselves mutually exclusive. The table is completed by calculating the row totals, the column totals and the grand total.

An on-going example will be used to illustrate each stage of the process.

Example 10.1

Table 10.1 was compiled by a personnel manager. It relates to a random sample of 180 staff taken from the whole workforce of the supermarket chain. We shall test for association between a member of staff's gender and his/her type of job, at the 5% level of significance.

Table 10.1

	Male	Female
Supervisor	20	15
Shelf stacker	20	30
Till operator	10	35
Cleaner	10	40

Cross tabulated data

Completing the row and column totals, as with the work on probability, gives the full table.

Table 10.2

	Male	Female	Total
Supervisor	20	15	35
Shelf stacker	20	30	50
Till operator	10	35	45
Cleaner	10	40	50
Total	60	120	180

10.3 Chi-square (X^2) test for independence

The hypothesis test which is carried out in order to see if there is any association between categorical variables, such as gender and eye colour, is known as the chi-square (X^2) test.

10.3.1 Expected values

If the two variables are completely independent, the proportions within the subtotals of the contingency table would be expected to be the same as those of the group totals for each variable. In practice we work with frequencies rather than proportions, distinguishing between observed and expected frequencies by putting the expected frequencies in brackets. If gender and eye colour are independent and if one-third of the population has blue eyes, we would expect one-third of males to be blue-eyed and one-third of females to be blue-eyed.

These proportions are obviously contrived so as to be easy to work with. How can we cope with more awkward numbers? In Example 10.1 the proportions are first calculated as fractions which are then multiplied by the total frequency to find the expected individual cell frequencies. This produces a formula which is applicable in all cases.

For any cell the expected frequency is calculated by:

$$\frac{\text{Row total} \times \text{Column total}}{\text{Overall total}}$$

where the relevant row and column are those crossing in that particular cell.

If the expected frequencies are observed to occur then we can deduce that the two variables are indeed independent. In practice we would obviously not expect to get exact agreement between the observed and the expected frequencies. Some critical amount of difference is allowed and we compare the difference from our observations with that allowed by the use of a standard table. Are the values observed so different from those expected that we must reject the idea of independence? Are the results just due to sampling errors, with the variables actually being independent? You should recognise the need for a hypothesis test!

Example 10.1 continued

We randomly selected a sample of 180 supermarket staff and found that 120 of them were female and 60 male, that is, two-thirds are female, one-third were male. Assuming there is no association between gender and job category and finding that we have 45 till operators, we would expect two-thirds (30) of them to be female and one-third (15) of them to be male.

Note that these figures are one-quarter of the total of each gender respectively, which checks because till operators (45) form one-quarter of the total staff of 180.

We could calculate the other **expected frequencies** from the probabilities and put them into the table: (see Section 4.7)

- P (Supervisor) = 35/180
- P (Male)   = 60/180
- P (Supervisor and male) = 35/180 × 60/180   assuming independence.

Therefore the expected **number** of male supervisors is

$$\frac{35}{180} \times \frac{60}{180} \times 180 = 11.67$$

This is the expected frequency for members of staff who are both male and a supervisor. Note that it is a theoretical number and does not have to be an integer. Alternatively the expected frequency is:

$$\frac{\text{Row total} \times \text{Column total}}{\text{Overall total}}, \quad \frac{35 \times 60}{180} = 11.67$$

Calculate the other expected frequencies and insert them in the table (in brackets):

Table 10.3

	Male	Female	Total
Supervisor	20 (11.67)	15 (23.33)	35
Shelf stacker	20 (16.67)	30 (33.33)	50
Till operator	10 (15.00)	35 (30.00)	45
Cleaner	10 (16.67)	40 (33.33)	50
Total	60	120	180

These are the frequencies which would be expected if there is no association between gender and job category at the supermarket. (Note: they sum to the same total.)

10.3.2 The chi-square (X^2) hypothesis test

To find the answer, we analyse the data and compare the result to a standard table figure. We carry out a formal hypothesis test at 5 per cent significance: the **chi-square test**.

10.3.2.1 Method

1) State null hypothesis (that of no association) and alternative hypothesis.
2) Record observed frequencies, O, in each cell of the contingency table.
3) Calculate row, column and grand totals.
4) Calculate expected frequency, E, for each cell:

$$E = \frac{\text{row total} \times \text{column total}}{\text{grand total}}$$

Note that: The test is invalid if any expected frequency is less than 1 and the number of expected frequencies below 5 is more than 20 per cent of the total number of cells.
5) Find critical value from chi-square table (Appendix D Table 5) with (r–1) x (c–1) degrees of freedom where r and c are the number of rows and columns respectively.
6) Calculate the test statistic:

$$\sum \frac{(O-E)^2}{E}$$

7) Compare the two values and conclude whether the variables are independent or not.

In Example 10.1, we have already carried out steps 2, 3 and 4 of the procedure by calculating the expected values. Whether these are calculated before, or during, the test depends on personal preference. Some statisticians also prefer to calculate the test statistic before starting the test and to then insert the calculated value in the formal hypothesis test.

The test statistic is an overall measure of the difference between the expected and observed frequencies. Each cell difference is squared so that positive and negative differences do not cancel out and are in proportion to the size of the expected cell contents. When the contributions from each cell are totalled their sum is compared with a critical value from the chi-square table. (See continuation of Example 10.1.)

Example 10.1 continued

Step 1 State both hypotheses

Null hypothesis (H_0): There is **no association** between gender and job category. (Remember that 'null' means none.)

Alternative hypothesis (H_1): There is an association between gender and job category.

Steps 2, 3 and 4 See Section 10.3.2.1.
Step 5 Find the critical value from the chi-square table

Number of degrees of freedom $(v) = (r - 1)(c - 1) = (4 - 1)(2 - 1) = 3 \times 1 = 3$
Level of significance = 5%
X^2 table, Appendix D Table 5 is always one-tailed as squares exclude the possibility of negative values.

Critical value: $X^2_{5\%, v=3} = 7.816$

Step 6 Calculate the test statistic, the X^2 value.
The test statistic is calculated from the contingency table, Table 10.3, which includes both the observed and the expected values for the frequency of staff. The data may be tabulated, as in Table 10.4, or the contribution of each cell may be calculated directly and then the test statistic found as the sum of these contributions:

$$\text{Test statistic} = \sum \frac{(O - E)^2}{E}$$

The observed and expected frequencies for each cell are transferred from Table 10.3 and used to complete Table 10.4.

Table 10.4

O	E	(O – E)	(O – E)²/E
20	11.67	8.33	5.946
15	23.33	−8.33	2.974
20	16.67	3.33	0.665
30	33.33	−3.33	0.333
10	15.00	−5.00	1.667
35	30.00	5.00	0.833
10	16.67	−6.67	2.669
40	33.33	6.67	1.335
Total			16.422

Statistic: 16.422

Conclusion: test statistic > critical value therefore reject H_0. We conclude that there is an association between gender and job category in the supermarket chain.

Looking again at the data (Table 10.3) we can see that far more males than expected were supervisors or shelf stackers and more females were cleaners or till operators.

10.4 Chi-square (X^2) test for independence – 2 by 2 tables

With only four cells the general method is the same as for larger tables but more error is involved unless we correct for it – Yate's correction.

When using the X^2 tables you may have noticed from the diagram that it represents a continuous distribution. But the data we are testing are categorical. This is an obvious source of error but fortunately it is not really serious unless we only have one degree of freedom, as in a 2×2 table.

For a 2×2 table we apply the **Yate's correction** in which each absolute difference between observed and expected values is reduced by 0.5. This smoothes out the 'stepped' effect of the discrete data. The formula for calculating the test statistic therefore becomes:

$$\sum \frac{\left(|O - E| - 0.5\right)^2}{E}$$

indicating that we subtract 0.5 from the absolute value of the difference before squaring. There is no problem with dropping the negative sign as the result is squared.

Otherwise the method is the same as used in Example 10.1.

Example 10.2

A small firm is investigating car ownership among its workforce. Are male employees more likely to own a car than female employees? In response to a questionnaire the following frequencies were observed.

Table 10.5

Gender\car ownership	Own a car	Do not own a car
Male	45	16
Female	60	34

We shall carry out a chi-square test, using a Yate's correction, to see if car ownership is associated with gender.

Completing the table and calculating the expected values:

Table 10.6

Gender\car ownership	Own a car	Do not own a car	Total
Male	48 (41.3)	13 (19.7)	61
Female	57 (63.7)	37 (30.3)	94
Total	105	50	155

For the first cell the expected value, $E = \dfrac{61 \times 105}{155} = 41.3$

As the expected values add up to the same total as the observed values for each row and column, all the other cells can be found by difference, hence the **one degree of freedom.**

For the second cell $E = 61 - 41.3 = 19.7$
For the third cell $E = 105 - 41.3 = 63.7$
For the fourth cell $E = 94 - 63.7 = 30.3$ or $E = 50 - 19.7 = 30.3$

We shall first transfer the observed and expected frequencies from Table 10.6, then calculate the test statistic and then use it in the formal hypothesis test.

Example 10.2 continued

Test statistic: $\sum \dfrac{\left(|O-E|-0.5\right)^2}{E}$

Table 10.7

O	E	$(|O-E|-0.5)$	$(|O-E|-0.5)^2/E$
48	41.3	6.2	0.931
13	19.7	6.2	1.951
57	63.7	6.2	0.603
37	30.3	6.2	1.269
Total			4.754

Hypothesis test

Null hypothesis (H_0): There is no association between gender and car ownership.
Alternative hypothesis (H_1): There is an association between gender and car ownership.
Level of significance: 5% level of significance.
Critical value:
Number of degrees of freedom $(v) = (r-1)(c-1) = (2-1)(2-1) = 1 \times 1 = 1$
Level of significance = 5%
C2 table (Table D5) is one-tailed only for this test.
$\quad X^2_{5\%,v=1} = 3.842$

Test statistic: 4.754 (from Table 10.7)
Conclusion: test statistic > critical value therefore reject H_0.
Conclude that there is an association between gender and car ownership in this firm.
    Looking again at the data (Table 10.6), we see that more males and fewer females than expected had a car.

10.5 Chi-square test for goodness of fit

If a particular distribution is hypothesised for a population then a chi-square test, with $(n-1)$ degrees of freedom, can be carried out to investigate whether or not the sample data could have come from a population with the hypothesised distribution. The observed values come from the sample and the expected values from the theoretical hypothesised distribution. The expected values are calculated by multiplying the sample size by the appropriate probability value from the statistical table to which the sample is being compared.

    The sample data are most easily explored in a computer package, such as SPSS, which can test them against any of the main distributions. Example 10.3 illustrates the method by comparing results from a single die to the uniform distribution which the data would follow if the die was a fair one.

Example 10.3

We wish to find our whether a die is fair or not. We throw the die 120 times and record the results. They are as follows:

Number shown on face	1	2	3	4	5	6
Frequency	20	10	10	20	20	40

If the die is unbiased the expected frequencies would be:

Number shown on face	1	2	3	4	5	6
Frequency	20	20	20	20	20	20

H_0: The die is fair: that is, not biased. H_1: The die is not fair: that is, it is biased.

Critical value: Chi-square tables, 5%, $n - 1 = 5$ degrees of freedom, Critical value = 11.07.

Test statistic: $\sum \dfrac{(O - E)^2}{E}$

Table 10.8

Value	Observed	Expected	O – E	(O – E)²/E
1	20	20	0	0
2	10	20	−10	5
3	10	20	−10	5
4	20	20	0	0
5	20	20	0	0
6	40	20	+20	20
Total				30

The value of the test statistic is therefore 30.
Conclusion: The test statistic exceeds the critical value so we reject H_0 and conclude that the die is biased.

10.6 A continuous chi-square test for independence

Example 10.4

In a recent survey within a supermarket chain, a random sample of 160 employees – stackers, sales staff and administrators – were asked to grade their attitude towards future wage restraint on the scale: very favourable; favourable; unfavourable; very unfavourable.

  Of the 40 stackers interviewed, 7 gave the response 'favourable', 24 the response 'unfavourable', and 8 the response 'very unfavourable'. There were 56 sales staff and from these, 10 responded 'very unfavourable', 9 responded 'favourable' and 3 responded 'very favourable'. The rest of the sample were administrators. Of these, 16 gave the response

Example 10.4 continued

'very favourable' and 2 gave the response 'very unfavourable'. In the whole survey, exactly half the employees interviewed responded 'unfavourable'.

We first draw up a contingency table showing these results and then test whether attitude towards future wage restraint is dependent on the type of employment.

Setting up the table

There are three types of employee giving four different responses, that is, we have a 3×4 (or a 4×3) table. Adding extra rows and columns for the subtotals and titles we need 5×6 cells.

Cover up Table 10.9 and have a go at compiling it for yourself. As you come to each number in the frequency of response above insert it into the appropriate cell. Find the missing figures by difference. There is sufficient information here to enable you to complete your table. When complete, check it against Table 10.9.

Table 10.9

	Very favourable	Favourable	Unfavourable	Very unfavourable	Total
Stackers	1	7	24	8	40
Sales staff	3	9	34	10	56
Administrators	16	24	22	2	64
Total	20	40	80	20	160

The expected values can next be calculated: $\dfrac{\text{Row total} \times \text{Column total}}{\text{Overall total}}$ and inserted into the table.

Table 10.10

	Very favourable		Favourable		Unfavourable		Very unfavourable		Total
Stackers	1	(5)	7	(10)	24	(20)	8	(5)	40
Sales staff	3	(7)	9	(14)	34	(28)	10	(7)	56
Administrators	16	(8)	24	(16)	22	(32)	2	(8)	64
Total	20		40		80		20		160

Hypothesis test

Null hypothesis (H_0): There is **no association** between job category and attitude towards wage restraint.

Alternative hypothesis (H_1): There is an association between job category and attitude towards wage restraint.

Level of significance: 5% level of significance

Critical value:

Number of degrees of freedom $(v) = (r - 1)(c - 1) = (3 - 1)(4 - 1) = 2 \times 3 = 6$

Level of significance = 5%

X^2 table (Table D5), 5%, 6 degrees of freedom = 12.59

Test statistic:

$$\sum \frac{(O - E)^2}{E}$$

Example 10.4 continued

Table 10.11

O	E	(O – E)	(O – E)²/E
1	5	–4	3.200
7	10	–3	0.900
24	20	+4	0.800
8	5	+3	1.800
3	7	–4	2.286
9	14	–5	1.786
34	28	+6	1.286
10	7	+3	1.286
16	8	+8	8.000
24	16	+8	4.000
22	32	–10	3.125
2	8	–6	4.500
Total			32.969

Test statistic: 32.969

Conclusion: test statistic > critical value therefore reject H_0.

Conclude that there is an association between job category and attitude towards future wage restraint. The administrators were in favour but the others were against it. (See Table 10.10.)

10.7 Further analysis of categorical data

If a chi-square test shows the presence of significant association between two variables, the researcher will probably wish to investigate further and find out more precisely which groups within the variables are the main source of the association.

One easy way of doing this is to look at the contribution each cell makes to the test statistic. The higher the contribution the stronger the association. A more formal method which permits testing sections of the table is partitioning. This involves the construction of a series of 2 x 2 subtables, one for each degree of freedom. Each sub-table is tested for significance.

If only a limited amount of data is available, it may be found that some of the expected values are too small for the chi-square test to be valid. Remember that no expected frequency should be less than 1 and the number of expected frequencies below 5 should not exceed 20 per cent of the total frequencies. If these conditions are infringed it is often possible to combine rows or columns in a meaningful way to increase cell contents, but this approach should only be used if the combinations are still sensible. The Fisher exact probability test is useful for small samples in 2 x 2 tables.

If the categories of each variable are ordered, concordance can be tested using Kendal's tau, or some other ordinal measure, instead of a chi-square value as the critical value.

Cross-tabulated categorical data can be displayed graphically by means of simple correspondence analysis for two variables and multiple correspondence analysis (optimal scaling) for two or more. This is best done by a computer package, such as SPSS or Minitab. The degree of association between two categories, one from each variable, is illustrated by their closeness in the correspondence diagram.

10.8 Summary

In this chapter we have considered categorical data with frequencies measured on subsets within two variables. This is the type of data which is very often collected in surveys and which cannot be analysed by many of the previous methods used in this course which require interval or ratio data.

The data were generally presented in cross-tabulated format and were then analysed by the following procedure in order to test for the independence of the two variables:

- present the data in a cross-table
- complete the table with row and column totals
- calculate the frequencies expected for each cell under the null hypothesis of independence
- state the null hypothesis of independence and the alternative hypothesis of association for a chi-square test
- find the critical value from the chi-square table with $(r - 1)(c - 1)$ degrees of freedom
- calculate the test statistic from the formula $\sum \dfrac{(O - E)^2}{E}$
- compare the two values and conclude whether the variables are independent or not
- if a significant association is found, inspect the data to find its main source.

This method of testing is not only very useful but it is easy to carry out in practice. During some part of your course you are quite likely to investigate a topic of interest by carrying out a small survey. Along with the graphical presentation (Chapter 2) chi-square tests should be the main tool for analysis (Weimer 1993, Chapter 12).

10.9 Computer output for chi-square tests – Example 10.1

Minitab and SPSS output are shown as Figure 10.1 and 10.2.

Excel

Excel will produce a chi-square test but you have to do most of the work yourself as you need to calculate the row totals, column totals and all the expected values for the individual cells using the spreadsheet functions. Only then will Excel carry out the test!

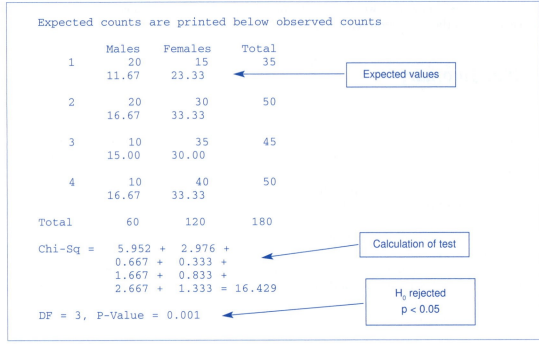

Figure 10.1 Minitab output

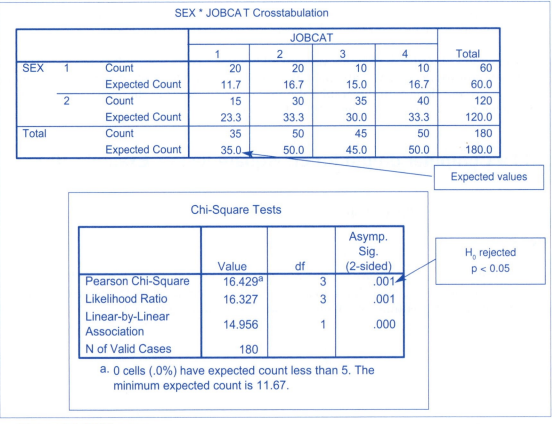

Figure 10.2 SPSS output

10.10 Case study

Your directors are interested in how owners of the different types of existing food outlets feel about the future.

Carry out a chi-square test to see if there is any association between business outlook and:

- type of outlet
- type of ownership
- size of establishment.

Tutorial 10: Chi-square test

The answers to all tutorial questions are to be found in Appendix A.

10.1 Purchases of different strengths of lager are thought to be associated with the gender of the drinker and a brewery has commissioned a survey to find out if this is true. A summary of the results is shown below:

	Strength		
	High	Medium	Low
Male	20	50	30
Female	10	55	35

Are gender and lager preference associated at 5% significance?

10.2 A firm is testing a new brand of coffee in three regions and wishes to see if the demand is regionalised. The demand at a random sample of 200 shops in each of the regions can be classified as high, medium or low and the results are summarised below. Test at 1% level whether or not there is a relationship between demand and region.

		Demand	
Region	High	Medium	Low
North	105	55	40
South	120	47	33
Midlands	125	38	37

10.3 The respondents of a survey were classified by magazine read and income as follows:

	Annual income (£)		
Magazine read	under 20,000	20,000 and under 40,000	40,000 and over
A	21	36	30
B	48	26	19

Test the hypothesis that the magazine read is independent of level of income using a 5% level of significance.

10.4 The management at Head Office wants to know how its employees feel about working conditions, particularly whether there are differences of opinion between various departments.

Conditions	A	Department B	C	D
Good	65	112	85	80
Average	27	67	60	44
Poor	8	21	15	16

Random samples are taken from each of the four departments with the above results. Do these data indicate that such differences of opinion exist at 5% significance?

10.5 During times of business decline and recession many suggestions are offered to spur the economy into a turnaround. A survey was conducted among 100 business executives, 100 economists and 100 government officials to find the opinion of each regarding the best way of reversing the trend of business decline. Their responses are tabulated below. Do these data represent sufficient evidence to assume that opinion regarding the best way to spur the economy into a turnaround during times of recession differs among business executives, economists and government officials? Test at a 1% significance level.

Opinion	Business executives	Economists	Government officials
Increase government spending	10	15	39
Cut personal income taxes	37	37	33
Decrease interest rates	24	34	15
Offer tax incentives to business	29	14	13
Total	100	100	100

Notes

For SPSS/Minitab/Excel worksheets see examples at the end of Worksheets 14.2.4 , 14.5.4 , and 14.8.4 respectively. Worksheets with computer output and its interpretation are on the companion website.

The supplementary exercise for Chapter 10, with answers, is on the companion website.

Index numbers

11

Objectives of this chapter

Chapters 1 to 5 were concerned with describing data – descriptive statistics. Chapters 6 to 10 have involved the use of the analytical results from a sample, with a variety of techniques, to infer the value for some unknown information about the population – inferential statistics.

In this chapter we start the final section which deals with changes over time – **time series**. We know that most values change with time and so we need some method of quantifying this change. We also need some method of comparing values at different times and comparing changes of two or more different items at different times. In order to compare relative changes over time we make use of **index numbers**. Your company knows that its sales are growing but how does this growth compare with that of its competitors, the industry as a whole or the Retail Price Index (RPI)?

Having completed this chapter you should:

- understand the relative importance of changes over time
- be able to compute indices to measure these changes
- be able to use an index to compare the values of different goods in different industries over time.

The main index we shall use for comparison will be the (RPI) so you should also:

- gain some understanding of how the RPI is computed and its general importance in business and economics.

11.1 Introduction: measuring changes over time

In business, managers and other decision makers may be concerned with the way in which the values of most variables change over time: prices paid for raw materials, numbers of employees and customers, annual income and profits, and so on. **Index numbers** are one way of describing such changes.

Index numbers were originally developed by economists for monitoring and comparing different groups of goods. It is necessary in business to understand and manipulate the different published index series, and be able to construct index series of your own. Once you have constructed your own index, it can then be compared to a national one (such as the RPI), a similar index for your industry as a whole, or to indices for your competitors. These comparisons are a very useful tool in decision making in business.

For example, an accountant of a supermarket chain could construct an index of the company's own sales and compare it to the index of the volume of sales for the general supermarket industry. A graph of the two indices, such as Figure 11.1, can illustrate the company's performance within the sector.

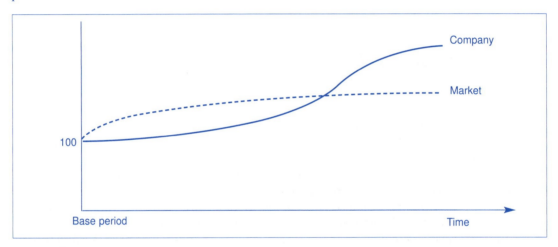

Figure 11.1 Two indices

It is immediately clear from Figure 11.1 that, after initially lagging behind the general market, the supermarket company caught up and then overtook it. In the later stages the company was having better results than the general market but, as with the whole industry, these were levelling out.

11.2 Index numbers

Index numbers can be used to describe the changes to any quantity over time. The measurements may be of industrial production, commodity prices, share prices, employment figures, and so on. They may refer to the whole world, the UK, or just your own company. Think of them as a mathematical tool for applying to any changes over time which may describe absolutely anything. In this chapter we will be mainly concerned with either prices or quantities or a combination of both.

An essential requirement is that index numbers measure the changing value of a variable over time in relation to its value at some fixed point in time, the **base period**, when the index is given the value of 100. They have no units because they are ratios and are always expressed as percentages.

Indices may be based at any convenient period, which is occasionally adjusted, and they are published with any convenient frequency such as:

Yearly   Gross National Product (GNP)
Monthly   Unemployment figures
Daily   Stock market prices.

11.2.1 Price indices

One of the most important uses of indices is to show how the price of a product **changes over time** due to changing costs of raw materials, variable supply and demand, changes in production processes, general inflation and so on. It is often of interest to compare an index to the RPI or to indices of competitors' prices.

Quantification of these changes, which are beyond the control of the producing company, may need some type of response and so form an essential part of the decision-making process. An increase in the price of raw materials may require a decision about selling prices; a change in supply may need the contracting of an additional source with a corresponding price adjustment; a change in demand may necessitate price adjustments so that the company can remain competitive, and so on.

11.2.2 The Retail Price Index – the RPI

Each month the government publishes a variety of indices that are designed to help us understand prevailing business and economic conditions. The most widely known of these is the **Retail Price Index (RPI).** This is the measure of inflation which is reported in the media and which influences all our lives. It is the measure used to revise social security and pension payments, forms the basis of many wage claims, and governs the increases in any payments or pensions which are 'index linked'.

The RPI is based on the amount spent by a typical household on a range of goods and services. Currently, around 120,000 separate price quotations are used every month in compiling the index, covering some 650 representative consumer goods and services for which prices are collected in around 150 areas throughout the UK. The relative importance of these goods and services is updated annually using weightings produced by the Central Statistical Office, mainly from the 'Family Expenditure Survey', which collects information on the spending habits of approximately 6500 households per year. Items and weights to be included are updated in February each year. For example, in February 2005 laptop computers and pre-pay mobile phones were included for the first time.

11.2.3 Quantity indices

Quantity indices are treated in exactly the same way as price indices but, as the name suggests, they are concerned with quantities and assume that prices remain the same or are of no relevance. We are used to seeing the index of unemployment figures regularly in the media, whether seasonally adjusted or not. A company, or industry, will be interested in changes in the quantity of goods produced from year to year. A country is concerned with its Gross National Product (GNP) which describes the annual total value of goods and services produced.

11.3 Simple indices

We first have to decide on the base period and then find the ratio of the value at any subsequent period to the value in that base period, the **price relative**. This ratio is then finally converted to a percentage.

Index for any time period, n $= \dfrac{\text{value in period n}}{\text{value in base period}} \times 100$

Example 11.1

The retail price of a particular model of car for the previous five years has been:

Year	1	2	3	4	5
Price (£)	12,380	12,490	12,730	13,145	13,750

Using Year 1 as the **base year** we can compare all the other prices to the value of £12,380 in that year.

Year 2: $\dfrac{12{,}490}{12{,}380} \times 100 = 100.9$ Year 3: $\dfrac{12{,}730}{12{,}380} \times 100 = 102.8$ and so on.

Year	1	2	3	4	5
Price (£)	12,380	12,490	12,730	13,145	13,750
Index	100.0	100.9	102.8	106.2	111.1

If we used Year 5 as the **base year** we would compare all the other prices to the value of £13,750 in that year.

Year 1: $\dfrac{12{,}380}{13{,}750} \times 100 = 90.0$ Year 2: $\dfrac{12{,}490}{13{,}750} \times 100 = 90.8$ and so on.

Year	1	2	3	4	5
Price (£)	12,380	12,490	12,730	13,145	13,750
Index	90.0	90.8	92.6	95.6	100.0

Alternatively if a series of index numbers is known and we know the price or quantity described by one of them the complete series of prices can be calculated. The price or quantity for an unknown period is found by just scaling up, or down, in the same ratio as the relevant index numbers.

11.4 Calculating changes

One essential use to which index numbers are put is that of monitoring changes over time. These changes may be calculated as **percentage point changes**, which can be misleading as the value depends on whether the two periods of measurement are near to the base year or not, or as **percentage changes** in which the change does not depend on which year is the base year.

Example 11.2

Table 11.1 shows the monthly price index for an item:

Month	1	2	3	4	5	6	7	8	9	10	11	12
Index	121	112	98	81	63	57	89	109	131	147	132	126

If the price in month 3 is £240, what is the price in month 8?

The index numbers for months 8 and 3 are 109 and 98 respectively so the value of £240 for month 3 needs scaling up by the ratio of 109:98 for month 8.

Price in month 3 is £240 $\Rightarrow$ Price in month 8 is £240 $\times \dfrac{109}{98} = 266.94$

If the price in month 7 is £218, what is the price in month 2?

Price in month 7 is £218 $\Rightarrow$ Price in month 2 is £228 $\times \dfrac{112}{89} = 274.34$

Filling in the table and giving the results to the nearest pound gives:

Month	1	2	3	4	5	6	7	8	9	10	11	12
Index	121	112	98	81	63	57	89	109	131	147	132	126
Price (£)	296	274	240	198	154	140	218	267	320	360	323	309

11.4.1 Percentage point change

The percentage point change is simply the difference between the index values for consecutive time periods. If the series is near the base period, when the index numbers are in the low hundreds, the changes will be small. If, on the other hand, the index is high and nearly due for rebasing, the numbers may be approaching 400 or 500 and the changes will appear comparatively large. These percentage point changes are therefore not comparable over time.

Example 11.3

Using the figures from Example 11.2 again, what are the percentage point changes between the consecutive months?

Month	1	2	3	4	5	6	7	8	9	10	11	12
Index	121	112	98	81	63	57	89	109	131	147	132	126

A simple subtraction provides these figures, negative for decrease, positive for increase:

Month	1	2	3	4	5	6	7	8	9	10	11	12
Index	121	112	98	81	63	57	89	109	131	147	132	126
% Point change		−9	−14	−17	−18	−6	+32	+20	+22	+16	−15	−6

11.4.2 Percentage change

Percentage changes are calculated by the usual percentage method of finding the ratio of the change to the previous value and multiplying by 100.

Example 11.4

Using the figures from Example 11.2 again, what are the percentage changes between the consecutive months?

Table 11.2

Month	1	2	3	4	5	6	7	8	9	10	11	12
Index	121	112	98	81	63	57	89	109	131	147	132	126

The points change is divided by the index it has come from and multiplied by 100 in same method as used for finding any percentage change.

For month 2: $\dfrac{112 - 121}{121} \times 100 = -7.4$ For month 9: $\dfrac{131 - 109}{109} \times 100 = -20.2$

Table 11.3

Month	1	2	3	4	5	6	7	8	9	10	11	12
Index	121	112	98	81	63	57	89	109	131	147	132	126
% change		−7.4	−12.5	−17.3	−22.2	−9.5	56.1	22.5	20.2	12.2	−10.2	−4.5

These values will be the same whether the index is near the base year or not; that is, they will not be affected by a change in the base period.

11.5 Changing the base period

The base period can be chosen as any convenient time. It is usual to update the base period fairly regularly to avoid:

- any significant change which makes comparison with earlier figures meaningless
- the numbers growing so large that a points change is many times a percentage change.

At one time, for political reasons, the method of measuring employment kept changing so a series across changes would not compare like with like. Just after rebasing, a change of 5 index points would equal a 5 per cent change. If the index was around the 250 level it would only equal 2.5% and if around the 500 level only 1%. An employment increase of 5% sounds much better than the 1%! Economic figures appear more stable after rebasing.

The Retail Price Index was last rebased January 13th 1987 when its value was 385.9. At the end of 2005 it stood at 194.1 so it will probably not be rebased again in the near future.

We need therefore to know how to change a base period. Published index numbers may include a sudden change, such as a series 470, 478, 485 becoming series 100, 103, 105, and so on. We need to convert one set of numbers so that they both have a common base year and can be analysed as a whole, continuous series. This is sometimes known as 'splicing' the two indices.

In order to change from one index series to another we need the value in the first series for the same period as that in which the rebasing to 100 for the second takes place. The ratio of these two values forms the basis of any conversion between them.

Example 11.5

The amount spent on advertising by a supermarket is index linked and is described by the following indices in Table 11.4.

Table 11.4

Year	1	2	3	4	5	6	7	8
Index 1	100	138	162	196	220			
Index 2					100	125	140	165

Typically each index series is completed and then, if we have, say, the advertising expenditure for any one year, we can use the figure to calculate that for any of the other years. First identify the base year for each series. Remember that in its base year the value of an index is 100.

Base year for each index: Index 1 = Year 1   Index 2 = Year 5
Both values known for year 5
From year 5: ratio of old : new = 220 : 100   (Note: All new values will be smaller)
From year 5: ratio of new : old = 100 : 220   (Note: All old values will be bigger)
These ratios will be applied when converting from 'old' to 'new' and vice versa.

Completing the table for Index 1 and Index 2:

Index 1: Old index = New index $\times \dfrac{220}{100}$

For year 6: Old index = $125 \times \dfrac{220}{100} = 275.0$ Year 7: Old index = $140 \times \dfrac{220}{100} = 308.0$

Index 2: New index = Old index $\times \dfrac{100}{220}$

For year 1: New index = $100 \times \dfrac{100}{220} = 45.5$ Year 2: New index = $138 \times \dfrac{100}{220} = 62.7$

Completing both index series and checking that each is adjusted in the right direction:

Table 11.5

Year	1	2	3	4	5	6	7	8
Index 1	100	138	162	196	220	275.0	308.0	363.0
Index 2	45.5	62.7	73.6	89.1	100	125	140	165

Advertising expenditure can be calculated for all years if that for any one year is known by multiplying its value by the ratio of the relevant index numbers from either series (see Table 11.6).

Table 11.6

Given that advertising expenditure was known to be £4860 in year 3, that for:

Year 1 $= 4860 \times \dfrac{100}{162} = 3000$ or $4860 \times \dfrac{45.45}{73.64} = 3000$

Year 2 $= 4860 \times \dfrac{138}{162} = 4140$ or $4860 \times \dfrac{62.73}{73.64} = 4140$ etc.

Year	1	2	3	4	5	6	7	8
Index 1	100	138	162	196	220	275	308	363
Index 2	45.5	62.7	73.6	89.1	100	125	140	165
Advert (£)	3000	4140	4860	5880	6600	8250	9240	10890

11.6 Comparing time series

A company knows that its sales are rising year by year but so too are those of its main competitor, which is a smaller company. How can the progress of the two companies be compared? An index for each company is produced with the same base year and the two indices compared.

Example 11.6

The sales, in £ million, of two companies over eight years are given in Table 11.7. Company B is smaller than Company A.

Table 11.7

Year	1	2	3	4	5	6	7	8
Company A	123.2	134.8	145.2	153.4	162.9	169.3	171.2	187.1
Company B	5.7	6.2	6.9	7.3	8.9	9.5	9.9	10.6

It is obvious that both companies are increasing their sales, but which one is doing better? A comparison can be made by calculating an index series for both companies with the same base year, in this example Year 1.

$$\text{Year 2}\quad\text{Company A:}\quad 100 \times \frac{134.8}{123.2} = 109.4 \quad\quad \text{Company B:}\quad 100 \times \frac{6.2}{5.7} = 108.8$$

Table 11.8

Year	1	2	3	4	5	6	7	8
Company A	123.2	134.8	145.2	153.4	162.9	169.3	171.2	187.1
Index A	100	109.4	117.9	124.5	132.2	137.4	139.0	151.9
Company B	5.7	6.2	6.9	7.3	8.9	9.5	9.9	10.6
Index B	100	108.8	121.2	128.1	156.1	166.7	173.7	186.0

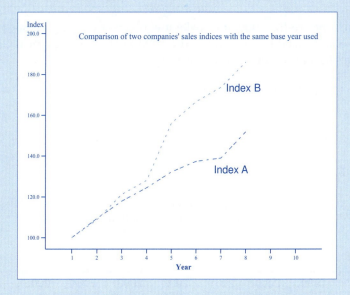

Figure 11.2

The smaller company, B, is doing comparatively better than the larger company, A.

11.7 Deflating an index

An index may be deflated to remove the effect of inflation over the long term. Workers expect their earnings to increase over their working lifetime due to promotions, annual increments, and cost of living rises. But has the purchasing power of their salaries increased? On the other hand, a company would like to keep its overall salary bill from rising, in real terms, even though individuals are earning more. This should be possible since, in general, high earners are retiring and lower earners are joining the workforce. How can they check?

The Retail Price Index is often used to compute real changes in earnings or expenditure as it compares the purchasing power of money at different points in time. It is generally accepted as a standard measure of inflation even though calculated from a restricted 'basket of goods'.

Example 11.7

Table 11.9 shows Tom's earnings, in £'000, between 1999 and 2005; the total wages bill for his company, in £million, and the published RPI figures for the same years.

Table 11.9

Years	1999	2000	2001	2002	2003	2004	2005
Tom's earnings	15.3	16.1	16.9	18.0	20.9	21.4	21.9
Total wages bill	5.41	5.62	5.83	6.04	6.25	6.46	6.67
RPI	165.4	170.3	173.3	176.2	181.3	186.7	192.0

In order to deflate a figure for 2000 and make it equivalent to the corresponding figure for 1999 it must be multiplied by the ratio of the 1999 to 2000 figures for the RPI.

In 2000, the purchasing power of Tom's earnings , in 1999 terms, is:

$$16.1 \times \frac{165.4}{170.3} = 15.64, \text{ that is, £15,640}$$

In 2000 the total salary bill for the company, in 1999 terms, is

$$5.62 \times \frac{165.4}{170.3} = 5.46, \text{ that is, £5,460,000}$$

Both these values are more in real terms than the actual 1999 values so real increases have taken place. If all the subsequent values are similarly deflated we get:

Table 11.10

Years	1999	2000	2001	2002	2003	2004	2005
Tom's earnings	15.30	15.64	16.13	16.90	19.07	18.96	18.87
Total wages bill	5.41	5.46	5.56	5.67	5.70	5.72	5.75

Tom's earnings rose steadily, in real terms, until 2003 when he got a substantial rise. Had he been promoted? After that the purchasing power of his earnings declined.

The total wages bill also rose steadily but in decreasing amounts until it levelled out.

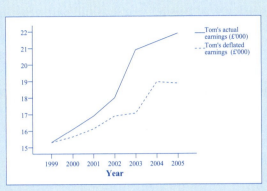 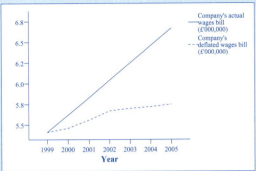

Figure 11.3

Tom's earnings in real terms were unfortunately actually decreasing, instead of rising, in recent years but the company's total wage bill has indeed levelled out as it hoped.

11.8 Simple aggregate indices

A simple aggregate is not a realistic approach to including more than one item in an index. For example, you would get some idea of the total price of a shopping basket by adding up all the unit costs of the items, but this assumes that you purchase exactly one of each. This is an unrealistic assumption for a household's weekly shopping outlay. If, however, the aim of the exercise is to compare prices from year to year then it is quite justified.

11.8.1 Aggregate price index

The relevant prices are summed year by year and the resulting sums treated as price relatives. Any variations in corresponding quantities (1 kg or 10 kg) and units (cost per g or cost per kg) are ignored.

Example 11.8

A company buys four items at the prices in Table 11.11.

Table 11.11

| Items | Price paid per unit | | |
	Year 1	Year 2	Year 3
A	10	11	13
B	23	25	26
C	17	17	18
D	19	20	23

Find the simple aggregate price index number for year 2 using year 1 as the base year:

$$\frac{\text{Sum of prices in Year 2}}{\text{Sum of prices in base year}} = \frac{11 + 25 + 17 + 20}{10 + 23 + 17 + 19} = \frac{73}{69} \times 100 = 105.8$$

Find the simple aggregate price index number for year 3 using year 1 as the base year:

$$\frac{\text{Sum of prices in Year 3}}{\text{Sum of prices in base year}} = \frac{13 + 26 + 18 + 23}{10 + 23 + 17 + 19} = \frac{80}{69} \times 100 = 115.9$$

11.8.2 Aggregate quantity index

The relevant quantities are summed year by year and the resulting sums treated as a single index. Any variations in corresponding price (£ or p) are ignored.

Example 11.9

A company buys the following quantities of four items:

Table 11.12

Items	Number of units bought Year 1	Year 2	Year 3
A	20	24	26
B	55	51	53
C	63	84	86
D	28	34	37

Find the **simple aggregate quantity index** number for year 2 using year 1 as the base year:

$$\frac{\text{Sum of quantities in Year 2}}{\text{Sum of quantities in base year}} = \frac{24 + 51 + 84 + 34}{20 + 55 + 63 + 28} = \frac{193}{166} \times 100 = 116.3$$

Find the **simple aggregate quantity index** number for year 3 using year 1 as the base year:

$$\frac{\text{Sum of quantities in Year 3}}{\text{Sum of quantities in base year}} = \frac{26 + 53 + 86 + 37}{20 + 55 + 63 + 28} = \frac{202}{166} \times 100 = 121.7$$

11.9 Weighted aggregate indices

Neither the simple aggregate price index nor the simple aggregate quantity index is completely realistic as both prices and quantities will vary. Some combination of both price and quantity variation is therefore needed. This is achieved by weighting the prices by their corresponding quantities. But which weights are to be used? Three variations will be described below:

- **Laspeyre index** which uses weights from the base year.
- **Paasche index** which uses weights from the current year.
- **Fisher index** is the geometric mean of Laspeyre's and Paasche's indices.

Because quantities as well as prices tend to rise in our consumer-based society, the base weights tend to underestimate reality and the current weights tend to overestimate it. Hence the Laspeyre index tends to overestimate changes and the Paasche index to underestimate them. It seems reasonable to suggest that reality lies somewhere between the two indices. Fisher has suggested that this is best described by the geometric mean of the other two:

$$\text{Fisher's index} = \sqrt{\text{Laspeyre's index} \times \text{Paasche's index}}$$

We shall look at all three indices combining the simple prices and quantities used in Examples 11.8 and 11.9.

11.9.1 The Laspeyre base-weighted index

This index compares prices from a current year to those of a base year with both being weighted by the quantities bought in the base year.

Example 11.10

A company buys four products with the following characteristics.

Table 11.13

Items	Number of units bought			Price paid per unit		
	Year 1	Year 2	Year 3	Year 1	Year 2	Year 3
A	20	24	26	10	11	13
B	55	51	53	23	25	26
C	63	84	86	17	17	18
D	28	34	37	19	20	23

Find the **base-weighted aggregate index, Laspeyre's index**, for year 2 using year 1 as the base year.

$$\text{Index for year 2} = \frac{\Sigma(\text{prices in year 2} \times \text{weights in base year})}{\Sigma(\text{prices in base year} \times \text{weights in base year})}$$

$$= \frac{11 \times 20 + 25 \times 55 + 17 \times 63 + 20 \times 28}{10 \times 20 + 23 \times 55 + 17 \times 63 + 19 \times 28} = \frac{3226}{3068} \times 100 = 105.1$$

Find the **base-weighted aggregate index, Laspeyre's index**, for year 3 using year 1 as the base year.

$$\text{Index for year 3} = \frac{\Sigma(\text{prices in year 3} \times \text{weights in base year})}{\Sigma(\text{prices in base year} \times \text{weights in base year})}$$

$$= \frac{13 \times 20 + 26 \times 55 + 18 \times 63 + 23 \times 28}{10 \times 20 + 23 \times 55 + 17 \times 63 + 19 \times 28} = \frac{3468}{3068} \times 100 = 113.0$$

11.9.2 The Paasche current-weighted index

This index compares prices from a current year to those of a base year with both being weighted by the quantities bought in the current year.

Example 11.11

A company buys four products with the following characteristics:

Table 11.14	Number of units bought			Price paid per unit		
Items	Year 1	Year 2	Year 3	Year 1	Year 2	Year 3
A	20	24	26	10	11	13
B	55	51	53	23	25	26
C	63	84	86	17	17	18
D	28	34	37	19	20	23

Find the **current period-weighted aggregate index, Paasche index**, for year 2 as current year using year 1 as the base year.

$$\text{Index for year 2} = \frac{\Sigma(\text{prices in current year} \times \text{weights in current year})}{\Sigma(\text{prices in Year 1} \times \text{weights in current year})}$$

$$= \frac{11 \times 24 + 25 \times 51 + 17 \times 84 + 20 \times 34}{10 \times 24 + 23 \times 51 + 17 \times 84 + 19 \times 23} = \frac{3647}{3487} \times 100 = 104.6$$

Find the **current period-weighted aggregate index, Paasche index**, for year 3 as current year using year 1 as the base year.

$$\text{Index for year 3} = \frac{\Sigma(\text{prices in current year} \times \text{weights in current year})}{\Sigma(\text{prices in Year 1} \times \text{weights in current year})}$$

$$= \frac{13 \times 26 + 26 \times 53 + 18 \times 86 + 23 \times 37}{10 \times 26 + 23 \times 53 + 17 \times 86 + 19 \times 37} = \frac{4115}{3644} \times 100 = 112.9$$

11.9.3 The Fisher index

The Laspeyre and the Paasche indices for these data are fairly close, with the former being higher than the latter, as expected. The Fisher index will now combine them.

Example 11.12

Fisher's index for year 2	=	$\sqrt{\text{Laspeyre's index} \times \text{Paasche's index}}$
	=	$\sqrt{105.1 \times 104.6} = 104.8$
Fisher's index for year 3	=	$\sqrt{\text{Laspeyre's index} \times \text{Paasche's index}}$
	=	$\sqrt{113.0 \times 112.9} = 112.9$ (4 sig. figs)

The type of aggregate index chosen is decided by the relative importance placed on the weightings by economic experts.

11.10 A continuous example using index numbers

In this example we will consider some data describing the salaries in a company, working through the different types of index number manipulations.

Example 11.13

The data in Table 11.15 describe the average salaries (£000) for the workers in a company over eight consecutive years. (The time of rebasing of the RPI (1987) is the reason for the choice of years.)

Table 11.15

Year	1982	1983	1984	1985	1986	1987	1988	1989	1990	1991
Average salary	10.9	11.4	12.0	12.7	13.6	14.4	15.0	15.5	16.3	17.6

a) Calculate an index for these average salaries using 1986 as the base year

$$1982: \frac{10.9}{13.6} \times 100 = 80.1 \qquad 1983: \frac{11.4}{13.6} \times 100 = 83.8 \text{ and so on.}$$

Table 11.16

Year	1982	1983	1984	1985	1986	1987	1988	1989	1990	1991
Index number	80.1	83.8	88.2	93.4	100	105.9	110.3	114.0	119.9	129.4

b) Calculate the percentage points change between consecutive years
This is found as the change in the index numbers themselves.

Table 11.17

Year	1982	1983	1984	1985	1986	1987	1988	1989	1990	1991
Index number	80.1	83.8	88.2	93.4	100	105.9	110.3	114.0	119.9	129.4
% point change		3.7	4.4	5.2	6.6	5.9	4.4	3.7	5.9	9.5

c) Calculate the percentage change between consecutive years
This is calculated as the change divided over the earlier value as a percentage.

Table 11.18

Year	1982	1983	1984	1985	1986	1987	1988	1989	1990	1991
Index number	80.1	83.8	88.2	93.4	100	105.9	110.3	114.0	119.9	129.4
% change		4.6	5.3	5.9	7.1	5.9	4.2	3.4	5.2	7.9

The RPI was rebased in January 1987 giving an average index for the year of 101.9. This is equivalent to 1987 in the salary index so we need to rebase the RPI figures for the earlier years in order to compare our whole range of salaries with the RPI.

d) Complete both indices and plot on the same diagram

Table 11.19

Year	1982	1983	1984	1985	1986	1987	1988	1989	1990	1991
Old RPI	320.4	335.1	351.8	373.2	385.9	394.5				
New RPI						101.9	106.9	115.2	126.1	133.5

Old index for 1988 $= 106.9 \times \dfrac{394.5}{101.9} = 413.8$; for 1989 $= 115.2 \times \dfrac{394.5}{101.9} = 446.0$

New index for 1986 $= 385.9 \times \dfrac{101.9}{394.5} = 99.7$; for 1985 $= 373.2 \times \dfrac{101.9}{394.5} = 96.4$

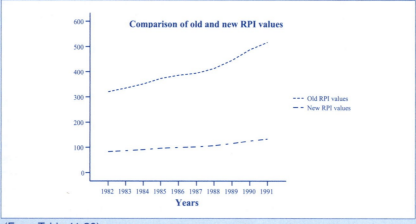

Figure 11.4 (From Table 11.20)

Table 11.20

Year	1982	1983	1984	1985	1986	1987	1988	1989	1990	1991
Old index	320.4	335.1	351.8	373.2	385.9	394.5	413.8	446.0	488.2	516.9
New index	82.8	86.6	90.9	96.4	99.7	101.9	106.9	115.2	126.1	133.5

You can see why the old index number was rebased. The new one gives a better impression of economic stability, even though they both describe the same situation.

e) How has the average salary fared compared with the RPI?
The indexed average salary is taken from Table 11.16 and the RPI from Table 11.20. Note that both are rebased at the same time, 1986/7; the RPI approximately.

Table 11.21

Year	1982	1983	1984	1985	1986	1987	1988	1989	1990	1991
Average salary	80.1	83.8	88.2	93.4	100	105.9	110.3	114.0	119.9	129.4
RPI	82.8	86.6	90.9	96.4	99.7	101.9	106.9	115.2	126.1	133.5

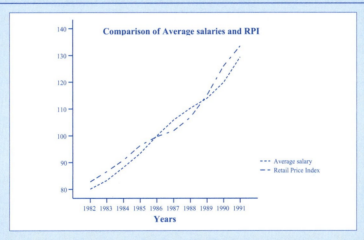

Figure 11.5

The average salaries have generally kept step with the RPI, using 1986 as the base year. If we next look at the percentage increases, a clearer picture may emerge.

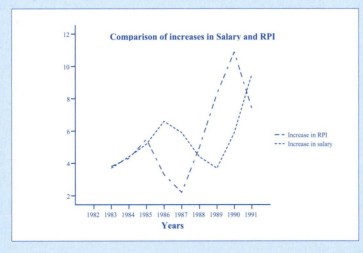

Figure 11.6

It becomes clearer from Figure 11.6 that the salary increases were keeping step with the RPI but were lagging one year behind, as might be expected if the management were responding to union claims following the published figures.

f) Deflate the salaries index by the RPI to see how the workers were faring in real terms, starting from 1982

$$1983: 11.4 \times \frac{82.8}{86.6} = 10.9 \quad 1984: 12.0 \times \frac{82.8}{90.9} = 10.9$$

Table 11.22

Year	1982	1983	1984	1985	1986	1987	1988	1989	1990	1991
Average salary	10.9	11.4	12.0	12.7	13.6	14.4	15.0	15.5	16.3	17.6
RPI	82.8	86.6	90.9	96.4	99.7	101.9	106.9	115.2	126.1	133.5
Deflated av. sal.	10.9	10.9	10.9	10.9	11.3	11.7	11.6	11.2	10.7	10.9

In real terms the average salaries had remained the same for the first few years, then they had risen over two years and finally settled back to their original purchasing value.

Table 11.23 gives the average salaries of different types of employees in your company and the numbers of each employed.

Table 11.23

	Average salary (£'000) Years				Number of employees Years			
	1	2	3	4	1	2	3	4
Administrative	27.2	28.9	31.8	33.0	35	42	53	63
Clerical	12.9	13.7	14.6	15.2	25	19	16	14
Manual	18.9	19.6	20.1	21.0	123	130	127	125
Security	15.0	16.0	17.1	17.9	5	4	6	7
Maintenance	11.5	12.3	13.1	14.0	23	26	24	21

g) Calculate the simple aggregate indices for both average salaries and number of employees, using year 1 as the base year

Sum up the totals for each year and then rebase them to year 1. (This is not valid for average saleries but illustrates the method.)

Table 11.24

	Average salary (£'000) Years				Number of employees Years			
	1	2	3	4	1	2	3	4
Administrative	27.2	28.9	31.8	33.0	35	42	53	63
Clerical	12.9	13.7	14.6	15.2	25	19	16	14
Manual	18.9	19.6	20.1	21.0	123	130	127	125
Security	15.0	16.0	17.1	17.9	5	4	6	7
Maintenance	11.5	12.3	13.1	14.0	23	26	24	21
Totals	85.5	90.5	96.7	101.1	211	221	226	230
Rebased	100	105.8	113.1	118.2	100	104.7	107.1	109.0

Index for average salaries is:

Table 11.25

Year	1	2	3	4
Index	100.0	105.8	113.1	118.2

Index for number of employees is:

Table 11.26

Year	1	2	3	4
Index	100.0	104.7	107.1	109.0

h) **Calculate the Laspeyre index for the average salaries for years 2, 3 and 4. Remember the base year is the same, year 1, giving the weights for each.**

Table 11.27

	Average salary (£'000) Years				Number of employees Years			
	1	2	3	4	1	2	3	4
Administrative	27.2	28.9	31.8	33.0	35	42	53	63
Clerical	12.9	13.7	14.6	15.2	25	19	16	14
Manual	18.9	19.6	20.1	21.0	123	130	127	125
Security	15.0	16.0	17.1	17.9	5	4	6	7
Maintenance	11.5	12.3	13.1	14.0	23	26	24	21

Year 2:
$$\frac{28.9 \times 35 + 13.7 \times 25 + 19.6 \times 123 + 16.0 \times 5 + 12.3 \times 23}{27.2 \times 35 + 12.9 \times 25 + 18.9 \times 123 + 15.0 \times 5 + 11.5 \times 23} = \frac{4127.7}{3938.7} = 104.8$$

Year 3:
$$\frac{31.8 \times 35 + 14.6 \times 25 + 20.1 \times 123 + 17.1 \times 5 + 13.1 \times 23}{27.2 \times 35 + 12.9 \times 25 + 18.9 \times 123 + 15.0 \times 5 + 11.5 \times 23} = \frac{4337.1}{3938.7} = 110.1$$

Year	2	3	4
Laspeyre index	104.8	110.1	115.0

i) **Calculate the Paasche index for the average salaries for years 2, 3 and 4. Remember the current year changes for each calculation.**

Year 2:
$$\frac{28.9 \times 42 + 13.7 \times 19 + 19.6 \times 130 + 16.0 \times 4 + 12.3 \times 26}{27.2 \times 42 + 12.9 \times 19 + 18.9 \times 130 + 15.0 \times 4 + 11.5 \times 26} = \frac{4405.9}{4203.5} = 104.8$$

Year 3:
$$\frac{31.8 \times 53 + 14.6 \times 16 + 20.1 \times 127 + 17.1 \times 6 + 13.1 \times 24}{27.2 \times 53 + 12.9 \times 16 + 18.9 \times 127 + 15.0 \times 6 + 11.5 \times 24} = \frac{4888.7}{4414.3} = 110.7$$

Year	2	3	4
Paasche index	104.8	110.7	115.9

j)   Calculate the Fisher index for Years 2, 3 and 4

Year 2: $\sqrt{104.8 \times 104.8} = 104.8$;   Year 3: $\sqrt{110.1 \times 110.7} = 110.4$

Year	2	3	4
Fisher index	104.8	110.4	115.4

11.11 Summary

In this chapter we have made use of index numbers to describe how the price, or quantity, of items varies over time. Their use provides a method of comparing characteristics at different points in time. We have seen that the numbers generally rise with time and so are periodically rebased to 100 so that they remain reasonably stable. We looked in some detail at the Retail Price Index (RPI), its construction and use.

From the index numbers themselves we have calculated and monitored changes. We then compared changes in, say, salaries with standard indices such as the RPI to see how they were changing in real terms.

We calculated simple aggregate and weighted aggregate indices which are used more often than simple ones in the world of business.

After studying Chapter 11 you should have the confidence to make use of the many tables of time-related data in government and other publications.

11.12 Case study

The case study does not include any time-related data so is not appropriate for the use of index numbers.

For that reason it is suggested that, at this stage, you take time to summarise the results of your previous case study exercises so that you are able to present them to the directors of Restful Restaurants plc. A formal report is not necessary. They are not asking you specifically for recommendations, but any points you would like to highlight will be appreciated by them.

Tutorial 11: index numbers

Answers are in Appendix A.
11.1 The retail price of a typical undergraduate text book over a period of four years is listed below:

Year	2003	2004	2005	2006
Price	£14.50	£15.25	£15.95	£16.40

a) Find the price index based on 2003 prices.

b) Find the percentage points change between consecutive years (base year = 2003).

c) Find the percentage increase between consecutive years.

11.2 A car showroom is giving a special offer on one type of car. The advertised price of this car in four consecutive quarters was £10,450, £10,800, £11,450 and £9,999.

a) Find the price index based on the first quarter's price.

b) Find the price index based on the final quarter's price.

c) What are the quarterly changes in (b) in terms of percentage points based on the last quarter?

d) What are the quarterly changes in terms of percentages?

11.3 The annual output of a company is described by the following indices:

Year	1	2	3	4	5	6	7	8
Index 1	100	125	153	167				
Index 2				100	109	125	140	165

a) Complete Index 1 and Index 2 for years 1 to 8.

b) If the factory made 23,850 units in year 1, how many did it make in each of the other years?

c) What was the percentage increase in output each year?

11.4 The following are two sets of retail prices of a typical student's shopping basket. The items were on sale in a London supermarket during the autumn of 2004 and 2006:

Item	2004 price	2006 price
1 pizza	£2.09	£2.59
1 loaf	£0.69	£1.00
1 pint of milk	£0.35	£0.48
Four-pack of lager	£2.65	£2.40
500g apples	£0.45	£0.67

Calculate the simple aggregate price index for 2006 using 2004 as the base year.

11.5 A company buys four products with the following characteristics (year 1 = base year):

	Number of units bought		Price paid per unit	
Items	Year 1	Year 2	Year 1	Year 2
A	121	141	9	10
B	149	163	21	23
C	173	182	26	23
D	194	203	31	33

a) Calculate the simple price aggregate for year 2 based on year 1.

b) Calculate the base-weighted price aggregate for year 2.

c) Calculate the current-weighted price aggregate for year 2.

11.6 Six companies from within the UK were selected at random from a directory of graduate employers. The following are the graduate and non-graduate earnings in 2005 from these companies; each employee has been in the company between two and three years.

Location	Graduate earning	Non-graduate earning
Company 1	£28,000	£23,500
Company 2	£34,000	£25,000
Company 3	£24,500	£28,800
Company 4	£56,000	£40,000
Company 5	£29,000	£24,000
Company 6	£32,000	£26,000

a) Find the simple aggregate index to compare graduate and non-graduate salaries in 2005.
b) What percentage more did the graduates get over the non-graduates?
c) What percentage less did the non-graduates get than the graduates?

Notes

The supplementary exercise for Chapter 11, with answers, is on the companion website.

Time series

12

Objectives of this chapter

A **time series** is simply a list of values measuring a single item such as sales, prices or quantities at regular intervals over time. In Chapter 11 we used time series in the form of index numbers to investigate changes over time. The main interest was in past time periods and the main objective comparison of different series.

In this chapter we again study the past but with the main purpose of identifying patterns in past events which can be used, in Chapter 13, to forecast future values and events.

Ideally we make use of computer packages to identify past patterns, or lack of them, and then fit the best possible model to the past data. This model will then be used in Chapter 13 to forecast values in the near future.

By the end of this chapter you should be able to:

- plot a time series of data
- identify the type of model likely to produce the best fit
- establish its formula, if appropriate, with the help of a computer package
- decompose any seasonal pattern present
- establish the goodness of fit of the model by analysing its residuals.

12.1 Introduction: inspection of a time series

There are many standard methods used in forecasting, as we shall see in Chapter 13. They all, however, follow the principle of finding the best model to fit the past time series of data and then using the same model to forecast future values.

The best method to use in any circumstance depends on the form taken by the past data so it seems reasonable to plot that data as the first step. The past values are plotted against the time periods as in a **scatter diagram**. This is often called a 'sequence diagram'. Inspection of the plotted data should give some indication of which type of model, or models, might be the most suitable to apply. The selected models can then be fitted, by a computer package such as SPSS or Minitab, which will be used to illustrate the methods in this chapter. More than one model is generally produced and the best of these selected by comparing how well each fits the data. In Chapter 13 the best fitting models for each set of data will be used for forecasting purposes.

Time series of past data ⇒ Suitable method ⇒ Best fitting model ⇒ Forecast

If the plotted data appear to follow a **linear pattern** on the sequence diagram then **linear regression** is a suitable model to use with the regular time periods, t, being used as the independent variable. The time periods should be regularly spaced but any missing values can be accommodated by adjusting the value of t in the following time periods.

Table 12.1 shows three typical patterns exhibited by time series with suggested types of suitable model. (It is by no means an exhaustive list of either past data time series or suitably fitting models.)

Table 12.1

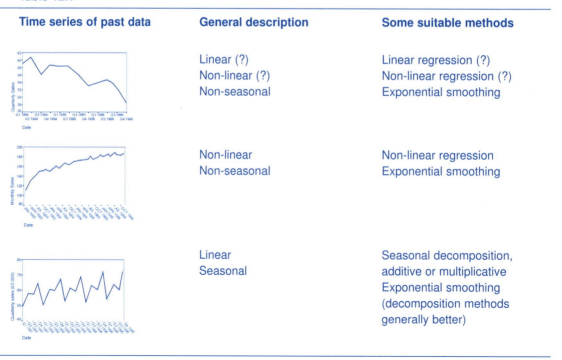

Time series of past data	General description	Some suitable methods
	Linear (?)	Linear regression (?)
	Non-linear (?)	Non-linear regression (?)
	Non-seasonal	Exponential smoothing
	Non-linear	Non-linear regression
	Non-seasonal	Exponential smoothing
	Linear	Seasonal decomposition, additive or multiplicative
	Seasonal	Exponential smoothing (decomposition methods generally better)

We shall consider each type of series in turn. For each we will produce two models by different methods; select the better of each pair and then use the selected model, in Chapter 13, to produce short-term forecasts for each type of series.

The decision regarding the best model for each series will be based visually on graphical assessment of closeness, and also numerically on the size of the errors as a measure of 'misfit'.

Generally, if a model fits past chronological data reasonably well, it can be used to predict values in the near future under the same prevailing conditions.

12.2 Non-seasonal time series

We shall try to model the first time series in Table 12.1 by using both linear and non-linear regression. We have previously found regression equations to describe the linear relationship between an independent and a dependent variable. The same method applies to time series analysis in which 'time' is the independent variable. Using SPSS, linear and non-linear models can be produced together and immediately compared. From the shape of the data in Figure 12.1 it is evident that any smooth model, whether a straight line or a curve, is unlikely to fit it well. Never expect miracles – all we aim for is the best possible fit. We judge this by comparing the 'misfit' of the models and selecting that with the lowest value. Finally we will fit exponential smoothing models to the same data and compare the results.

12.2.1 Time series plot

We shall first produce the time series plot and decide on suitable models to try.

Example 12.1

The data in the first series describes the quarterly sales (£'000) for 12 consecutive quarters of a particular item made by your company:

39 41 36 39 38 38 36 33 34 35 33 28

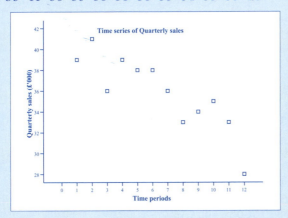

Figure 12.1

The general shape appears to be slightly convex upwards but a straight line might fit equally well, especially to the first eleven points. It is definitely not seasonal as this would be expected to show a repeated pattern of fours for quarterly data. We shall first try fitting linear, quadratic and cubic models to this data.

12.2.2 Regression models

The calculation of the linear regression model is the same as in Chapter 9. In this example the independent variable (x) is the time periods and the dependent variable is the sales.

There are many models available in SPSS. We shall apply the simplest:

- The linear model: $y = a + bx$ (12.1)
- The quadratic model: $y = a + bx + cx^2$ (12.2)
- The cubic model: $y = a + bx + cx^2 + dx^3$ (12.3)

Often it is not easy to judge which model is the better fit from a diagram. From SPSS we can produce coefficients for the formula for each model and also a numerical measure of how well each fits the data. This measure is the same R-squared value as we used, in percentage form, to judge the goodness of fit of a linear regression model in Chapter 9.

Example 12.1 continued

Fitting the linear, quadratic and cubic models to this data:

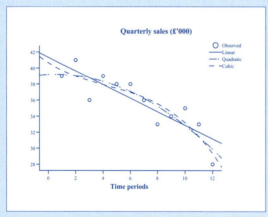

Figure 12.2

It is not easy to judge which model gives the best fit so we need the regression analysis.

```
Independent:   TIMES
Dependent Mth  Rsq   d.f.    F   Sigf      b0       b1      b2      b3
  SALES   LIN  .744   10  29.02  .000  41.3333  -.8462
  SALES   QUA  .792    9  17.19  .001  39.1818    .0759  -.0709
  SALES   CUB  .802    8  10.83  .003  40.6667  -1.0717   .1412  -.0109
```

For the linear model, b0 gives the value of the constant, a, and b1 the value of the slope, b. Similarly for the other models the coefficient of x^2 is under b2 and that of x^3 under b3.

These three models are described by linear, quadratic and cubic equations which are respectively:

$$y = 41.33 - 0.846x \qquad \text{(from 12.1)}$$
$$y = 39.18 + 0.076x - 0.071x^2 \qquad \text{(from 12.2)}$$
$$y = 40.67 - 1.072x + 0.141x^2 - 0.011x^3 \qquad \text{(from 12.3)}$$

where y = sales and x = the time period which takes the values 1 to 12 for this data.

Which of these models gives the best fit? The Rsq value, which has not been adjusted for the differing degrees of freedom, suggests that it is the cubic model. With adjustment this may not be the case.

We will check further by analysing the residuals.

We are looking for the set of residuals with a mean of zero and the smallest spread about that mean. As a rule of thumb, this can be assessed by a comparison of standard deviations, box plots, and so on.

Example 12.1 continued

The preference for the cubic model is borne out by a simple analysis of the residuals.

```
Variable      Mean Std Dev  Minimum  Maximum  N Label
ERR_1 (lin)   .00   1.79  -3.17949  2.12821 12 Residuals from Linear model
ERR_2 (quad) .00   1.61  -2.77123  2.15185 12 Residuals from Quadratic model
ERR_3 (cubic).00   1.57  -2.55977  1.99900 12 Residuals from Cubic model
```

All have a mean of zero as required, so we choose the model with the smallest standard deviation: the cubic model. We shall use this model in Chapter 13 to produce a forecast for the sales for each of the following two months.

12.2.3 Exponential smoothing models

Exponential smoothing is a technique for averaging out the random components (errors) in a series. It is particularly useful for short-term forecasting. A variety of models are available, allowing for different combinations of trend and seasonality. The type of trend and/or seasonality determines how many parameters are included in the exponential smoothing model.

The general idea is that the estimate for the next value in time will be the same as for the present estimated value adjusted for how far the present estimate was out; that is, some proportion of the error at this stage is used to correct for the next stage. The proportional adjustment varies between models. Do we adjust by 10 per cent of the error or 50 per cent of the error?

Trial and error is used to produce the 'best' model. The initial values for the level and trend can also be selected rather than accepting the automatic values produced by SPSS.

The best model is that which produces the smallest errors, as measured by the SSE. This is the sum of the squares of the errors already met in analysis of variance (Chapter 8).

12.2.3.1 Steady model

This model assumes that the data have no general trend, either up or down, and that there is no seasonal variation; that is, variations are at random around some steady mean value.

The proportion of the error by which the next estimate is adjusted is described by the symbol, α (alpha), which is usually between 0.1 and 0.5 and is always between 0 and 1. The closer the value of α is to 0, the less influence the current observation has in determining the forecast. Low values of α are suitable for fairly smooth data with few fluctuations as a smooth model is produced.

Steady model: New forecast = old forecast + alpha × error in previous forecast (12.4)

12.2.3.2 Growth model (Holt's model)

The method for the growth model is similar to the steady model but it also includes a second smoothing constant, β (beta), which is generally smaller than alpha and adjusts for error in the forecast trend. The trend may be positive or negative but the model is still referred to as a 'growth' model. The use of β corrects for a portion of the most recent error in the slope. (Some text books, and also SPSS, use γ (gamma) rather than β as the second smoothing constant.)

Growth model:
New forecast = previous forecast + α × error in previous forecast
New trend = previous trend + β × error in previous trend   **(12.5)**

12.2.3.3 Seasonal model

Exponential smoothing can also be used for seasonal data by using a third smoothing constant for the seasonality. It does not, however, seem to give nearly as good a model as the method of seasonal decomposition (see Section 12.4).

Although the data in Example 12.1 appear to follow a downward trend we shall first demonstrate a few steady models before finding the best-fitting growth model.

Example 12.1 continued

Steady models

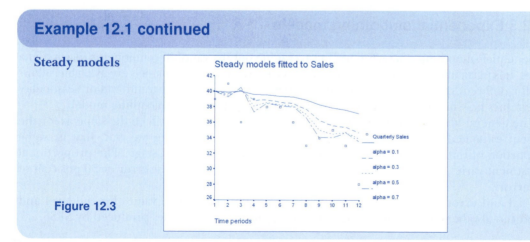

Figure 12.3

Even with an alpha figure of 0.7 the model lags behind the actual data.

```
Initial values:          Series              Trend
                         40.00000            Not used
The SSE is:              Alpha          SSE
                         .1000000       201.0
                         .3000000       105.2
                         .5000000        82.6
                         .7000000        78.6
```

The value for the smoothing constant of 0.7 gives the best model but a trend is clearly needed. A growth model seems likely to improve the fit considerably.

If a growth model correcting for the error in slope is applied, does the model improve?

Example 12.1 continued

Figure 12.4

It is difficult to tell which is the best model, but the use of a trend has certainly improved the general fit.

```
Initial values:          Series              Trend
                         40.00000            -1.00000

The SSE is:   Alpha          Gamma              SSE
              .5000000       .1000000           57.1
              .5000000       .2000000           59.7
              .5000000       .0000000           54.1
```

The best model of these is alpha = 0.5; beta (gamma) = 0.0 This has a lower SSE than any of the steady models. (Note that this is not the same model as the previous one for alpha = 0.5 as a trend of −1 has been applied.)

The best regression and best exponential smoothing models will be compared in Section 12.5, residual analysis.

We shall use this model for forecasting sales for each of the following two months in Chapter 13.

12.3 A continuous example of non-seasonal modelling

Example 12.2

Figure 12.5 describes the monthly sales of an item produced by your company during four years.

Figure 12.5

Considering the shape of the graph, it is evident that the data is not seasonal, that the plot rises fairly steadily and although a straight line might fit it reasonably well for the second half, the overall fit would probably require a curve.

We shall again use SPSS to produce the best exponential smoothing model and the best-fitting regression curve.

SPSS has a useful weapon known as a 'grid search'. Instead of the analyst using trial and error to produce innumerable models and then comparing their respective SSEs to select the best, a general, fairly coarse, trawl through all possible parameters will produce an approximation of the best model quickly. This model can then be finely tuned to find an improved version giving the lowest SSE.

Example 12.2 continued

Just showing part of the output indicates that the best model is a growth (Holt's) model with $\alpha = 0.4$ and β (γ) $= 0.7$ giving a SSE of 931.

```
Initial values:          Series               Trend
                         95.00000             10.00000
The 10 smallest SSE's are:   Alpha     Gamma          SSE
                             .400      .700          931.12
                             .400      .600          933.84
                             .400      .800          939.41
                             .300     1.000          947.76
                             .500      .500          948.43
```

How well does this model appear to fit the data?

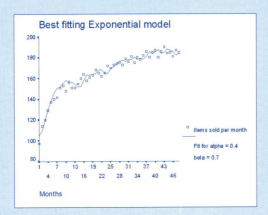

Figure 12.6

This model fits the data reasonably well but a smoother model might be preferable. We shall next look for a smooth-fitting curve using regression.

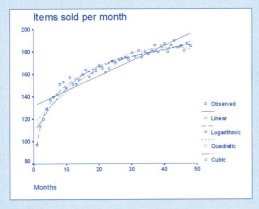

Figure 12.7

The smoother models look better. Clearly the linear model is not the best but we need some numerical comparison of the three curves. (Using the right mouse button in SPSS explains and gives the formula of each model so unfamiliar ones can be tried without worrying about any awkward formulae.)

```
Independent:   MONTHS
```

Dependent	Mth	Rsq	d.f.	F	Sigf	b0	b1	b2	b3
SALES	LIN	.825	46	216.88	.000	131.892	1.3471		
SALES	LOG	.977	46	1991.96	.000	97.0253	23.1584		
SALES	QUA	.930	45	299.88	.000	116.030	3.2505	−.0388	
SALES	CUB	.950	44	278.31	.000	107.376	5.2666	−.1407	.0014

Judged by the Rsq value the logarithmic model is very good.

This model is of the form y = a + b × ln(t) where ln is the natural logarithm. In this case using the coefficients produced: Sales = 97.0 + 23.2 ln(month).

Plotting the two models selected by the regression and exponential smoothing methods gives Figure 12.8.

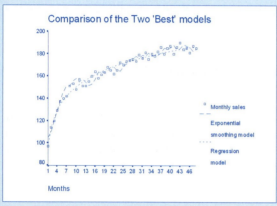

Figure 12.8

These are obviously very different types of models. One follows the general curve, the other tries to follow the individual items on it, but which one fits the data better and so is likely to give the better forecast?

In Section 12.5, residuals analysis, we shall look for the preferable set of residuals and in Chapter 13 we shall consider the forecasts made by each of these models for the following two months.

12.4 Decomposition of seasonal time series

12.4.1 Additive model – by calculation and graph

In a time series diagram you may find a repeated pattern demonstrating periodicity. If this is the case then this periodicity, which is caused by some seasonal factor, must form part of the model.

The model for a seasonal time series is:

Value = Trend + Seasonal component + a random amount   (12.6)

The trend is the line of best fit, usually non-linear, through the data. The seasonal component is the amount by which the trend is adjusted because in that particular time period, for example in a particular quarter of the year, some regular factor influences the data. The trend and seasonal component both need to be identified from the past data.

The trend is first found as the running average of the appropriate number of periods. If the data is monthly, groups of twelve would be averaged; if quarterly, the groups would contain four consecutive time periods.

We shall analyse a seasonal time series describing the sales of ice-cream by a particular company over a period of four years. In Chapter 13 we will then use the results of the analysis to estimate sales for the four quarters of the following year accompanied by the maximum likely errors to be found in the estimates. We shall first assume that the best model to use is an additive one and tackle the analysis by hand. For comparison, the data will be analysed using SPSS for the same model (see Section 12.4.2). Finally we shall consider, from SPSS output only, whether a multiplicative model might give a better fit to this data (see Section 12.4.3).

Example 12.3

A small ice-cream manufacturer who supplies your company's supermarket chain reports sales figures of £50,000 for the last quarter. Can this be used to estimate his sales in the following quarter?

A single figure is never sufficient to provide the answer unless the sales are constant. We also need the figures for many earlier quarters so that we can identify any past pattern and use it for future sales predictions.

Table 12.2

| Year | Sales (£'000) | | | |
	Quarter 1	Quarter 2	Quarter 3	Quarter 4
2002	40	60	80	35
2003	30	50	60	30
2004	35	60	80	40
2005	50	70	100	50

This time series should be plotted accurately on a full sheet of graph paper, leaving room for the forecasts for the four quarters of the following year (to save drawing the graph again). The graph in Figure 12.9 has been produced by SPSS.

Example 12.3 continued

If consecutive points are connected the periodicity of four becomes evident.

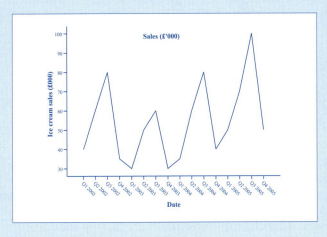

Figure 12.9 Quarterly sales

The next step is to calculate the values for the trend by finding a cycle average for each cycle of four values. The first value is calculated from quarters 1 to 4 of year 2002; the second from quarter 2 of 2002 to quarter 1 of 2003; the third from quarter 3 of 2002 to quarter 2 of 2003, and so on.

Unfortunately, because there are an **even** number of time points in a cycle, the first cycle average is centred half way between quarters 2 and 3; the second between quarters 3 and 4; and so on. We cannot therefore compare them directly with the sales in order to find the difference between them. The next stage is to find the moving average of each two consecutive cycle averages to give the trend values which will then be against a quarter. (For an odd number of points see end of Section 12.4.1.)

These figures are plotted on the graph, taking care that the series starts at quarter 3. By this method the trend values for either the first two or the last two quarters are unfortunately lost.

Additive model	Observed sales value	=	Trend value	+	Seasonal variation	+	Random amount	
	A	=	T	+	S	+	R	(12.6)

The **trend value** is the value of the sales if the seasonal effect had been 'averaged out'.
The **seasonal variation** is the average effect of it being a particular quarter.
The **random amount** is the random variation due to neither of the previous variables.

Example 12.3 continued

Table 12.3 is built up in columns from the left to the right.
After the dates, the sales figures are entered in chronological order.

The first cycle average: $\dfrac{40+60+80+35}{4} = \dfrac{215}{4} = 53.75$

The second cycle average: $\dfrac{60+80+35+30}{4} = \dfrac{205}{4} = 51.25$

The first moving average trend figure: $\dfrac{53.75+51.25}{2} = 52.50$

The second moving average trend figure: $\dfrac{51.25+48.75}{2} = 50.00$

Plotting the trend (Figure 12.10) with the data in Table 12.3 we can see that it is a smoothed average through the quarterly sales.

Later the smoothed trend line needs extending into the near future and then adjusting by the appropriate seasonal factor to give the forecasts. Figure 12.10 could, in theory, be used to extend the trend but it would be difficult to read values from it accurately. A large hand drawn graph is therefore preferable.

We next need the 'seasonal factors'. Calculate the first residuals (R_1) by subtracting the trend (T) from the sales value (A). For this data we can see that the sales are always high in

Table 12.3

Date	Sales (A) (£'000)	Cycle (C) Average	Trend (T) Mov. aver.	First Resid. $R_1 = A - T$	Fitted value $F = (T + SF)$
2002 Q1	40				
2002 Q2	60				
		53.75			
2002 Q3	80		52.50	+27.50	75.42
		51.25			
2002 Q4	35		50.00	−15.00	33.75
		48.75			
2003 Q1	30		46.25	−16.25	32.08
		43.75			
2003 Q2	50		43.13	+6.87	49.17
		42.50			
2003 Q3	60		43.13	+16.87	66.04
		43.75			
2003 Q4	30		45.00	−15.00	28.75
		46.25			
2004 Q1	35		48.75	−13.75	34.58
		51.25			
2004 Q2	60		52.50	+7.50	58.54
		53.75			
2004 Q3	80		55.63	+24.37	78.54
		57.50			
2004 Q4	40		58.75	−18.75	42.50
		60.00			
2005 Q1	50		62.50	−12.50	48.33
		65.00			
2005 Q2	70		66.25	+3.75	72.29
		67.50			
2005 Q3	100				
2005 Q4	50				

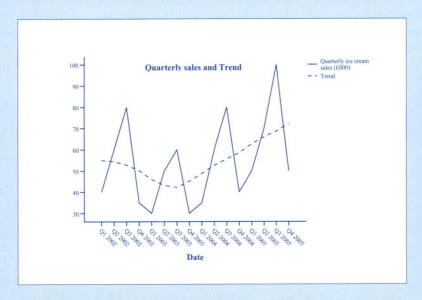

Figure 12.10 Quarterly sales and trend

quarter 3, but what value do we put on the seasonal factor for quarter 3? It seems reasonable that it should be the average of the differences from the trend, the first residuals, for that particular quarter. Check the values in the table of the first residuals.

Example 12.3 continued

Seasonal Factor (S) is the average seasonal deviation from the trend.

Table 12.4		Quarter 1	Quarter 2	Quarter 3	Quarter 4
		–	–	+27.50	−15.00
		−16.25	+6.87	+16.87	−15.00
		−13.75	+7.50	+24.37	−18.74
		−12.50	+3.75		
	Total	−42.50	+18.12	+68.74	−48.74
	Average (S)	−14.17	+6.04	+22.91	−16.25

The additive model to which we shall fit the data is:

Additive model   **Fitted   = Trend   + Seasonal**
                        sales value   value   factor
                        F   = T   + S   (12.7)

The fitted model values are calculated by adding together the trend values and the appropriate seasonal factors. Check in the table that the fitted values (F) are the sums of the trend values (T) and the appropriate seasonal factors from Table 12.4. Plotting the fitted values with the data gives an idea of how well the model would have performed in the past.

The differences between the observed values and the model values are referred to as the 'second residuals'. These will be analysed in Section 12.5 and, in Chapter 13, we shall use them to estimate how good any forecasts made from this model are likely to be.

If we add a graph of the fitted sales values to our actual sales data on the graph we can compare the theoretical model with observed sales data.

Example 12.3 continued

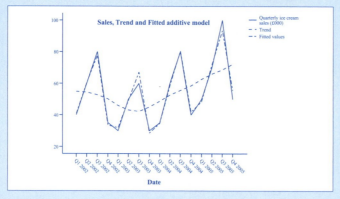

Figure 12.11 Sales, trend and fitted additive model

It is evident that this model is a good fit for the past sales of ice cream. The 'differences' between the observed values and the model values are obviously small. We shall analyse them in Section 12.6.

If we have an **odd** number of points per cycle, the trend values are the same as the cycle average as this is positioned in the required quarter and so may be subtracted from the observed data for that quarter without needing any further manipulation.

12.4.2 Additive model by computer package

Figures 12.1 to 12.11 have all been produced from SPSS. Here we will take a look at the SPSS analysis which is an extension of our hand-calculated method and a little more sophisticated.

Example 12.3 continued (SPSS output)

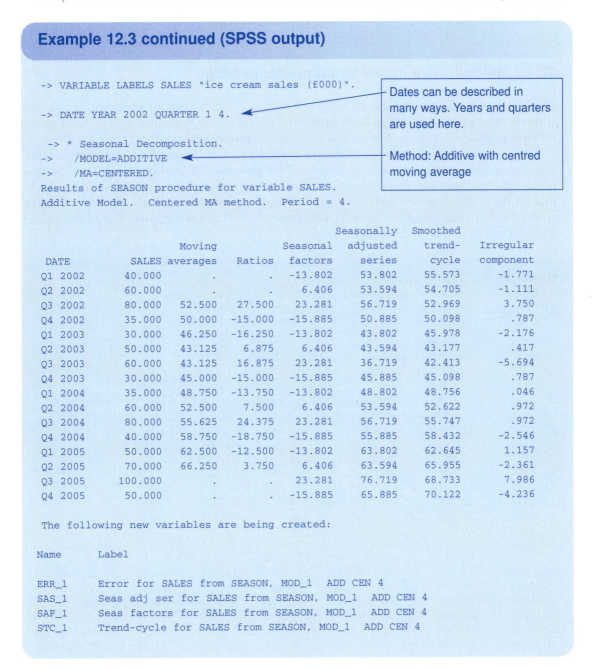

```
-> VARIABLE LABELS SALES "ice cream sales (£000)".

-> DATE YEAR 2002 QUARTER 1 4.

 -> * Seasonal Decomposition.
->    /MODEL=ADDITIVE
->    /MA=CENTERED.
Results of SEASON procedure for variable SALES.
Additive Model.  Centered MA method.  Period = 4.
```

Dates can be described in many ways. Years and quarters are used here.

Method: Additive with centred moving average

DATE	SALES	Moving averages	Ratios	Seasonal factors	Seasonally adjusted series	Smoothed trend-cycle	Irregular component
Q1 2002	40.000	.	.	-13.802	53.802	55.573	-1.771
Q2 2002	60.000	.	.	6.406	53.594	54.705	-1.111
Q3 2002	80.000	52.500	27.500	23.281	56.719	52.969	3.750
Q4 2002	35.000	50.000	-15.000	-15.885	50.885	50.098	.787
Q1 2003	30.000	46.250	-16.250	-13.802	43.802	45.978	-2.176
Q2 2003	50.000	43.125	6.875	6.406	43.594	43.177	.417
Q3 2003	60.000	43.125	16.875	23.281	36.719	42.413	-5.694
Q4 2003	30.000	45.000	-15.000	-15.885	45.885	45.098	.787
Q1 2004	35.000	48.750	-13.750	-13.802	48.802	48.756	.046
Q2 2004	60.000	52.500	7.500	6.406	53.594	52.622	.972
Q3 2004	80.000	55.625	24.375	23.281	56.719	55.747	.972
Q4 2004	40.000	58.750	-18.750	-15.885	55.885	58.432	-2.546
Q1 2005	50.000	62.500	-12.500	-13.802	63.802	62.645	1.157
Q2 2005	70.000	66.250	3.750	6.406	63.594	65.955	-2.361
Q3 2005	100.000	.	.	23.281	76.719	68.733	7.986
Q4 2005	50.000	.	.	-15.885	65.885	70.122	-4.236

```
The following new variables are being created:


Name     Label


ERR_1    Error for SALES from SEASON, MOD_1   ADD CEN 4
SAS_1    Seas adj ser for SALES from SEASON, MOD_1   ADD CEN 4
SAF_1    Seas factors for SALES from SEASON, MOD_1   ADD CEN 4
STC_1    Trend-cycle for SALES from SEASON, MOD_1   ADD CEN 4
```

The moving averages are the trend figures calculated by hand previously and the 'Ratios', (a description more suited to the following multiplicative model) are the same first residuals. The 'seasonal factors' and the 'smoothed trend cycle' describe the average effect due to a particular quarter and the sales level without that effect. These differ slightly from our calculated figures as they have been further smoothed and also extended to cover the first and last two time periods. We shall look at seasonally adjusted series later.

No fitted values from the model have been produced by default but they can easily be obtained as the sum of smoothed trend cycle and seasonal factors which have automatically been produced and saved by SPSS as STC_1 and SAF_1. The errors, ERR_1, and deseasonalised sales, SAS_1, have also been saved.

Minitab produces similar analysis using a moving average model.

12.4.3 Multiplicative model by computer package

In order to have a second seasonal model of these ice-cream sales for comparison with the additive one, we shall produce a multiplicative model in SPSS, analyse its residuals to see which is preferable, and use it as well as the additive model to make short term forecasts.

If the seasonal adjustment is proportional to the level of the series (the trend) then a multiplicative model may be more appropriate. The processes of multiplication and division replace those of addition and subtraction at each stage. Otherwise the procedure is similar to that for the additive model. Using SPSS, the multiplicative model is selected as the method of analysis rather than an additive model, otherwise the method is the same. Could this model give a better fit to the ice-cream sales data?

Example 12.3 continued

SPSS output

```
Results of SEASON procedure for variable SALES.
Multiplicative Model.  Centered MA method.  Period = 4.
```

DATE	SALES	Moving averages	Ratios (* 100)	Seasonal factors (* 100)	Seasonally adjusted series	Smoothed trend-cycle	Irregular component
Q1 2002	40.000	.	.	72.158	55.434	54.903	1.010
Q2 2002	60.000	.	.	114.864	52.236	54.338	.961
Q3 2002	80.000	52.500	152.381	144.548	55.345	52.201	1.060
Q4 2002	35.000	50.000	70.000	68.430	51.147	49.228	1.039
Q1 2003	30.000	46.250	64.865	72.158	41.575	45.659	.911
Q2 2003	50.000	43.125	115.942	114.864	43.530	43.527	1.000
Q3 2003	60.000	43.125	139.130	144.548	41.509	43.261	.960
Q4 2003	30.000	45.000	66.667	68.430	43.841	45.257	.969
Q1 2004	35.000	48.750	71.795	72.158	48.505	48.280	1.005
Q2 2004	60.000	52.500	114.286	114.864	52.236	51.856	1.007
Q3 2004	80.000	55.625	143.820	144.548	55.345	56.135	.986
Q4 2004	40.000	58.750	68.085	68.430	58.454	59.757	.978
Q1 2005	50.000	62.500	80.000	72.158	69.292	63.466	1.092
Q2 2005	70.000	66.250	105.660	114.864	60.942	65.699	.928
Q3 2005	100.000	.	.	144.548	69.181	67.730	1.021
Q4 2005	50.000	.	.	68.430	73.068	72.140	1.013

```
The following new variables are being created:

    Name        Label

    ERR_2       Error for SALES from SEASON, MOD_2   MUL CEN 4
    SAS_2       Seas adj ser for SALES from SEASON, MOD_2   MUL CEN 4
    SAF_2       Seas factors for SALES from SEASON, MOD_2   MUL CEN 4
    STC_2       Trend-cycle for SALES from SEASON, MOD_2   MUL CEN 4
```

The moving average is the same as previously but the rest of the figures are quite different as multiplication and division have replaced addition and subtraction. Do not worry if you cannot reproduce the figures, just trust SPSS! As for Model 1, the errors, deseasonalised values, seasonal factors and trend values have been saved for Model 2.

Example 12.3 continued

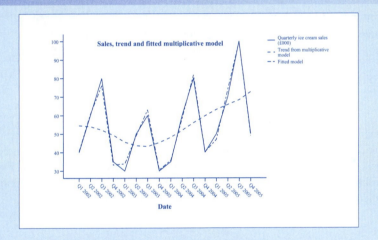

Figure 12.12 Sales, trend and fitted multiplicative model

Comparing this graph with Figure 12.11 it is not easy to see which model fits the 'ice-cream sales' data better. In Section 12.6, we will compare them by analysing each set of residuals.

12.4.4 Seasonal effects and deseasonalised values

In order to find fitted model values in the additive model we added the appropriate seasonal factor to the smoothed trend cycle values. In the multiplicative model the smoothed trend cycle values are multiplied by the corresponding seasonal factors.

These same seasonal factors are also used for deseasonalising data. We may hear in the media that unemployment has gone down but that the deseasonalised value has gone up. What does this mean? For some items, such as unemployment and ice-cream sales for which there is obviously a seasonal component, it is reasonable to remove that component before comparing different quarters.

For the additive model the seasonal factor is subtracted from the observed data in order to deseasonalise it. For the multiplicative model it is divided by it. These are the values in the columns of seasonally adjusted series in the SPSS output.

Consecutive quarters can be compared using this series to see whether sales have improved without the effect of, for example, the amount of sales due to the higher summer temperatures coming into the equation.

It now makes sense to calculate percentages changes to compare with appropriate published indices, and so on. The deseasonalised values can be compared to the trend value at any point in time to see whether, for example, sales were better or worse than the general trend at that time.

Example 12.3 continued

How can we compare the ice-cream sales in summer with those in winter? We shall 'deseasonalise' the observed sales figures for 2005.

Table 12.5

Date	Observed sales	_	Seasonal factor	=	Deseasonalised sales	Trend (from SPSS output)
2005 Q1	50	–	−14.17	=	64.17	62.65
2005 Q2	70	–	+6.04	=	63.96	66.00
2005 Q3	100	–	+22.91	=	77.09	68.73
2005 Q4	50	–	−16.25	=	66.25	70.12

Having removed the amount due to each quarter we can see that quarters 1 and 2 were very similar but that quarter 3 showed an increase, in real terms, of £13,130 over quarter 2. This was followed by a decrease in sales of £10,840 between quarters 3 and 4. Compared with the trend, quarters 1 and 3 performed well but quarters 2 and 4 did not.

12.5 Residual analysis

The main requirement of a model, no matter which method has been used to produce it, is that it should fit the observed data well. The differences between the model values and those observed should therefore be as small as possible. Ideally they should be normally distributed with a mean of zero and a small standard deviation. They should be randomly distributed against time. If, for example, they are positive for the early data and negative for the later data, then there is some factor missing from the model. Normality can be judged graphically by histograms or box plots and numerically by **Kolmogorov-Smirnov (K-S) tests** for normality. Each of these methods will be demonstrated in the following examples.

Graphically we can examine the plots of the observed and model values to see how closely they fit. The vertical differences between the pairs of values indicate the magnitude of the separate residuals. These residuals can be saved and analysed to see which set best fulfils the conditions above.

In this chapter we have analysed three sets of data and produced two good models for each. We have considered each graphically and we are satisfied that good models have been produced. Some measure of the goodness of fit has been produced for each model but these are not immediately comparable as we have R-squared and SSE values for the regression and exponential smoothing models respectively, and irregular components for the two seasonal decomposition models. Even the seasonal decomposition models cannot be directly compared as one measures differences with a mean of 0, and the other ratios with a mean of 1.

For each model we shall find the differences between the observed and model values – residuals or errors – by subtraction and analyse them to see which set best fulfils the required conditions for residuals.

Two measures often used to compare residuals are **mean absolute deviation (MAD)** and **mean square error (MSE)**. (See Appendix C for formulae.) We shall use their standard deviation which is immediately available and is equivalent to $\sqrt{MSE}$.

We now return to Examples 12.1 to 12.3 for **residual analysis**. The sizes of the mean and standard deviation are found as descriptive statistics. The normality is judged graphically by histograms or box plots, or numerically using the Kolmogorov-Smirnov normality test. The chronological randomness is judged by sequence plots.

Example 12.4 Residual analysis of Example 12.1

Our two preferred models for this data were the cubic regression model and the growth exponential smoothing model with alpha = 0.5, beta = 0.0, and with initial conditions of 40 for the starting value and –1.0 for the trend.

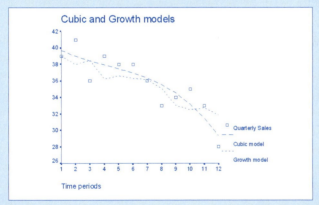

Figure 12.13

It is still not easy to decide which is best from the graph. The residuals can be calculated and analysed to produce the results in Table 12.6.

Table 12.6 Descriptive statistics

	N	Minimum	Maximum	Mean	Std. deviation
Quarterly sales	12	28	41	35.83	3.54
Errors from cubic model	12	−2.55977	1.99900	−5.3E-15	1.5723984
Errors from growth model	12	−3.87988	3.000000	.3233236	2.1914435

As judged by the descriptive statistics of the errors the cubic model was preferable, with the smaller mean and smaller standard deviation.

As this is only a small sample, graphical judgements of normality will be poor. A Kolmogorov-Smirnov (K-S) test is more appropriate.

Table 12.7 One-sample Kolmogorov-Smirnov test

		Errors from cubic model	Errors from growth model
N		12	12
Normal parameters[a,b]	Mean	.0000000	.3233236
	Std. deviation	1.5723983	2.1914434
Most extreme	Absolute	.161	.163
differences	Positive	.105	.113
	Negative	−.161	−.163
Kolmogorov-Smirnov Z		.556	.566
Asymp. sig. (two-tailed)		.917	.906

a   Test distribution is normal.

b   Calculated from data.

Both sets of residuals are normal with significance values >0.05. The cubic two-tailed significance is slightly higher.

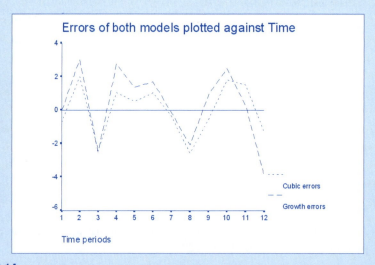

Figure 12.14

Both graphs of errors in Figure 12.14 appear random against time. For most of the sequence the cubic errors are the smaller of the two as they appear nearer the zero line.

Cubic model: $40.67 - 1.072x + 0.141x^2 - 0.011x^3$ is judged to be the better one.

For this set of data, even though the cubic model has been judged to give the better fit, both it and the growth model will be used to demonstrate forecasting in Chapter 13.

Example 12.5   Residual analysis of Example 12.2

The two best fitting models for this data were a logarithmic model with coefficients 97.0 and 23.2 and a growth exponential model with alpha = 0.4 and beta = 0.7, initial conditions of 95 for the position and 10 for the trend.

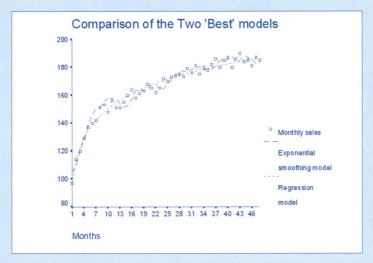

Figure 12.15

In Figure 12.15 one model is smooth and the other undulating so they are not easy to compare graphically. Better to use residual analysis (Table 12.8).

Table 12.8 Descriptive statistics

	N	Minimum	Maximum	Mean	Std. deviation
Items sold per month	48	97	190	164.90	20.76
Errors from growth model	48	−10.15796	7.40862	−.7421744	4.3873240
Errors from logarithmic model	48	−6.60895	5.87125	5.67E-15	3.1194525

The logarithmic model is better and the errors from that model appear normal.

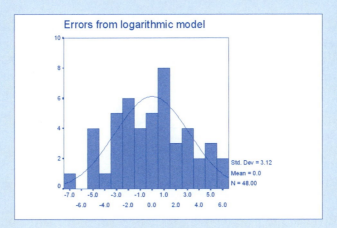

Figure 12.16

Table 12.9 One-sample Kolmogorov-Smirnov test

		Errors from growth model	Errors from logarithmic model
Normal parameters[a,b]	Mean	−.7421744	−1.61E-08
	Std. deviation	4.3873239	3,1194525
Most extreme	Absolute	0.64	.053
differences	Positive	.064	.053
	Negative	−.061	−.048
Kolmogorov-Smirnov Z		.443	.370
Asymp. sig. (two-tailed)		.989	.999

a   Test distribution is normal.

b   Calculated from data.

Both models produce normal residuals as checked by the K-S test for normality (Figure 12.17).

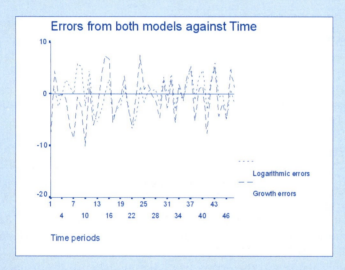

Figure 12.17

From Figure 12.17 the errors from both models are random against time, although the logarithmic errors are generally smaller.

This gives the selected model: Number of items sold = 97.0 + 23.2 ln(t)

The growth and logarithmic models will be used in Chapter 13 for forecasting.

Example 12.6   Residual analysis of Example 12.3

For this seasonal data we produced additive and multiplicative models.

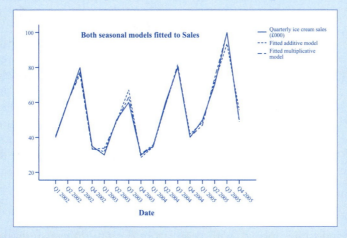

Figure 12.18

Both models give a good fit to the observed data. Residual analysis produces the output in Table 12.10.

Table 12.10 Descriptive statistics

	N	Minimum	Maximum	Mean	Std. deviation
Ice cream sales	16	30	100	54.38	20.24
Additive model	16	−6.81	7.99	−.2865	3.4499
Multiplicative model	16	−5.46	4.54	−.1614	2.5643

The residuals from the multiplicative model looks better. Box plots are generated for both sets of residuals (Figure 12.19).

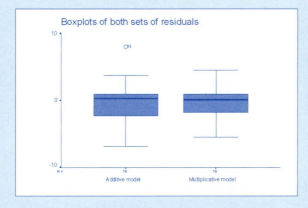

Figure 12.19

Both plots are symmetrical. Multiplicative errors have a smaller spread about zero.

Table 12.11 One-sample Kolmogorov-Smirnov test

		Additive	Multiplicative
N		16	16
Normal parameters[a,b]	Mean	−.2865	−.1614
	Std. deviation	3.4499	2.5643
Most extreme	Absolute	.213	.128
differences	Positive	.213	.128
	Negative	−.131	−.101
Kolmogorov-Smirnov Z		.851	.512
Asymp. sig. (two-tailed)		.464	.956

a Test distribution is normal.

b Calculated from data

Both sets of errors judged to be normal, with those from the multiplicative model being better.

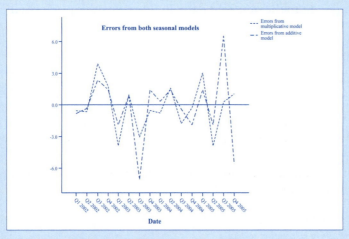

Figure 12.20 Both sets of errors against time

Both sets of errors in Figure 12.20 appear random against time. With a quarterly seasonal model it is important that the pattern of four in a repeat is no longer evident.

The multiplicative model is judged to be the better model but both will be used for forecasting in Chapter 13.

12.6 Further analysis of time series

There are many other procedures for the analysis of a time series. You may come across multiple regression models, autoregression models which take into account the correlation between successive observations, Box-Jenkins methods which use autoregression, differencing and moving average combined; or spectral analysis which analyses the periodic components of the series as a whole. You may find that it often makes sense to add a time-delay (lagging) to a time series as the next term may not depend on the previous one but on the one before that.

Further details of all these more advanced methods can be found in books (such as Groebner and Shannon, 1993, Chapters 17 and 18). They are more difficult to understand than the methods we have studied but they can all be automated by computer packages such as SPSS and Minitab so they are no problem to carry out. The results are, however, more difficult to interpret.

12.7 Summary

In this chapter you have met three of the main methods of time series analysis, so one of those is likely to be suitable for most of the data you will meet on your course.

The most appropriate method to use is generally dictated by the data itself, so the first step is always to plot the modelling data in chronological order. The graph can then be considered to see whether the data might:

- be described by a function, whether a linear or non-linear function
- have an upward or downward trend, or generally have a steady level
- show any seasonality and, if so, identify its periodicity.

The best method can then be identified.

If more than one model is produced, comparison is usually made with the sum of the squared errors (SSE) but eventually the true test of any model is how well it will make predictions in the future, so the true verdict has to await the judgement of time!

More specifically, we have studied three methods of forecasting in this chapter with variations of each. These were:

- regression models
  - linear
  - curved
- exponential smoothing models
  - steady
  - growth
- seasonal decomposition models
  - additive
  - multiplicative.

12.7.1 Method summary

Any data:

1 Enter the data into SPSS or Minitab and plot the data **in chronological order** as a graph against time. Study the result to see which type of model is appropriate.

Non-seasonal data:

2 If the time series plot indicates no seasonality try both curve fitting and exponential smoothing in order to find the best model.
3 Use curve fitting regression, which includes linear models, to identify the best model; save the predicted values and residuals; plot the predicted with the observed values to see how close the fit is and finally analyse the residuals to see that they satisfy the required conditions.
4 Use the exponential smoothing method with a grid search in the first instance to get a suitable model. Try to improve on this model by altering the initial conditions and the parameters slightly, using the SSE as the criterion for improvement. Plot the saved fitted values regularly to see how well the model fits the observed data. Finally analyse the residuals to see that they satisfy the required conditions.
5 Compare the two models both graphically and by residual analysis in order to select the better model.

Seasonal data:

May be analysed by hand or by using SPSS or Minitab.

Computer analysis:

2 If using a **computer package**, type in the data in chronological order produce a time series plot and identify its periodicity.
3 Select an additive model and analyse the time series, saving the fitted values and the errors.
4 Select a multiplicative model and analyse the same time series, saving the fitted values and the errors.
5 Compare both models graphically and by means of residual analysis and so select the model which fits the data better.

Non-computer analysis:

2 If **analysing the data by hand**, calculate and tabulate the moving cycle of four averages $(Q_1 + Q_2 + Q_3 + Q_4)/4$, $(Q_2 + Q_3 + Q_4 + Q_1)/4$, (see Table 12.3) and so on. Hence calculate the centred **Trend values (T)** and **plot them on the same graph as your data, A**. Note that the first value is plotted against the third time slot as the extreme values have been lost in the averaging.
3 Calculate values for the **First residuals (R₁)**: $R_1 = A - T$ (see Table 12.4) for each separate quarter and from them calculate the average **Seasonal factor (S),** for each of the four quarters. Check that the average of these averages is not very far from zero.
4 Calculated the **Fitted values (F)**: $F = T + S$ (see Table 12.3)
   If the model is a 'perfect fit' these will be the same as the observed sales. We expect them to be close, indicating that we have a 'good' model.
5 Calculate the **Second residuals (R₂)**: $R_2 = A - F$
   These are the random amounts by which the model has 'mismatched' the observed data in the past and give an indication of how good forecasts are going to be. They should be small and randomly distributed about a value of zero.

For all methods:

• Assess your model.

- The fitted and observed values should be similar.
- The discrepancy between them should be very small and randomly distributed about zero.

In the next chapter we shall:

Produce forecasts for the next time cycle for all these methods using the work done in this chapter and assess how precise the forecasts are likely to be. Only time will tell how accurate they are!

Tutorial 12: Time series analysis

In Tutorial 12 you will construct and draw a graph of a time series in each question for a set of data, and in Tutorial 13 you will use the same series in order to produce short term forecasts using the same graphs.

12.1 The quarterly sales, (£'0,000) of a departmental store have been monitored for the past five years with the following results:

Year	Total quarterly sales (£'0,000)			
	Q1	Q2	Q3	Q4
2001	48	58	57	65
2002	50	61	59	68
2003	52	62	59	69
2004	52	64	60	73
2005	53	65	60	75

a) Plot the given data as a time series leaving room for the four forecasts for 2006.
b) Calculate the three values missing in the table on the next page, where they are indicated by question marks.
c) Plot the trend line on the same graph as your observed values.
d) Calculate the seasonal averages for each of the four quarters.
e) Find the deseasonalised data for the first quarter of 2005.

12.2 A group of hotels has returned these figures for their quarterly turnover. (£'0,000):

Year	Turnover (£'0,000)			
	Q1	Q2	Q3	Q4
2002	337	410	438	374
2003	321	416	462	414
2004	335	428	447	369
2005	311	399	422	

a) Calculate the three values missing in the table overleaf, produced from the above data, which are indicated by question marks.
b) Plot the turnover figures and the trend figures on one graph leaving room for four forecasts.

Table for question 12.1

Date		Sales (£'0,000)	Cycle average	Trend	First residual	Second residual
2001	Q1	48				
	Q2	58				
			57.00			
	Q3	57		57.250	−0.250	+0.969
			57.50			
	Q4	65		57.875	+7.125	−1.281
			58.25			
2002	Q1	50		58.500	−8.500	+0.406
			58.75			
	Q2	61		59.125	+1.875	−0.063
			59.50			
	Q3	59		59.750	−0.750	+0.469
			60.00			
	Q4	68		60.125	+7.875	−0.531
			60.25			
2003	Q1	52		60.250	−8.250	+0.656
			60.25			
	Q2	62		60.375	+1.625	−0.313
			60.50			
	Q3	59		60.500	−1.500	−0.281
			60.50			
	Q4	69		60.750	+8.250	−0.156
			61.00			
2004	Q1	52		61.125	−9.125	−0.219
			61.25			
	Q2	64		?	?	+0.312
			?			
	Q3	60		62.375	−2.375	−1.156
			62.50			
	Q4	73		62.625	+10.375	+1.969
			62.75			
2005	Q1	53		62.750	−9.750	−0.844
			62.75			
	Q2	65		63.000	+2.000	+0.062
			63.25			
	Q3	60				
	Q4	75				

Table for question 12.2

Date		Sales (£'0,000)	Cycle average	Trend	First residual	Second residual
2002	Q1	337				
	Q2	410				
			389.75			
	Q3	438		387.750	50.250	−3.917
			385.75			
	Q4	374		386.500	−12.500	−4.875
			387.25			
2003	Q1	321		390.250	−69.250	0.583
			393.25			
	Q2	416		398.250	17.750	−4.938
			403.25			
	Q3	462		405.000	57.000	2.833
			406.75			
	Q4	414		408.250	5.750	13.375
			409.75			
2004	Q1	335		407.875	−72.875	−3.042
			406.00			
	Q2	428		400.375	27.625	4.938
			394.75			
	Q3	447		?	?	1.083
			?			
	Q4	369		385.125	−16.125	−8.500
			381.50			
2005	Q1	311		378.375	−67.375	2.458
			375.25			
	Q2	399				
	Q3	422				

12.3 The following figures represent the quarterly number of cars sold by a group of car distributors.

	Cars sold			
Year	Q1	Q2	Q3	Q4
2002	727	767	779	811
2003	777	811	818	838
2004	816	853	847	872
2005	851	881		

a) Plot the number of cars sold and the trend figures on a graph leaving room for the forecast for the next four quarters. Make use of the Minitab output below.

Minitab output

Row	Cars	Trend	Ist.resid	Seasonal	Fitted	2nd.resid
1	727	*	*	*	*	*
2	767	*	*	*	*	*
3	779	777.250	1.750	-0.1670	777.083	1.91669
4	811	789.000	22.000	15.5830	804.583	6.41669
5	777	799.375	-22.375	-20.6250	778.750	-1.75000
6	811	807.625	3.375	6.8130	814.437	-3.43750
7	818	815.875	2.125	-0.1670	815.708	2.29169
8	838	826.000	12.000	15.5830	841.583	-3.58331
9	816	834.875	-18.875	-20.6250	814.250	1.75000
10	853	842.750	10.250	6.8130	849.563	3.43750
11	847	851.375	-4.375	-0.1670	851.208	-4.20831
12	872	859.250	12.750	15.5830	874.833	-2.83331
13	851	*	*			
14	881	*	*			

Summary statistics

Variable	N	Mean	StDev
Turnover	14	817.7	43.5
Ist.resi	10	1.86	13.97
2nd.resi	10	0.00	3.63

Notes

For SPSS/Minitab/Excel worksheets on graphical display see Chapter 14, Sections 14.2.6, 14.5.6 and 14.8.6 respectively. Worksheets with computer output and its interpretation are on the companion website.

The supplementary exercise for Chapter 12, with answers, is on the companion website.

Forecasting

13

Objectives of this chapter

In the previous chapter you modelled different types of time series with the objective of producing the model which best fitted the observed data. This chapter continues the same theme, with the preferred models selected in Chapter 12 being used to predict the values to be taken in the near future by these same models. As this is likely to be the last topic studied it has deliberately been kept short to allow time for organising and starting revision before the final examination. (You will find comprehensive revision materials on the companion website.)

Having completed this chapter, and already knowing how to select the best model, you should be able to:

- make reasonable predictions
- assess how good they are likely to be.

13.1 Introduction: the importance of forecasting

The role of forecasting is extremely important in the forward planning of any company. Unfortunately it is never an exact science as too many unknown quantities are inevitably left out of the model. These may be things over which the company has no control and/or the forecaster has no knowledge. It is obvious that any company which knew exactly all demands on its future production would have a tremendous advantage over its competitors who might be over- or under-producing.

Forecasts covering the whole economic environment enable the company's corporate planners to make decisions as to the future development of the company. Product and market forecasts will enable them to take advantage of potential growth areas. These predictions combined with good sales forecasts should give them the edge over competitors in producing appropriate quantities of goods. Financial forecasts should enable a company to manage its finances smoothly, taking advantage of good times while avoiding problems in the leaner years.

13.2 Forecasts

The forecasts we make from identified models all make the same basic assumption that the conditions prevailing for the time periods over which the modelling data was collected will continue into the future. In other words, any trends or patterns identified in building up the model will still apply when the model is being used to make forecasts.

This is common sense but should always be checked using a plot of the modelling data. You may find that the pattern changed part way through data collection and only the later part of the data is suitable for projection into the future. If that is the case then only the relevant part should contribute to the forecasting process.

No forecast can claim to be exact, so it should always be quoted with a margin of error. The size of this will reflect how well the model fitted the past data from which it was constructed. Hopefully it was a good fit and will produce a precise forecast. Unfortunately this may not be the case and, at the other extreme, this month's figure may still be the best estimate for next month's!

Be careful not to confuse precision with accuracy. Precision can be measured from past errors but only the future will measure accuracy by revealing whether your forecast was on target or not.

13.3 Forecasting with a non-seasonal time series model

Whether using regression or an exponential smoothing the best model is identified by the estimation of its parameters. These are the coefficients for regression and the smoothing constants for exponential smoothing.

The two best models estimated in Chapter 12 will be used for each series and their forecasts, with expected precision, estimated. We can use the expected precision to compare the models but it is also useful to plot the estimated forecast along with the previous data to check that it seems reasonable. If the forecasts from both models are close, it might seem reasonable to take their average as the reported forecast.

Example 13.1

We analysed the following time series in Chapter 12 (Example 12.1):

39 41 36 39 38 38 36 33 34 35 33 28

The data described the quarterly sales, (£'000) of a particular item made by your company for 12 consecutive quarters. The plotted series looked like the graph in Figure 13.1.

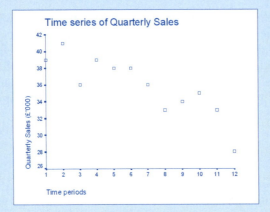

Figure 13.1

These data were rather scattered and obviously not close to any recognisable model and so are unlikely to provide a 'good' forecast. They were definitely not seasonal so regression and exponential smoothing models were fitted. The best of each type was found to be the cubic regression model with coefficients 40.67, –1.07, 0.141 and –0.011 and the growth model with smoothing constants $\alpha = 0.5$, $\beta = 0.0$ with initial conditions 40 and –1.0 (Example 12.4).

Regression model

The best model was identified as:

$$y = 40.67 - 1.07x + 0.141x^2 - 0.011x^3 \tag{13.1}$$

where x is the time period which took the values of 1 to 12 in the time series model.
    The next time period would be period 13 so substituting 13 for x we calculate the forecast to be:
    Sales = $40.67 - 1.07 \times 13 + 0.141 \times 13^2 - 0.011 \times 13^3 = 26.4$

So the forecast would be £26,400 if we think three significant figures are suitable.

Exponential smoothing model

The model which best fitted the data was found to be a growth model with initial value 40 and initial trend –1.0. The smoothing constants were $\alpha = 0.5$, $\beta = 0.0$. (SPSS used gamma (γ) instead of beta (β) for the second smoothing constant.) SPSS analysis produced the following output for the fitted values and errors.

Case Summaries^a

		Quarterly Sales	Fit for SALES from EXSMOOTH, MOD_1 HO A .50 G .00	Error for SALES from EXSMOOTH, MOD_1 HO A .50 G .00
1		39	39.00000	.00000
2		41	38.00000	3.00000
3		36	38.50000	-2.50000
4		39	36.25000	2.75000
5		38	36.62500	1.37500
6		38	36.31250	1.68750
7		36	36.15625	-.15625
8		33	35.07813	-2.07813
9		34	33.03906	.96094
10		35	32.51953	2.48047
11		33	32.75977	.24023
12		28	31.87988	-3.87988
Total	N	12	12	12

a. Limited to first 100 cases.

Figure 13.2

Remember the growth model is:

New forecast = previous forecast + α × error in previous forecast
                      + previous trend + β × error in previous forecast trend.
New trend = previous trend + β × error in previous trend

Example 13.1 continued

Because the value of beta in this case is zero the model simplifies to:

New forecast = previous forecast + 0.5 × error in previous forecast −1.0   (13.2)

as the initial value for the trend will remain unchanged at −1.0 for the whole series. It can be seen that for period 12 the forecast was 31.88 and its error −3.88. The new forecast is therefore 31.88 + 0.5 × (−3.88) + (−1) = 28.94 giving **£28,900** (3sf).

In summary, the regression model and the exponential smoothing model have produced forecasts of £26,400 and £28,900 from a poorly fitting model. Looking back at Figure 13.1, the figure of £28,900 is probably the more likely but only time will tell which is actually nearer the true figure.

13.4 A further non-seasonal time series forecast

Example 13.2

Four years of monthly sales were analysed in Example 12.2. The plotted series looked like Figure 13.3.

Figure 13.3

These data were less scattered than in Example 13.1 and follow a fairly smooth curve so are likely to provide a 'better' forecast. They were definitely not seasonal so regression and exponential smoothing models were fitted. The best of each type was found to be the logarithmic regression model with coefficients 97.03 and 23.16 and the growth model with smoothing constants $\alpha = 0.4$, $\beta = 0.7$ with initial conditions 95 and 10.0 for the start and trend respectively.

Regression model

The best model was identified as

$$y = 97.03 + 23.16 \times \ln(t) \tag{13.3}$$

where t is the time period, and ln(t) is its natural logarithm.

The model was constructed from periods 1 to 48 so the next time period would be period 49. Substituting 49 for t we calculate the forecast to be:

$$\text{Sales} = 97.03 + 23.16 \times \ln(49) = 187.16$$

So the forecast would be **187 items**.

Exponential smoothing model

The exponential smoothing model which best fitted this data was found to be a growth model with initial value of 95 and initial trend of 10. The smoothing constants were $\alpha = 0.4$, $\beta = 0.7$. SPSS analysis produced the output in Figure 13.4 for fitted values and errors, the last part of which is shown below. This output also includes the forecast for period 49.

		Items sold per month	Fit for SALES from EXSMOOTH, MOD_6 HO A .40 G .70	Error for SALES from EXSMOOTH, MOD_6 HO A .40 G .70
40		187	185.53669	1.46331
41		180	187.66264	-7.66264
42		186	183.99266	2.00734
43		190	184.75273	5.24727
44		184	188.27801	-4.27801
45		185	186.79533	-1.79533
46		181	185.80303	-4.80303
47		187	182.26280	4.73720
48		185	183.86508	1.13492
49			184.34423	.
Total	N	48	49	48

Case Summaries [a]

a. Limited to first 100 cases.

Figure 13.4

So the forecast by the best exponential smoothing model is **184 items**.

Summary

Both methods have come up with similar forecasts: 187 and 184.

Looking back at Figure 13.3, or the latter part of Figure 13.4 there is no reason to discard either forecast so perhaps the average is as good a figure as any. Again, only time will tell the value of the true figure.

13.5 Forecasting with a seasonal model

When analysing a seasonal model (see Section 12.4), we identified a moving average trend and also a set of four seasonal factors. The trend was only defined in the past and, if the model was analysed by hand, was missing for the first two and the last two periods. The seasonal factors were calculated from the past but can also be applied in the near future.

13.5.1 Additive model

The first model used was the **additive model**:

Additive model   **Fitted value** = **Trend value** + **Seasonal factor**
A   = T   + S

The future fitted values become the **forecasts** so the process of forecasting by this method is to extend the trend into the future and apply the seasonal factors to it to complete the model:

Additive model Forecast value = **Trend value** + **Seasonal factor**
F   = T   + S   (13.4)

The trend could be extended by eye using your own best judgement because it is a smooth line. An alternative is to produce an 'optimistic' line and a 'pessimistic' line and from them produce a range for the forecasts.

In Example 13.3 we shall use the decomposition of the time series as analysed in Example 12.3. We shall first make use of the hand-calculated additive model, then the SPSS analysis of the additive model and finally the SPSS analysis of the multiplicative model.

Example 13.3

Figure 13.5 reproduces Figure 12.10 with extra space for forecasts.

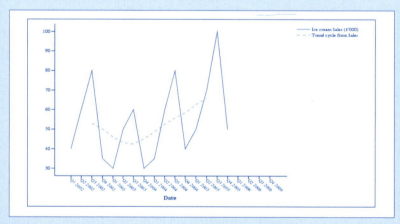

Figure 13.5 Quarterly sales and trend

You should have a hand-drawn graph from Example 12.3 which is a larger version of Figure 13.5. Extend the trend line by hand to cover the four quarters of 2006 and read off and record the value at each of the quarters.

Example 13.3 continued

One suggestion is shown below but your judgement is just as good as anyone else's and you may have chosen a different route. Stick with yours, then read off and record your trend values for the four quarters of 2006 from your large-scale graph.

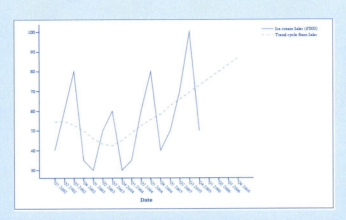

Figure 13.6 Trend extended into the near future

Suggested values: Q1 =76.4; Q2 =79.9; Q3 =83.4; Q4 =86.9 (from a large graph).

Additive model	**Forecast value**	**= Trend value**	**+ Seasonal factor**	
	F	**= T**	**+ S**	**(13.4)**

Table 13.1

		Trend +	Seasonal factor =	Forecast	
2006	Q1	76.4 +	−14.17 =	62.23	£62,200
	Q2	79.9 +	+6.04 =	85.94	£85,900
	Q3	83.4 +	+22.91 =	106.31	£106,300
	Q4	86.9 +	−16.25 =	70.65	£70,700

Remember **your** forecasts are just as good as these since you have calculated them from your chosen trend line extension.

Example 13.3 continued

Alternatively the trend may be modelled using SPSS output from the additive model and finding the best fitting curve for the trend. Using non-linear regression produced reasonable fits with a quadratic or cubic model.

```
Independent:  Time

Dependent Mth  Rsq  d.f.    F Sigf     b0     b1     b2     b3

   STC_1     QUA .933   13 89.95 .000 59.5863 -4.0527 .3158
   STC_1     CUB .951   12 77.95 .000 64.2215 -6.9021 .7224 -.0159
```

From the Rsq and looking at the graph in Figure 13.7 to see which fitted best towards the end of the past data the cubic model should be used:

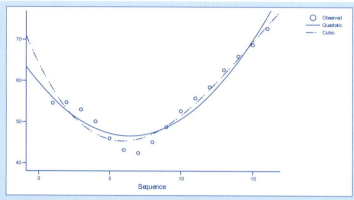

Figure 13.7 Trend from the additive model with fitted quadratic and cubic lines

Using the cubic model to find the next four trend values:
Trend $= 64.2 - 6.90t + 0.722t^2 - 0.016t^3$
Q1 (t = 17) Trend $= 64.2 - 6.90 \times 17 + 0.722 \times 17^2 - 0.016 \times 17^3 = 76.95$
Q2 (t = 18) Trend $= 64.2 - 6.90 \times 18 + 0.722 \times 18^2 - 0.016 \times 18^3 = 80.62$
Q3 (t = 19) Trend $= 64.2 - 6.90 \times 19 + 0.722 \times 19^2 - 0.016 \times 19^3 = 84.00$
Q4 (t = 20) Trend $= 64.2 - 6.90 \times 20 + 0.722 \times 20^2 - 0.016 \times 20^3 = 87.00$

Using these trend figures with the seasonal figures for the SPSS output:

Table 13.2		Trend +	Seasonal factor =	Forecast	
2006	Q1	76.95 +	−13.80 =	63.15	£63,200
	Q2	80.62 +	+6.41 =	87.03	£87,000
	Q3	84.00 +	+23.28 =	107.28	£107,300
	Q4	87.00 +	−15.89 =	71.11	£71,100

These two methods of trend extrapolation have been fairly consistent with their forecasts.

13.5.2 Multiplicative model

Alternatively the trend may be modelled using the SPSS output from the **multiplicative model** and finding the best fitting curve for the trend. Non-linear regression produced reasonable fits with a quadratic or cubic model.

```
Dependent Mth Rsq d.f.    F Sigf       b0       b1      b2      b3
   STC_2    QUA .931  13 87.08 .000  58.9065 -3.8648  .3052
   STC_2    CUB .960  12 95.67 .000  64.6602 -7.4018  .8099  -.0198
```

From the Rsq and the graph in Figure 13.8, to see which fitted best towards the end of the past data, the cubic model is best. The quadratic looks much too high, as can be seen from Figure 13.8.
Using the cubic model with the higher Rsq value to find the next four trend values:
Trend $= 64.7 - 7.40t + 0.810t^2 - 0.020t^3$
Q1 (t = 17) Trend $= 64.7 - 7.40 \times 17 + 0.810 \times 17^2 - 0.020 \times 17^3 = 74.73$
Q2 (t = 18) Trend $= 64.7 - 7.40 \times 18 + 0.810 \times 18^2 - 0.020 \times 18^3 = 77.30$
Q3 (t = 19) Trend $= 64.7 - 7.40 \times 19 + 0.810 \times 19^2 - 0.020 \times 19^3 = 79.33$
Q4 (t = 20) Trend $= 64.7 - 7.40 \times 20 + 0.810 \times 20^2 - 0.020 \times 20^3 = 80.70$

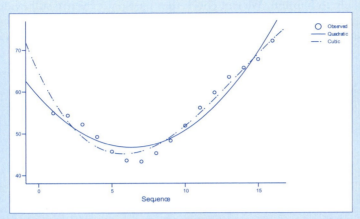

Figure 13.8 Trend from Multiplicative model with fitted quadratic and cubic lines

Using these trend figures with the seasonal figures for the SPSS output:

Table 13.3		Trend	x	Seasonal factor =	Forecast	
2006	Q1	74.73	x	0.7216=	53.93	£53,900
	Q2	77.30	x	1.1486=	88.79	£88,800
	Q3	79.33	x	1.4455=	114.67	£114,700
	Q4	80.70	x	0.6843=	55.22	£55,200

Tabulating the results from Table 13.1 to Table 13.3 gives Table 13.4.

Table 13.4		Hand-drawn additive	Additive (SPSS)	Multiplicative (SPSS)
2006	Q1	£62,200	£63,200	£53,900
	Q2	£85,900	£87,000	£88,800
	Q3	£106,300	£107,300	£114,700
	Q4	£70,700	£71,100	£55,200

It looks as though the multiplicative is out of line with the two additive models.

13.6 How good is a forecast?

A good forecast needs to be both precise and accurate.

We judge the precision of a forecast by considering the errors (residuals) that would have been produced had that model been used to 'back forecast' in the past when we knew the true values for comparison. Assuming that the prevailing conditions continue into the near future, we check that the residuals are normally distributed and then quote a 95 per cent confidence for the forecast. Its maximum likely error is 1.96 standard deviations on either side of the forecast. This is a rule of thumb which is useful for making comparisons.

We cannot judge accuracy until the future event actually happens so we can compare its true value with that which has been predicted for it. We can however check that forecast values are not unlikely to happen. We can check that past patterns are still evident in future values and that past trends have been carried through into the future.

We have forecasts for Examples 13.1 to 13.3. We shall now look to see how 'good' they are.

Example 13.1 continued

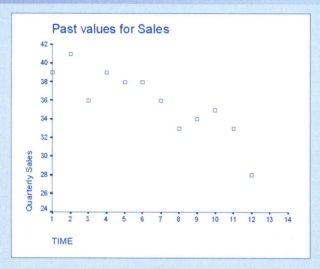

Figure 13.9

Our forecasts for period 13 are £26,400 for the regression model and £28,900 for the exponential smoothing model. The higher one seems more likely but we have no reason to reject either.

We now look at the maximum likely error of the two forecasts:

Regression model

In Section 12.5 (Table 12.7) the standard deviation of the residuals from this model was found to be 1.57 giving intervals of £3100 either side of the forecast. Our forecast therefore becomes from **£23,300** to **£29,500**. Not very precise!

Exponential smoothing model

These errors (Section 12.5 Table 12.7), had a standard deviation of 2.19 giving an interval of ± 4.4 and a forecast estimation of from **£24,500** to **£33,300**. Even worse!

A precise forecast was never expected from this irregular data.

Example 13.2 continued

Our forecasts for period 49 are **187** for the regression model and **184** for the exponential smoothing model. Both seem equally likely from Figure 13.10.

We now look at the precision of the two models.

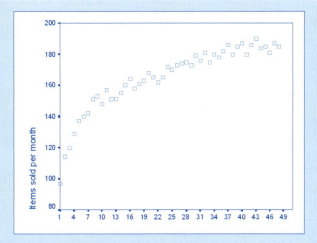

Figure 13.10

Regression model

In Section 12.5, Table 12.8, we saw that the standard deviation of the errors from the logarithmic model was 3.12, giving a maximum likely error of ± 6.2 on either side of this forecast, or 3% which is obviously an improvement on the last model. Our forecast is therefore between **181** and **193 items**.

Exponential smoothing model

These errors (Section 12.5, Table 12.8) had a standard deviation of 4.39 giving a maximum likely error of ± 8.8 and a forecast estimation of between **175** and **193 items**.

Example 13.3 continued

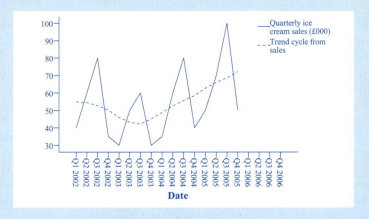

Figure 13.11 Quarterly sales and trend

The forecasts from the three models for this time series are:

	Hand-drawn additive	Additive (SPSS)	Multiplicative (SPSS)
Q1	£62,200	£63,200	£53,900
Q2	£85,900	£87,000	£88,800
Q3	£106,300	£107,300	£114,700
Q4	£70,700	£71,100	£55,200

Substituting your own forecasts for the hand-drawn additive model, plot these figures on your graph paper and see which set you think is most likely to produce the better forecast.

Moving average model

The summary statistics for the residuals from the three models are:

Model	Mean	Standard deviation
Hand-drawn additive	0.0167	2.77
Additive from SPSS	−0.265	3.45
Multiplicative from SPSS	−0.161	2.56

Forecasts from the multiplicative model will be the most precise, but time only will tell if they are the most accurate!

Do note that there is no correct answer when looking for a forecast, all we can do is produce the most likely figure given the prevailing conditions. We can never allow for unexpected changes in circumstances, such as a particularly cold and wet August which could play havoc with ice-cream sales.

13.7 Further methods of forecasting

Basically any time series can be used for producing forecasts, so any of the models described briefly in Section 12.6 can be applied when appropriate.

Alternatively autoregression models are particularly useful if it is felt that there is some time lapse before a series responds to changing conditions as they also depend on older values of the time series.

There are many forecasting models generated by Box-Jenkins techniques. These may be autoregressive models, moving average models or a combination of the two. They are effective in producing small errors but are often complicated and generally not easy to understand.

If future estimations can be found for the independent variables, multiple regression will often produce good forecasts as the influences of many factors are taken into consideration. Because these forecasts do not depend on just one variable they may be more robust to small changes and they will be better for slightly longer-term forecasting than the models used in this chapter which are essentially suitable for short-term forecasting only.

Multiple regression can also cope with seasonality if a 'dummy' variable is assigned to each of the four seasons. The value of the dummy variable is 1 for that particular season and 0 for the other three. This may seem involved but it works well in practice.

13.8 Summary

This chapter has been a continuation of Chapter 12. We have made use of the time series identified in Chapter 12 to make forecasts for the near future.

We have used three types of model: regression with time as the independent variable; exponential smoothing models; and seasonal decomposition in which the model needed to include a seasonal factor as well as a trend.

In every case the best fitting model was continued into the near future. The future values it produced were taken as the required forecasts. These forecasts were each quoted with a margin of error which reflected the quality of fit of the model to data in the past on the assumption that the modelling conditions would continue unchanged into the near future.

None of these models are suitable for long term forecasting because any change from the conditions under which the model was built up would require the use of a completely new model.

Forecasting is still considered to be an art rather than a science and a 'gut feeling' by an experienced operative may be as justified as any statistical analysis!

Tutorial 13: forecasting

These questions should be answered making use of the graphs you drew for Tutorial 12. Question 13.1 corresponds to Question 12.1, 13.2 to 12.2, etc. Note that there are no exact answers, only reasonable ones.

13.1 a) Extend the trend line and use it to forecast the sales of the departmental store for each of the quarters of 2006, describing clearly the method used. State your forecasts and add them to your graph to check that they look reasonable.
   b) Calculate the standard deviation of the second residuals and estimate the maximum likely error in your forecasts

13.2 a) Using an additive model forecast the turnovers for 2005 Quarter 4, 2006 Quarter 1, 2006 Quarter 2, 2006 Quarter 3. Add them to your graph and check the continuity of the seasonal pattern.
   b) What is the maximum error likely in your forecasts?
   c) Obtain deseasonalised data for 2004 Quarter 4, 2005 Quarter 1, 2005 Quarter 2, 2005 Quarter 3.
   d) Is the model used appropriate for forecasting with this data? Explain your answer.

13.3 a) Using an additive model forecast the turnovers for 2005 Quarter 3, 2005 Quarter 4, 2006 Quarter 1, 2006 Quarter 2. Add them to your graph.
   b) What is the maximum error likely in your forecasts?
   c) Obtain deseasonalised data for 2004 Quarter 3, 2004 Quarter 4, 2005 Quarter 1, 2005 Quarter 2.
   d) Assess the suitability of your model for forecasting with this data.

Notes

For SPSS/Minitab/Excel worksheets on graphical display see Chapter 14, Sections 14.2.6, 14.5.6, and 14.8.6 respectively. Worksheets with computer output and its interpretation are on the companion website.

The supplementary exercise for Chapter 13, with answers, is on the companion website.

Computer analysis

14

This chapter includes SPSS and Minitab worksheets for all the topics included in the course. Some Excel worksheets are also included but their application is limited to the analysis available in Excel. The versions used in this chapter are SPSS 12.0.1, Minitab 14 and Microsoft Office Excel 2003. Each worksheet should take about one hour to complete though this will depend on the ability of the individual student. Some topics are short and so more than one are combined in one single worksheet. There is also annotated output from all the worksheets in the lecturers' materials on the companion website. This is aimed at helping the student to interpret the results of the analysis.

This is obviously an 'either/or' situation in which you are only expected to use one of the computer packages depending on availability. Minitab is a popular teaching package and SPSS is commonly met in the working environment. Both are widely used so should be employed in preference to Excel which is an excellent spreadsheet rather than a statistical analysis package. SPSS and Minitab include excellent tutorials and Excel offers good training online.

14.1 Introduction to SPSS

SPSS, the Statistical Package for the Social Sciences, was originally developed in the USA to enable data from surveys and experiments to be analysed 'fully and flexibly'. It includes a wide range of procedures for both simple and highly complex methods which allow for very sophisticated analysis. Its weaknesses are mainly in the output from the simpler forms of analysis which may not be immediately interpretable, although this is improving with each new version.

SPSS offers the facilities common to all Windows applications. It is supplied with an excellent tutorial which you should either work through or refer to as needed.

On initially entering SPSS you are offered some choices (Figure 14.1). If you wish to use a file which you previously created you can select it from 'Open an existing data source'. If you wish to create a new file then select 'Type in data'. If you don't wish to use this box you can cancel it and select 'Don't show this dialogue in the future'.

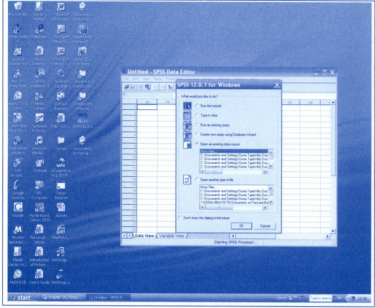

Figure 14.1

Figure 14.2

Whatever you choose, the 'SPSS Data Editor' opens automatically. This has two windows: the Variable View (Figure 14.2) for entering the names and descriptions of the variables and the Data View (Figure 14.3), which is used for entering their data values. A pair of tabs on the lower right hand side of the window indicates which view is which.

If you enter data from an existing file the heading changes to the name of that file.

As soon as you do any work the 'SPSS Viewer' window opens to keeps a listing of all your commands and output including the charts.

Each of these windows can be edited, saved, pasted to another Windows application and printed out.

Numerical data is entered into the grid in Data View in the usual manner with each

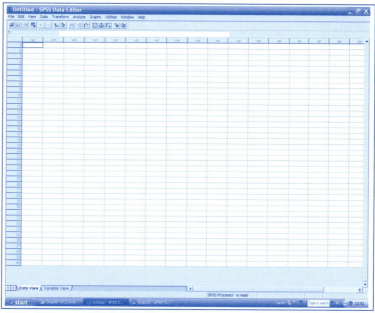

Figure 14.3

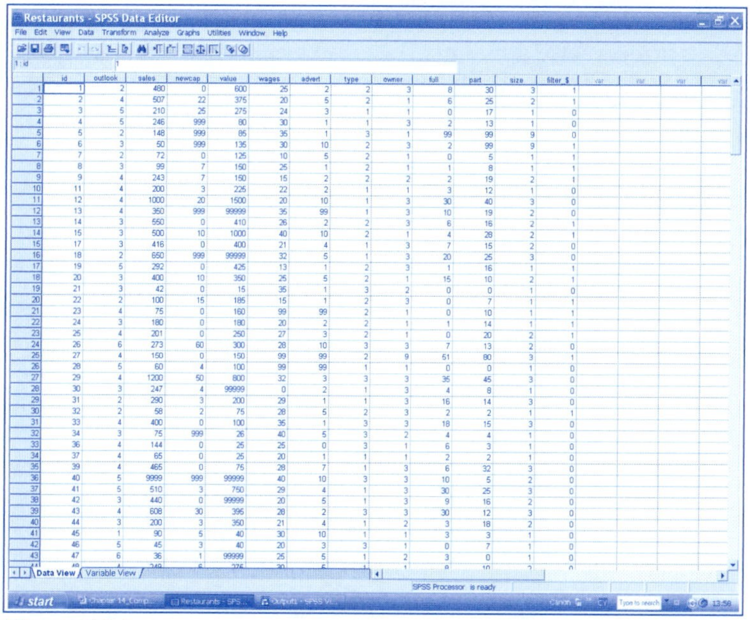

Figure 14.4

column containing the measurements on one particular variable and each row containing the measurements for a particular case (Figure 14.4). The characteristics of each variable are described in the Variable View grid (Figure 14.5). The variable name is limited to eight letters but its label, which appears on graphs and tables, can be any length.

The output which appears in the Viewer (Figure 14.6) is in the form of 'Objects' which can be edited in SPSS, saved, deleted, printed out, or exported to other applications. The amount of output is rather copious so it is a good idea to delete regularly any output which is not needed, especially before copying and pasting into a word processor for assignments, projects, and so on.

Each of the following sections, expanded into practical worksheets, is available on the companion website.

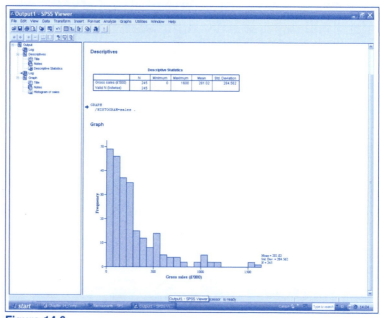

Figure 14.5

14.2 SPSS worksheets

Note: The commands in these worksheets are from SPSS Version 12.0.1.

Throughout this tutorial, *selections from menus, dialogue boxes or buttons* are shown in bold italics separated by the slash sign (/); VARIABLES in capitals; and **characters you need to type** in bold.

The assumption is that you have not used SPSS previously even though you are probably familiar with Windows.

Numerical answers to all the questions in these worksheets are to be found in Section 14.3. (The full output from all the worksheets, including the graphics, is included in the lecturers' material on the companion website.)

14.2.1 Graphical presentation with SPSS

During this tutorial you will learn how to use SPSS to explore data

Figure 14.6

graphically and also how to edit your graphs. In this tutorial screen prints are included initially to illustrate some of the instructions. We shall use the data from Tutorial 2 Question 2. (More graphics follow in Worksheet 14.2.2.)

14.2.1.1 Opening SPSS

The main menu on your local network may be set up in a variety of ways and the method of opening SPSS will differ from one to another.

Now open SPSS for Windows

You are now in the opening dialogue box. Select *Type in Data* / *OK* for a new file. The SPSS Data Editor opens in either Data View or Variable View.

14.2.1.2 Entering your data into SPSS

The following numbers represent the ages of a sample of 60 employees of a firm Merlin plc:

35	44	54	33	46	20	32	19	50	39	33	37
42	40	20	25	34	52	27	22	18	40	23	17
41	45	21	34	49	27	60	46	32	58	23	52
24	64	41	47	54	37	40	41	40	36	46	29
34	39	39	40	37	50	41	34	47	34	45	36

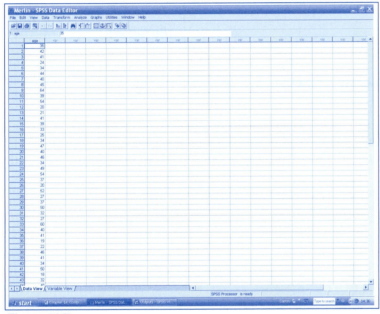

Figure 14.7

In Variable View row 1, name the variable **AGE**. Label it **Age of Employee** and, if necessary, change the decimal places to 0.

In Data View type all the ages in column 1 under Age, working systematically through them down the columns above from 35 to 34, 44 to 39, and so on, all in one column. Check that the final row number is 60 (Figure 14.7).

14.2.1.3 Checking your input

By printing the data into the SPSS Viewer you can check it at this stage and also have a record of it for printing out at the end of the session.

Analyse / *Reports* / *Case Summaries* Select AGE and then click on the arrow to move it over to the active Variables box (Figure 14.8).

Any analysis is performed on the variables in this right-hand box and not on the others which remain unselected in the original list.

On pressing OK the data is printed into the SPSS Viewer window (Figure 14.9). Check the values with those above. If any of them are incorrect, just overtype the correct version into the data editor.

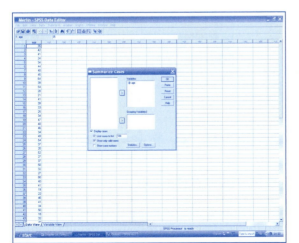

Figure 14.8

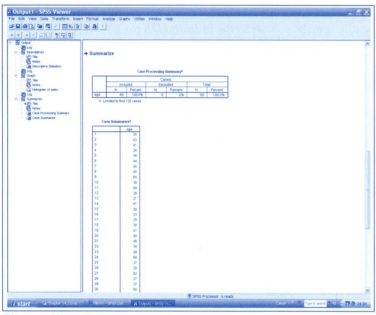

Figure 14.9

14.2.1.4 Saving your data as a file

If you are happy with the data save it to a disk, CD or onto your hard disk.

With the data window on top *File / Save as* **Merlin1** and *Save*. Your data has now been saved as an SPSS data file 'Merlin1.sav' onto your preferred type of storage.

14.2.1.5 Producing a histogram

We shall first produce the default histogram and then another more refined version.

Graphs / Histogram Select AGE as your variable and then *OK*.

The default histogram appears as a chart in the SPSS Viewer which can be printed out, saved as a separate file or exported into a Word file. It has no title and the default bar width is not a sensible one. We shall improve on this.

Graphs / Histogram Select AGE, then *Titles* and type in something like **Histogram of Ages**, and *Continue* then *OK* (Figure 14.10).

Now we can improve on the default bar width. From the toolbar, with the histogram selected: *Edit / SPSS Chart Object / Open / Edit / Properties / Histogram options / Bin sizes / Custom interval width 5 / Apply / Close / X* (on the toolbar)/*Scale / Range Custom / Minimum 10 / Maximum 70 / Major increments 5 / Apply / Close* (Figure 14.11).

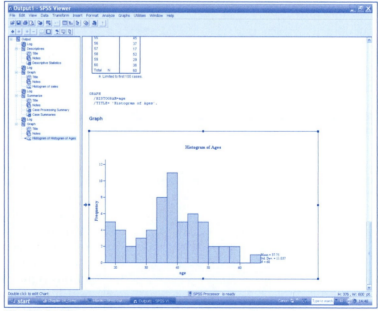

Figure 14.10

(Alternatively the Chart Editor can be opened by double clicking on the histogram in the SPSS Viewer.)

Your graph has a title and the scale on the horizontal axis is more reasonable (Figure 14.12). Don't worry about the mean and standard deviation; those are considered in Chapter 3. We shall edit this histogram further as the next task.

14.2.1.6 Editing a graph further

Double click anywhere within the graph to open up the Chart Editor with its tool bar. Pointing with the mouse at any of the icons tells you its specific purpose. Single clicking on any element within the chart window selects it, double clicking opens the Properties dialogue box. Colour and pattern can be applied to the histogram bars using *Fill* and *Border*. Try changing colours and patterns. Text and fonts can be altered using *Text*.

SPSS does not offer the options of producing frequency or cumulative frequency polygons.

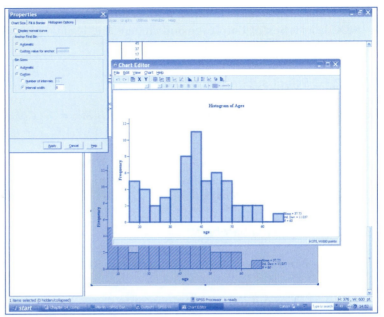

Figure 14.11

14.2.1.7 Producing a stem-and-leaf plot and a box plot

Analyse / Descriptive Statistics / Explore Move AGE into the Dependent List, Display *Plots* rather than *Both*.

Among other output you will find a stem-and-leaf plot with stem width of 10 and each case represented by one leaf

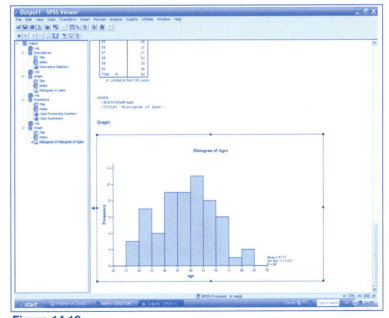

Figure 14.12

and a box plot. You can see from both that the data distribution is symmetrical, that the lowest value is 17 and the highest 64 and, from the box plot, that the middle half of the data ranges from about 31 to about 46. Make sure you can interpret both these graphs.

14.2.1.8 Include a second variable

Next split the employees into two separate groups, male and female, by coding the data.

Click the *Goto Data* grid button. Click on column 2 in Data View and then type **1** in the first 40 cells of column 2 and **2** in the remainder. In Variable View name this new variable **SEX**, label it **Sex of Employee** and change the decimal places to 0. Code the variable label as **1** for **Male** and **2** for **Female**.

14.2.1.9 Select subgroups of data

Data / Select cases / If condition is satisfied / If Sex = 1 / Continue / OK
For the males only, repeat tasks 14.2.1.5 and 14.2.1.6.
Data / Select cases / All cases
Data / Select cases / If condition is satisfied / If Sex = 2 / Continue / OK
For the females only, repeat tasks 14.2.1.5 and 14.2.1.6.
Data / Select cases / All cases

14.2.10 Produce a barchart

Graphs / Bar / Simple / Define / Category axis **SEX**. Give your barchart a suitable title.

14.2.1.11 Print out the session contents

When you have completed your tutorial you probably have some errors in your session window. These can be deleted by selecting each of the unwanted sections in turn by clicking on them and deleting them with the Delete key. When you are happy with the remaining material print it out, making sure that your cursor is in the Viewer window, then:
   File / Print / OK

14.2.1.12 Saving data and session output (if required)

   Data / Select cases / All cases
   With the cursor in the data sheet:
   File / Save as **Merlin2.sav** to save the data as an SPSS file.
   With the cursor in the SPSS Viewer:
   File / Save window as **Merlin1.spo** to save your output window if you wish.

14.2.2 Summary statistics with SPSS

We shall again use the data which you typed into SPSS in Worksheet 14.2.1 as the file Merlin2.sav and then saved. (If, by any chance you do not have it, refer to Worksheet 14.2.1 and instructions 14.2.1.2 and 14.2.1.8 and input the tabulated data again.) Look carefully at your screen before finding appropriate answers.

   This file contains information about the ages of 60 employees, male and female, of the firm Merlin plc.

14.2.2.1 Opening an SPSS data file:

1 Open SPSS and select *Merlin2* from the opening dialogue box under 'More files'. Your data appears in the Data Editor window.

2 Look at the data sheet. The ages of the 60 employees are displayed in the first column and the sex of each in the second.

If you have just typed them in, then check the numbers carefully with the tabulated data.

14.2.2.2 Data summary

1 Summarise the data by its mean and standard deviation.
Analyse / Descriptive Statistics / Descriptives and select AGE. This is a quick way to obtain the main summary statistics.
- What is the mean age of the employees?
- What is the standard deviation of these ages?
2 More information can be obtained by exploring the data:
Analyse / Descriptive Statistics / Explore and select AGE.
Display both. Add *Percentiles* to *Statistics* and *Histogram* to *Plots*.
- What is the median of the ages?
- State the minimum, maximum and range of the ages.
- State the quartiles and interquartile range of the ages.
- Does the histogram appear to be reasonably symmetrical?
3 Double click anywhere within the histogram to open up the Chart Editor.
Double click within the histogram / *Histogram Options* and tick *Display / Normal curve / Apply / Close* to check for symmetry. *File / Close* returns you to the Viewer.

14.2.2.3 Comparing groups of data

Check that the number in each group is correct:
Analyse / Descriptive Statistics / Frequencies. Select SEX as the variable.
Charts / Piecharts.
Double click anywhere within the piechart produced to open up the Chart Editor. Double click within the piechart, or on the legend, to open *Properties / Data value labels*. Select *Frequency / Sex of Employee / Percent / Apply / Close*. Select the icon for *Data ID mode* on the tool bar and click on each sector.
- What percentage of the employees are male?
2 Compare the two groups:
Analyse / Compare means / Means. Move AGE into the Dependent List and SEX into the Independent List. From Options add Median to the Cell Statistics.
- State the median for each group.
- State the mean and standard deviation for each group.
- Compare the median with the mean for each group.
3 Looking for a more detailed comparison, Explore can be used on each group:
Analyse / Descriptive Statistics / Explore. Move AGE into the Dependent list and SEX into the Factor list. *Plots* / select *Boxplots / Factor levels together*.
- For which sex are the ages higher, on average? Give two reasons.
- For which sex are the ages more spread out, on average? Give two reasons.
- Do the box plots illustrate the same results?
4 Print out your output:
In the Viewer window *File / Print / all*

14.2.3 Estimation and hypothesis testing with SPSS

In this worksheet we shall use the data saved in previous Worksheet 14.2.1 as Merlin1.sav as our population. We shall calculate its summary statistics, and use it as a population to provide a random sample from which we shall estimate the population parameters and then test various hypotheses about that population (conveniently forgetting that we actually know the true values for the population!).

1 Open SPSS and your file, Merlin1.sav, saved in Worksheet 14.2.1. If you have not saved the data turn back to that section and type it in.
2 Calculate the summary statistics for all the ages and look at their graphical descriptions:
   Analyse / Descriptive Statistics / Descriptives Select AGE
   • Make a note of the mean value.
3 Take a random sample of 10 cases:
   Data / Select cases / Random sample of cases / Sample. Sample size exactly **10** from the first **60**. Leave unselected cases as *Filtered*.
   Check in your data window and name the filter variable as Sample1 in Variable View.
   Note: Different samples will produce differing results.
4 Check the sample for normality:
   *Analyse / Nonparametric tests / 1 sample K-S / Select AGE and make sure that **Normal** is ticked.
   The 'Assymp. sig.' is the probability that the data is normal.
   • What is its value?
   You will probably find that it is over 0.05 and so the population is normally distributed
5 Find a confidence interval for the mean of all the ages:
   Analyse / Descriptive Statistics / Explore Select AGE.
   Under Descriptives you will find the upper and lower bounds of the 95 per cent Confidence interval for the mean.
   • State the 95 per cent confidence interval.
   • Does this interval include the mean age found in task 2?
6 Forgetting that we actually know the true value of the population mean, test the hypothesis that the mean age of all the employees is 50.
   Analyse / Compare means / One-Sample T Test Selecting AGE for the variable, set the test value at 50, leaving the confidence interval at 95 per cent.
   The 'Sig. 2 tailed' gives the probability that the null hypothesis of 50 years is correct.
   • State this value.
   You will probably find that this is lower than 0.05.
   Repeat for **40** years.
   • State this value.
   You will probably now find that it is higher than 0.05 so 40 is acceptable as a claim for the mean age of the population at 5 per cent significance.
   • What do you conclude?
   From the task bar *Data / Select cases / All cases / OK*.
7 In a new column Type **1** in rows 1 to 30 and **2** in rows 31 to 60. Name the column **Sex** and label **1 = Male, 2 = Female**.
   Take a random sample of 20 to give a large enough sample from each sex (See task 14.2.3.3).
   Name this new variable as **Sample2**.
   Save this file as **Merlin3**.
8 Calculate separate confidence intervals to see if they overlap.
   Analyse / Descriptive Statistics / Explore / Select AGE / *Factor list* SEX

- Do the intervals overlap?
- What does this mean?

9 Carry out a two-sample t-test to see if the males and females in the whole population have different mean ages.

Analyse / Compare means / Independent Samples T Test Select AGE for the Test variable, SEX for the Grouping variable. Define groups **1** and **2**, leave the confidence interval at 95 per cent. The Sig. (2-tailed) value on the last line gives the probability that there is no difference between the means.

- State this value.
- What do you conclude?

10 Carry out a Mann–Whitney U test to see if the males and females in the whole population have different mean ages if the data were not normally distributed.

Analyse / Nonparametric tests / 2 Independent Samples Select AGE for the Test variable, SEX for the Grouping variable. Test Type: Mann–Whitney.

The Assymp.Sig. (2-tailed) value on the last line gives the probability that there is no difference between the means.

- State this value.
- What do you conclude?

14.2.4 Analysis of variance with SPSS

14.2.4.1 One-way ANOVA

One-way ANOVA can be thought of as an extension to the two-sample t-test.

1 *Open file*: Merlin3.sav
2 Check by describing the variable, AGE, to be used in this analysis:

Analyse / Descriptive Statistics / Descriptives / AGE

You should find a mean of 37.75 and a standard deviation of 11.04.

3 Carry out a two-sample t-test on AGE grouped by SEX. (Reminder from last worksheet.)

Analyse / Compare means / Independent Samples T Test / Select AGE for the Test Variable and SEX as the Grouping Variable, and Define groups: **1** and **2**.

- State the mean values for the males and the females.
- The null hypothesis for this test is that the means are the same, that is that the difference is zero. What is the probability that this is true?
- Assuming equal variances, what do you conclude?

4 *Analyse / Compare means / One-Way ANOVA* / Select AGE as the dependent variable and SEX as the factor.

From the *Options* activate *Descriptives* for the addition of the separate group means.

- State the null hypothesis.
- What is the probability that it is true?
- What do you conclude?
- Look at the confidence interval for each of the means. Indicate why these lead to the same conclusion.
- Compare with results of task 3.

5 With the next empty column selected in the Variable View input the Job Category of each employee: Name the variable JOBCAT. Use **Job Category** for the variable label with values: **1 = Clerical**, **2 = Management**, **3 = Production**, **4 = Security** (See Worksheet 14.2.1 if unsure of the method.)

Type in the following two rows of codes all down in one column without any spaces:

4 3 4 1 1 3 3 3 2 1 2 1 1 3 4 1 4 4 2 1 2 1 3 2 3 1 3 3 1 2
1 3 3 3 3 1 1 2 4 1 2 1 1 3 3 1 3 2 3 3 3 1 1 2 3 3 1 3 3 3

Save this updated data file as **Merlin4.**

6 *Analyse/ Compare means / One-Way ANOVA* / Select AGE as the dependent variable and JOBCAT as the factor. From the *Options* activate *Descriptives* and from *Post Hoc* select *Least significant difference (LSD)*.
   * State the null hypothesis.
   * State the alternative hypothesis.
   * What is the probability that the null hypothesis is true?
   * What do you conclude?
   * Look at the confidence interval for each of the means. Indicate why these lead to the same conclusion.
   * Which levels of JOBCATS differ in their mean ages?

14.2.4.2 Two-way ANOVA

Two-way ANOVA is the simplest extension of One-way ANOVA.
   We shall now split AGE by *both* factors simultaneously.

1 *Analyse / General Linear Model / Univariate* / Select AGE as the Dependent Variable and JOBCAT and SEX as the Fixed Factors.
   * State the three null hypotheses.
   * State the three alternative hypothesis.
   * What are the probabilities that each null hypothesis is true?
   * What do you conclude?
   Since the interactions are not significant we can just consider the main effects
2 *Analyse / General Linear Model / Univariate* / Select AGE as the *dependent variable and JOBCAT and SEX as the factors. From Model select Custom*. Build JOBCAT and SEX into the model and select *Main effects* (under *Build terms*)
   * State the two null hypotheses.
   * State the two alternative hypothesis.
   * What are the probabilities that each null hypothesis is true?
   * What do you conclude?
   We can compare our groups graphically using the methods from earlier Worksheets.
3 *Graphs / Bar / Clustered / Define / Category Axis JOBCAT / Define clusters by SEX*
4 *Graphs / Interactive / Pie / Clustered / Slice by JOBCAT / Cluster by SEX*
5 Carry out a chi-square test to see if there is any association between Job Categories and Sex:
   Analyse / Descriptive statistics / Crosstabs / Rows JOBCAT / Columns SEX / Statistics Chi-square / Cells Observed and Expected
   * State the null hypothesis.
   * State the alternative hypothesis.
   * What is the probability that the null hypothesis is true?
   * What do you conclude?
6 Carry out a two-way Analysis of Variance using a main effects model as in the table for the laboratories and brands of peanut butter as given in Tutorial 8 Question 3.

You will need one column for all the fat contents, another column for the Laboratory codes: 1 = A, 2 = B, and so on, and a third for the brands.
Use the output to answer Tutorial 8 Question 3.
7 Carry out a two-way Analysis of Variance using a main effects model for the electronics firm data in Tutorial 8 Question 4.
You will need one column for all numbers of monitors produced, another column for the employees: 1 = A, 2 = B, and so on, and a third for the times of day.
Use the output to answer the Tutorial 8 Question 4.

14.2.5 Correlation and regression analysis with SPSS

During this tutorial you will learn how to use SPSS to investigate the association between two continuous variables and how to describe it graphically
1 In this practical session you will analyse some bivariate data.
To enter the data:
File / *Open worksheet* / **Merlin4** (saved in the ANOVA Worksheet, 14.2.4).
In order to see what this file contains:
Analyse / *Descriptive Statistics* / *Descriptives*. Select all the variables but not the filters.
We have three variables. Each is measured on 60 cases. There are no missing values.
We shall give each of the employees a salary and then see if this is associated with their age.
In Variable View, in the first empty row name a new variable SALARY and label it **Annual salary** (£'000).
In Data View type the following in one column (work down these columns one after the other):

38.1	38.9	23.2	22.9	19.8	19.7	15.6	31.7	17.3	37.8
18.7	42.8	19.6	47.5	31.3	8.5	28.5	14.1	33.5	32.9
42.3	60.1	15.5	15.8	59.3	15.9	37.3	20.3	13.7	9.8
25.9	60.7	20.7	35.9	33.8	39.3	32.9	19.8	6.4	15.2
53.6	75.2	40.2	25.3	24.5	14.5	23.9	28.2	35.3	8.7
37.6	10.9	28.5	63.2	32.0	10.2	8.6	25.3	12.5	38.4

The variables of interest in this practical session are the continuous variables SALARY and AGE. We shall investigate the relationship between the Salaries earned by the employees of Merlin and their ages.
2 Save revised datafile as **Merlin5.**
3 Produce a scatter plot.
Graphs / *Scatter* / *Define as Simple*/ Select SALARY for Y and AGE for X.
Give your graph a suitable title.
Examine the plot. You should find it does suggest a rather poor linear relationship.
• Does there appear to be a relationship?
• Have a guess as to whether this is likely to be significant or not.
4 Calculate the correlation coefficient.
Analyse / *Correlate* / *Bivariate*
Select SALARY and AGE as the variables.
• What is the value of the correlation coefficient?
• What is the probability of it being zero?
• Is this significant at 5 per cent?

If the p value is less than 0.05 the correlation coefficient is significant at the 5 per cent level of significance.

5 Find the regression equation:
   Analyse / Regression / Linear/ Select SALARY as *Dependent*, AGE as *Independent*.
   Use Method Enter.
   The regression equation, as produced by SPSS, is not at all obvious.
   In the Coefficients table, under unstandardised coefficients and in the column under B you will find the constant, a, and the coefficient of Age, b.
   • Write down the regression equation.

6 Produce the regression line on your scatter plot.
   Graphs / Scatter / Define as simple / Select SALARY for Y and AGE for X and *OK*
   Double click on the graph to get into editing mode.
   Click on the points to select them.
   Chart / Add chart element / Fit line at total

7 Carry out residual analysis (this could have been added at step 5).
   Analyse / Regression / Linear / Select SALARY as dependent and AGE as independent variables. Select *Plots / Standardised residual plots / histogram*. Select *Save / Residuals / Unstandardised.*
   Save this data as **Merlin6.mtw**
   You should see that your residuals appear reasonably normal on the histogram.
   To see if the mean is zero and the standard deviation low:
   Analyse / Descriptive Statistics / Descriptives / Select the SALARY and UNSTANDARDISED RESIDUALS.
   You should see that the mean of the residuals is zero. The standard deviation has been reduced (but not by much for these data).
   In the next three tasks we look at the males and females separately.

8 Produce the two regression lines on your scatter plot.
   Graphs / Scatter / Define as Simple. Select SALARY for Y and AGE for X and Set marker by SEX. OK
   Double click on the graph to get into editing mode.
   Click on the male points to select them (this is easiest to do in the legend).
   Chart / Add chart element / Fit line at total.
   Repeat for the female points.
   • Describe the general differences between the male and the female salaries.

9 In the Data editor: *Data / Select cases / If condition is satisfied / If Sex = 1 / Continue*
   Leave unselected cases as Filtered. *OK*
   Repeat task 4 and, if the correlation coefficient is significant, task 5 for the males only.
   • Write down the correlation coefficient and the regression equation, if appropriate

10 In the Data editor: *Data / Select cases / All cases*. Then *If condition is satisfied / If Sex = 2*.
   Leave unselected cases as Filtered.
   Repeat task 4 and, if the correlation coefficient is significant, task 5 for the females only.
   • Write down the correlation coefficient and the regression equation, if appropriate.

14.2.6 Time series analysis and forecasting with SPSS

In this worksheet we will analyse seasonal data. Exponential smoothing and curve fitting can be carried out quite easily for non-seasonal data in SPSS by following the instructions in the Help menu.

The quarterly sales of a departmental store have been monitored for the past five years with the following information being produced (Tutorial 12 Question 1):

Total quarterly sales (£'000)				
Year	Q1	Q2	Q3	Q4
2001	48	58	57	65
2002	50	61	59	68
2003	52	62	59	69
2004	52	64	60	73
2005	53	65	60	75

1 Type all the sales figures in chronological order in one column heading it **Sales.**
   *Then Data / Define dates / Select **Years, quarters** / First case in Year 2001 quarter 1.*
   Look at the new variables in both Data Editor grids. They describe the year, the quarter
   and their combination for use in time series diagrams. Save this file as **Sales**.
2 Plot a sequence graph of sales with dates to see if an additive model is appropriate.
   Graphs / Sequence / Variables: Sales / Time axis labels: Date.

14.2.6.1 Additive model

1 Assuming it is, carry out the seasonal decomposition using that model:
   *Analyse / Time Series / Seasonal Decomposition / Additive model / Endpoints weighted by 0.5
   / Display casewise listing* Variable SALES.
2 Some new variables have been produced. Produce a sequence plot, as in task 14.2.6.2,
   adding the trend STC_1 to the graph.
3 Make use of the seasonal factors and the smoothed trend cycle for making forecasts.
   For an Additive model: Fitted values = Trend + Seasonal Factor so compute a new
   variable, named FITTED_1, describing the fitted values:
   Transform / Compute / Target variable type FITTED_1 = STC_1 + SAF_1
4 Plot a sequence graph of the Sales and the Fitted_1 values.
   Graph / Sequence / Variables: Sales, Fitted_1 / Time axis labels: Date.
5 Residual analysis:
   Remember that the residuals should: (a) be small, (b) have a mean of 0, (c) have a standard
   deviation which is much smaller than that of Sales, (d) be normally distributed and (e) be
   random time-wise. The residuals have been saved as ERR_1.
   (a), (b) and (c) Produce descriptive statistics of Sales and ERR_1.
   (d) For ERR_1 produce a box plot and a histogram with a normal plot.
      Carry out the K-S hypothesis test for normality:
      Analyse / Nonparametric tests / 1 sample K-S / Normal distribution.
   (e) Produce a sequence plot of the errors
      Edit the chart to put a reference line at ERR_1 = 0.

14.2.6.2 Multiplicative model

1 Repeat task 14.2.6.1.1 but use a multiplicative model
2 Repeat task 14.2.6.1.2 but use a multiplicative model
3 Make use of the seasonal factors and the smoothed trend cycle for making forecasts.
   For a multiplicative model: Fitted values = Trend × Seasonal Factor so compute a new
   variable, named FITTED_2, describing the fitted values:
   *Transform / Compute / Target variable type FITTED_2 = STC_2 * SAF_2*
   *Save file as **Quarterly sales.sav.***
4 Plot a sequence graph of the Sales and the Fitted_2 values.
   Graph / Sequence / Variables: Sales, Fitted_2 / Time axis labels: Date
5 For the multiplicative model, subtract the fitted values from the sales figures to find a set
   of errors, ERR_3, which are comparable with those from the additive model.

14.2.6.3 Comparing models

1 (a), (b), (c) Produce descriptive statistics of sales and ERR_1, ERR_3.
   (d) Produce boxplots and histograms with a normal plots on ERR_1, ERR_3.
       Carry out the K-S hypothesis tests for normality:
   Analyse / Nonparametric tests / 1 sample K-S / Normal distribution.
   (e) Produce sequence plots of both sets of errors
       Edit the charts to put a reference lines at 0.
       Which is the better model in your opinion? Why?
2 Assuming that the trend from the additive model is increasing by 0.3 per quarter, what
   would be your forecasts for the four quarters of 2006?

14.3 Numerical answers to SPSS worksheets

(Full output can be found in the Instructor's materials on the companion website.)

14.2.1 Graphical presentation

All output graphical.

14.2.2 Summary statistics

14.2.2.2

1 37.75, 11.04 years.
2 39.00; 17, 64, 47; 32, 45.75, 13.75 years; Yes.

14.2.2.3

1 66.7%.
2 Male 39.5, Female 36.5 years,
   Male 38.25, 11.08, Female 36.75, 11.17 years.
3 Males 'averages' higher; Females 'spreads' higher.

14.2.3 Estimation and hypothesis testing

(Different answers for different samples.)
2 37.75 years.
4 0.530.
5 27.38 to 44.02 years; Yes.
6 0.004; 0.272.
8 Yes, so mean ages could be the same.
9 0.083, mean ages could be the same.
10 0.359, median ages could be the same.

14.2.4 Analysis of variance

14.2.4.1

3 38.9, 36.6 years; 0.411; they are the same.
4 0.411; they are the same; the confidence intervals overlap.

6 0.000; at least two are different; many don't overlap; all different apart from Production and Security.

14.2.4.2

1 0.000, 0.804, 0.713; different for Jobcat, same for Sex and Interaction.
2 0.000, 0.229; different for Jobcat, same for Sex.
3 Sig. (Labs) = 0.383, sig.(Brands) = 0.079; both same at 5% significance.
4 Sig. (Shifts) = 0.028, sig.(Employees) = 0.276, only shifts different.

14.2.5 Correlation and regression analysis

4 0.398; 0.002; Yes.
5 Salary = 7.73 + 0.554 × Age.
9 Males: 0.483, Salary = 6.88 + 0.734 × Age; Females: not significant.

14.2.6 Time series analysis and forecasting

Graphical output with most answers approximate only.

14.4 Introduction to Minitab

Minitab is a powerful tool originally developed at Pennsylvania State University as a teaching aid for introductory statistics courses. It is now one of the most widely accepted statistical analysis packages for college instruction and is also an established research tool. It is becoming more sophisticated with each version and now includes many forms of multivariate analysis.

Minitab offers the facilities common to all Windows applications. The version used here is 14.0. It is upgraded regularly so that one problem is keeping up with the literature. It offers an excellent series of tutorials which should be worked through. It also includes a comprehensive Help facility at any stage.

On initially entering Minitab a split window is automatically set up. The lower half, the Worksheet, is for entering data. If you enter data from an existing file the heading changes to the name of that file. The Session window keeps a listing of all your commands and output. Each of these

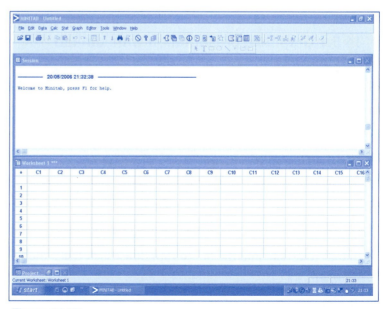

Figure 14.13

windows can be edited, saved, pasted to another Windows application and/or printed out in the usual manner.

Numerical data only are typed into the grid with each column containing the measurements on one particular variable and each row containing the measurements for a particular case. The variables are named (name limited to eight characters) in the cells between the column numbers and row 1 of the data cells.

The output in the Session window can be edited before being saved, printed out or copied and pasted to another application such as Word.

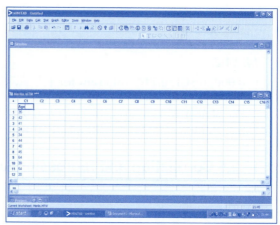

Figure 14.14

14.5 Minitab worksheets

Throughout this tutorial, *selections from menus, dialogue boxes or buttons* are shown in bold italics separated by the slash sign /; VARIABLES in capitals; and **characters you need to type** in bold. As your experience increases the degree of detail in the instructions decreases.

The assumption is that you have not used Minitab previously and that you are familiar with Windows.

Minitab is not fussy about capitals but is very fussy about **having only numbers in its worksheet**. It remembers that letters have been typed into the grid even after they have been deleted so take care! In the Data menu there is 'Change Data Type' which can be used to rectify this problem.

(The full output from all the sheets, including the graphics, is included in the Instructor's material on the companion website.)

14.5.1 Graphical presentation with Minitab

During this tutorial you will learn how to use Minitab to explore data graphically and also how to edit your graphs. In this tutorial screen prints have been included initially to help you understand the instructions. We shall use the data in Tutorial 2 Question 2.

(More graphics follow in Worksheet 14.5.2)

14.5.1.1 Opening Minitab

Menus on your local network may be set up in a variety of ways and the method of opening Minitab will differ from one to another.

Now open Minitab for Windows.

You are now in Minitab with two windows open: the Worksheet window into which you will put all your data and the Session window which holds the record of all your commands and the resulting output. (See Figures 14.13 and 14.14.) Later you will use the Information window and the Chart window. Each of these windows can be saved and/or printed out during or at the end of the session.

14.5.1.2 Putting your data into Minitab

The following figures represent the ages of a sample of 60 employees of a firm, Merlin plc:

35	44	54	33	46	20	32	19	50	39	33	37
42	40	20	25	34	52	27	22	18	40	23	17
41	45	21	34	49	27	60	46	32	58	23	52
24	64	41	47	54	37	40	41	40	36	46	29
34	39	39	40	37	50	41	34	47	34	45	36

Place the cursor over the data window, the Worksheet, in the first cell of the row below C1, column 1, and click the mouse. You are now in the cell which will contain the column heading for the first variable. You can move around the worksheet using the arrow keys.

Type the word **Age** and then, with the down arrow, move the cursor down to row 1 of C1. Type all the values in the table into column 1, one number per cell, using the down arrow between each. Work down the first column from 35 to 34 then continue down with 44 to 39, and so on, until you have all 60 ages in the first column. Be very careful not to type any words into the data cells. Check that your final number is in row 60.

14.5.1.3 Checking your input

By printing the data into the Session Window you can check it at this stage and also have a record of it printed out at the end of the session.

Data / Display Data / Click on AGE to select your variable and then *Select*. This variable is entered into the Display box (Figure 14.15).

On pressing *OK* the data is printed into the Session window. Check the values with those above. If any are incorrect, just over-type the correct version into the worksheet (Figure 14.16).

14.5.1.4 Saving your data as a file

Once you are happy with the data, save it onto a disc, CD or onto your hard disc.

File / Save Current Work-sheet as **Merlin1**. This has now been saved as a Minitab data file Merlin.mtw on the storage of your preference.

14.5.1.5 Producing a histogram

We shall produce a simple histogram and then refine it.

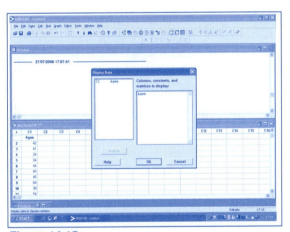

Figure 14.15

Figure 14.16

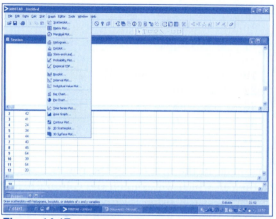

Figure 14.17

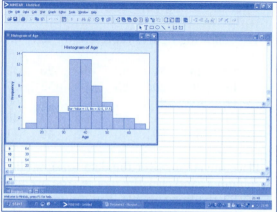

Figure 14.18

Graph / Histogram / Simple / Click on AGE, then *Select / Labels / Title* / **Histogram of Ages** then *OK*.(Figures 14.17 and 14.18)

Double click on one of the X axis values to use the editor:

Binning / Interval type / Cutpoint

Interval definition: Mid-point/Cutpoint positions 15 20 . . . . 60 65

Scale: Major tick positions / Position of ticks 15 20 . . . . . . .60 65 *OK*. (Figure 14.19).

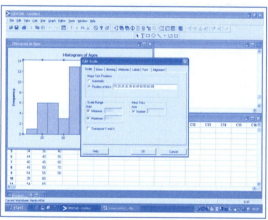

Figure 14.19

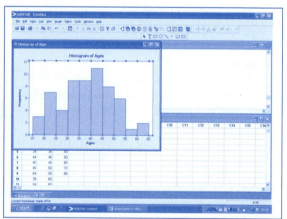

Figure 14.20

Have we too many bars (Figure 14.20)?

Try a different grouping. Type a new set of cut-off points and Major tick positions: **0 10 20 30 40 50 60 70 80**, and produce a new histogram (Figure 14.21).

Which histogram do you prefer? We shall use the second one for the following tasks.

Note that all your graphs can be viewed using the 'Show Graphs Folder' icon on the top toolbar.

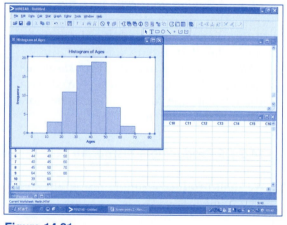

Figure 14.21

14.5.1.6 Editing a graph

Right click anywhere within the graph to use editing mode. ***Edit bars***. Colour and pattern can be applied to the histogram bars using the ***Fill pattern and Borders*** and ***Fill line*** options. Text and fonts can be altered, lines added to the graph, and so on. Try making many changes!

Save this graph before editing it further: Right click on the green cross in the top left corner and ***Save graph as*** **Histogram of Ages**.

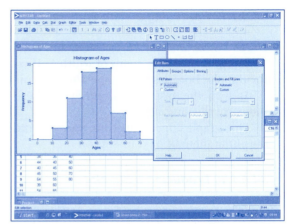

Figure 14.22

14.5.1.7 Adding a frequency polygon to a histogram

Right click the title: ***Edit title / add polygon to the title***.

Click on your histogram for editing mode. In the editing toolbar, click on the open polygon icon to use the line drawing tool. In the graph, click on the position (5,0), then, in turn, on the centre of the top of each bar and finally on position (75,0). Double click on the final point to drop the line drawing tool.

14.5.1.8 Producing a cumulative frequency ogive

The F3 key will clear the contents of the dialogue box. Produce a histogram as in task 14.5.1.5 but from ***Scale*** select ***Y scale / Accumulate values across bars***. Give it a suitable title. Alter the intervals as in task 14.5.1.5. Edit as for the polygon, using the open-ended polygon icon to click on the cumulative frequencies at the end of each interval starting with (10,0), then (20,3) through to (80,60).

Does the ogive look a bit untidy? It would be clearer if the histogram were removed. Double click within the histogram to select it; from the Edit bars dialogue box select ***Custom*** for Fill patterns and borders. Select blank fill pattern, white background, white colour and no lines. You will be left with just the cumulative frequency polygon.

14.5.1.9

Next split the employees into two separate groups, male (1) and female (2), by coding the data. If the worksheet is not visible click the Show worksheets folder on the top toolbar.

Type the word **Sex** in the heading of the first empty column. Type **1** in the first 40 cells of the column and **2** in the remaining 20 cells.

14.5.1.10 Producing a histogram of subgroups of data

Data / Split worksheet by / Sex. You now have two extra separate worksheets.

Repeat task 14.5.1.5 for each new worksheet.

14.5.1.11 Producing a bar chart of the subgroups of data

Graph / Barchart / Simple / Select SEX.

14.5.1.12 Producing a stem-and-leaf plot from Worksheet Merlin1

Graph / Stem-and-leaf / Select AGE and *OK*.

You probably have stems of width 5. If you would prefer wider ones, repeat the command for the plot but, this time, type **10** in the increment box.

As with the histograms, either of these plots is quite acceptable. Make sure you can interpret this output.

This graph appears in your session window and can be printed out with the rest of this output at the end of your session.

14.5.1.13 Producing a dot plot

Graph / Dotplot / Simple / Select AGE and *OK*.

For this plot each case is represented by a single dot, that is, the data is ungrouped. Replace the major ticks at 0 10 20, and so on.

14.5.1.14 Producing a box plot

Graph / Boxplot / Simple / Select AGE and give your graph a title.

We can see that the middle half of the data ranges from about 31 to about 46 and that the extreme values are at about 17 and 64.

14.5.1.15 Printing out the session contents and your graphs

When you have completed your tutorial you probably have some errors in your session window. These can be deleted by highlighting the unwanted sections and deleting them as you would in Word. When you are happy with the remaining material print it out, make sure that your cursor is in the session window before you print it out:

File / Print Session Window / OK.
Each graph needs printing separately when on top.
File / Print Graph / OK.

14.5.1.16 Saving your work onto your preferred type of storage

All your work (data, session and graphs) can be saved as a project:

File / Save Project as **Merlin1.MPJ** to save as a project file.
The data can be saved separately as a data file:
File / Save Current Worksheet as **Merlin2.MTW** to save as a data file. (Already saved.)
The session output can be saved separately as a text file:
File / Save Session Window as **Merlin1.TXT** to save your session window as a text file.

14.5.2 Summary statistics with Minitab

14.5.2.1 Inputting data from a Minitab datafile

We shall again use the data which you typed into Minitab in Worksheet 14.5.1.2 as the file Merlin1.mtw and then saved. (If, by any chance you do not have it, refer to Worksheet 14.5.1 (14.5.1.2 and 14.5.1.9) and input the tabulated data again.)

This file contains information about the age and sex of 60 employees of the firm Merlin plc.

1 Inputting a Minitab datafile. Open Minitab and then from the Data Editor window select *File / Open Worksheet* and select *Merlin2* from your file list. Your data appears in the Worksheet window.

2 Look at the data sheet. The ages of the 60 employees and their sex are displayed in the first and second columns. If you have just typed them in, then check the numbers carefully with the tabulated data.

14.5.2.2 Data summary

1 Summarise the data by its main summary statistics.
Stat / Basic Statistics / Display Descriptive Statistics and select AGE as your Variable.
   - What is the mean age of the employees?
   - What is the standard deviation of these ages?
   - What is the median of the ages?
   - State the minimum, maximum and range of the ages.
   - State the quartiles and interquartile range of the ages.

2 Repeat the descriptive statistics above but also produce some graphs.
Stat / Basic Statistics / Graphical summary/ Select AGE.
   - Do the histogram and box plot show the data to be to be reasonably symmetrical?
Note that the graphical summary is an excellent source of information.

14.5.2.3 Comparing two groups

1 Check that the number in each group is correct:
Stat / Tables / Tally individual variables / Display Counts. Select SEX as the variable.

2 *Graph / Pie Charts*. Click in *Categorical variables*. Select SEX and *Percent, Frequency, Category name* for *Slice labels*.
What percentage of the employees are male?

3 The two groups can now be compared numerically:
Stat / Basic Statistics / Display Descriptive Statistics and select AGE as your Variable, click in the *By variable* box and select *SEX. / Graphs / Boxplot* of data
   - State the median for each group.
   - State the mean and standard deviation for each group.
   - State the interquartile range for each group.
   - For which sex are the ages higher, on average? Give two reasons?
   - For which sex are the ages more spread out, on average? Give two reasons.
   - Do the box plots illustrate the same results?

4 Save whichever type of file you prefer; it is not necessary to save all your work after every session.

5 Print out whichever output you wish either as the session or as individual graphs.

14.5.3 Estimation and hypothesis testing with Minitab

In this worksheet we shall use the data input in Worksheet 14.5.1, Merlin1.mtw, as our population. We shall calculate its summary statistics, and use it as a population to provide a random sample from which we shall estimate the population parameters and then test various hypotheses about that population (conveniently forgetting that we actually know the true values for the population!).

1   Open Minitab and your file, Merlin1.mtw, saved in Worksheet 14.5.1. If you have not saved the data turn back to that section and type it in.
    With your cursor in the worksheet *File / Open Worksheet* and select *Merlin1.*

2   Calculate the summary statistics for all the ages and look at their graphical descriptions:
    Stat / Basic statistics / Display Descriptive statistics / Select AGE.
    Make a note of the mean value.

3   Take a random sample of 10 cases:
    Calc / Random data / Sample from Columns. Type **10** in *Samples rows*, click in the box underneath and select AGE. *Store samples in C3*. Check in your data window and label column 3 as **Sample1**.

4   Test your sample for normality:
    Stat / Basic Statistics / Normality Test / Kolmogorov-Smirnov / Select Sample1 as variable
    The P-value at the end gives the probability that the population is normal.
    • What is your value? You will probably find that it is over 0.05 so the data can be considered to be normally distributed.

5   Find a confidence interval for the mean of all the ages:
    Stat / Basic Statistics / Graphical Summary / Select Sample1.
    • Does this interval include the mean age found in task 2?
    Repeat, changing the confidence interval to 90%. Compare the two intervals.

6   Forgetting that we actually know the true value of the population mean, test the hypothesis that the mean age of all the employees is 50.
    Stat / Basic Statistics / 1-Sample t / Select Sample1 for the variable, test the mean of 50, leaving the alternative hypothesis in the options as *not equal*.
    The P-value gives the probability that the null hypothesis of 50 years is correct.
    • State this value. You will probably find that this is lower than 0.05.
    Repeat for 40 years.
    • State this value. You will probably now find that it is higher than 0.05 so 40 is acceptable as a claim for the mean age of the population at 5 per cent significance.

7   In a new column, C4, Type **1** in rows 1 to 30 and **2** in rows 31 to 60. Label the column **Sex**. We shall assume that the first 30 employees are male and the last 30 female.
    Take a new sample of 20 (see task 3 if uncertain) selecting AGE and SEX as the columns and store the data in the next two unused columns to give a large enough sample from each sex. Label these two new columns **Age2** and **Sex2**.

8   Calculate separate confidence intervals and see if they overlap.
    Stat / Basic Statistics / Graphical summary / Select AGE2 for *Variables*, tick *By variable* and select *SEX2*. *Produce 95% confidence intervals*.
    • Do the intervals overlap?
    • What does this mean?

9   Carry our a two-sample t-test to see if the males and females in the whole population have the same mean ages.
    Stat / Basic Statistics / 2-Sample t / Samples in one column / Samples AGE2 / Subscripts SEX2.
    The P-value on the last line gives the probability that there is no difference between the means.
    • State this value.
    • What do you conclude?

10 Carry out a non-parametric test. (The two groups need to be in different columns.)
    Data / Sort / Sort column / AGE2 SEX2 / By column SEX2 / Store sorted data in original columns.
    Copy and paste the male ages into C7 and the female ages into C8. Label these **MAge** and **FAge**.
    Stat / Nonparametrics / Mann–Whitney / First Sample MAge / Second Sample FAge

11 Save this updated file as Merlin3.mtw on your preferred storage.
   File / Save Current Worksheet as **Merlin3.mtw.**

14.5.4 Analysis of variance with Minitab

14.5.4.1 One-way ANOVA

One-way ANOVA can be thought of as an extension to the two-sample t-test.
1 *Open Worksheet* Merlin3 saved while working through the Worksheet 14.5.3.
2 Check by describing the variable, AGE, to be used in this analysis:
   Stat / Basic Statistics / Display Descriptive Statistics / AGE.
3 Carry out a two-sample t-test on ages grouped by sex.
   Stat / Basic Statistics / 2-Sample t / Samples in one column / Samples AGE /
   Subscripts SEX / Options / Alternative / not equal.
   • State the mean values for the males and the females
   • The null hypothesis for this test is that the means are the same, that is, that the
     difference is zero. What is the probability that this is true?
   • What do you conclude?
4 *Stat / ANOVA / One-way / Response AGE / Factor SEX.*
   • State the null hypothesis.
   • What is the probability that it is true?
   • What do you conclude?
   • Look at the confidence interval for the difference.
     Indicate why this leads to the same conclusion.
   • Compare with results of task 14.5.4.3.
5 In the first empty column type **Jobcat** for the heading and the following list of codes (with-
   out spaces which are here just to ease checking)

   4 3 4 1 1 3 3 3 2 1 2 1 1 3 4 1 4 4 2 1 2 1 3 2 3 1 3 3 1 2
   1 3 3 3 3 1 1 2 4 1 2 1 1 3 3 1 3 2 3 3 3 1 1 2 3 3 1 3 3 3

   (1 = Clerical, 2 = Management, 3 = Production, 4 = Security)
   Save your revised current worksheet as **Merlin4**
6 *Stat / ANOVA / One-way / Response AGE / Factor JOBCAT.*
   • State the null hypothesis.
   • State the alternative hypothesis.
   • What is the probability that the null hypothesis is true?
   • What do you conclude?
   • Look at the confidence interval for each of the means.
     Indicate why these lead to the same conclusion.
   • Which levels of JOBCATS differ in their mean ages?

14.5.4.2 Two-way ANOVA

Two-way ANOVA is the simplest extension of one-way ANOVA.
   We shall now split the ages by both factors simultaneously.
1 *Stat / ANOVA / General Linear Model / Responses AGE / Model JOBCAT, SEX* and *JOBCAT*
   * SEX.

- State the three null hypotheses.
- State the three alternative hypothesis.
- What are the probabilities that each null hypothesis is true?
- What do you conclude?

Since the interactions are not significant we can just consider the main effects.

2 *Stat / ANOVA / General Linear Model / Responses AGE / Model JOBCAT* and *SEX.*
- State the two null hypotheses.
- State the two alternative hypothesis .
- What are the probabilities that each null hypothesis is true?
- What do you conclude?

3 Compare the subgroups graphically.
   Graph / Barchart / Cluster / Select JOBCAT and *SEX.*

4 Carry out a chi-square test to see if there is any association between Job categories and Sex:
   Stat / Tables / Crosstabulations and Chi-Square / For Rows JOBCAT / For columns Columns SEX / Chisquare / Display Chi-Square analysis / Expected Cell Counts.
- State the null hypothesis.
- State the alternative hypothesis.
- What is the probability that the null hypothesis is true?

5 Carry out a two-way analysis of variance, without interactions, for the Laboratories and Brand of Peanut Butter as given in Tutorial 8 Question 3.
   You will need one column for all the fat contents, another column for the Laboratory codes: 1 = A, 2 = B, and so on, and a third for the Brands.
   Use the output to answer Tutorial 8 Question 3.

6 Carry out a two-way analysis of variance for the electronics firm data, without interactions, in Tutorial 8 Question 4.
   You will need one column for all numbers of monitors produced, another column for the employees: 1 = A, 2 = B, and so on, and a third for the times of day.
   Use the output to answer Tutorial 8 Question 4.

14.5.5 Correlation and regression with Minitab

During this tutorial you will learn how to use Minitab to investigate the association between two continuous variables and how to describe it graphically

In this practical session you will analyse the some bivariate data.

1 To enter the data:
   File / Open Worksheet / Merlin1 (saved in the ANOVA worksheet, 14.5.1).
   In order to see what this file contains: open the Information window: *Window / Info*. This window gives details of the data stored in the file Merlin4.mtw which you are going to analyse.
   We shall give each of the cases a salary, in £'000, and then see if it is associated with their age. In the first empty column: name the variable **Salary**, in £'000, and type the following in one column (work down these columns one after the other):

38.1	38.9	23.2	22.9	19.8	19.7	15.6	31.7	17.3	37.8
18.7	42.8	19.6	47.5	31.3	8.5	28.5	14.1	33.5	32.9
42.3	60.1	15.5	15.8	59.3	15.9	37.3	20.3	13.7	9.8
25.9	60.7	20.7	35.9	33.8	39.3	32.9	19.8	6.4	15.2
53.6	75.2	40.2	25.3	24.5	14.5	23.9	28.2	35.3	8.7
37.6	10.9	28.5	63.2	32.0	10.2	8.6	25.3	12.5	38.4

The variables of interest in this practical session are the continuous variables SALARY and AGE. We shall investigate the relationship between the Salaries earned by the employees of Merlin and their ages.

2   Save revised worksheet as **Merlin5.mtw.**

3   Produce a scatter plot to see if there appears to be a relationship.
    Graph / Scatterplot / Simple / Select SALARY for Y and AGE for X
    * Examine the plot. Does it suggest a linear relationship?

4   Calculate the correlation coefficient.
    Stat / Basic Statistics / Correlation / Select SALARY and AGE as the variables.
    * What is the value of the correlation coefficient?
    * What is the probability of it being zero?.
    * Is this significant at 5 per cent?.
    If the p value is less than 0.05 the correlation coefficient is significant at the 5 per cent level of significance.

5   Find the regression equation:
    Stat / Regression / Regression / Select SALARY for Response, AGE for Predictors.
    * Write down the regression equation.
    The last output was for the default setting. Minitab can calculate and store the fitted values and the standardised residuals for each observation.
    Edit / Edit Last Dialog. The last dialogue box reopens.
    Under *Storage* select *Residuals / Standardised residuals and Fits / OK* and check that three new columns have been added to your worksheet.

6   Save this altered version of your file at this stage under a new name Merlin6
    File / Save Worksheet as **Merlin6.**

7   Investigate the fitted values:
    Graph / Scatterplot Select FITS1 as the Y-variable and AGE as the X-variable.
    This produces a straight line as all the fitted values lie on the regression line.
    To fit this line to a scatter plot requires a graphics plot:
    Graph / Scatterplot / With regression SALARY against AGE as before.

8   To print this graph which will not appear in your session file:
    File / Print Graph.

9   To predict a Y-value for a given X-value, in this case a 40 year old:
    Stat / Regression / Regression.
    Select SALARY and AGE as before and then select *Options*.
    Type **40** in the Prediction intervals for new observations.
    The output gives the predicted value for y when x is 40 with a confidence interval and prediction interval for this predicted y-value.
    * What is the predicted salary of a 40 year old employee?

10 To produce the regression line with its confidence interval and prediction interval:
    Stat / Regression / Fitted Line Plot / Options: Display Confidence and Prediction bands. Select SALARY and AGE as before. Print this window as before.

11 Print your session and/or graphs if required.

14.5.6 Time series analysis and forecasting with Minitab

Unfortunately Minitab does not combine a moving average trend with seasonal decomposition. We shall therefore look at its default method of combining a linear trend with seasonal decomposition and compare its output with reproduction of the previous analysis worked by hand.

In this worksheet we will just analyse seasonal data. Exponential smoothing and curve fitting can be carried out quite easily in Minitab by following the instructions in the Help menu.

The quarterly sales, (£'0,000), of a departmental store have been monitored for the past five years with the following information being produced (Tutorial 12 Question 1):

Total quarterly sales (£'0,000)				
Year	Q1	Q2	Q3	Q4
2001	48	58	57	65
2002	50	61	59	68
2003	52	62	59	69
2004	52	64	60	73
2005	53	65	60	75

1 Enter the data: Type all the sales figures **in chronological order** in one column heading it **Sales**.

2 Plot a Sequence graph of Sales to see if an additive model seems appropriate.
   Graph / Time Series Plot / Simple / Series SALES / Time scale / Calendar / Quarter Year / Start values / Quarter 1 Year 2001.

3 Assuming the data to be seasonal, carry out the seasonal decomposition using an additive model:
   Stat / Time Series / Decomposition / Variable SALES / Seasonal length 4 / Additive Model / Trend plus seasonal / Store Trend, Fits and Residuals. Graphs / Do not display plots / Generate forecasts 4 / Starting from origin 20.
   Save this data as **Quarterly sales.mtw.**

4 Plot a Sequence graph of Sales with Trend to see if an additive model seems appropriate.
   Graph / Time Series Plot / Multiple SALES and TREND.
   The trend produced is a straight line. With this particular data that looks reasonable.
   Plot the sales and fitted values on the same graph to check the model fit.

5 Residual analysis:
   Remember that the residuals should: (a) be small, (b) have a mean of 0, (c) have a standard deviation which is much smaller than that of sales, (d) be normally distributed and (e) be random time-wise. The residuals have been saved as RESI1.
   (a), (b) and (c) Produce descriptive statistics of Sales and RESI1.
   (d) For RESI1 produce a box plot and a histogram with a normal plot.
       Carry out the K-S hypothesis test for normality:
       Stat / Basic Statistics / Normality Test / Kolmogorov-Smirnov.
   (e) Produce a time series plot of the errors.
       Stat / Time Series / Decomposition / Seasonal length 4 / Additive Model / Trend plus seasonal / Select SALES. and storing Trend, Fits and Residuals / Graphs / Residual plots / Four in one.
   Do these look to be a good set of residuals?
   We are now going to build up a moving trend plus seasonal factor model.

6 Using Minitab to produce the moving average:
   Stat / Time Series / Moving Average / Variable SALES / MA length 4 / Centre the moving averages / Store Moving averages.
   (You may need to plot a separate sequence graph of sales and moving average as the AV line seems displaced on the default production.)

7 Head the next column **Seasonal** and type in the appropriate seasonal factors as produced

by the deseasonal composition in task 14.5.6.3. These were −8.83, +1.92, -1.14 and +8.05 for quarters 1 to 4 respectively.
Calculate the FITTED values as AVER1 + SEASONAL
Calc / Calculator / Store result in variable Fitted / Expression **AVER1 + SEASONAL.**

8   Plot a Sequence graph of Sales and Fitted values to see if this model is better.
Graph / Time Series Plot / Multiple SALES and FITTED.
Does this model look a closer fit? It probably does but we need to compare the residuals.

9   Calculate the residuals from this model as RESI2 = SALES − FITTED
Save data as **Quarterly sales2.mtw.**

10 Compare residuals:
(a), (b) and (c) Produce descriptive statistics of Sales and RESI1, RESI2.
(d) For both sets of errors produce box plots and histograms with a normal plots.
    Graphs / Boxplots / Multiple Ys / Simple
    Graphs / Histogram / With fit and groups.
    Carry out the K-S hypothesis test for normality:
    Stat / Basic Statistics / NormalityTest / Kolmogorov-Smirnov.
(e) Produce a time series plots of both sets of errors.
    Graph / Time Series Plot **RESI1 RESI3**
Which set looks preferable? The set from the moving average model is better.

11 Assuming that the trend from the moving average model, AVER1, is increasing by 0.3 per quarter, what would be your forecasts for the four quarters of 2006? Compare with those produced in task 14.5.6.3.

14.6 Numerical answers to Minitab worksheets

14.5.1 Graphical presentation

All graphical output. (Full output in Instructor's materials on the Internet)

14.5.2 Summary statistics

14.5.2.2

1   37.75; 11.04; 39.00; 17, 64, 47; 32.0, 45.75, 13.75 years.
2   Yes.

14.5.2.3

2   66.7%.
3   Male 39.5, Female 36.5 years.
    Male 38.3, 11.1, Female 36.8, 11.2 years.
    Male 13.5, Female 16.0.
    Males 'averages' higher; Females 'spreads' higher.
    Yes.

14.5.3 Estimation and hypothesis testing

Answers from samples, so may differ.

2 37.75 years.
4 > 0.05.
5 Yes.
6 < 0.05; >0.05 most likely answers.
8 Yes, so mean ages could be the same.
9 The result depends on your sample. (Results marginal so may be same or not.)
10 CI = –17.99 to 2.01. Confidence interval includes zero so mean ages could be the same.

14.5.4 Analysis of variance

14.5.4.1

3 38.9, 36.6 years; 0.41; they are the same.
4 0.411; they are the same; the confidence interval includes zero.
6 0.000; at least two are different; many don't overlap;
   Management different from all the others; clerical different from production.

14.5.4.2

1 Sex 0.804, Jobcat 0.000, Jobcat*Sex 0.713.
2 Sex 0.229, Jobcat 0.000 different for Jobcat, same for Sex.
3 Sig. (Labs) = 0.383, sig.(Brands) = 0.079; both same at 5%significance.
4 Sig. (Shifts) = 0.028, sig.(Employees) = 0.276 only shifts different.

14.5.5 Correlation and regression analysis

4 0.398; 0.002; Yes.
5 Salary = 7.73 + 0.554 x Age.
9 29.9, £29,900.

14.5.6 Time series analysis and forecasting

Graphical output for most of the answers.
3 Forecasts: 55.8, 66.9, 64.2, 73.8 (£'0,000)

10	Sales	Resids1	Resids3
Mean	60.50	0.00	0.05
St dev	7.40	1.23	0.84
KS test	P-value > 0.150		

11 Forecasts: 63.9 – 8.8 = 55.1
   (£'0,000)   64.2 + 1.9 = 66.1
                 64.5 – 1.1 = 63.4
                 64.8 + 8.1 = 72.9

14.7 Introduction to Excel

Excel is a 'spreadsheet, graphics and database management tool' produced by Microsoft. It is widely used as a spreadsheet in business and finance but makes no claim to be a statistical package. Even with the 'Add-in' capabilities available, its scope is limited and there is occasionally conflict between the answers produced by the 'Add-in' and by the equivalent function in Excel itself. The Data Analysis Add-in was not produced by Microsoft and they are not willing to support it at present. However some types of statistical analysis, both graphical and numerical, can be carried out in Excel so it can be useful if neither SPSS nor Minitab is available, but its results must be interpreted with caution. Excel 2003 claims to have many improved statistical functions and states that some analytical results will differ from those in previous versions. However Microsoft still recommends the use of dedicated statistical packages for other than very basic statistical analysis. It is possible to produce the required statistical formulae using the spreadsheet functions but this is a rather laborious task compared to the use of SPSS or Minitab.

Excel offers the facilities common to all Windows applications and is part of Microsoft Office. The version used in these worksheets is Excel 2003 which is included in the Office 2003 suite. No tutorial is included in the package but it includes a fairly comprehensive Help facility and excellent training is offered on line. Many business rather than statistics textbooks include the use of Excel.

14.8 Excel worksheets

Because of the limitations of Excel as a statistical package these worksheets are shorter than ideal. The aim of these worksheets is to carry out statistical analysis in the most efficient manner available with Excel. No use will be made of formulae but rather of the functions provided by Excel itself or its data analysis ToolPak from the Add-ins under Tools on the Toolbar.

Throughout these tutorials *selections from menus, dialogue boxes or buttons* are shown in bold italics separated by the slash sign / and the **characters you need to type** in bold. The degree of detail decreases as your experience increases. The assumption is made throughout that you have not used Excel for statistical analysis previously even though you are familiar with Windows.

All numerical answers to these worksheets are to be found in Section 14.9 but note that some are from the analysis of random samples so your answers will be different. (The full output from all the sheets, including the graphics, is included in the lecturers' materials on the companion website.)

When you enter Excel, Book 1 opens containing three spreadsheets with the help facility pane at the side. This can be closed if not required.

Numerical data and variable names are typed into the worksheet and the results may be produced on a different sheet or included in the current one. The output can be edited, saved or printed out. Probably the neatest method of display is to cut and paste it into Word, especially if it is to form part of a report or project.

14.8.1 Graphical presentation with Excel

Screen prints are included initially to illustrate the instructions. (More graphics follow in Worksheet 14.8.2.)

14.8.1.1 Opening Excel

Menus on your local network may be set up in a variety of ways and the method of opening Excel will differ from one to another.

Now open Microsoft Excel.

You are now in Excel with Sheet 1 of Book 1 open (Figure 14.23). This is where you will put all your data with appropriate variable names and present the graphs produced from it. Each cell, starting at A1, is identified by a letter for its column and a number for its row. The sheet has far more rows and columns than you will need for these worksheets.

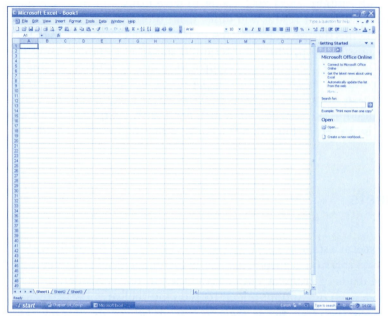

Figure 14.23

14.8.1.2 Putting your data into Excel

The data we shall use in this worksheet represent the ages of a sample of 60 employees of a firm, Merlin plc. Place the cursor in A1 and type **Ages of a sample of employees at Merlin plc**. In cell A3 type **Ages (years)**, this is the variable to be described. You can move around the worksheet using the arrow keys.

Now place the cursor in A4 and type in the first age, 35, which will appear in the formulae bar and also in the appropriate cell. Carry on down column 1 filling in all the ages in that column, then work down column 2, and so on. Your final figure should be in cell A63.

The following figures represent the ages of a sample of 60 employees of a firm Merlin plc:

35	44	54	33	46	20	32	19	50	39	33	37
42	40	20	25	34	52	27	22	18	40	23	17
41	45	21	34	49	27	60	46	32	58	23	52
24	64	41	47	54	37	40	41	40	36	46	29
34	39	39	40	37	50	41	34	47	34	45	36

14.8.1.3 Checking your input

You may find it easier to check figures on a hard copy so print out the data:

File / Print / Active sheet

Check the values with those above. If any is incorrect, just overtype the correct version into the worksheet.

14.8.1.4 Saving your data as a file

Now that you are happy with the data save it to a disk, CD or onto your hard disk.

File / Save As **Merlin1**. This has now been saved as an Excel data file Merlin1.xls on your preferred type of storage.

14.8.1.5 Producing a histogram

Excel produces an ordered bar chart rather than a histogram.

We shall first produce the default histogram and then another more refined version.

Tools / Data analysis /Histogram / Input range. Either type in **A4:A63** or select the same range with the cursor. Select *Output range* **E4** to determine the position of the output. (Any other suitable location, or a fresh sheet, may be used.) See Figure 14.24.

If Data Analysis is not immediately available, go to Tools, Add-ins and select the Analysis Toolpaks.

By default the output has produced a frequency table split into 8 equal intervals which do not have very convenient limits. It also lacks a graph (Figure 14.25).

Type the numbers **20 30 40 50 60** and **70** in cells C4 to C9 and repeat the last commands adding the range **C4:C9** as the *'Bin range'*. Also select *Chart output*. (Figure 14.26).

14.8.1.6 Improving the graph

This improves the horizontal axis but the vertical may still leave much to be desired. Select the histogram by clicking on it. Increase its vertical scale by pulling down on one of the bottom black handles. This diagram is not a true histogram which

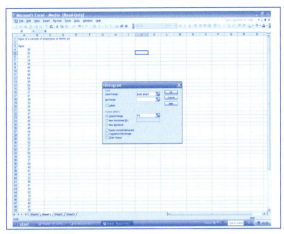

Figure 14.24

Figure 14.25

should be continuous on the horizontal scale. It is really an ordered bar chart (Figure 14.27).

You can edit your histogram by selecting it and the appropriate dialogue box, colours, fonts, patterns, and so on. *Chart / Options* also allows editing. Have a play!

Charts can be positioned anywhere in the spreadsheet by selecting and dragging.

Figure 14.26

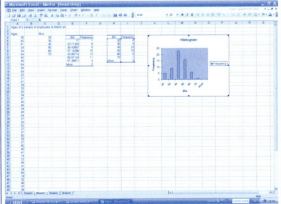

Figure 14.27

14.8.1.7 Producing a cumulative frequency diagram

Repeat the histogram command with the bin ranges as already selected and an output range somewhere free, probably E25. This time click on *Cumulative Percentage*.

14.8.1.8

Next split the employees into two separate groups, male (1) and female (2), by coding the data. Type the word **Sex** in the heading of column B. Type **1** in the first 40 cells of the column and **2** in the remaining 20 cells.

14.8.1.9 Producing a histogram of subgroups of data

Insert two new columns after column B. With cursor in column C *Insert / Columns.*
Copy and paste the male ages into new column C and all the female ages into column D. Repeat task 14.8.1.5 for each new column.

14.8.1.10 Producing a bar chart of subgroups of data

Type the numbers **40** and **20** in cells D4 and D5.
Chart Wizard / Column / Data range **D4:D5.**
There are no facilities for drawing stem-and-leaf, box and whisker or dot plots in Excel.

14.8.1.11 Printing out the worksheet

When you have completed your session you probably have some errors in your worksheet. These can be deleted by highlighting the unwanted sections and deleting them as you would in Word. Charts may be dragged around to tidy the sheet up. When you are happy with the remaining material, print it out:
File / Print Active Worksheet for everything.
Alternatively all the output except the long column of data may be selected with the cursor and:
File / Print Selection can be used.

14.8.1.12 Saving data and graphical output (if required)

File / Save as **MerlinGr** to indicate that graphs have been added to Merlin.xls.

14.8.1.13 Saving data only

Delete all but the data then *File / Save as* **Merlin2.**

14.8.2 Summary statistics with Excel

14.8.2.1 Inputting data from an Excel data file

We shall again use the data which you typed into Excel in Worksheet 14.8.1 as the file Merlin2.xls and then saved. This file contains information about the age and sex of 60 employees of the firm Merlin plc. (If, by any chance you do not have it, refer to Worksheet 14.8.1 (14.8.1.2 and 14.8.1.8) and input the tabulated data again.)

1 Inputting data from an existing Excel file: Open Microsoft Excel and then:
File / Open and select *Merlin2*. The data appears in the Worksheet.
2 Look at the data sheet. The ages of the 60 employees are displayed in the first column with their sex in the second column.
If you have just typed them in, check the numbers carefully with the tabulated data in Section 14.8.1.2.
Make your own choice of output ranges; remember that new columns can be inserted if output is in the way.

14.8.2.2 Data summary

1 Summarise the data by its main summary statistics.
Tools / Data analysis / Descriptive Statistics / Input range **A3:A63.**
Tick *Labels in first row* and *Summary statistics*. Widen column D to read the terms.
- What is the mean age of the employees?
- What is the standard deviation of these ages?
- State the mode and the median of the ages?
- State the minimum, maximum and range of the ages.

14.8.2.3 Comparing two groups

1 Check that the number in each group is correct:
Type **1, 2** in cells C4 C5 respectively.
fx / Select a category / Select a function / FREQUENCY / Data array B4:B63 / Bins_array C4:C5 / Output Range D4.
2 *Insert / Chart*. Select *Pie* for Chart / *Next* Data range **E5:E6** (from frequency output) / *Next / Data Labels / Show category, value and percent / Title Male (10) and Female (2) Employees / Finish*
- What percentage of the employees are male?
Drag the graph to a reasonable position and resize it.
3 The two groups can now be compared:
Tools / Data analysis / Descriptive Statistics / Input range **A3:A43.**
Tick *Labels in first row* and *Summary statistics*. (Add **Ages(male)** to title of this output.)
Tools / Data analysis / Descriptive Statistics / Input range **A44:A63**
Untick *Labels in first row* keep *Summary statistics*. (Add **Ages (female)** to the title.)
- State the median for each group.
- State the mean and standard deviation for each group.
- For which sex are the ages higher, on average? Give two reasons.
- For which sex are the ages more spread, on average? Give two reasons.
4 Print out your output:
Select the output you wish to print out. *File / Print selection.*
5 Save your output:
File / Save as **Merlin2Gr** to indicate that graphs have been added to Merlin2.xls.

14.8.3 Estimation and hypothesis testing with Excel

In this worksheet we shall use the data input in Worksheet 14.8.1, Merlin1.xls, as our population. We shall again calculate its summary statistics, and then use it as a population from which to provide a random sample. From this sample we shall estimate the population parameters and then test various hypotheses about that population, (conveniently forgetting that we actually know the true values for the population!).

1 Open Excel and input your file, Merlin1.xls, saved in Worksheet 14.8.1. If you have not saved the data, turn back to that section and type it in.
   With your cursor in the worksheet *File / Open* and select **Merlin1**.

2 Calculate again the summary statistics for all the ages:
   Tools / Data analysis / Descriptive Statistics. / Input range A3:A63
   Tick *Labels in first row* and *Summary statistics*. Widen column I to read the terms.
   • Make a note of the mean value.

3 Take a random sample of 10 cases:
   Tools / Data analysis / Sampling / Input range A4:A63 / Method Random / No. of samples 10 / Output range C4.
   Label column **Age Sample** in C3.

4 Test your sample for normality: (Excel does not offer a normality test so a histogram will be used as an indication.)
   Type the numbers **20, 30, 40, 50** and **60** into D4:D8 to set as the bin range.
   Tools / Data analysis /Histogram / Input range C4:C13 / Bin range D4:D8 / Output range C15 and ask for *Chart* output.
   • Does your histogram look reasonably normal?
   (Unless it seems a long way off normal, assume normality. If it does seem very skewed take a new sample.)

5 Find a confidence interval for the mean of all the ages. (Don't use the function wizard as this uses 'z' instead of 't' in the calculation, giving an incorrect result.)
   Tools / Data analysis / Descriptive statistics / Input range C4:C13 / Summary statistics and *Confidence level for mean*.
   • Make a note of your sample mean (note: samples differ).
   Despite Excel's description this result is not the confidence interval but the half interval on either side of the mean, $ts/\sqrt{n}$. If your result is 'c' then your confidence interval is $\bar{x} \pm c$
   Calculate your interval:
   • Does this interval include the mean age found in task 2?
   Repeat, changing the confidence level to 90 per cent.
   Label these outputs **Age Sample** and compare the two intervals.

6 As Excel does not offer a one-sample t-test the sample cannot be used to test for the value of the population mean. This is assumed to be within the 95 per cent confidence interval found in the last task.

7 Insert a new column. Type **1** in rows 4 to 33 and **2** in rows 34 to 63, (see task 14.8.2.4). Label the column **Sex**. We shall assume that the first 30 employees are male and the last 30 female.
   Take two new samples of 10 (see task 14.8.3.3 if uncertain), one for the males and one for the females and store the data in the next two unused columns. Label these columns **Male Age** and **Female Age** respectively.

8 Calculate separate confidence intervals for the males and females and see if they overlap. Produce summary statistics for each sex separately, as in task 14.8.3.5. Label the outputs **Male Ages** and **Female Ages** respectively.
   Calculate each 95 per cent confidence interval as in task 14.8.3.5.
   • Do the intervals overlap?
   • What does this mean?

9 Carry out a two-sample t-test to see if the males and females in the whole population have

the same mean ages. In order to decide which test to use, the variances of the two samples must be compared for equality.

Tools / Data analysis / F-Test Two-sample Variances / Variable ranges for male and female samples respectively.

- State value of $p(F \leq f)$ one-tail.

If this value is ≥ 0.05 the two variances are not significantly different, that is they are equal; if this value is < 0.05 they are unequal. Select the next test accordingly.

Tools / Data analysis / tTest for Two Samples assuming (Un)Equal variance / Variable ranges for male and female samples respectively / *Hypothesised difference 0 / Alpha 0.05*.

The $P(T \leq t)$ two-tail is the probability of there being no difference between the population means.

- State this value.
- What do you conclude?

10 Save this updated file as **Merlin3Gr**.

11 Copy the data into an unused Worksheet and save as **Merlin3**.

14.8.4 Analysis of variance with Excel

14.8.4.1 One-way ANOVA

One-way ANOVA can be thought of as an extension to the two-sample t-test.

1 *Open file* **Merlin3** saved while working through the Worksheet 14.8.3.

2 Check by describing the variable Age, to be used in this analysis:

   Tools / Data analysis / Descriptive Statistics / Input range **A3:A63**

   Tick **Labels in first row** and **Summary statistics**. Widen column C to read the terms.

   - Make a note of the mean and standard deviation.

3 Carry out an appropriate two-sample t-test on Ages grouped by Sex. (Reminder from last worksheet.)

   Tools / Data analysis / tTest for Two Samples assuming (Un)Equal variance / Variable ranges male and female sample ranges for male and female samples respectively / **Hypothesised difference 0 / Alpha 0.05 / Output range L4**.

   The $P(T \leq t)$ two-tail is the probability of there being no difference between the population means.

   - State this value.
   - What do you conclude?

4 *Tools / Data analysis / Anova:Single factor / Input range* male and female sample ranges together / *Alpha 0.05 / Output range* **I20**

   - State the null hypothesis.
   - What is the probability that it is true?
   - What do you conclude?

   Compare with results of task 3. You should reach the same conclusion even though this is an F-test and the previous one a t-test.

5 Insert a new column after column A. Type **Jobcat** (Job category) for the heading and type in following list of codes (top row first):

   4 3 4 1 1   3 3 3 2 1   2 1 1 3 4   1 4 4 2 1   2 1 3 2 3   1 3 3 1 2
   1 3 3 3 3   1 1 2 4 1   2 1 1 3 3   1 3 2 3 3   3 1 1 2 3   3 1 3 3 3

   (1 = Clerical, 2 = Management, 3 = Production, 4 = Security)

6 Separating the ages for each of the job categories.
   Select A4 to B63, the ages and job categories, *Data / Sort / by JOBCAT in ascending order*. Copy and paste the ages for each of the four JOBCAT groups into separate columns labelling them accordingly.
   Save your revised file as **Merlin4** (to save typing in this data again.)
7 Repeating task 5 but for all the data as we now have four groups:
   Tools / Data analysis / Anova: single factor / Input range all four job categories / Alpha 0.05 / Output range I35.
   - State the null hypothesis.
   - State the alternative hypothesis.
   - The figure of 1.3×10^{-48} is so small that you can take it as zero.
   - What do you conclude?
8 Excel asks for the expected values as well as the observed values, so a chi-square test is not a reasonable test to carry out in Excel.
9 Save this updated file as **Merlin4Gr.**

14.8.5 Correlation and regression with Excel

During this tutorial you will learn how to use Excel to investigate the association between two continuous variables and how to describe it graphically.
1 In this practical session you will analyse some bivariate data. To enter the data:
   File / Open **Merlin** (saved in the first Worksheet, 14.8.1).
   We shall give each of the cases a salary, in £'000, and then see if this is associated with their age. In this column B name the variable **Salary**, and type the following figures into one column (Work down these columns one after the other):

38.1	38.9	23.2	22.9	19.8	19.7	15.6	31.7	17.3	37.8
18.7	42.8	19.6	47.5	31.3	8.5	28.5	14.1	33.5	32.9
42.3	60.1	15.5	15.8	59.3	15.9	37.3	20.3	13.7	9.8
25.9	60.7	20.7	35.9	33.8	39.3	32.9	19.8	6.4	15.2
53.6	75.2	40.2	25.3	24.5	14.5	23.9	28.2	35.3	8.7
37.6	10.9	28.5	63.2	32.0	10.2	8.6	25.3	12.5	38.4

   The variables of interest in this practical session are the continuous variables Salary and Age. We shall investigate the relationship between the salaries earned by the employees of Merlin and their ages.
2 Save revised worksheet as **Merlin5.**
3 Produce a scatter plot.
   Select the Chart wizard on the top tool bar. Select the *XY (Scatter)* and then the version without any lines. *Next / Data range A4:B63 / Series in columns / Next / Chart title Salary v Age / Value (X) Axis Age / Next / Value (Y) Axis Salary (£'000) / Place as object in Sheet 1 / Finish*. Right click on a gridline and select *Clear*.
   (You may need to reposition and increase the height of the chart.)
   - Examine the plot. Does it suggest a linear relationship?
4 Calculate the correlation coefficient.
   Tools / Data analysis / Correlation
   Input range A3:B63 / Labels in first row.

- What is the value of the correlation coefficient?
- Given the critical value is 0.250 for a sample of 64 (Appendix D Table 6), is it significant at 5 per cent?

5 Find the regression equation:

Tools / Data analysis / Regression / Input Y range **B4:B63**/ *Input X range* **A4:A63.**

The equation is not immediately apparent. You will find the values of 'a' and 'b' under 'coefficients'.

- What is the regression equation?

The last output was for the default setting. Excel can also calculate and store the fitted values and the residuals for each observation.

Tools / Data analysis / Regression / Input Y range **B4:B63**/ *Input X range* **A4:A63**
Add Residuals, Residual plots, Line fit plots and Normality plots.

This command has put the regression line through the data, the residuals and predicted values have been saved and also some residual plots produced. (You may need to separate out your plots and possibly change their vertical scales for easier interpretation.)

6 Save this altered version of your file at this stage under a new name, Merlin6:

File / Save as **Merlin6.**

7 Investigate the graphs in the output:

- Consider the fitted line plot: does the data seem a close fit to the line?
- Consider the X Variable 1 residual plot: do the residuals seem to be random when plotted against X?
- Consider the normal probability plot: are the residuals plotted on a straight line, indicating normality?

All are reasonable but none ideal.

8 The residuals have rather large values so we shall analyse them.

Move your residuals next to the column containing the salaries.

Tools / Data analysis / Descriptive statistics / Input range (the range of cells holding your residuals and salaries).

The mean is nearly zero but the standard deviation should be much smaller. This reflects the wide spread of the original data about the regression line.

14.8.6 Time series analysis and forecasting with Excel

Unfortunately Excel does not combine the calculation of a moving average trend with seasonal decomposition. We shall therefore look at its default method of calculating a centred moving average of four values but cannot use this package for forecasting as the only method available for this is linear regression, which is unsuitable for seasonal data.

You can, of course, use the spreadsheet to calculate the first residuals, the seasonal deviations and the fitted values as in Chapter 12, Section 12.5.1.

The quarterly sales (£'0,000) of a departmental store have been monitored for the past five years with the following information being produced (Tutorial 12 Question 1):

	Total quarterly sales (£'0,000)			
Year	Q1	Q2	Q3	Q4
2001	48	58	57	65
2002	50	61	59	68
2003	52	62	59	69
2004	52	64	60	73
2005	53	65	60	75

1 Enter the data all in column A headed **Quarterly Sales (£0 000s)**: Type all the sales figures in chronological order in this one column.
   Save the data as **Quarterly sales.**

2 Plot a sequence graph of Sales to see if an additive model seems appropriate:
   Chart wizard / Line / Next / Input data A2:A21/ Series in columns / Next / Chart title Quarterly Sales / Category (X) axis Quarters / Value (Y) axis Sales / Next / As object in sheet 1 / Finish.
   Increase the height of the graph and double click within the Y axis to alter the Scale Minimum to 40. The pattern looks promising, doesn't it? Clear the gridlines.

3 Assuming quarterly data, carry out a moving average analysis of time period 4:
   Tools / Data analysis / Moving average / Input range A1:A21 / Labels in first row / Interval 4 / Chart output.
   Edit this graph as in task 14.8.6.2. Note that the 'forecast' in the legend is the moving average trend for the seasonal data and not the appropriate forecast for seasonal data.

4 Print out the graphs.
   Excel cannot carry out seasonal decomposition so no further analysis is possible.

14.9 Numerical answers to Excel worksheets

The full output is given in the lecturers' materials on the companion website.

14.8.1 Graphical presentation

All graphical output.

14.8.2 Summary statistics

14.8.2.2
1 37.75; 11.04; 34, 39; 17, 64, 47 years.

14.8.2.3
2 67%
3 Male 39.5, female 36.5 years.
   Male 38.3, 11.1, female 36.8, 11.2 years. Male averages are higher.
   Female spreads are wider.

14.8.3 Estimation and hypothesis testing

Note: Most of these answers are produced from random samples, so your values will probably be different from these.
2 37.75 years.
4 Not particularly.
5 21.7 to 38.1 years; 23.3 to 36.5 years; second interval narrower.
8 34.2 to 48.8 years; 34.2 to 49.8 years; yes, overlap so could be the same.
9 0.454, 0.089, Mean ages of male and female populations could be the same.

14.8.4 Analysis of variance

14.8.4.1

2 37.75, 11.04 years.
3 0.95; no significant difference.
4 0.95; no significant difference.
7 6.62×10^{-10}; at least two means different.

14.8.5 Correlation and regression

3 Yes but not strong.
4 0.398; yes.
5 Salary (£'000) = 7.73 + 0.554 x Age.

14.8.6 Time series analysis and forecasting

All output graphical.

Appendix

A Answers to tutorial questions

Tutorial 2: Graphical presentation

(Numerical answers are accurate but diagrams are only sketches.)

2.1 a)

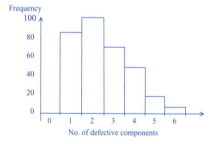

b)

Defectives	Freq.	Cum.Freq.
0	25	25
1	85	110
2	99	209
3	70	279
4	51	330
5	14	344
6	6	350

2.2 a)

Age	Freq.
less than 10	0
10 and < 20	3
20 and < 30	11
30 and < 40	18
40 and < 50	19
50 and < 60	7
60 and < 70	2

(b)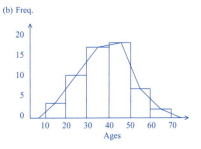

c)

Frequency	Stem & Leaf
3	1 | 789
11	2 | 00123345779
18	3 | 223344444566777999
19	4 | 0000011112455666779
7	5 | 0022448
2	6 | 04

Stem width: 10
Each leaf: 1 case(s)

d)

Age	C. F.	% C.F.
< 10	0	0.0
< 20	3	5.0
< 30	14	23.3
< 40	32	53.3
< 50	51	85.0
< 60	58	96.7
< 70	60	100.0

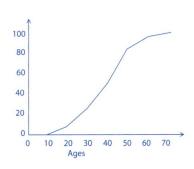

2.3 a)

Height	Freq.	Range	Freq./inch	(c) Cum. Freq.	% C.F.
60" and < 64"	2	4"	0.5	2	4
64" and < 66"	6	2"	3.0	8	16
66" and < 68"	11	2"	5.5	19	38
68" and < 69"	9	1"	9.0	28	56
69" and < 70"	10	1"	10.0	38	76
70" and < 72"	8	2"	4.0	46	92
72" and < 74"	2	2"	1.0	48	96
74" and < 80"	2	6"	0.3	50	100

b)

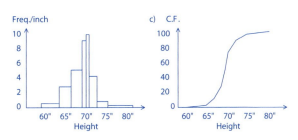

Tutorial 3: Summary statistics

(Answers from calculators are accurate but those from graphs are estimates only.)

3.1 a) 18 b) 199 c) 200 d) 4.944
3.2 a)   A $\bar{x} = 4.50$ s = 0.301   0.86 g/denier
              B $\bar{x} = 4.40$ s = 0.154   0.47 g/denier
3.3 n = $1000\,\bar{x} = 2.00$ s = 0.999 defective components
3.4 n = 50 $\bar{x} = 64.0$ s = 6.36 hours
3.5 n = 100 $\bar{x} = 97.0$ s = 9.27 marks
3.6 Mode = 2 defectives; median = (175th/ 176th box) containing 2 defectives
3.7 Estimated mode = 41 years, estimated median = 39 years, estimated upper quartile = 47 years and estimated lower quartile = 31 years, giving an interquartile range of 16 years.
       6% under 21 and 15% over 50 years old.
3.8 Estimated mode = 69.2 inches, estimated median = 68.7, estimated upper quartile = 70.0 inches and estimated lower quartile = 66.8 inches, giving an interquartile range of 3.2 inches. 8% of students are over 6 ft tall.

Tutorial 4: Probability

4.1   0.8
4.2   (a) 1/6 b) 1/2 (c) 1/3 (d) 0
4.3   (a) 1/13 (b) 1/4 (c) 1/52 (d) 4/13 (e) 3/13 (f) 1/2 (g) 1/26 (h) 3/26
4.4   (a) 8 (b) 1/8 (c) 3/8 (d) 3/8 (e) 1/8 (f) 1
4.5   (a) 3/36 (b) 5/12 (c) 1/6 (d) 1/2 (e) 1/4 (f) 5/12
4.6   (a) 1/3 (b) 1/2 (c) 5/6 (d) 1/6
4.7   (a) 0.042 (b) 0.543 (c) 0.415
4.8   (a) 0.850 (b) 0.818 (c) 0.889 (d) 0.471 (e) 0.529
4.9   (a) 0.700 (b) 0.500 (c) 0.500 (d) 0.600 (e) 0.800 (f) 0.571 (g) 0.429
4.10 (a) 0.640 (b) 0.128 (c) 0.240 (d) 0.144 (e) 0.872 (f) 0.776 (g) 0.550 (h) 0.075 (i) 0.710
       (j) 0.290

Tutorial 5: Normal distribution

5.1   (a) 0.0161 (b) 0.746 (c) 0.21% (d) 8.41 metres
5.2   (a) 0.0284 (b) 5 days (c) 171 cups (d) 26 sandwiches
5.3   928
5.4   (a) 382 (b) 6888 (c) 730 (d) 1.04 kg
5.5   (a) 64% (b) 87%
5.6   (a) 4.78% (b) 0.9044 (c) 4 cups (d) 0.04%
5.7   (a) 5.48% (b) 33.6% (c) 21 working days (d) 0.38%
5.8   3 years 7 months
5.9   (a) 99.7% (b) 68.5% (c) 0.62%
5.10 (a) 0.202 (b) 0.0487 (c) 27.9 kg

Tutorial 6: Confidence intervals (mainly to 3 s.f.)

6.1 (a) $27.6 < \mu < 29.0$ (b) $27.4 < \mu < 29.2$ (c) $27.1 < \mu < 29.5$
6.2 £26.12 $< \mu <$ £30.08
6.3 $0.979 < \mu < 1.043$
6.4 $63.1\% < \pi < 70.2\%$
6.5 Firm A: £338.90 $< \mu <$ £347.10, Firm B: £335.40 $< \mu <$ £342.50
     Overlap, so could be same, Firm B correct.
6.6 $-0.104 < \mu < 0.722$ Zero included, no difference between methods.
6.7 $12.7 < \mu < 15.3$ and $15.7 < \mu < 20.3$ No overlap, two different population means.
6.8 $-2.1 < \mu_d < +12.1$ Training may not be effective.
6.9 $62.2\% < \pi < 73.8\%$ 75% outside range so claim not upheld.
6.10 $92.9\% < \mu < 99.1\%$ Claim not upheld, mark lower than 100.

Tutorial 7: Hypothesis testing

7.1   C.V. = 1.64   T.S. = 1.94 H_0 rejected, mean less than £95.
7.2   C.V. = 2.33   T.S. = 4.63 H_0 rejected, she does spend longer.
7.3   C.V. = 1.81   T.S. = 4.38 H_0 rejected, mean weight more than 1 kg.
7.4   C.V. = 2.58   T.S. = 1.58 H_0 not rejected, mean life could be 1500 hrs.
7.5   C.V. = 1.83   T.S. = 2.87 H_0 rejected, drug gives more hours sleep.
7.6   C.V. = 2.58   T.S. = 1.40 H_0 not rejected, coin could be fair.
7.7   C.V. = 1.89   T.S. = 1.70 H_0 not rejected, training may be ineffective.
7.8   C.V. = 1.64   T.S. = 1.86 H_0 rejected, could be less than 84 scoops.
7.9   C.V. = 2.82   T.S. = 2.27 H_0 not rejected, yields could be same.
7.10 C.V. = 1.83   T.S. = 1.20 H_0 not rejected, study has not been effective.

Tutorial 8: Analysis of variance

8.1 T.S. = 0.20 $F_{0.05}(3,16) = 3.24$
     We have no evidence that the mean typing speeds of the four trainees are different.
8.2 T.S. = 4.41 $F_{0.05}(2,37) = 3.26$
     Results of all three instructors are not the same.
8.3 Brands: T.S. = 4.05 $F_{0.05}(2,6) = 5.14$; Laboratories: T.S. = 1.25 $F_{0.05}(3,6) = 4.76$.
     There is no difference between the mean results of the brands or laboratories.
8.4 Employees: T.S. = 1.55, $F_{0.05}(4,8) = 3.84$ Shifts: T.S. = 5.76, $F_{0.05}(2,8) = 4.46$.
     There is a significant difference in mean production between shifts but not between workers.
8.5 (a) Employees $F_{Emp} = 0.02$, $F_{0.05}(2,18) = 3.55$ No significant difference.
     (b) Employees $F_{Emp} = 0.05$, $F_{0.05}(2,12) = 3.89$ Still no significant difference.
     (c) Weeks $F_{Week} = 4.59$, $F_{0.05}(2,12) = 4.59$ At least one week's sales different.
     Week 1 different from weeks 2, 4, 5, 6 and 7; week 3 different from weeks 5 and 7; week 5 different from week 6. All other differences non-significant.

Tutorial 9: Correlation and regression

9.1   r = 0.560, C.V. = 0.576, no correlation between expenses and profits.
9.2   r = 0.968, y = 0.068 + 0.705x, 5.4% increase in Sales
9.3   b) r = 0.247, not significant c) not appropriate d) 6.1% e) not valid
9.4   b) r = 0.976 c) y = 21.7 + 3.47x e) 95.3% f) 74% g) 143%! h) outside range of given data.
9.5   r = −0.668, y = 20.5 − 0.564x, for every additional £1000 salary an extra half day is likely to be missed, 6.4 days.
9.6   r = 0.987, C.V. = 0.765, correlation significant.
      y = 0.113 + 0.103x, for every extra £1000 turnover an extra profit of £103 is expected.

Tutorial 10: Chi-square test

10.1 C.V. 5.99   T.S. 3.96   Lager preference is not gender dependent.
10.2 C.V. 13.28   T.S. 5.63   Demand for new brand is not regionalised.
10.3 C.V. 5.99   T.S. 14.46   Magazine read is associated with income.
10.4 C.V. 12.59   T.S. 4.57   No differences of opinion between departments.
10.5 C.V. 16.81   T.S. 38.86   Opinions differ among the different professions.

Tutorial 11: Index Numbers

Some values will vary slightly due to rounding errors depending upon the method taken for calculating them. One decimal place shown but final answer may be an integer.

11.1 a)   100, 105.2, 110.0, 113.1
      b)   5.2, 4.8, 3.1
      c)   5.2%, 4.6%, 2.8%
11.2 a)   100, 103.3, 109.6, 95.7
      b)   104.5, 108.0, 114.5, 100.
      c)   3.5, 6.5, −14.5
      d)   3.3% 6.0% −12.7%
11.3 a)   182.0, 208.8, 233.8, 275.6; 59.9, 74.9, 91.6
      b)   23,850 29,810 36,490 39,830 43,410 49,790 55,760 65,720 (4 s.f.)
      c)   25%, 22.4%, 9.2%, 9.0%, 14.7%, 12.0%, 17.9%
11.4   114.2
11.5 a)   102.3, b) 102.0, c) 102.1
11.6 a)   133.7, b) 33.7%, c) 25.2%

Tutorial 12: Time series

12.1 a)   graph of time series
      b)   62.25, 61.75, 2.250.
      c)   addition of trend to graph
      d)   −8.906, +1.938, −1.219, +8.406.
      e)   £619,100

12.2 a) 388.750, 391.750, 55.250
     b) graph of time series and trend
12.3 a) graph of time series and trend

Tutorial 13: Forecasting (continuation of questions from Exercise 12)

NB Forecasts are only estimates, so the answers are here for guidance only.

13.1 a) forecast = extended trend value + seasonal factor.
          £547,000 £657,000 £628,000 £726,000
     b) £8150 ± £16,300
13.2 a) Seasonal factors: −69.83 +22.69 +54.17 −7.63
          Forecasts: 1999 Q4   £3,490,000
                        2000 Q1   £2,801,000
                        2000 Q2   £3,655,000
                        2000 Q3   £3,902,000
     b) ± £120,000
     c) £3,766,000 £3,808,000 £3,763,000 £3,678,000
     d) First residuals mean = −2.23, s.d. = 49.95
         Second residuals mean = −0.0001, s.d. = 6.03
         Zero mean, small standard deviation. Model reasonable.
13.3 a) £8,840,000 £9,080,000 £8,800,000 £9,160,000
     b) ± £727,600
     c) £8,470,000 £8,560,000 £8,720,000 £8,740,000
     d) First residuals mean = 1.86 s.d. = 14.0
         Second residuals mean = 0.0002 s.d. = 3.63

B Glossary of terms

(Intended for explanation rather than definition)

Accuracy Ability to hit a target.

A priori approach to probability Probability from symmetry which therefore needs no experiment.

Additive model A model which assumes that any data is composed of a trend plus a seasonal effect plus some random variation.

Adjusted R^2 R^2 (correlation coefficient squared) figure adjusted for the reduction of the degrees of freedom as additional independent variables are added to a regression equation.

Aggregate price index Composite price index for groups of items which may or may not be weighted by their relative importance.

Alternative hypothesis The hypothesis concluded to be true if the null hypothesis is rejected.

Analysis of variance A statistical procedure for determining whether the means of several different populations are equal.

Anova table A standard table used to summarise the analysis of variance calculations and results.

Arithmetic mean The 'normal' mean calculated as the sum of the values divided by the number of the values.

Assumptions about data Conditions on which standard probability tables are based and which must be met by data if the result of its analysis is to be validly compared with those tables.

Bar chart (graph) A graphical method of presenting qualitative frequency data, with the length of the bar being proportional to the frequency.

Base period The time at which the particular index had a value of 100.

Binomial distribution A probability distribution showing the probability of x successes in n trials of a binomial experiment.

Blocking The removal of a source of variation from the error term in the analysis of variance if it can be assigned to the levels of a second variable.

Box plot A graphical summary of data displaying the median, interquartile range, range and outliers.

Categorical data Data which can be categorised but not measured.

Census A complete enumeration of the whole population.

Centrality Any measure which identifies the 'centre' of the data. Usually a mean, mode or median.

Central limit theorem states that, whatever the distribution of the population, the distribution of the sample means will be approximately normal for large samples.

Chi-square test A test for association between two categorical variables.

Class interval A range of values bounded by class limits.

Cluster sampling The population is first divided into a number of natural clusters and then the clusters are randomly sampled.

Conditional probability The probability associated with a second event which depends on the outcome of a preceding event.

Confidence interval The interval within which the population parameter is expected to lie.

Confidence level The probability that the true population parameter is included in a confidence interval.

Confidence limits The boundaries of a confidence interval.

Contingency table A cross-table for displaying the frequencies of all possible groupings on two categorical variables.

Continuous data Data which can take values at any point within an interval.

Correlation The degree of association between two continuous variables.

Critical value A table value stating the number of standard errors with which a test statistic is compared to determine whether H_0 should, or should not, be rejected.

Cross-tables A table which includes the frequencies of all possible groupings counted on two categorical variables.

Cumulative frequency The number or percentage of items below the end of the relevant interval.

Cumulative frequency polygon (ogive) A graphical display of the number, or percentage, of items up to and including the end of the relevant interval.

Data A collection of observations on one or more variables of interest.

Decision analysis The application of statistical concepts, such as expected values, in the making of decisions.

Decomposition of time series The splitting of any value in a time series into its component parts of trend and seasonal effect (and cycle).

Degrees of freedom The number of free observations associated with the computation of a sample statistic.

Dependent variable The variable, usually denoted by y, which is being predicted or explained by the independent variable.

Descriptive statistics Tabular, graphical and numerical methods of classifying and presenting data.

Discrete data Data which can take values only at certain points within an interval.

Empirical probability A method of assigning probabilities based on past frequencies or experimentation.

Estimation The method of inferring the value of a population parameter from the value of the equivalent sample statistic.

Event A subcollection of the outcomes of an experiment.

Exclusive events Any outcome included in one and one only event.

Exhaustive events All possible outcomes have been included in the stated events.

Expected frequencies The frequencies which would be expected in the sample if a null hypothesis were true.

Expected values Mean of a random variable. Also value which would be expected if the null hypothesis were true.

Experiment The collection of data with control over the factors which may affect the variable of interest.

Exponential distribution (negative) A continuous probability distribution often used for describing the probability of time between occurrences of events.

Exponential smoothing A forecasting technique which uses a weighted average of past time series values to produce a smoothed time series.

First smoothing constant, alpha (α) The proportion of the error in the previous forecast value which is to be applied as a correction in the production of the next forecast value.

Fisher index $\sqrt{\text{(Laspeyre index value} \times \text{Paasche index value)}}$

Fitted value A 'predicted value' for past data used to judge the fit of a model.

Forecasting The method of using the forward projection from a time series for predictive purposes in the near future.

Frequency density Ratio of class frequency to width of class.

Frequency distribution A summary of data grouped into exclusive class intervals and frequencies.

Frequency polygon A graph produced from frequency data by joining the mid-intervals at the top of the histogram bars.

F-test A hypothesis test for comparing the variance of two independent populations using the variances of two small samples. Used in the analysis of variance and the two-sample t-test.

Geometric mean The nth root of the product of n numbers.

Goodness of fit A measure of how closely the observed values fit those predicted by a model.

Graphical description Any diagrammatic representation of a set of data.

Grouped data Data organised into a **frequency distribution**.

Growth model The exponential smoothing model in which the trend does not remain fairly level.

Histogram A graphical method of presenting continuous data, with the area of the bar being proportional to the relative frequency within the interval, the frequency density.

Hypothesis testing The process of testing a hypothesis about a population parameter by the use of information collected from a sample or samples.

Independent probability The probability associated with a second event which does not depend on the outcome of a preceding event.

Independent samples t-test A hypothesis test for comparing two independent population means using the means of two small samples.

Independent variable A variable, usually denoted by x, which can be decided independently and then used to predict or explain a dependent variable.

Index numbers A set of values, based on 100, used to measure changes in magnitude of single items or sets of items over time.

Inferential statistics Statistics gathered from a sample and used to infer some parameter of the population from which the sample was drawn.

Interactions The effect produced when the levels of one factor in an analysis of variance interact with the levels of another factor in influencing the response variable.

Interquartile range The spread of the middle half of ordered data.

Interval data Data which must be numeric and for which intervals between values must be measurable in terms of standard units.

Interval estimate The interval calculated from a sample expected to include the corresponding population parameter.

Kolmogorov–Smirnov test A test for the goodness of fit of sample data to some probability distribution such as the normal distribution.

Kruskal–Wallis test The non-parametric equivalent of analysis of variance.

Laspeyre's price index A weighted aggregate price index in which the weight of each item is its base period quantity.

Least critical difference The least difference between group means necessary for two of them to be judged significantly different.

Least squares regression The method of calculating the Pearson's correlation coefficient.

Level of significance The probability of rejecting a true null hypothesis due to sampling error.

Linear regression The straight line relationship between two continuous variables.

Log-linear regression A form of regression which describes the relationship between variables which are other than continuous.

Main effects The differences between group means in analysis of variance assuming no interactions.

Mann–Whitney U test (Wilcoxon rank sum test) A non-parametric equivalent of a two-sample t-test.

Mean The sum of all the data values divided by their number.

Mean absolute deviation (MAD) The mean of the absolute deviations from the mean used to judge the quality of a set of errors.

Mean square error (MSE) The mean of the squared errors used to judge the quality of a set of errors.

Median The location of the middle value of an ordered data.

Mode The location of the most frequently occurring value of a set of data.

Modelling The representation of reality by a set of data or an equation from which predictions and explanations can be made.

Moving average A method of smoothing a time series by taking an average of each successive group of data points, the group being determined by any periodicity present.

Multiple regression The relationship between one dependent and more than one independent variables.

Multiplicative model A model which assumes that any data is composed of a trend multiplied by a seasonal effect multiplied by some random variation.

Multi-stage sampling A method of successively selecting smaller samples from within larger ones.

Negatively skewed distribution A distribution with a left-hand tail.

Nominal data Data which may be numeric or non-numeric. It can only be classified and not ordered or measured.

Non-linear regression Any relationship between two continuous variables which is best described by a function other than a straight line.

Non-parametric tests The tests which can be used validly when the assumptions needed for parametric testing cannot be met.

Non-seasonal data Data which exhibit no seasonal pattern.

Normal probability distribution A widely occurring, symmetrical, continuous, bell-shaped asymptotic distribution.

Null hypothesis The hypothesis, which always includes equality, initially assumed to be true, though it may in fact be either true or false. The hypothesis challenged by the sample data.

Observed frequencies The frequencies actually counted in the sample.

Odds The ratio of the probability of an event occurring to the probability of it not occurring.

Ogive The shape of the graphical presentation of a cumulative frequency distribution.

One-sample t-test A hypothesis test for a population mean using the analysis of data from a small sample.

One-tailed test The test of a null hypothesis which can only be rejected when the sample statistic is in one extreme end of the distribution.

One-way analysis of variance Analysis of variance in which only one variable is being analysed for group mean differences.

Ordinal data Data which may be numeric or non-numeric and which can be ordered but not measured.

Outcome A single result from an experiment.

Paasche's price index A weighted aggregate price index in which the weight of each item is its current period quantity.

Paired data Data describing two variables measured for each case which can be sensibly related by change or difference.

Paired samples t-test A hypothesis test for comparing population means of paired data using a small paired sample.

Pascal's triangle A triangular array useful for calculating binomial coefficients.

Pearson's correlation coefficient A measure of the degree of the pairwise association between continuous variables.

Percentage change The difference between the relevant index numbers as a percentage of the earlier of the two values.

Percentage point change The difference between the relevant index numbers.

Percentile The value below which a specified percentage of all the values in a distribution are to be found.

Pie chart A graphical method of presenting qualitative frequency data in sectors of a circle with the sector angle being proportional to the frequency.

Point estimate The single value estimate of a population parameter calculated from a corresponding sample.

Poisson distribution A probability distribution showing the probability of x occurrences of an event over a specified interval.

Polygon A many-sided figure depicting, in statistics, an absolute or relative frequency distribution.

Population The collection of all elements of interest.

Positively skewed distribution. A distribution with a right-hand tail.

Power of a test The ability of a test to reject H_0 when it is false.

Precision The width of an interval estimate.

Predicted value The value expected to be taken by the dependent variable for a given value of the independent variables.

Price relative The price in the current period relative to that in the base period. (Price index)

Probability A numerical measure of the likelihood that an event will occur.

Probability tables A systematic list of all the values of a random variable with associated probabilities.

Probability tree diagram Graphical method of displaying the probabilities of multiple events.

p-value The probability of getting the sample statistic, or a more extreme value, when H_0 is true.

Qualitative data Data which may be numeric or non-numeric but are measured on the nominal or ordinal scales only.

Quantitative data Numerical data measured on the interval or ratio scales to describe 'how much' or 'how many'.

Quartiles The values which divide ordered data into four equal parts.

Quota sampling The population is first divided into homogeneous subgroups and then sampling takes place within each subgroup.

Randomised block design A two-way analysis of variance designed to eliminate any assignable extraneous variation from the analysis.

Random sampling A sample in which the members are selected at random so that every member of the sample has an equal probability of being selected.

Range The complete spread of ordered data.

Ratio data Data which must be numeric, have intervals measurable in standard units, and a meaningful zero.

Raw data The original data as collected.

Regression A description of the relationship between two continuous variables.

Regression equation The mathematical equation relating the dependent and independent variables.

Regression line Usually the straight line describing the regression between two continuous variables.

Regression model The equation describing the relationship between two continuous variables.

Relative frequency Favourable proportion of all possible outcomes.

Residual analysis The analysis of the differences between the observed and expected values in order to assess the model.

Sample A subset of a population, usually intended for analysis.

Sample space All the possible outcomes from an experiment.

Sampling The selection of a subset of a population to represent that population.

Sampling distribution of means The distribution of the means of every possible sample combination from a population.

Sampling error Error arising from the incomplete enumeration of a population.

Scale of measurement Scale which classifies the data as being either nominal, ordinal, interval or ratio.

Scatter diagram A graph of bivariate data used to identify any relationship which might be present.

Seasonal data Data which shows a periodic pattern related to a set of time periods such as months or quarters.

Seasonal factor (effect) The component of a time series model which is due to it being a particular season.

Seasonally adjusted series A time series from which the seasonal effects has been removed.

Second smoothing constant beta (β) [gamma (γ] The proportion of the error in the previous forecast trend which is to be applied as a correction in the production of the next forecast trend.

Semi-interquartile range Half the **interquartile range**.

Sign test A simple non-parametric equivalent of a one-sample t-test.

Significance level The maximum probability of rejecting H_0 when it is true.

(Simple) random sampling Sampling such that every member of the population has an equal chance of being included in the sample.

Skewness Lack of symmetry in a distribution.

Spearman's rank correlation coefficient, r_s (ρ) A measure of the degree of the pair-wise association between ordinal variables also known as 'Spearman's rho'.

Spread Any measure which describes the closeness of data about its centre. Usually, range, interquartile range, standard deviation or variance.

Standard deviation The square root of the variance.

Standard deviation of the population A measure of spread found by taking the square root of the average of all the squared deviations from the mean.

Standard deviation of the sample A measure of spread found by taking the square root of all the squared deviations from the mean divided by (n–1).

Standard error The standard deviation of the distribution of sample estimators. In hypothesis testing the critical value and the test statistic are compared by their number of standard errors.

Standardised (normalised) value The number of standard deviations a data point is away from the mean.

Steady model The exponential smoothing model in which the trend is comparatively level.

Stem-and-leaf plot A data display which shows the shape of the data and also retains the numbers.

Stratified random sampling The population is first divided into strata and then a simple random sample is taken from each stratum.

Subjective probability A method of assigning probabilities based on judgement.

Summary statistics Numbers which give concise summaries of data distributions, usually in terms of centrality and spread.

Sums of squares The sum of the squared deviations from the mean used as a measure of variation, especially in the analysis of variance.

Survey A process designed to produce information about a population with evidence collected from a sample.

Systematic sampling A method of sampling by randomly selecting a first member and then selecting the others at regular intervals.

Test statistic A value measuring a number (of standard errors) calculated from the sample for comparing with the critical value from a standard table.

Time series A set of observations measured at successive points in time or over successive periods of time.

Treatments The traditional term for the levels of a variable of interest in the analysis of variance.

Trend The movement of a time series observable over many time periods often found from calculating moving averages.

T-tests Hypothesis tests for population means using data from small samples.

Two-tailed test The test of a null hypothesis which can be rejected when the sample statistic is in either extreme end of the distribution.

Two-way analysis of variance Analysis of variance in which the interest may be in the difference between the group means of one or more variables but in which at least two are being analysed.

Types of error Type I: the rejection a true null hypothesis. Type II: failing to reject a false null hypothesis.

Validity of test The satisfying of the specified assumptions needed to be met for any particular test.

Variance A measure of dispersion based on the squared deviations of the data values from the mean.

Wilcoxon matched pairs (signed rank) test A non-parametric equivalent of a paired t-test or one sample t-test.

Wilcoxon rank sum test (Mann–Whitney U test) A non-parametric equivalent of a two-sample t-test.

Yate's correction A continuity correction made when calculating the test statistic for a chi-square test of a 2×2 contingency table.

C Notation and formulae

Greek alphabet

α A Alpha	ι I Iota	ρ P Rho
β B Beta	κ K Kappa	σ Σ Sigma
γ Γ Gamma	λ Λ Lambda	τ T Tau
δ Δ Delta	μ M Mu	υ Y Upsilon
ε E Epsilon	ν N Nu	ϕ Φ Phi
ζ Z Zeta	ξ Ξ Xi	χ X Chi
η H Eta	o O Omicron	ψ Ψ Psi
θ Θ Theta	π Π Pi	ω Ω Omega

Notation

Parameter	Population	Sample
Mean	μ	$\bar{x}$
Standard deviation	σ	s
Variance	σ^2	s^2
Proportion	Π	p
Size	N	n
Correlation coefficient	ρ	r
Rank correlation coefficient	ρ_s	r_s
Regression coefficients	α, β for y-intercept and slope respectively	a, b for y-intercept and slope respectively

x is the independent variable and y the dependent variable in regression.

O and E are the observed and expected frequencies respectively in chi-square testing.

$\hat{\mu}$ and $\hat{\sigma}$ are estimates for μ and σ respectively.

d represents differences between the paired values when working with paired data.

Σ (sigma) indicates 'the sum of'.

f represents the number of items in a group of frequency data.

z is shorthand for the standardised value.

t is shorthand for the t value.

Formulae

Summary statistics

Mean: $\bar{x} = \dfrac{\sum x}{n}$ for single numbers $\bar{x} = \dfrac{\sum fx}{n}$ for frequency data

Population standard deviation

$$\sigma = \sqrt{\frac{\sum (x - \bar{x})^2}{n}} \quad \text{or} \quad \sqrt{\frac{\sum f(x - \bar{x})^2}{n}} \quad \text{for frequency data}$$

An equivalent formula which is often used is:

$$\sigma = \sqrt{\frac{\sum x^2}{n} - \left(\frac{\sum x}{n}\right)^2} \quad \text{or} \quad \sigma = \sqrt{\frac{\sum fx^2}{n} - \left(\frac{\sum fx}{n}\right)^2} \quad \text{for frequency data}$$

Sample standard deviation

$$s = \sqrt{\frac{\sum (x - \bar{x})^2}{n-1}} \quad \text{or} \quad \sqrt{\frac{\sum f(x - \bar{x})^2}{n-1}} \quad \text{for frequency data.}$$

An equivalent formula which is often used is:

$$s = \sqrt{\frac{\sum x^2}{n-1} - \left(\frac{\sum x}{n-1}\right)^2} \quad \text{or} \quad s = \sqrt{\frac{\sum fx^2}{n-1} - \left(\frac{\sum fx}{n-1}\right)^2} \quad \text{for frequency data}$$

Probability

Binomial: For n trials with the probability of success in any one trial being p, the probability of getting r successes is:

$$\frac{n!}{r!(n-r)!} \times p^r (1-p)^{(n-r)}$$

where n! stands for factorial n, i.e. $n \times (n-1) \times (n-2) \dots 2 \times 1$
Poisson: The probability of a particular number, x, occurring is given by

$$P(x) = \mu^x \frac{e^{-\mu}}{x!}$$

where μ is the mean and e $\cong$ 2.718. ($\cong$ means 'approximately equal to')
Exponential: The probability of an event occurring x times is given by:
$P(x) = \lambda e^{-\lambda x}$, where λ (lambda) is the mean time between successive events.

Normal distribution

Standardised value $\quad z = \dfrac{x - \mu}{\sigma}$

Confidence intervals

Percentage or a proportion, π, is given by:

$$\pi = p \pm z \sqrt{\frac{p(100-p)}{n}} \quad \text{for a percentage or} \quad \pi = p \pm z \sqrt{\frac{p(1-p)}{n}} \quad \text{for a proportion}$$

Mean from large sample and/or from sample with known standard deviation

$$\mu = \bar{x} \pm z \frac{s}{\sqrt{n}}$$

Mean from small sample with unknown standard deviation

$$\mu = \bar{x} \pm t \frac{s}{\sqrt{n}}$$

Difference of means of paired data

$$\mu_d = \bar{x}_d - t\frac{s_d}{\sqrt{n_d}} \quad \bar{x}_d, s_d \text{ and } n_d \text{ refer to the calculated differences}$$

Hypothesis testing – test statistics

Percentage: $\dfrac{|p - \pi|}{\sqrt{\dfrac{\pi(100 - \pi)}{n}}}$

Mean: σ known, $z = \dfrac{|\bar{x} - \mu|}{\sigma/\sqrt{n}}$ or σ unknown so s needed $t = \dfrac{|\bar{x} - \mu|}{s/\sqrt{n}}$

Difference of two means with known population standard deviations

$$z = \frac{|\bar{x}_1 - \bar{x}_2|}{\sqrt{\dfrac{\sigma_1^2}{n_1} + \dfrac{\sigma_2^2}{n_2}}}$$

where $\bar{x}_1, \bar{x}_2$ are the sample means, σ_1, σ_2 are the known standard deviations, n_1, n_2 are the sample sizes.

Difference of two means with unknown population standard deviations

F test: $F = \dfrac{s_1^2}{s_2^2}$ where s_1 refers to the larger standard deviation so that F is always > 1

The formula used for 'pooling' the standard deviations is:

$$s_p = \sqrt{\frac{(n_1 - 1)s_1^2 + (n_2 - 1)s_2^2}{n_1 + n_2 - 2}}$$

Where s_1 and s_2 are the standard deviations of samples 1 and 2 respectively.

Test statistic:

$$t = \frac{|\bar{x}_1 - \bar{x}_2|}{s_p\sqrt{\dfrac{1}{n_1} + \dfrac{1}{n_2}}} \quad \text{or} \quad t = \frac{||\bar{x}_1 - \bar{x}_2| - c|}{s_p\sqrt{\dfrac{1}{n_1} + \dfrac{1}{n_2}}} \quad \text{for a hypothesised value c}$$

Mann–Whitney non-parametric test:

$$U = R - \frac{n_1(n_1 + 1)}{2}$$

where R is the smaller sum of ranks and n_1 the size of the same sample.

Analysis of variance

The least critical difference $CD = t\sqrt{MSE\left(\dfrac{1}{n_1} + \dfrac{1}{n_2}\right)}$ t has the MSE d. of f. and one tail.

Correlation and regression

The formula used to find the Pearson's Product Moment Correlation, r, coefficient is (least squares method):

$$r = \dfrac{S_{xy}}{\sqrt{S_{xx}S_{yy}}} \qquad (-1 \le r \le +1)$$

where $\quad S_{xx} = \sum x^2 - \dfrac{\sum x \sum x}{n}$

$$S_{yy} = \sum y^2 - \dfrac{\sum y \sum y}{n}$$

$$S_{xy} = \sum xy - \dfrac{\sum x \sum y}{n}$$

The **regression line** is described, in general, as the straight line with the equation:

$$y = a + bx$$

The **gradient, b**, is calculated from:

$$b = \dfrac{S_{xy}}{S_{xx}} \text{ where } S_{xy} = \sum xy - \dfrac{\sum x \sum y}{n} \text{ and } S_{xx} = \sum x^2 - \dfrac{\sum x \sum x}{n}$$

Since the regression line passes through the centroid, both means, its equation can be used to find the value of a, the **intercept** on the y-axis:

$$a = \overline{y} - b\overline{x}$$

Spearman's rank correlation coefficient, r_s
The formula for calculating this is

$$r_s = 1 - \dfrac{6\sum d^2}{n(n^2 - 1)}$$

where d is the difference in rankings and n the sample size.

Chi-square testing

For any cell the expected frequency is calculated by: $\dfrac{\text{Row total} \times \text{Column total}}{\text{Overall total}}$

Test statistic for larger than 2 × 2 table: $\sum \dfrac{(O - E)^2}{E}$

Test statistic for 2 × 2 table (Yate's correction): $\sum \dfrac{(|O - E| - 0.5)^2}{E}$

Index numbers

Index for any time period n $= \dfrac{\text{value in period n}}{\text{value in base period}} \times 100$

Time series

Regression models:

- The linear model: $y = a + bx$
- the quadratic model: $y = a + bx + cx^2$
- the cubic model: $y = a + bx + cx^2 + dx^3$

Exponential smoothing models

Steady model: New forecast = old forecast + alpha × error in previous forecast
where alpha (α) is the first smoothing constant.

Growth model

New forecast = previous forecast + alpha × error in previous forecast + previous trend + beta × error in previous forecast trend.

New trend = previous trend + beta × error in previous trend
where beta (β) is the second smoothing constant.

Seasonal decomposition – Additive model

D Tables

Table 1 Areas under the standard normal curve
Table 2 Percentage points of the t-distribution
Table 3 Percentage points of the standard normal curve
Table 4 Percentage points of the F-distribution $\alpha = 5\%$
Table 5 Percentage points of the X^2 distribution
Table 6 Critical values for Pearson's correlation test
Table 7 Critical values for Spearman's rank correlation test
Table 8 Critical values for the sign test (5% significance)
Table 9 Critical values for Wilcoxon matched pairs (Wilcoxon Signed Rank) Test
        (5% significance level)
Table 10 Critical values for the Mann–Whitney U test

For further or more detailed tables see *Elementary Statistics Tables for all Users of Statistical Techniques* by Henry R. Neave published by Routledge.

Table 1 Areas under the standard normal curve

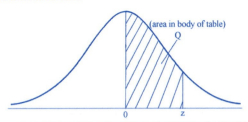

z	0.00	0.01	0.02	0.03	0.04	0.05	0.06	0.07	0.08	0.09
0.0	0.0000	0.0040	0.0080	0.0120	0.0160	0.0199	0.0239	0.0279	0.0319	0.0359
0.1	0.0398	0.0438	0.0478	0.0517	0.0557	0.0596	0.0636	0.0675	0.0714	0.0753
0.2	0.0793	0.0832	0.0871	0.0910	0.0948	0.0987	0.1026	0.1064	0.1103	0.1141
0.3	0.1179	0.1217	0.1255	0.1293	0.1331	0.1368	0.1406	0.1443	0.1480	0.1517
0.4	0.1554	0.1591	0.1628	0.1664	0.1700	0.1736	0.1772	0.1808	0.1844	0.1879
0.5	0.1915	0.1950	0.1985	0.2019	0.2054	0.2088	0.2123	0.2157	0.2190	0.2224
0.6	0.2257	0.2291	0.2324	0.2357	0.2389	0.2422	0.2454	0.2486	0.2517	0.2549
0.7	0.2580	0.2611	0.2642	0.2673	0.2704	0.2734	0.2764	0.2794	0.2823	0.2852
0.8	0.2881	0.2910	0.2939	0.2967	0.2995	0.3023	0.3051	0.3078	0.3106	0.3133
0.9	0.3159	0.3186	0.3212	0.3238	0.3264	0.3289	0.3315	0.3340	0.3365	0.3389
1.0	0.3413	0.3438	0.3461	0.3485	0.3508	0.3531	0.3554	0.3577	0.3599	0.3621
1.1	0.3643	0.3665	0.3686	0.3708	0.3729	0.3749	0.3770	0.3790	0.3810	0.3830
1.2	0.3849	0.3869	0.3888	0.3907	0.3925	0.3944	0.3962	0.3980	0.3997	0.4015
1.3	0.4032	0.4049	0.4066	0.4082	0.4099	0.4115	0.4131	0.4147	0.4162	0.4177
1.4	0.4192	0.4207	0.4222	0.4236	0.4251	0.4265	0.4279	0.4292	0.4306	0.4319
1.5	0.4332	0.4345	0.4357	0.4370	0.4382	0.4394	0.4406	0.4418	0.4429	0.4441
1.6	0.4452	0.4463	0.4474	0.4484	0.4495	0.4505	0.4515	0.4525	0.4535	0.4545
1.7	0.4554	0.4564	0.4573	0.4582	0.4591	0.4599	0.4608	0.4616	0.4625	0.4633
1.8	0.4641	0.4649	0.4656	0.4664	0.4671	0.4678	0.4686	0.4693	0.4699	0.4706
1.9	0.4713	0.4719	0.4726	0.4732	0.4738	0.4744	0.4750	0.4756	0.4761	0.4767
2.0	0.4772	0.4778	0.4783	0.4788	0.4793	0.4798	0.4803	0.4808	0.4812	0.4817
2.1	0.4821	0.4826	0.4830	0.4834	0.4838	0.4842	0.4846	0.4850	0.4854	0.4857
2.2	0.4861	0.4864	0.4868	0.4871	0.4875	0.4878	0.4881	0.4884	0.4887	0.4890
2.3	0.4893	0.4896	0.4898	0.4901	0.4904	0.4906	0.4909	0.4911	0.4913	0.4916
2.4	0.4918	0.4920	0.4922	0.4925	0.4927	0.4929	0.4931	0.4932	0.4934	0.4936
2.5	0.4938	0.4940	0.4941	0.4943	0.4945	0.4946	0.4948	0.4949	0.4951	0.4952
2.6	0.4953	0.4955	0.4956	0.4957	0.4959	0.4960	0.4961	0.4962	0.4963	0.4964
2.7	0.4965	0.4966	0.4967	0.4968	0.4969	0.4970	0.4971	0.4972	0.4973	0.4974
2.8	0.4974	0.4975	0.4976	0.4977	0.4977	0.4978	0.4979	0.4979	0.4980	0.4981
2.9	0.4981	0.4982	0.4982	0.4983	0.4984	0.4984	0.4985	0.4985	0.4986	0.4986
3.0	0.4987	0.4987	0.4987	0.4988	0.4988	0.4989	0.4989	0.4989	0.4990	0.4990
3.1	0.4990	0.4991	0.4991	0.4991	0.4992	0.4992	0.4992	0.4992	0.4993	0.4993
3.2	0.4993	0.4993	0.4994	0.4994	0.4994	0.4994	0.4994	0.4995	0.4995	0.4995
3.3	0.4995	0.4995	0.4995	0.4996	0.4996	0.4996	0.4996	0.4996	0.4996	0.4997
3.4	0.4997	0.4997	0.4997	0.4997	0.4997	0.4997	0.4997	0.4997	0.4997	0.4998

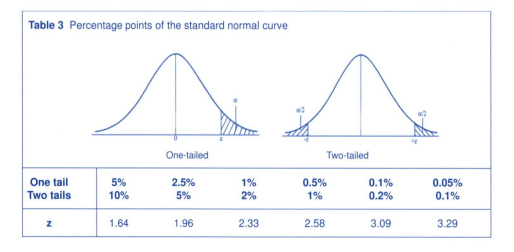

Table 2 Percentage points of the t-distribution

One-tailed   Two-tailed

One tail α	5%	2.5%	1%	0.5%	0.1%	0.05%
Two tails α	10%	5%	2%	1%	0.2%	0.1%
$\nu = 1$	6.31	4.30	12.71	31.82	63.66	636.6
2	2.92	4.30	6.96	9.92	22.33	31.60
3	2.35	3.18	4.54	5.84	10.21	12.92
4	2.13	2.78	3.75	4.60	7.17	8.61
5	2.02	2.57	3.36	4.03	5.89	6.87
6	1.94	2.45	3.14	3.71	5.21	5.96
7	1.89	2.36	3.00	3.50	4.79	5.41
8	1.86	2.31	2.90	3.36	4.50	5.04
9	1.83	2.26	2.82	3.25	4.30	4.78
10	1.81	2.23	2.76	3.17	4.14	4.59
12	1.78	2.18	2.68	3.05	3.93	4.32
15	1.75	2.13	2.60	2.95	3.73	4.07
20	1.72	2.09	2.53	2.85	3.55	3.85
24	1.71	2.06	2.49	2.80	3.47	3.75
30	1.70	2.04	2.46	2.75	3.39	3.65
40	1.68	2.02	2.42	2.70	3.31	3.55
60	1.67	2.00	2.39	2.66	3.23	3.46
∞	1.64	1.96	2.33	2.58	3.09	3.29

ν = degrees of freedom   α = total percentage in tails

Table 3 Percentage points of the standard normal curve

One-tailed   Two-tailed

One tail	5%	2.5%	1%	0.5%	0.1%	0.05%
Two tails	10%	5%	2%	1%	0.2%	0.1%
z	1.64	1.96	2.33	2.58	3.09	3.29

α = total percentage in tails

Table 4 Percentage points of the f distribution   α = 5%

					Numerator degrees of freedom				
v_2	v_1	1	2	3	4	5	6	7	8	9
	1	161.40	199.50	215.70	224.60	230.20	234.00	236.80	238.90	240.50
	2	18.51	19.00	19.16	19.25	19.30	19.33	19.35	19.37	19.38
	3	10.13	9.55	9.28	9.12	9.01	8.94	8.89	8.85	8.81
	4	7.71	6.94	6.56	6.39	6.26	6.16	6.09	6.04	6.00
	5	6.61	5.79	5.41	5.19	5.05	4.95	4.88	4.82	4.77
	6	5.99	5.14	4.76	4.53	4.39	4.28	4.21	4.15	4.10
	7	5.59	4.74	4.35	4.12	3.97	3.87	3.79	3.73	3.68
	8	5.32	4.46	4.07	3.84	3.69	3.58	3.50	3.44	3.39
	9	5.12	4.26	3.86	3.63	3.48	3.37	3.29	3.23	3.18
	10	4.96	4.10	3.71	3.48	3.33	3.22	3.14	3.07	3.02
	11	4.84	3.98	3.59	3.36	3.20	3.09	3.01	2.95	2.90
	12	4.75	3.89	3.49	3.26	3.11	3.00	2.91	2.85	2.80
	13	4.67	3.81	3.41	3.18	3.03	2.92	2.83	2.77	2.71
	14	4.60	3.74	3.34	3.11	2.96	2.85	2.76	2.70	2.65
	15	4.54	3.68	3.29	3.06	2.90	2.79	2.71	2.64	2.59
	16	4.49	3.63	3.24	3.01	2.85	2.74	2.66	2.59	2.54
	17	4.45	3.59	3.20	2.96	2.81	2.70	2.61	2.55	2.49
	18	4.41	3.55	3.16	2.93	2.77	2.66	2.58	2.51	2.46
	19	4.38	3.52	3.13	2.90	2.74	2.63	2.54	2.48	2.42
	20	4.35	3.49	3.10	2.87	2.71	2.60	2.51	2.45	2.39
	21	4.32	3.47	3.07	2.84	2.68	2.57	2.49	2.42	2.37
	22	4.30	3.44	3.05	2.82	2.66	2.55	2.46	2.40	2.34
	23	4.28	3.42	3.03	2.80	2.64	2.53	2.44	2.37	2.32
	24	4.26	3.40	3.01	2.78	2.62	2.51	2.42	2.36	2.30
	25	4.24	3.39	2.99	2.76	2.60	2.49	2.40	2.34	2.28
	26	4.23	3.37	2.98	2.74	2.59	2.47	2.39	2.32	2.27
	27	4.21	3.35	2.96	2.73	2.57	2.46	2.37	2.31	2.25
	28	4.20	3.34	2.95	2.71	2.56	2.45	2.36	2.29	2.24
	29	4.18	3.33	2.93	2.70	2.55	2.43	2.35	2.28	2.22
	30	4.17	3.32	2.92	2.69	2.53	2.42	2.33	2.27	2.21
	40	4.08	3.23	2.84	2.61	2.45	2.34	2.25	2.18	2.12
	60	4.00	3.15	2.76	2.53	2.37	2.25	2.17	2.10	2.04
	120	3.92	3.07	2.68	2.45	2.29	2.17	2.09	2.02	1.96
	∞	3.84	3.00	2.60	2.37	2.21	2.10	2.01	1.94	1.88

Denominator degrees of freedom

v = degrees of freedom   α = total percentage in tails

Table continued overleaf

Table 4 continued Percentage points of the F distribution   α = 5%

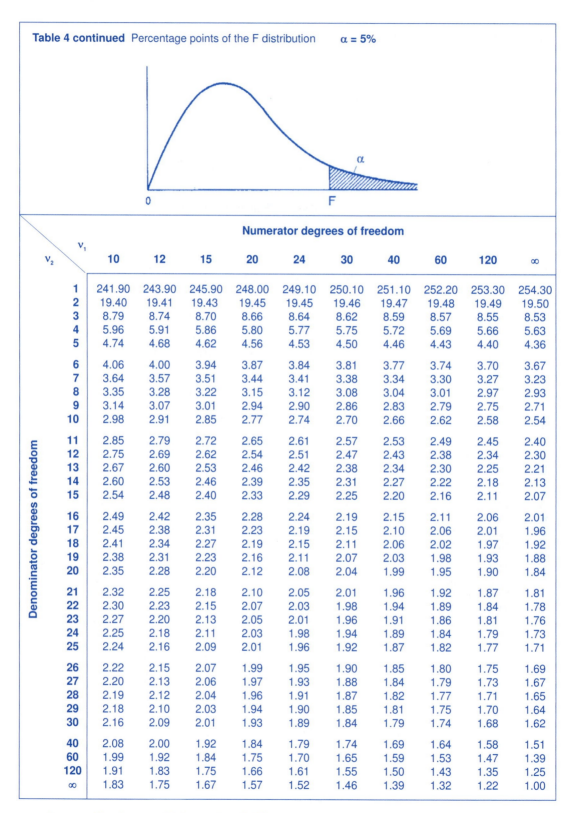

	ν_1										
ν_2		**10**	**12**	**15**	**20**	**24**	**30**	**40**	**60**	**120**	**∞**
	1	241.90	243.90	245.90	248.00	249.10	250.10	251.10	252.20	253.30	254.30
	2	19.40	19.41	19.43	19.45	19.45	19.46	19.47	19.48	19.49	19.50
	3	8.79	8.74	8.70	8.66	8.64	8.62	8.59	8.57	8.55	8.53
	4	5.96	5.91	5.86	5.80	5.77	5.75	5.72	5.69	5.66	5.63
	5	4.74	4.68	4.62	4.56	4.53	4.50	4.46	4.43	4.40	4.36
	6	4.06	4.00	3.94	3.87	3.84	3.81	3.77	3.74	3.70	3.67
	7	3.64	3.57	3.51	3.44	3.41	3.38	3.34	3.30	3.27	3.23
	8	3.35	3.28	3.22	3.15	3.12	3.08	3.04	3.01	2.97	2.93
	9	3.14	3.07	3.01	2.94	2.90	2.86	2.83	2.79	2.75	2.71
	10	2.98	2.91	2.85	2.77	2.74	2.70	2.66	2.62	2.58	2.54
	11	2.85	2.79	2.72	2.65	2.61	2.57	2.53	2.49	2.45	2.40
	12	2.75	2.69	2.62	2.54	2.51	2.47	2.43	2.38	2.34	2.30
	13	2.67	2.60	2.53	2.46	2.42	2.38	2.34	2.30	2.25	2.21
	14	2.60	2.53	2.46	2.39	2.35	2.31	2.27	2.22	2.18	2.13
	15	2.54	2.48	2.40	2.33	2.29	2.25	2.20	2.16	2.11	2.07
	16	2.49	2.42	2.35	2.28	2.24	2.19	2.15	2.11	2.06	2.01
	17	2.45	2.38	2.31	2.23	2.19	2.15	2.10	2.06	2.01	1.96
	18	2.41	2.34	2.27	2.19	2.15	2.11	2.06	2.02	1.97	1.92
	19	2.38	2.31	2.23	2.16	2.11	2.07	2.03	1.98	1.93	1.88
	20	2.35	2.28	2.20	2.12	2.08	2.04	1.99	1.95	1.90	1.84
	21	2.32	2.25	2.18	2.10	2.05	2.01	1.96	1.92	1.87	1.81
	22	2.30	2.23	2.15	2.07	2.03	1.98	1.94	1.89	1.84	1.78
	23	2.27	2.20	2.13	2.05	2.01	1.96	1.91	1.86	1.81	1.76
	24	2.25	2.18	2.11	2.03	1.98	1.94	1.89	1.84	1.79	1.73
	25	2.24	2.16	2.09	2.01	1.96	1.92	1.87	1.82	1.77	1.71
	26	2.22	2.15	2.07	1.99	1.95	1.90	1.85	1.80	1.75	1.69
	27	2.20	2.13	2.06	1.97	1.93	1.88	1.84	1.79	1.73	1.67
	28	2.19	2.12	2.04	1.96	1.91	1.87	1.82	1.77	1.71	1.65
	29	2.18	2.10	2.03	1.94	1.90	1.85	1.81	1.75	1.70	1.64
	30	2.16	2.09	2.01	1.93	1.89	1.84	1.79	1.74	1.68	1.62
	40	2.08	2.00	1.92	1.84	1.79	1.74	1.69	1.64	1.58	1.51
	60	1.99	1.92	1.84	1.75	1.70	1.65	1.59	1.53	1.47	1.39
	120	1.91	1.83	1.75	1.66	1.61	1.55	1.50	1.43	1.35	1.25
	∞	1.83	1.75	1.67	1.57	1.52	1.46	1.39	1.32	1.22	1.00

Numerator degrees of freedom (column header)

Denominator degrees of freedom (row axis label)

ν = degrees of freedom   α = total percentage in tails

Table 5 Percentage points of the χ^2 distribution

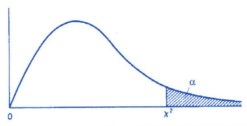

ν	10%	5%	2.5%	1%	0.l%
1	2.706	3.841	5.024	6.635	10.83
2	4.605	5.991	7.378	9.210	13.82
3	6.252	7.816	9.351	11.35	16.27
4	7.780	9.488	11.14	13.28	18.47
5	9.236	11.07	12.83	15.08	20.51
6	10.64	12.59	14.45	16.81	22.46
7	12.02	14.07	16.02	18.49	24.36
8	13.36	15.51	17.53	20.09	26.13
9	14.68	16.92	19.02	21.67	27.89
10	15.99	18.31	20.48	23.21	29.59
11	17.28	19.68	21.92	24.72	31.26
12	18.55	21.03	23.34	26.22	32.91
13	19.81	22.36	24.74	27.69	34.51
14	21.06	23.68	26.12	29.14	36.12
15	22.31	25.00	27.49	30.58	37.70
16	23.54	26.30	28.85	32.00	39.25
17	24.77	27.59	30.19	33.41	40.79
18	25.99	28.87	31.53	34.81	42.31
19	27.20	30.14	32.85	36.19	43.82
20	28.41	31.41	34.17	37.57	45.32
21	29.62	32.67	35.48	38.93	46.80
22	30.81	33.92	36.78	40.29	48.27
23	32.01	35.17	38.08	41.64	49.73
24	33.20	36.42	39.36	42.98	51.18
25	34.38	37.65	40.65	44.31	52.62
26	35.56	38.89	41.92	45.64	54.05
27	36.74	40.11	43.19	46.96	55.48
28	37.92	41.34	44.46	48.28	56.89
29	39.09	42.56	45.72	49.59	58.30
30	40.26	43.77	46.98	50.89	59.70
40	51.81	55.76	59.34	63.69	73.42
50	63.17	67.50	71.42	76.15	86.66
60	74.40	79.08	83.30	88.38	99.61
70	85.53	90.53	95.02	100.4	112.3
80	96.58	101.9	106.6	112.3	124.8
90	107.6	113.1	118.1	124.1	137.2
100	118.5	124.3	129.6	135.8	149.5

Table 6 Critical values for Pearson's correlation test

| One-tailed | Two-tailed |

v	α					
One tail	**5%**	**2.5%**	**1%**	**0.5%**	**0.1%**	**0.05%**
Two tails	**10%**	**5%**	**2%**	**1%**	**0.2%**	**0.01%**
2	.900	.950	.980	.990	.998	.999
3	.805	.878	.934	.959	.986	.991
4	.729	.811	.882	.917	.963	.974
5	.669	.754	.833	.875	.935	.951
6	.621	.707	.789	.834	.905	.925
7	.582	.666	.750	.798	.875	.898
8	.549	.632	.715	.765	.847	.872
9	.521	.602	.685	.735	.820.	.847
10	.497	.576	.658	.708	.795	.823
11	.476	.553	.634	.684	.772	.801
12	.457	.532	.612	.661	.750	.780
13	.441	.514	.592	.641	.730	.760
14	.426	.497	.574	.623	.711	.742
15	.412	.482	.558	.606	.694	.725
16	.400	.468	.543	.590	.678	.708
17	.389	.456	.529	.575	.662	.693
18	.378	.444	.516	.561	.648	.679
19	.369	.433	.503	.549	.635	.665
20	.360	.423	.492	.537	.622	.652
25	.323	.381	.445	.487	.568	.597
30	.296	.349	.409	.449	.526	.554
40	.257	.304	.358	.393	.463	.490
60	.211	.250	.295	.325	.385	.408

v = degrees of freedom α = total percentage in tails

Table 7 Critical values of Spearman's rank correlation test

$$r_s = 1 - \frac{6\Sigma d^2}{n(n^2 - 1)}$$

n	5	6	7	8	9	10
Q%						
10	0.900	0.771	0.679	0.643	0.582	0.549
5		0.829	0.759	0.738	0.666	0.632

For $10 < n < 20$, $\dfrac{r_s}{\sqrt{1-r_s^2}} \sqrt{n-2}$ is distributed as t with $(n - 2)$ d. of f.

For $n > 20$, $r_s \sqrt{n-1}$ may be treated as normally distributed $(0, 1)$.

Table 8 Critical values for the sign test   (5% significance)

n	One-tailed	Two-tailed	n	One-tailed	Two-tailed
5	0		25	7	7
6	0	0	26	8	7
7	0	0	27	8	7
8	1	0	28	9	8
9	1	1	29	9	8
10	1	1	30	10	9
11	2	1	35	12	11
12	2	2	40	14	13
13	3	2	45	16	15
14	3	2	50	18	17
15	3	3	55	20	19
16	4	3	60	23	21
17	4	4	65	25	24
18	5	4	70	27	26
19	5	4	75	29	28
20	5	5	80	32	30
21	6	5	85	34	32
22	6	5	90	36	35
23	7	6	95	38	37
24	7	6	100	41	39

Mark all differences as + or − and find the total of each. S is the smaller of the two totals.
If S ≤ critical value, null hypothesis is rejected.

Table 9 Critical values for Wilcoxon matched pairs test (Wilcoxon signed rank test) (5% significance level)

n	One tail	Two tails	n	One tail	Two tails
5	0		25	100	89
6	2	0	26	110	98
7	3	2	27	119	107
8	5	3	28	130	116
9	8	5	29	140	126
10	10	8	30	151	137
11	13	10	35	213	195
12	17	13	40	286	264
13	21	17	45	371	343
14	25	21	50	466	434
15	30	25	55	573	536
16	35	29	60	690	648
17	41	34	65	820	772
18	47	40	70	960	907
19	53	46	75	1112	1053
20	60	52	80	1276	1211
21	67	58	85	1451	1380
22	75	65	90	1638	1560
23	83	73	95	1836	1752
24	91	81	100	2045	1855

Rank the non-zero differences, ignoring the sign of the difference. Find $T^+ =$ sum of ranks for positive difference and $T^- =$ sum of ranks for negative differences.
Test statistic: $W = \min (T^+, T^-)$.
Reject null hypothesis if $W \leq$ critical value.

Table 10 Critical values of the Mann–Whitney U test
(Wilcoxon rank sum test)

5% one tail

n_1 n_2	4	5	6	7	8	9	10	12	15	20
4	1	2	3	4	5	6	7	9	12	18
5		4	5	6	8	9	11	13	18	25
6			7	8	10	12	14	17	23	32
7				11	13	15	17	21	28	39
8					15	18	20	26	33	47
9						21	24	30	39	54
10							27	34	44	62
12								42	55	77
15									72	100
20										138

5% two tails

n_1 n_2	4	5	6	7	8	9	10	12	15	20
4	0	1	2	3	4	4	5	7	10	14
5		2	3	5	6	7	8	11	14	20
6			5	6	8	10	11	14	19	27
7				8	10	12	14	18	24	34
8					13	15	17	22	29	41
9						17	20	26	34	48
10							23	29	39	55
12								37	49	69
15									64	90
20										127

Order the two samples together and indicate by A or B whether a mark comes from the first or second sample.

Then form the sum R_A of the ranks of observations from sample A and similarly R_B from sample B. R is the smaller of the two rank sums.

The test statistic: $U = R - \dfrac{n(n+1)}{2}$ n is the size of the sample which produced R.

Reject the null hypothesis if u ≤ critical value

E Students' materials available on the companion website

At www.palgrave.com/business/taylor
(Materials available as separate files or batches of associated files within folders.)
The topics covered by the extra materials available to students on the companion website:

- Graphical data description.
- Summary statistics.
- Probability.
- Normal probability.
- Estimation.
- Hypothesis testing: means and proportions.
- Hypothesis testing: ANOVA.
- Correlation and regression.
- Contingency tables and chi-square tests.
- Index numbers.
- Time series.
- Time series – forecasting.

A file is available on the companion website containing each of the following materials for each of the topics listed above:

- Supplementary exercises with answers.
- Computer output for practical session worksheets, with interpretation and answers.
- Revision material, with answers, for in-class tests and examinations.
  - Sample multi-choice questions with answers.
  - Sample examination questions with answers.

Also:

- Case study output with suggested solutions.

F Lecturers' materials available on the companion website

A very comprehensive instructor's pack on the companion website includes:

- Handouts for each lecture.
- Masters of overhead projector slides for the same lectures.
- PowerPoint presentations for the same lectures.
- Worked solutions to at least one tutorial question
- Computer worksheets wih output, interpretation and answers to all worksheets; also all the data sets created or used by the students.
- Revision materials with overheads for the twelve lecture topics.
- Extra revision materials to those in the book.
- Extra multi-choice questions suitable for in-class tests for large groups.
- Extra examination questions from which an examination paper could be compiled.
- A numeracy pre-test on the basic mathematical techniques required for the course.

The materials above are included for each of the following topics:

- Graphical data description.
- Summary statistics.
- Probability.
- Normal probability.
- Estimation.
- Hypothesis testing: means and proportions.
- Hypothesis testing: ANOVA.
- Correlation and regression.
- Contingency tables and chi-square tests.
- Index numbers.
- Time series.
- Time series – forecasting.

In addition there are:

- Worked solutions to at least one tutorial question on each topic.
- Revision materials with overheads for each topic.

In addition to the revision materials available to the students on the companion website there are:

- Revision materials on all topics with overhead transparencies and answers.
- Multi-choice questions suitable for in-class tests for large groups.
- Examination questions from which examination papers can be compiled.
- A numeracy pre-test on the basic mathematical techniques required for the course.

G References

No extra books are really necessary for this course but more depth of information can be obtained from the following sources.

For all topics:

Groebner, David F. and Shannon, Patrick W. *Business Statistics: A decision-making approach*, fourth edition (New York: Macmillan, 1993).

For nonparametric statistics:

Siegel, Sidney and Castellan, N. John Jr. *Nonparmetric Statistics for the Behavioural Sciences* (Singapore: McGraw-Hill, 1988).

For more statistical depth:

Weimer, Richard C. *Statistics*, second edition (Dubuque, Iowa: Wm. C. Brown, 1993).

For multivariate analysis:

Everitt, Brian S. and Dunn, Graham. *Applied Multivariate Data Analysis* (London: Arnold, 2001).

For light relief:

Huff, Durrell. *How to Lie with Statistics* (Harmondsworth: Penguin, 1991).

Reichman, W. J. *The Use and Abuse of Statistics* (Harmondsworth: Penguin, 1964).

Comprehensive tables:

Neave, Henry R. *Elementary Statistical Tables for all Users of Statistical Techniques* (London: Routledge, 1992).

Index